Mandell Creighton

A History of the Papacy During the Period of the Reformation

Volume 3

Mandell Creighton

A History of the Papacy During the Period of the Reformation
Volume 3

ISBN/EAN: 9783337835774

Printed in Europe, USA, Canada, Australia, Japan

Cover: Foto ©Lupo / pixelio.de

More available books at **www.hansebooks.com**

THE PAPACY

VOL. III.

A HISTORY

OF

THE PAPACY

DURING

THE PERIOD OF THE REFORMATION

BY

M. CREIGHTON, M.A.

DIXIE PROFESSOR OF ECCLESIASTICAL HISTORY IN THE UNIVERSITY OF CAMBRIDGE
AND CANON RESIDENTIARY OF WORCESTER CATHEDRAL : LL.D. OF GLASGOW
AND HARVARD : D.C.L. OF DURHAM ; FELLOW OF THE
SOCIETÀ ROMANA DI STORIA PATRIA

VOL. III.

THE ITALIAN PRINCES

1464—1518

BOSTON

HOUGHTON, MIFFLIN, & CO.

1887

PREFACE.

THE period of history with which these volumes are concerned
has called forth in late years a great amount of literature. The
Italian Renaissance has been dealt with in its literary, artistic,
social, and religious aspects by specialists of great merit; and its
leading personages have been made the subjects of many excellent biographies. Perhaps one result of this special treatment has been to unduly isolate this period and exaggerate
some of its characteristics; it has been regarded as entirely
abnormal, its large historic features have been blurred by the
mass of details, and its place in the development of human
affairs has been somewhat obscured. I have striven to treat it
with the same sobriety as any other period, and, while endeavour-
ing to estimate the temper of the times, I have not forgotten
that that temper affected chroniclers as much as it affected those
who were the subjects of their chronicles. If the writers of the
Middle Ages are to be reduced to the scientific view of historical
progress which we now adopt, the same treatment ought in all
fairness to be applied to the literary men of the Renaissance.
The credulity displayed in the gossip of the one has to be
appraised as carefully as the credulity of the miraculous records
of the other. I have attempted to found a sober view of the
time on a sober criticism of its authorities.

Amongst these authorities there has been opened up in late
years a great number of the records of contemporary diplomacy,
especially that of Venice, of which we have a consecutive abstract
in the diary of Marin Sanuto. There are no questions which

require more consideration in the present condition of historical studies than the use to be made of, and the weight to be attached to, the letters of ambassadors. Really an ambassador requires as much criticism as a chronicler. The political intelligence of the man himself, the source of his information in each case, the object which he and his government had in view, and the interest which others had in deceiving him—these and other considerations have to be carefully weighed. I have endeavoured to do this to the best of my power, and have selected the negotiations which I thought it best to emphasise. Diplomatic dealings need not always be recorded simply because we know that they took place ; but the ideas of diplomatic possibility give us an insight into the politics of the times, which cannot be disregarded. I have, however, tried to reduce diplomatic history to its due proportion in my pages.

The epoch traversed in these volumes is one of the most ignoble, if not the most disastrous, in the history not only of the Papacy, but of Europe. It is scarcely fair to isolate the Popes from their surroundings and hold them up to exceptional ignominy ; yet it is impossible to forget their high office and their lofty claims. I have tried to deal fairly with the moral delinquencies of the Popes, without, I trust, running the risk of lowering the standard of moral judgment. But it seems to me neither necessary to moralise at every turn in historical writing, nor becoming to adopt an attitude of lofty superiority over anyone who ever played a prominent part in European affairs, nor charitable to lavish undiscriminating censure on any man. All I can claim is that I have not allowed my judgment to be warped by a desire to be picturesque or telling.

There are many important subjects which I have only slightly touched, and many interesting men who are little more than names in my pages. My book, as it is, threatens to become unduly long, and I have felt myself bound to exercise self-restraint at every turn. I am not writing a history of Italy, or of the Renaissance, or of the Reformation, but of the Papacy ;

and I think it best to pass by important questions till such times as their importance in reference to my main subject becomes apparent.

I owe an apology on one point to my readers. My final revision of the sheets was unfortunately hurried owing to unexpected engagements, and I notice with regret that I have not been sufficiently careful in securing uniformity in the spelling of proper names and in the use of titles, especially as regards Cardinals. Though this may cause annoyance to fastidious readers, I think it will not be a source of confusion to any.

I have to acknowledge a debt of gratitude to Dr. Richard Garnett, of the British Museum, who, when I was far from libraries during the greater part of the time in which these volumes were written, was of great service to me by bringing to my notice sources of information which I might otherwise have overlooked.

CAMBRIDGE : *Jan.* 1887.

Erratum.

Page 199, line 10, *for* Renaud *read* Perraud.

CONTENTS

OF

THE THIRD VOLUME.

BOOK V.

THE ITALIAN PRINCES.

1464–1518.

CHAPTER I.

PAUL II.

1464–1471.

CHAPTER II.

PAUL II. IN HIS RELATIONS TO LITERATURE AND ART.

CHAPTER III.

SIXTUS IV. AND THE REPUBLIC OF FLORENCE.

1471–1480.

CHAPTER IV.

ITALIAN WARS OF SIXTUS IV.

1481-1484.

CHAPTER V.

INNOCENT VIII.

1484–1492.

CHAPTER VI.

BEGINNINGS OF ALEXANDER VI.

1492–94.

CHAPTER VII.

CHARLES VIII. IN ITALY.

1494-95.

CHAPTER VIII.

ALEXANDER VI. AND FRA GIROLAMO SAVONAROLA.

1495-98.

APPENDIX.

BOOK V.

THE ITALIAN PRINCES.

1464–1518.

CHAPTER I.

PAUL II.

1464–1471.

So long as the struggle against the conciliar movement continued, the objects of the papal policy were determined; it was only when the papal restoration had been practically achieved that the difficulties of the Papal position became apparent. Nearly a hundred years had passed since there was an undoubted Pope who had his hands free for action of his own; and in those hundred years the central idea on which the Papacy rested—the idea of a Christian Commonwealth of Europe—had crumbled silently away. A dim consciousness of decay urged Pius II. to attempt to give fresh life to the idea before it was too late. The expulsion of the Turks from Europe was clearly an object worthy of united effort, and the old associations of a Crusade would set up the Papacy once more as supreme over the international relations of Europe. But Pius II.'s well-meant effort for a Crusade was a total failure, and only his death prevented the failure from being ludicrous. He left unsolved the difficult problem, In what shape was the Papacy to enter into the new political system which was slowly replacing that of the Middle Ages? A still more difficult problem, as yet scarcely suspected, lay behind, How was the ecclesiastical system which the Middle Ages had forged to meet the spirit of criticism which the New Learning had already called into vigorous life.

Some sense of these problems was present to Pius II. as he lay upon his deathbed; but few of the Cardinals were so farseeing. Pius II.'s corpse was brought to Rome, and his obsequies were performed with befitting splendour. Then on August 24 the twenty Cardinals who were in Rome entered the Conclave in the Vatican. The first day was spent in preliminaries. On the second day the electors, before proceeding to the election of an absolute monarch, attempted to impose on him constitutional restraints. They framed a series of regulations which each swore that he would observe in case he were elected. These regulations began with an undertaking to continue the war against the Turks, and summon a General Council within three years for the purpose of stirring up princes to greater enthusiasm for the faith. But this was only the formal prelude to promises which more nearly affected the interests of the College. The future Pope undertook to limit the number of Cardinals to twenty-four, who were to be created only after a public vote in a Consistory. None were to be created who were not of the age of thirty at least, graduates in law or theology, and not more than one relative of the Pope was to be amongst them. The Cardinals were to be consulted on appointments to the more important posts, and the wills of members of the Curia were to be respected on their death. As a guarantee for the observance of this agreement a clause was added empowering the Cardinals to meet twice a year and consider if it had been duly regarded; if not, they were to admonish the Pope, 'with the charity of sons towards a father,' of his forgetfulness and transgression.

Election of
Cardinal
Barbo,
August 30.

When this agreement had been drafted and signed by all, the Cardinals proceeded to a scrutiny. The majority seem to have made up their minds, for the first voting showed twelve votes in favour of Pietro Barbo, Cardinal of S. Marco. As soon as this was announced four Cardinals at the same moment declared their accession, and then to make the election unanimous Bessarion asked each separately if they agreed. Cardinal Barbo was elected with a unanimity and a rapidity which were of rare occurrence in the annals of papal elections. Only the old Scarampo was opposed to one against whom he had a long-standing grudge, for Barbo had consistently opposed his influence over Eugenius IV.

Early life
of Paul II.

Pietro Barbo was a nephew of Eugenius IV., by whom he had been made Cardinal. He was a man of handsome appearance, naturally suave and courteous, with all a Venetian's love of splendour. He learned in the Curia how to use his natural gifts to good purpose. He could easily ingratiate himself into the favour of his superiors, and was a favourite of Nicolas V. and Calixtus III. To the keen-sighted Pius II. his supple manners were not so acceptable, and he did not so readily have his wishes satisfied. Yet he was an incorrigible beggar, and had recourse even to tears if entreaties failed, so that Pius II. laughed at him and gave him the name of 'Maria pientissima.' But the complacency of Barbo was not confined to his superiors. He was fond of popularity and was genuinely kindly. He never abandoned the cause of any whom he took under his protection. He visited members of the Curia when they were sick, tended them carefully, and supplied them with unguents and medicines which he obtained from Venice. His enemies attributed his kindliness to interested motives, and accused him of hunting legacies;[1] but this could not be the reason of his affability to the Roman citizens, whom he delighted to entertain with refined magnificence. His first act in the Conclave after his election showed that his natural impulse was towards considerate courtesy. He advanced to embrace his old enemy Scarampo, who was so crippled with gout that he could not leave his chair: seeing a crestfallen look upon his face he consoled him and bade him be of good cheer, assuring him that the past was forgotten.

To his personal popularity and his supposed sympathy with the objects of the Cardinal College, Barbo chiefly owed his election, though the political cause which brought him into prominence was the alliance with Venice against the Turks which Pius II. bequeathed to the Papacy. Barbo was in the prime of life, of the age of forty-eight; when asked what name he would bear as Pope, he said 'Formosus.' The Cardinals were afraid that this would be interpreted as his own estimate of his handsome appearance. At their request he chose another name; but his next choice of Mark did not please them better, for it was the Venetian war cry. Finally he took the title of Paul II., and was consecrated on September 16.

The Cardinals, who had counted on the complaisance of the new Pope, soon found themselves mistaken. In spite of his promises Paul II. intended to be as absolute as his predecessors.

Paul II. and his Cardinals.

---

[1] So says Platina, who never fails to drop ill-natured hints about Paul II.

born 1421—d. 1481

He had signed the agreement drawn up in the Conclave with the remark that, even if its provisions had not been drafted, he would have observed them for their intrinsic usefulness. But his first act as Pope was to set aside this compact. He drew up another of his own, which he said was better, but which was full of ambiguities. He summoned the Cardinals one by one into his chamber and requested them to sign his draft as preferable to their own. When they remonstrated he overwhelmed them with reproaches; when they wished to read the document and discuss its contents, he covered it with his hand and bade them sign. When Bessarion refused and tried to escape, the Pope seized him, dragged him back, locked the door, and threatened him with excommunication if he did not immediately obey. Dismayed and overborne the Cardinals one by one complied, except the brave and upright Carvajal, who said, ' I will not do in my old age what I never did as a youth. I will not repent of my integrity; but I will bear you no grudge.' When Paul II. had extorted all the signatures except that of Carvajal, he flung his document into a chest and locked it up; the Cardinals were not allowed even to have a copy of the amended regulations which the Pope consented to observe. It was a bitter disappointment to them. Under Nicolas V., Calixtus III., and Pius II. the College had not been able to mould the papal policy. Under Paul II. it hoped for a return to power; but the Pope burst its bonds as a lion breaks through a net. The Cardinals were downcast; but at last a dim consciousness that probably each of them would have behaved in a like manner found expression in a joke which the Cardinal of Avignon made to the Pope: ' You have made good use of your twenty-four years' study of the College to deceive us once.' [1]

We cannot blame the conduct of Paul II. in this matter. The attempt to bind the Pope was a legacy of the Schism, and rested upon the principles laid down by the conciliar movement. But it had appeared earlier than the Schism, and was distinctly forbidden by a Constitution of Innocent VI. in 1353.[2]

---

[1] These details are taken from two very frank letters of Cardinal Ammannati, one to the Pope, the other to the Cardinal of Teano; Cardinalis Papiensis *Epistolæ*, 181, 182.

[2] Raynaldus, *Annales*, 1353, § 29.

It was natural that the electors to the Papacy should try to secure their own interests; but such a proceeding was entirely contrary to the canonical conception of the plenitude of the papal power. The method adopted of signing a joint agreement was singularly unfortunate. To refuse to sign would have meant exclusion from office : to fulfil the agreement after election would have been an unlawful diminution of his authority, which the new Pope was bound to maintain and hand down intact.

But though Paul II. did not intend to increase the power of the Cardinals, he had no objection to increase their grandeur. He reserved to the Cardinals the privilege of wearing red hats, and allowed them to use purple cloaks and trappings for their horses, which had been formerly reserved for the Pope; he gave them also raised seats in consistories and in churches. Moreover, he made a monthly allowance of 100 gold florins to Cardinals whose yearly revenues were below 4,000 florins, and he showed a like liberality to poor Bishops. All this was part of his policy to make his pontificate remarkable by personal splendour. If Nicolas V. aimed at making Rome the literary and artistic capital of Christendom, Paul II. aimed at making the grandeur of the papal court a model to the princes of Europe. He loved magnificence, and claimed it as a special prerogative of the Papacy. He delighted to walk in procession, where his tall figure overtopped all others; his dignity and impressiveness in celebrating the mass enchanted even his assistants in the ceremony. His love of ornaments was shown by his revival of the use of the Regnum or triple crown, first worn by Urban V., but since abandoned;[1] he had one made studded with jewels valued at 120,000 ducats. 'When he appeared in public it was,' says Platina, 'like another Aaron, with form more august than man.'[2]

Paul II. was a zealous collector of cameos and medals, and a lucky opportunity soon threw in his way a means of acquiring

Magnificence of Paul II.

[1] Papiensis *Commentarii*, p. 371. 'Mitram, quæ tribus educta coronis Regnum appellatur, atque a Pontificibus multis ante sæculis desita erat gestari, novam confecit atque adhibuit.'

[2] Platina maliciously adds that he painted his face. 'Fuere qui dicerent eum dum in publicum prodiret, faciem sibi fucis concinnare;' but as even Platina only gives it as a rumour, we may fairly reject it as a calumny.

Death of
Cardinal
Scarampo.
March
1465.

a large collection. Cardinal Scarampo died in March 1465, and by his will left all his possessions to two nephews, who were by no means fit persons to enjoy the vast treasures which Scarampo had amassed at the expense of the Church. He was suspected of having appropriated the wealth of Eugenius IV., and when he carried his enmity against Paul II. so far as to make no restitution to the Church at his death, everyone thought that the Pope was amply justified in setting aside his will, and seizing his goods. Men even wondered at Paul II.'s clemency towards Scarampo's nephews; when they attempted to flee with some of their uncle's treasures they were only imprisoned for a few days, and Paul II. made them a handsome allowance out of the money which he received.

Apathy
about a
Crusade.

Paul II. was not a practised politician like Pius II.; he was averse from war, as was natural in one who loved the splendours of peace. He had no desire to meddle unnecessarily with the affairs of Europe, and the results of the journey to Ancona were not encouraging for a continuance of crusading schemes. Still Paul II. sent subsidies to Mathias of Hungary, and declared himself ready to contribute 100,000 ducats for the purpose of a crusade if other powers would contribute in proportion. But Europe was apathetic: North Italy was disturbed by the death of Cosimo de' Medici, and the Venetians hung back. Nothing was done, and the Turks continued to advance steadily, checked only by the brave resistance of Scanderbeg in Albania.

Paul II.
and the
reform of
the Church.

Perhaps Paul II. was not sorry to find that no heroic measures were expected from him. His interests lay in the arts of peace, and he took a large view of the obligations of the work that lay immediately at his doors. For a time, at the beginning of his pontificate, he seems to have seriously contemplated a reform of some of the worst abuses of the papal system. He consulted a Consistory about the desirability of abandoning grants of benefices in expectancy. Different opinions were given, but that of Carvajal prevailed. He said that the Papacy had laboured long to break down the opposition of ordinaries to papal provisions; now that the prerogative had been established, it would be dangerous to let it fall into abeyance.[1] It was an argument unfortunately only

[1] Cardinalis Papiensis *Epistolæ*, 92.

too plausible at all times. Abuses soon pass into rights, and the technical mind deprecates the surrender of claims which it cannot undertake to defend. Paul II. did not venture to decree the abolition of grants in expectancy; but for his own part he declined to make such grants. Though he loved magnificence, he was too high-minded to resort to unworthy means for raising money. He did his utmost to put down simony and repress the sale of indulgences,[1] and his efforts to check abuses were sincere. It is a sign how deeply rooted these abuses were that one so strong as Paul II. should have hesitated to go further than bequeath to his successors a fruitless example of personal purity.

In matters concerning the Church at large Paul II. might be guided by the opinion of his Cardinals, but in reforming the Curia he followed his own judgment. The army of officials, who composed the administrative staff of the papal court, were divided into several departments, chief of which was the Chancery, presided over by a Cardinal who took the title of Vice-Chancellor. The Chancery preserved the papal archives, and conducted the papal correspondence. For this last purpose there were two sets of officials, the papal secretaries and the abbreviators. Since the reorganisation of the Curia by Martin V. it had been recognised that the secretaries stood in confidential relations towards the Pope, and their office frequently ended with the death of their patron. The abbreviators who were not concerned with the private correspondence of the Pope, but only prepared formal documents, held office for life, and were appointed by the Vice-Chancellor.[2] The lucrative post of Vice-Chancellor had been bestowed by Calixtus III. on his nephew Cardinal Borgia. Pius II. had no friendly feelings towards Borgia, and liked to exercise patronage himself. Accordingly he formed the abbreviators into a College, fixed their number at seventy, and limited the nominations of the Vice-Chancellor to twelve.[3] He filled the College so constituted with

---

[1] Filelfo to Sixtus IV., *Ep.* bk. xxiii. : ' Indulgentias item ipsas temporum necessitate concessas, quoniam lucrativæ viderentur, magna ex parte abrogavit. Quæ vero vel gratiæ vel expectativæ appellantur, ex quibus ipsis grandes thesauri conflantur, eas quam inhibuerit, omnes sciunt.'

[2] Ciampini, *De Abbreviatorum Antiquo Statu.* Rome, 1691, p. 23-34.

[3] See Voigt, *Æneas Sylvius Piccolomini*, iii. 552 &c.

favourites of his own, Sienese friends and literary dependents. Paul II., probably with justice, regarded the abbreviators as the source of much corruption and venality; perhaps he was not sorry to rid himself of the Sienese element which Pius II. had so largely introduced into the Curia. He abolished the arrangements of Pius II., ejected his nominees from their posts, and did away with the order of abbreviators altogether. This again was a barren attempt at reform. Sixtus IV. restored the College, and Innocent VIII. increased it that he might make money out of the sale of offices.

Wrath of abbreviators.

No step is more unpopular than one of administrative reform, and Paul II.'s reputation has suffered in consequence. Great was the dismay, bitter the indignation, and loud the cries of the dispossessed officials. Many of them were scholars and men of letters, and according to the temper of their class considered that they conferred more distinction on the Curia than they received from it. The Pope's action was resented as an insult to the entire literary fraternity, and the abbreviators were at first sure that if they raised their complaints the Pope would be forced by public opinion to give way. Moreover, as the office of abbreviator was frequently bought by candidates, they put in a legal claim to its possession as a freehold for life. Platina, the most distinguished of their number, urged their cause with warmth, and demanded that their claims should be submitted to the legal decision of the auditors of the Rota. He little knew the resoluteness of the Pope. Paul II. looked at him with a scowl; 'Do you talk of bringing us before judges, as if you did not know that all law is seated in our breast? If you talk in that way, all shall be dismissed. I care not; I am Pope, and can at my good pleasure rescind or confirm the acts of others.' Platina found Paul II. as immovable as a rock, and when remonstrance failed he determined to have recourse to threats. He wrote a haughty letter to the Pope, saying that if he persisted in depriving the abbreviators of their legal rights, they would complain to the princes of Europe and entreat them to summon a Council which would call the Pope to account for his illegal conduct. It is a striking testimony to the power of the revived literature of Italy that such a threat should have been conveyed to such a Pope. The humanists must indeed have had a high sense of their own importance before they could dream of disturbing the peace of Europe by a question concerning their position in the papal court.

The answer of Paul II. was quick and decided. He ordered Platina to be put in prison on a charge of treason. In vain Platina justified his action by reference to the censorial power in the Roman Republic; for four months he lay in his cell, bound by heavy chains, without a fire in the wintry weather. He was at length released through the entreaties of Cardinal Gonzaga, who warned him not to leave Rome, but to stay there quietly. 'If you were to go to India,' he added, 'Paul would find means to bring you back.' Platina was humbled, and on his release from prison lived quietly in Rome, till he again excited the Pope's anger and suffered still worse treatment at his hands.

With equal decision Paul II. applied himself to the practical details of the government of Rome. He inquired into the prices of provisions, and when the corn merchants pleaded scarcity as a reason for their high charges, the Pope sent envoys of his own to procure corn and meat for the Roman market. So successful was he in this undertaking that prices fell more than a half. While he thus provided for the comfort of the people, he sternly repressed disorder and demanded obedience to the laws. He had a horror of violence and wished all men to live in peace. In carrying out his measures he showed a happy mixture of firmness and mercy. Turbulent spirits were cooled by a few days' imprisonment; no malefactors were allowed to escape; but Paul II. was averse from severity, and above all from bloodshed. Though willing to remit the full penalty inflicted on smaller crimes, his sense of justice would not allow him to pardon homicide, while his clemency shrank from the infliction of capital punishment. The prisons were filled with culprits, and the magistrates clamoured for their execution. 'Do you think it a small thing,' said the Pope, 'to put to death a man, so admirable a piece of God's workmanship, and moulded for use by human society through so many years of toil?' He devised a new punishment for grave offenders by sending them to serve in his galleys, with strict orders to the captains that they should be mercifully treated. Compassion was inherent in the tempera-

ment of Paul II. He rescued birds from their captors and let
them go free. He could not even endure to see a bullock being
led to the shambles, but would stop and buy it from the
butcher that its life might be spared. [1]

In other matters which affected the well-being of the city,
Paul II. showed equal sagacity. He cleansed the sewers and
aqueducts, and repaired the bridges over the Tiber. He preferred to take part in the city life rather than enjoy the somewhat solitary grandeur of the Vatican. He lived chiefly in the
Palazzo of S. Marco, which he had built as Cardinal, and which
still stands as a memorial of his architectural taste. From its
windows he could enjoy the sight of the Roman Carnival which
he delighted to organise and encourage. There were races of
all kinds in the long straight street which led to his palace,
and which took from his day the well-known name of the Corso.
All classes and all ages might enjoy themselves; there were
foot races for the Jews, for youths, for adults and for old men.
There were horse races, donkey races, and races for buffaloes.
There were pageants of giants and cupids, Diana and her
nymphs, Bacchus and his attendant fauns; there were processions of civic magistrates escorted by waggons laden with grotesque figures, while songs in honour of the Pope resounded on
all sides. On the last day of the Carnival, Paul II. gave
a magnificent banquet to the magistrates. The remnants,
including all the furniture of the table, were distributed
amongst the people, and the Pope himself threw small silver
coins to be scrambled for by the crowd. Some shook their
heads at these heathenish vanities as unbefitting a Pope; [2] but
Paul II., while desirous to check abuses, had none of the spirit
of asceticism, though he himself was most temperate in his
pleasures, and seldom took more than one meal a day, and that
a simple one. He possessed, however, the spirit of genuine
charity, and besides showing liberality in cases of conspicuous
need, chose almoners, men and women of high character, whom
he supplied with money, which they expended secretly in the
relief of the destitute.

[1] Canesius in Quirini, p. 40.

[2] Papiensis *Epistolæ*, 282 : ' Æmulator vanitatis antiquæ sæculares ludos
et epulum populo Romano exhibes. . . Veram laudem ista non habent.
Sacerdotalis non putantur officii.'

CHAP.
I.

Paul II.
recovers
the Patri-
mony.
1465.

In the States of the Church Paul II. did what he could to stop administrative corruption. He forbade the governors of cities to receive presents, except of provisions, and of these not more than a supply for two days. He gave the castles into the hands of prelates, thinking that they were more trustworthy than the neighbouring barons. Moreover he was enabled to take an important step towards securing the peace of Rome, which since the days of Eugenius IV. had been disturbed by the turbulent baron Everso, Count of Anguillara, who was little better than a bandit, and made the approaches to Rome dangerous by the robber hordes whom he encouraged. He held his power by virtue of opposition to the Popes; he intrigued with the discontented in Rome and kept the city in constant disquiet. At his death, in September, 1464, he was master of most of the towns in the Patrimony. Paul II. resolved to recover the possessions of the Church from the two sons of Everso who promised to restore the castles which their father had seized. The promise was not kept, and in June 1465 Paul II. sent his troops against them. There was a party in Rome which was in their favour, a party which wished to maintain any sort of check on the power of the Pope. Paul II. acted with the wisdom of a statesman. He summoned an assembly of the Roman people, and plainly put before them his policy and his aims.[1] The opposition was at once overborne, and Rome was united in desiring to be rid of a horde of robbers at its gates.[2] Not a blow was struck in behalf of Everso's sons: one fled to Venice, the other was made prisoner. Thirteen castles were at once surrendered to the Church, and by the end of 1465 Paul II. was master of the Patrimony. Towards the general politics of Italy the attitude of Paul II. was at once wise and dignified. He studied above all things to maintain peace, and refused to join in any of the leagues, or countenance any of the plans, which the Italian States were so fertile in forming against their neighbours. He would not offend anyone, but he would seek no one's favour. He had no objects of his own to pursue, but aimed at holding an independent position as arbiter amongst conflicting interests.

In the external relations of the Papacy Pius II. had left

[1] Canesius in Quirini, 56, &c., gives the Pope's speech.
[2] Ammannati *Epistolæ*, 121, expresses the general feeling of the Romans.

one important question for settlement, and when the need for action was clearly apparent Paul II. could act with a resolution unknown to his predecessor. The last thing that Pius II. had done before departing for Ancona was to summon to Rome the heretical King of Bohemia, George Podiebrad. It was reserved to Paul II. to bring to an end the Bohemian difficulty, and the fact that he entertained no political projects of his own enabled him to concentrate his attention on the purely ecclesiastical side of George Podiebrad's position. We have seen how George of Bohemia strove to emerge from the isolation in which as a Utraquist he stood amongst the powers of Europe. He tried every means, and even threatened to break down the hierarchical basis of the state system of Europe. First he endeavoured to win the Imperial crown, and failing that, to reform the Empire according to his ideas ; finally he set on foot a scheme for a new organisation of international affairs, by means of a parliament of European princes. This last attempt had warned the Papacy of its danger, and Pius II. resolved to crush George by every means in his power. The death of Pius II. suspended for a time the process against George which the Pope had threatened. George had a short period of respite while Paul II. paused to survey the ground.

Difficulties
of King
George.

Though George Podiebrad had done great things in restoring order into Bohemia and raising its credit abroad, he was still no nearer to a permanent settlement than he was at the beginning of his reign. The Catholics of Breslau refused to recognise him as their king, and were under the protection of the Pope. Bohemia was still distracted, and the key to the papal policy was to be found in the saying of the Archbishop of Crete to the complaint of the men of Breslau, that not the Rhine, the Danube, and the Tiber could quench the flame of heresy in Bohemia. 'The Moldau alone will suffice,' was his answer. In truth, the Bohemian nobles looked with some suspicion on the king who had risen from their own ranks, and whose efforts were directed to increase the kingly power. They were gradually becoming more discontented ; and though they would not venture to take up arms simply at the Pope's bidding, for the large majority of the people was Utraquist, they were ready to seek a political pretext which might bring them into alliance with the Pope. Early in 1465 a baron who had been always hostile to King George, Hynek of Lichtenberg, rose against the King, and the States of Moravia declared war against him as a disturber of the peace. His castle of Zornstein was besieged, whereupon Hynek fled to Rome and besought the Pope to take cognisance of his case. The Bishop of Lavant, who had been appointed legate for Bohemian affairs in Germany, wrote from Rome, forbidding all Catholics in Moravia and Bohemia to continue the siege of Zornstein; Hynek, as being a good Catholic, was under the protection of the Pope.

King George now knew what he had to expect from the new Pope. He wrote to Paul II. assuring him that Hynek was not persecuted on account of his faith, but was being punished for his rebellious conduct. The Bishop of Lavant from Neustadt threatened with interdict all who took part in the siege of Zornstein. Paul II. answered George's letter, not to himself, but to the Bohemian States, saying that he was sorry to hear charges against an orthodox man like Hynek; as he who ordered proceedings to be taken against Hynek had no power and authority, since he refused obedience to the Church, the Pope declared Hynek to be no rebel, and repeated his orders that the siege of Zornstein should be raised. Of course the Papal letter did not carry conviction, and Zornstein fell before its besiegers in June 1465.

The letter of Paul II. was meant to be a declaration of war; by his defence of Hynek he showed the means by which he intended to wage it, and invited allies. He did not act without knowledge; by his side stood the stubborn Carvajal, who since the days of Eugenius IV. had directed the papal diplomacy in Germany and Bohemia. George was not long in feeling the results of this policy. The discontented barons, who dreaded the steady growth of the royal power, gathered together secretly and formed themselves into a League under the guidance of Bishop Jost of Breslau. At the head of these nobles stood Zdenek of Sternberg, once the firm friend of King George, but who had gradually been estranged from him. It was agreed that the religious question was to be carefully excluded from their complaints, and that their action was to be founded on the grounds of national patriotism. A list of grievances was drawn up and presented to the King in a Diet held at Prag on September 25, 1465. The discontented barons absented themselves; but their written complaint contained twelve articles accusing the King of diminishing the rights of the nobles, employing foreigners rather than Bohemians, and allowing Rokycana and his priests to disturb the peace of the land. To these complaints the King returned a dignified answer; but it was clear that the grievances were merely a pretext, and that the object of the League was hostility against George. On November 28, the discontented barons, with the Bishops of Breslau and Olmütz, entered into a League for five years for the purpose of mutual defence.

Paul II.
cites
George
to Rome.
August
1465.

Side by side with this action of the Bohemians the Pope proceeded on his way. Indignant at the fall of Zornstein he nominated a commission of three Cardinals, amongst whom were Carvajal and Bessarion, to report on the process which Pius II. had instituted against George. On receiving their report he renewed, on August 2, the citation to ' George of Podiebrad, who calls himself King of Bohemia,' to appear within 180 days to answer to the charges of heresy, perjury, sacrilege, and other crimes. On August 6 the Pope further commissioned the Bishop of Lavant to loose all ties of allegiance or alliance between George and his subjects or allies. The Pope did not wait to give George a chance of appearing to his citation. The notoriety of his misdeeds was held to be apparent, and the legate was bidden to lodge complaints against him in all the courts of Germany.

King George at once realised the danger in which he stood. He saw that the papal policy tended to isolate him, not only in Europe, but in his own kingdom. He judged it wise to make a movement of retreat, to try and renew the position in which he had first stood towards Pius II. He looked for mediators with the Pope. In the Emperor he could put little trust; from Mathias of Hungary, who stood high in the Pope's favour, he hoped much; from Lewis of Bavaria he borrowed the pen of his chancellor, Dr. Martin Mayr. Acting on Mayr's advice he pleaded his inability to come to Rome, and demanded a Council in the neighbourhood of Bohemia before which he would willingly appear. Lewis of Bavaria sent an envoy to Rome in November 1465, bearing George's proposals for reconciliation. He offered to lead a Crusade against the Turks, and drive

them from Constantinople, on condition that he received as a
reward the Imperial crown of the Eastern Empire: in Bohemia
the existing condition of the religious question was to continue:
the Compacts were to rest on their own basis without any papal
recognition: George's son was to succeed him on the Bohemian
throne, and another son was to receive the archbishopric of
Prag, which he was to hold from the Pope: much of the possessions and privileges of the Church should be restored to the
Catholic clergy.

Paul II. was not captivated by this fantastic proposal. He
was of a practical turn of mind and had no taste for daring and
adventurous schemes. His mind was made up about George,
and he was resolved to give no quarter. He gave a decisive
proof of his intractability by his treatment of a Bohemian envoy
who brought him a letter from George in December. 'Holy
Father,' said the envoy, 'this letter is sent by your faithful son
the King of Bohemia.' The Pope took the letter and flung it
on the ground. 'How, you beast, can you be so bold as in our
presence call him king whom you know to be a condemned
heretic? To the gallows with you and your heretical ruffian.'[1]
Paul II. could be both plain-spoken and resolute when he
chose; and we are not surprised to find that the envoy waited
for three weeks for an answer, but none was given. Finally
at Christmas the Pope, seeing him in the church of S. Maria
Maggiore, sent a chamberlain to turn him out. Lewis of
Bavaria, in answer to his mediation, received a sharp reproof,
and a vigorous criticism of George's proposals. A forsworn
heretic, said the Pope, asks for further favours: let him first
keep his promises: better the infidel who knows not the truth
than a heretic and schismatic. Diplomacy was no longer possible
between the Pope and the King.

Though a breach was now imminent, all parties hesitated.
George had everything to gain by moderation and still hoped
to escape the storm. The League of Bohemian nobles was not
strong enough to attack him, and negotiated with the Pope for
money and support. The Pope answered that they were not
fighting for the Catholic cause, but only for their own interests;
if they declared themselves on the side of Breslau and the
Catholic faith he would help them, but not otherwise. The

CHAP.
I.

Paul. II.
refuses to
negotiate.
December
1465.

Sentence
given
against
King
George.
December
1466.

---

[1] Klose, *Documentirte Geschichte von Breslau*, iii., pt. i., p. 352.

League hesitated and made a truce with George, who was constant in his desire for peace. The Pope meanwhile did not venture to proceed to extremities and declare George deposed till he saw some means of enforcing the sentence. George could not be overcome save by the arms of some foreign power, and it was not easy to find a prince who was ready to undertake the difficult task of attacking so powerful an adversary. The Emperor was of course hopeless, and the Princes of Germany were too busy with their own schemes of aggrandisement. There remained Mathias of Hungary and Casimir of Poland; but Mathias, though professing himself ready to obey the Pope in all matters, was occupied against the Turks in his own dominions, and Casimir maintained a doubtful attitude towards the Pope's proposals. The time passed by for George's appearance in Rome to answer the charges against him, and still the Pope hesitated to proceed to extremities. The question was discussed in a Consistory on December 21, 1466, till Carvajal, true to his inflexible principles, confirmed the wavering minds of the Cardinals. 'Why do we measure all things by human judgments? Must not something in difficulties be left to God? If the Emperor and the Kings of Poland and Hungary will not help us, God will help us from His holy seat and will bruise the head of the wicked. Let us do our duty; He will perform the rest.'[1] His view prevailed, and on December 23, in an open Consistory, sentence was given against George as a heretic; he was deprived of all his dignities, and his subjects were released from their allegiance.

The effect of this determined attitude of the Pope was at once felt in Germany, where the old antipathy against the Bohemians began in some measure to revive. The students of Leipsic and Erfurth sold their books and bought arms for a crusade against the heretic: the Emperor and the German Princes began to draw further away from George. The Barons' League formed itself definitely into a Catholic League, and elected as its leader Zdenek of Sternberg; but it was clear that the League would be powerless unless it found allies outside the kingdom. George had a wise adviser and a skilful diplomat in Gregory of Heimburg, whose skilful appeals to the German Princes did much to strengthen George's posi-

---

[1] Papiensis *Commentarii*, 437.

tion. Acting under Heimburg's advice, George on April 14, 1467, met the Pope's Bull by a formal appeal. On the grounds that the proceedings against him were contrary to justice, and were dictated merely by personal hatred, he appealed first to the Roman See itself, against which, George added, he had no grievances, but only against its present occupant, who was a mortal man, subject to mortal passions; secondly, he appealed to a General Council; and thirdly, to Paul's successor, and to all corporations in Christendom which loved right and justice.[1] This appeal produced no results save that it gave a technical ground for Catholics to continue on the side of George without severing their allegiance to the Pope.

War now broke out between the Barons' League and King George; but it was a war of plundering raids and sieges of castles in which George had the balance of success. Both sides grew weary of this fruitless devastation, and a truce was made in November. George behaved with singular moderation; he wished only for a lasting peace, and did not care to pursue a temporary advantage. The Pope fulminated against George, but that produced little effect; the real question was whether the Polish or Hungarian King would come to the help of the League. There were long negotiations with Casimir of Poland; but he shrank from the arduous task and offered his services as a mediator. Mathias of Hungary was more easily won over. Though bound by many ties to George Podiebrad, he had become gradually estranged from him and regarded him with feelings akin to jealousy. He had married George's daughter, but her death in 1464 loosened his personal ties to the Bohemian King. In truth the attitude of Bohemia was a stumbling block in the way of the policy of Mathias. The existence of the Hungarian kingdom was threatened by the invasion of the Turks, and Mathias needed the help of Europe to repulse them. A close alliance with Bohemia was the most natural means of gaining help; but an alliance with Bohemia, in the existing condition of the papal policy, meant isolation from the rest of Europe. Mathias had to choose between an alliance with Bohemia against Rome and the Turk, or an alliance with Rome against Bohemia and the Turk. By identifying himself

The Bohemian League seeks for help.

---

[1] In Palacky, *Urkundliche Beiträge*, 455.

with the cause of the Church he saw a means of convincing Europe that his war against the Turk was waged in the cause of Christendom; he saw also a chance of obtaining for himself the crown of Bohemia, and thereby uniting the resources of the two countries. He resolved to cast in his lot with the Papacy, if it were necessary for him to take one side or the other.[1]

Mathias of
Hungary
declares
against
George.
March
1468.

The opportunity for which Mathias waited was not long in coming. King George had made a truce with the Catholic League that he might have his hands free to strike a blow against the Emperor. He regarded Frederick III. with growing animosity, and saw in him a centre for papal intrigues which might unite Germany as well as Hungary against Bohemia. Frederick had submitted to the German Diet at Nürnberg, in June, letters from the Pope demanding help against George, and the election of a new King of Bohemia. Though the Diet did not entertain these proposals, yet Frederick had shown his hostility towards George, who now resolved to meet it. He hoped by striking at Austria to raise up troubles within the Emperor's dominions, and convince Mathias of the need of an alliance with Bohemia against the Turk. In the beginning of 1468 George's son, Prince Victorin, defied Frederick III. as Duke of Austria, and advanced into his territory. The stroke was not decisive, as the Austrians managed to make some sort of resistance, and Frederick III. turned for help to Mathias. The decision of Mathias was at once taken. Summoned by the Pope, summoned by the Catholic League, and summoned by the Emperor to attack Bohemia, he saw himself supported on so many sides that victory would be sure to bring him the Bohemian crown. At the end of March he declared war against King George.

That Mathias Hunyadi should at the Pope's bidding turn his arms against George Podiebrad was the irony of history on the policy of the restored Papacy. As head of Christendom the Pope summoned Europe to war against the Turk; as head of the ecclesiastical system of Christendom the Pope strove to restore the outward unity of the Church; and these two objects proved to be contradictory. Pius II. hoped to combine them by his Crusade, which should again unite Europe under the

---

[1] See Jordan, *Das Königthum Georg's von Podiebrad*, 250.

papal leadership, and sweep away the dangerous and revolutionary schemes of George Podiebrad. Events showed that Pius II. had striven after what was unattainable, and Paul II. had to consider which aim he should put foremost. If Europe as a whole would not advance against the Turk, the best chance of holding the Turk at bay was the maintenance in Eastern Europe of a strong power, such as might be formed by a close alliance between Bohemia and Hungary. Paul II. cast to the winds all thought of the real interests of Europe, that he might secure the interests of the Church. To reduce Bohemia to obedience to the Papacy he did not scruple to plunge into warfare—which could only end in mutual destruction—the two most capable rulers in Europe, whose territories were the natural bulwarks against the advance of the Turk. When we deplore the selfish and grasping policy which prevailed universally in the succeeding age, we must regret that such a Pope as Paul II. did not bequeath an example of greater care for the general good.

The news of Mathias' decision awakened the wildest joy in Rome. Cardinal Ammannati wrote to the Pope, 'On reading to-day copies of two letters of the truly most Christian King of Hungary, I raised my eyes and hands to heaven, and gave thanks to God's goodness which at length has regarded us, and raised us to a hope of salvation, and kindled the spirit of Daniel who will tread down Satan under our feet . . . The Lord has awakened, as it were, from sleep, like a giant refreshed with wine. The vengeance for the blood of His servants which has been shed, has entered into His sight. Our enemies, in the words of the Apostle, will be made a footstool under our feet . . . The issue is grave ; for nothing can be more joyous for the Catholic people, nothing more glorious for the Apostolic Seat, than victory, nothing more sorrowful than defeat. The torch is destructive which may spread a daily conflagration on our heads and those of all faithful people. Wherefore we must the more propitiate the God of Hosts, and aid the pious King by the prayers of the Church, that while he fights there may rain over the Bohemian sinners snares, fire and sulphur, and the breath of storms may be the portion of their cup, for which they shed their own and others' blood.' [1]

Joy of Cardinal Ammannati.

[1] Cardinalis Papiensis *Epistolæ*, No. 265.

With these aspirations of Ammannati it is worth while to compare the words of Gregory of Heimburg, who still remained a keen critic of the Papal policy, convinced of the mischief which it had wrought in Germany, and prepared to withstand it to the last. Yet Heimburg had learned from his experiences with Sigismund of Tyrol, that it was hard to fight against the Papacy ; and though the keenness of his pen is the same as at first, his expressions are more moderate, and the joy in battle has cooled. Heimburg is no longer acting on the offensive, but uses all his skill to parry the blows of an adversary whom he feels to be too powerful for him. His last appeal in behalf of George was written in the middle of 1467 ; and in it Heimburg put forth all his skill. His object is to defend George against the Pope's procedure, and he carefully narrows the issue before him. Beginning with an apology for venturing to speak against dignitaries, he says that he is distracted between reverence and patriotism ; if he speaks, it is after the example of S. Paul, who raised his voice even against the High Priest, when he behaved wrongfully. He then declares George's fervent desire to clear himself of the charge of heresy, and by giving an account of arguments used in George's Council, he skilfully manages to set George's highmindedness in contrast with the corruption of the Curia, representing him as combating the suggestions made by his advisers, who recommended him to take advantage of the venality and prevarication which prevailed at Rome. He enlarges on the injustice of the Pope's procedure, and to explain the hatred of the Pope against George he tells once more the story of the means by which the Papacy overcame the German neutrality, and points out how it wishes to keep Germany in chains by means of its alliance with the feeble Emperor. He dwells on the papal arrogance in German and Bohemian affairs, and then continues :—' O Paul, Paul, bishop of bishops, who have received the sheep of Christ, not to shear, or milk, or slaughter, but to feed ; would it not have become your office of Shepherd to have granted the King's request for a fair trial, especially as he offered to bring into accordance with the Compacts anything that might be found contrary to the ritual of the Roman Church ? Could you not have granted a certain latitude to Bohemia, as Gregory the Great did to Augustine of Canterbury when he wrote, "If the same Christ is worshipped, variance of ritual matters not"? But you were afraid that the authority of General Councils, which you and the Emperor had trampled under foot, might again revive, and your filthiness be spread abroad throughout the world. You would have lacked also the delight that you have received from the slaughter of women great with child, whom your cut-throats, beneath the banner of the Cross of Christ, have massacred . . . Remember, Holy Father, that as long as you are weighed down with the burden of the flesh, you are a man liable to sin, and therefore may reckon true what is other than the truth . . . What gain do you hope to obtain if so much blood be shed in war that the Danube, red with the blood of the slain, dyes the Scythian sea? Will the Bohemians be heard at length even in your despite, and peace again be restored? God will provide what is best.'[1]

Heimburg writes as though the time for the pen were past, and matters must be decided by the sword. Mathias entered Bohemia in April 1468. Paul II. supported him by issuing Bulls of extraordinary severity against those who in any way helped George, or had any commercial dealings with him; and by holding out extraordinary inducements to those who joined in the Crusade against him. George was attacked by three enemies at once: Mathias of Hungary, the Catholic League, and the hosts of Crusaders who assembled at the Pope's bidding. They naturally gained some advantage; but Mathias soon saw that the conquest of Bohemia was no easy matter. He tried to win over Casimir of Poland, but George offered to procure from the Estates of Bohemia the election of a son of Casimir for his successor, and the Polish King listened more readily to George than to Mathias. The war went on, and George was sorely pressed; but as the schemes of Mathias became more apparent, the Emperor grew terrified at his too mighty ally. He wished to be rid of George Podiebrad, but he hoped to secure the crown of Bohemia for the Austrian house. Mathias, on his side, aimed not only at the throne of Bohemia, but at the dignity of King of the Romans, as a reward for his labours for the good of Christendom.

In his helplessness Frederick III. resolved to try what could be gained from the old alliance which he had formed with the

---

[1] Palacky, *Urkundliche Beiträge*, 647, &c.

BOOK
V.

Frederick
III. goes
to Rome.
November
1468.

Papacy. Under the pretext of fulfilling a vow which he had made in his troubles of 1462, he started on a pilgrimage to Rome in November 1468. He placed Austria under the protection of Mathias, whose interests he professed to have chiefly at heart in seeking an interview with the Pope. In fact, however, he regarded Mathias with terror, while Mathias looked on him with suspicion.

Italian
affairs.
1464-8.

Paul II. was not well pleased at the news of the Emperor's coming. In spite of the Pope's efforts for peace, Italy was not very quiet, and Imperial visits gave opportunities for disturbance. The death of Cosimo de' Medici in 1464, and of Francesco Sforza in 1466, had placed the direction of affairs in North Italy in less experienced hands. In the South, Ferrante of Naples looked with a jealous eye on the success of the Pope in consolidating the possessions of the Church. It is true that in February 1468 Paul II. had succeeded in bringing about a general pacification of Italy ; but the Italian League existed in name rather than in reality. A prudent counsellor pointed out to the Pope that a general disarmament would only cast adrift a number of mercenary soldiers who would seek some occupation for their arms. ' It is our duty,' said the Pope, ' to be true to our pastoral office ; God who rules all things will dispose matters according to His will.' Paul II. was personally averse from war. He kept only a few troops, enough to act as mounted police. He used to say that the only expense which he grudged was the pay of his soldiers.[1] But the more the Pope showed a pacific disposition, the more did Ferrante push his claims. He wished to recover the territory with which Pius II. had enriched his nephew Antonio, and he made difficulties about the payment of the tribute due from Naples. Paul II., though peaceful, was firm, and refused to accept the merely formal tokens of the vassalage of Naples, the white horse and the hawk. When the Neapolitan envoy urged that this refusal would anger the King, who could not afford to pay the tribute, Paul II. answered, ' We will wait : some day he will pay us.'

Affairs of
Rimini.
1468.

While matters were in this unstable condition, a small thing sufficed to create a disturbance. In October 1468 died Gismondo Malatesta, lord of Rimini, who since his humiliation

---

[1] Canesius in Quirini, 83.

by Pius II. had been warring against the Turks in the Morea. On his death Paul II. claimed Rimini, as Gismondo died without any legitimate heir, and his possessions therefore reverted to their lord the Pope. Venice acted as protector of Rimini during the absence of Gismondo, who was fighting on their behalf; and Rimini itself was held by Gismondo's famous wife Isotta. Paul II. had taken into his employment Roberto, a natural son of Gismondo, and Roberto offered to win the city for the Pope. He was successful in his conquest, but held Rimini for himself, and entered into alliance with Ferrante of Naples. It seemed only too probable that round the walls of Rimini would rage a war into which all the Italian powers would be drawn.

When the time of Frederick III.'s arrival at Rome drew near, Paul II. showed all a Venetian's suspiciousness and foresight. He called his troops into the city, and awaited Frederick's movements with some anxiety. But the feeble Frederick III. was equally powerless for good or evil. Attended by six hundred knights, he entered Rome on the evening of December 24, 1468, and was welcomed by the Cardinals, who, in a torchlight procession, conducted him to S. Peter's, where the Pope was awaiting his arrival. Twice the Emperor knelt as he approached the Pope's throne ; then the Pope, slightly rising from his seat, gave him his hand and kissed him. The seat assigned to him was no higher than the Pope's feet, and there Frederick sat while lauds were sung. He retired to the Vatican, and after a few hours' rest attended mass on Christmas Day and read the Gospel attired as a deacon. In all the festivities that followed Frederick III. showed himself desirous to pay all respect to the Pope, who treated him with patronising condescension. In processions he took the Emperor's right hand with his left, and with his right blessed the people. According to custom, the Emperor dubbed knights on the Bridge of S. Angelo, while the Pope looked on. Strict attention was paid to ceremonial usage, and the papal Master of Ceremonies, Agostino Patrizzi, drew up an elaborate account of all that was done, that it might serve as precedent to future times.

The record of Patrizzi was of little use for this purpose, as the visit of Frederick III. was the last appearance of an Emperor in Rome. Certainly the Empire had never sunk lower

than in the hands of Frederick III. Patrizzi writes:[1] 'Great
was the kindness which the Pope on all occasions showed
the Emperor; and it was esteemed all the greater because the
Papal authority is no less than it was in old times, while its
power and strength are much greater. For the Roman Church,
by God's will, through the diligence of the Popes, especially of
Paul, has so grown in power and wealth that it is comparable
with the greatest kingdoms. On the other hand the authority
and strength of the Roman Empire have been so diminished
and reduced that, save the name of Empire, scarcely anything
remains. I do not forget that former Popes have shown themselves respectful to Emperors, and sometimes to Kings. The
power of the Pope used to be what princes allowed; but now
things are changed—a trifle at their hands, a mere act of
courtesy, is held a very great matter.' Patrizzi tells us the
abiding policy of the Curia—it advanced pretensions, and
time turned them into realities. But precedents become
dangerous after a certain point, and we are not surprised that
Frederick III.'s successors gave the Curia no chance of enforcing
the precedent which it so triumphantly established.

Of course the Pope and the Emperor solemnly discussed the
project of a Crusade. The Pope asked the Emperor what he
advised, and Frederick judiciously answered that he had come
to receive, not to give, counsel: but at last he proposed a conference of princes at Constance, where he promised that he and
Mathias of Hungary would be present. Paul II. doubted the
expediency of this course, and nothing was decided. A Crusade
was indeed hopeless; but Frederick III. wished to gain from
the Pope a recognition of his claim to inherit the crowns of
Bohemia and Hungary, and to transfer the Electoral dignity of
Bohemia to Austria. But the papal cause was identified for
the present with that of the Hungarian king, and Paul II. would
not displease so necessary an ally; as to Bohemia, he wished
to strike it out of the number of kingdoms and divide it into
a number of duchies. The Imperial visit was productive of no
results to the Emperor, who on January 9, 1469, left Rome to
find on his return to his own dominions that a revolt had broken
out in Styria. Mathias of Hungary was not sorry to see his
uneasy ally employed at home.

[1] *De Adventu Frederici III.*, in Muratori, xxiii. 215.

After Frederick's departure from Rome Paul II. turned his attention to the affairs of Rimini. Venice, equally with the Pope, resented the position of Roberto Malatesta, and in May 1469 an alliance was made between them. Roberto was supported by Milan, Florence, and Naples; Federigo of Urbino, who saw with alarm the spread of the papal power over the neighbouring barons, deserted the Pope's service and put himself at the head of the army which marched to Roberto's defence. In August the papal forces were defeated and obliged to retreat, and in face of the menacing attitude of Ferrante of Naples and the advance of the Turks upon Negroponte, Paul II. did not judge it wise to prolong the war. Negotiations were set on foot which ended, on December 22, 1470, in the renewal of the League of Lodi, made in 1454, and in a general pacification of Italy. Roberto Malatesta was left in quiet possession of Rimini, where he strengthened himself by marriage with a daughter of Federigo of Urbino.

Paul II. resigns his claim on Rimini. December 1470.

Meanwhile Paul II. pursued his design of organising the government of the city of Rome. Paul II. in 1469 issued a commission for the revision of its statutes, which dated from 1363,[1] on the grounds that some were of ancient and popular origin, others contrary to the liberty of the Church, others useless and obsolete, while others needed amendment.[2] The reforms were made after consultation between the citizens and the Curia, between the magistrates and the prelates. The revised statutes were printed soon afterwards, probably in 1471,[3] and their publication marked an epoch in the legislation of the Roman city. They are divided into three books, dealing with civil and criminal law and administration. Paul II. did not attempt to destroy the old liberties of the city: its political power had been merged in the Papacy, and the Pope did not limit its old right of self-government. Senator, conservators, and captains of regions remained as before, and formed a court whose decrees were laid before the general assembly, in which every male over the age

Paul II.'s statutes for Rome. 1470.

[1] These earliest statutes have been published by Del Re, *Statuti della Città di Roma del Secolo xiv.* 1883.

[2] The commission in Theiner, *Codex Diplomaticus*, iii. 460, is a statesman-like document.

[3] This edition of the Statutes of Rome is extremely rare; of seven copies known to exist one is in England, in the library of Earl Spencer.

of twenty had a place. The clergy were excluded from the
government, and no Roman layman was to answer before an
ecclesiastical court. To put down the murders which the blood
feuds of the Romans made so frequent, a special court was
established and special penalties prescribed. The only striking
point in the administrative regulations are the sumptuary laws
forbidding luxury in clothing and festivals. The magnificent
Paul II. wished to appropriate splendour and display as a prerogative of the papal office.[1]

In Bohemia Mathias of Hungary found his task more
difficult than he expected. Early in 1469 he entered the
country and George gathered his forces to repel him. Owing
to a heavy fall of snow Mathias was surprised in the narrow
passes of Wilemow, where he could neither advance nor retreat.
George was ready to listen to overtures for a truce : he wished
for peace and determined to trust to the generosity of Mathias:
he thought that a renewal of the old alliance with Hungary was
still possible, and was more likely to be brought about by negotiation than by a victory in the field. Accordingly he allowed
Mathias to withdraw after promising to make peace. Great
was the dismay of the Papal Legate Rovarella, who threatened
Mathias with excommunication if he carried his promise into
effect. The possibility of a pacification ensuing from the
meeting between George and Mathias, which took place in
Olmütz on March 24, filled the nobles of the Catholic League
with terror. They resolved to bind Mathias to the cause which
he had undertaken, and on April 12 formally elected him King
of Bohemia. Mathias had now a position to fight for; he
informed George that he had agreed to the conditions of
Wilemow on the understanding that George would abjure his
heresy.

War again broke out; but George was now filled with
personal hostility against Mathias. He saw that his scheme of
forming a powerful Bohemian kingdom on a Utraquist basis
had failed, and he saw that the failure prevented him from
handing down to his sons the heritage of a kingdom. Resolved to secure Bohemia against the ambitious designs of

[1] The history of the Statutes of Rome has recently been illustrated by
La Mantia, *Origini e Vicende degli Statuti di Roma* in *Rivista Europea*,
vol. xii. 1879 ; also, more fully, *La Legislazione d' Italia*, 1884, i. 172, &c.

Mathias, he suggested to the Diet, which met in June at Prag,
the election of Ladislas, son of Casimir of Poland, as his
successor. The election was accepted, and George renewed the
war with a feeling that he had gained an ally. Everywhere
was disturbance. There were troubles in the dominions of the
Emperor as well as in Hungary, and a Turkish host invaded
Bosnia and Croatia. The papal policy had plunged Eastern
Europe into helpless confusion.

The King of Poland and Mathias both looked to the Pope
for confirmation of their pretensions to the Bohemian throne;
but Paul II.'s answers were ambiguous. He wished to use
them both to crush George, and thought it best to leave both
the claimants with much to hope from his decision. The war
went on, and Mathias found Bohemia hard to subdue. The
political interests of Germany again centred in Bohemia; there
was even talk of an alliance between George and Charles of
Burgundy. Even the Catholics of Silesia began to tire of war,
and in Breslau there were preachers who spoke of the blessings
of peace. But in March 1471 George Podiebrad died;
Rokycana died a month before him. With them the ideas that
animated the policy of the Utraquist party passed away. The
Bohemian question entered into a new phase; and Ladislas
and Mathias were left to fight for the Bohemian crown.

Paul II. did not long survive his great antagonist. On July
26 he was struck with apoplexy and was found dead in his bed.
Men said that he had been strangled by a spirit which he kept
imprisoned in one of his many rings.[1] He had done nothing
worthy of note in his last years, save that he decreed to lessen
to twenty-five years the interval between the years of jubilee,
and found a field for his magnificence in the reception of
Borso of Este, on whom he conferred the title of Duke of
Ferrara in April 1471.

It is impossible to suppress a feeling of regret that so strong
a man as Paul II., who possessed many of the qualities of a
statesman, did not succeed in giving a more decided impulse
towards the settlement of the future policy of the Papacy. He
saw the dangers that beset it, and for his own part he was
resolved to escape them. He would not allow the Papacy to
sink to the level of an Italian principality, nor would he adopt

[1] Allegretti, *Ephemerides Senenses*, in Mur. xxiii. 771.

the dangerous plan of identifying it with the New Learning. He would not permit the abuses of the Curia to become stereotyped, but did what he could to repress their more flagrant forms. All these were tendencies difficult to resist, and by his resistance Paul II. exposed himself to much obloquy and misunderstanding. These negative merits would in ordinary times have constituted a high claim on our respect. Unfortunately the days of Paul II. demanded in the Pope a constructive policy, and Paul II. was not sufficiently experienced in statesmanship to make his meaning clear and impress it upon others. The good that he did was rapidly swept away. His one great undertaking, the reduction of Bohemia, was of doubtful service to the Papacy.

Paul II.'s Bohemian policy.

As the nephew of Eugenius IV., Paul II. had been brought up amidst the traditions of the papal restoration. Amidst his search after other objects to pursue he seems to have clung to these traditions as founded on such certain wisdom that hesitation was impossible. Bohemia was the abiding memorial of the papal degradation, and he was resolved that that memorial should be obliterated. Of his force and resoluteness there can be no question; they are expressed even in the formal documents of his Chancery, which discard the graces of style which Pius II. loved, and speak with a directness that is rare in diplomatic records. Paul II. died with a belief that he had reduced Bohemia. George and Rokycana were dead: Heimburg took refuge in Saxony, was reconciled with the Church under Paul's successor, and died early in 1472. The loss of its leaders destroyed the political power of the Utraquist party in Bohemia, and again left free course to the current of the Catholic reaction. But the papal candidate did not succeed to the Bohemian throne; the Diet chose Ladislas of Poland, and in spite of all that Mathias could do, Ladislas made good his position. Eastern Europe was distracted by the contest, and the Turkish arms reaped the advantage of this disunion amongst their Christian opponents. Ladislas succeeded because his weakness compelled him to be tolerant; he needed the help of the Utraquists against the Hungarians. The Compacts were tacitly recognised; the existing condition of religious matters was maintained. All that the Papacy gained was the substitution of a Catholic for a Utraquist King of Bohemia, and the

price which it paid was the advance of the Turkish arms. No
doubt there was in this more gain than appears at first sight.
A man with the political sagacity and wide aims of George
Podiebrad threatened a dangerous revolution in the international
organisation of Europe.

Moreover, the papal policy had unexpected influence on
the course of religious feeling in Bohemia ; it did much to call
into existence a new organisation that was more decidedly
opposed to the principles of the Roman Church. George
Podiebrad in his desire for a strong national unity had done his
utmost to put down the more fanatical sects which had been
formed out of the remnants of the Taborites; he wished to
stand simply but decidedly on the basis of the Compacts, and
in this he was seconded by Rokycana. This position no doubt
corresponded to the desires of the nation, but it was not in
itself a strong one for opposition to the Roman Church. The
religious movement in Bohemia was so closely united in its
origin with political feeling, that it spread only amongst the
Tchechs and was powerless to influence the German element
within Bohemia itself. The Compacts expressed the compromise which a general desire for peace rendered necessary ; and
the Council of Basel succeeded in paring down Utraquism to
its lowest point. Still, however the actual details might be
diminished, the fundamental position of Utraquism remained —
it asserted the authority of the Scriptures against the authority
of the Church. The weakness of Utraquism lay in the fact
that after establishing this principle it limited the sphere of
its application to the single question of the reception of the
Communion under both kinds. Rokycana, in his desire to
save Bohemia from its isolation, adhered to the Catholic ritual
and doctrine, discarded all that was adverse to the system of
the Church, and retained only the cup for the laity. The
probability was that such a symbol would become meaningless,
and that a protest restricted within such narrow limits would
lose all real power.

In this state of things we are not surprised to find that
some earnest minds reverted to the principles from which the
Hussite movement originally began, and in deep moral seriousness went back to the position assumed by Mathias of Janow
and other precursors of Hus. Chief amongst such men was

Peter Chelcicky, who was dissatisfied alike with the yielding attitude of Rokycana and with the savage spirit of the Taborites. He could not follow Rokycana in admitting Transubstantiation, the priestly power of Absolution, or the doctrine of Purgatory and Indulgences ; about the Sacrament of the Altar he reverted to the position of Wyclif, that by virtue of the words of consecration, the substance of bread and the Body of Christ were alike present in the hands of the priest.

But it was not doctrine so much as practice that occupied the mind of Peter Chelcicky ; he thirsted for a moral reformation, which the fury of the Hussite wars had thrust far into the background. Chelcicky sought for the real basis of the life of the individual Christian, and found it in the love of God apart from all human ordinances. He defined Christianity as the kingdom of the spirit and of freedom, in which man pursues what is good, and in which war and contention are unknown. Heathenism is servitude to the flesh ; from it spring dissension and wickedness, which must be compelled to order by means of temporal government. Thus temporal authority rests on no Christian basis, but is founded on heathenism—that is, on the wickedness of man's carnal nature ; it is in itself an evil, but a necessary evil. Historically, the Primitive Church was destroyed when under Constantine it became associated with the Empire. The union of the priesthood with the temporal power turned the priests into 'satraps of the Emperor,' and made them forget their Christian duties. From this destruction of the idea of the state followed in Chelcicky's teaching the unholiness of war and bloodshed ; even defensive war was no better than murder.[1]

Rise of the Bohemian Brothers. The ideas of Chelcicky received an impulse from the progress of the Catholic reaction under Ladislas I., which filled Rokycana with dismay and led him to preach earnestly against the prevailing lukewarmness and sin. Amongst his hearers was one whose soul was deeply moved, and who is known only by the name of Brother Gregory. He was referred by Rokycana to the writings of Chelcicky, which so impressed him that he soon outstripped the zeal of Rokycana, which began to cool when the accession of George Podiebrad opened out better

[1] For further details see Palacky's *Geschichte von Böhmen*, iv. part 1, 475 &c. ; also Gindely, *Die böhmischen Brüder*, i. 12, &c.

hopes for the moderate Utraquists. Rokycana prevailed on
King George to give Gregory and his adherents a settlement at
Kenwald in 1457. The colony rapidly increased and counted
amongst its members men of every class and occupation. They
called themselves 'Brothers' and formed a community on a
religious basis, according to the principles of Chelcicky. At
first they employed the ministrations of a neighbouring priest,
but in 1467 they went so far as to ordain priests of their
own; following the precedent of the Apostles in the choice of
Mathias, they selected nine and then cast lots for three. This
act marked a breach not only with the Roman Church, but
also with the Utraquists, and Rokycana demanded that the
Brotherhood should be suppressed. King George saw in these
'Brethren of the Law of Christ,' as they now called themselves,
the heretics whom the Pope called on him to root out of his
kingdom. They defended themselves by offering to prove from
Scripture ' that men are right in laying aside obedience to the
Roman Church, that the authority of the Pope is not grounded
on the power of God's Spirit, that his rule is an abomination
before God, that Christ's word gives him no power of blessing or
of cursing, that he has not the keys to decide between right and
wrong, nor the power to bind and to loose.' There could be no
clearer expression of the difference between the new church and
the old. King George prepared to put down these heretics in
1468, but the inroad of Mathias called him to employ his
energy elsewhere. What George could have accomplished was
too hazardous for his successor. The Bohemian Brothers were
sometimes threatened and sometimes persecuted; but they
continued to hold together, living a life of Christian socialism.
At the end of the century their numbers were computed at
100,000, and they formed a compact body whose power of
protest against the Roman Church was far more influential than
that of the vacillating Utraquists whom the Papacy was so keen
to destroy. By its violent proceedings against Bohemia the
Papacy only intensified, by concentrating, the opposition which
it strove to overcome.

However we regard the Bohemian policy of Paul II., we
see that, if the gain was dubious, the loss was manifest.

CHAPTER II.

PAUL II. IN HIS RELATIONS TO LITERATURE AND ART.

BOOK
V.

The Pa-
pacy and
the revival
of learning.
WHILE considering the pontificate of Nicolas V. we saw one
side of the revival of learning in Italy, when the movement
retained its first freshness, when its tendencies were as yet
undeveloped, and the Papacy hoped to use it as a means of
spreading its new glories. Besides the prevailing fashion of
the age, the struggle against the Council of Basel and the
negotiations with the Greeks had led the Papacy to feel the
need of learned and literary champions of the new school.
While the Italian courts patronised literary adventurers who
were ready, like Lorenzo Valla, to use their pens against the
Pope, even a monk like Eugenius IV. did not venture to
repulse the new learning. While the Council of Basel was a
field where ambitious scholars might flesh their pens in invective against the Pope, the Papacy could not afford to dispense
with literary gladiators. The Council of Florence brought to
the West a train of learned Greeks, whose help was useful to
the Latin theologians in combating the metaphysics of the
orthodox party among the Greeks. The Papacy was too much
indebted to the Humanists to repudiate them. Nicholas V.
placed himself at their head, and was a patron of scholars
whom he employed in making known the records alike of
classical and biblical antiquity. He was without fear of the
results, and showed no consciousness of the antagonism
between the traditions of the Church and the lore of the
ancients.

The literary glories of the pontificate of Nicolas V. were but
an episode in the history of Rome. Nicolas V. had been
trained in Florence, and the literary men of his court had
mostly been formed under the patronage of Cosimo de' Medici.
Rome did not long contend with Florence as the centre of
Humanism. The work of Nicolas V. was short-lived, and

Pius II. did not attempt to carry it on. Perhaps he felt a little uneasy about the future. Perhaps he had a dim remembrance of his own attitude towards religious and moral questions in his early days. At all events, he stood aloof from the main current of the Renaissance, and did not try to enlist the Humanists in the service of the Papacy.

There were, indeed, manifold signs that the new learning was eating out the heart of the religious sentiment of Italy, and that in so insidious a way that it was hard to see when and how the voice of protest should be raised. The Renaissance did not set before its votaries a definite system of thought, nor did it oppose any of the doctrines of the Church. It was an attitude of mind rather than a scheme of life. It did not attack Christianity, but it turned men's eyes away from Christianity. It did not contradict ecclesiastical dogma, but it passed it by with a shrug as unworthy of the attention of a cultivated mind. The discovery of antiquity showed so much to be done in this world that it was needless to think much of the next. The Humanists were content to pursue their studies, to steep themselves in classical ideas, and to leave theology to those whose business it was. They were in no sense reformers of the world around them. So long as they were respected and patronised, they found the world a very pleasant place, and did not wish to change it. Their studies did not lead them to action, but supplied a mental emancipation. Outward affairs might go as they pleased: the man of culture had a safe refuge within himself. He lived in a world of beauty which was his own possession, won by his own learning. For him there were no fetters, no restraints; he regarded himself as privileged, and his claim was generally allowed. To him the aim of life was to develop the powers of the individual, who was justified in using any means to find a sphere in which these powers could be fully exercised.

The danger of these tendencies must have been apparent to many minds, but it was not so obvious how the danger was to be met. A heresy might be condemned; an intellectual attitude could scarcely even be defined. Pius II. did nothing more than refuse to patronise the Humanists, who repaid his neglect by insulting his memory. Meanwhile the new learning was making strides. It was raising up a new school of philo-

sophy, whose bearing towards the Church at first seemed orthodox, and round the new philosophy it was attaining to a definite
organisation.

The new philosophy was a direct result of the Council of
Florence, and the consequent introduction into Italy of Greek
scholars, more numerous and more learned than had been
known before. Amongst those who came to Italy with John
Palæologus in 1438 was a remarkable man who is known by
the name of Gemistos Plethon. Georgios Gemistos was born at
Constantinople in 1355, and travelled in pursuit of occult knowledge in various quarters. He finally settled at Mistra, near the
site of the ancient Sparta, in the Peloponnese. There he became
famous as a teacher, and gathered round him many scholars,
chief amongst whom was Bessarion. He was summoned, as
the most learned of the Greeks, to take part in the disputes
against the Latins. But though he came to Italy at the
bidding of the Greek Church, theological questions had no
interest for him. He was already convinced that the spirit of
the Greeks was degenerate, and could only be restored by a
new religion and a revived philosophy. He told his views to
his scholars, though probably they only regarded them as the
visions of a student. When he came to Florence, a venerable
old man of eighty-three, with long flowing beard and calm dignified mien, he created an enthusiasm amongst the Florentine
scholars. There was a general curiosity in Italy to know something of Plato, and Gemistos was well versed in Plato's writings.
Instead of attending the Council, he poured forth his Platonic
lore, and uttered dark sentences to a circle of eager Florentines.
Cosimo de' Medici was delighted with him, and hailed him as
a second Plato. Gemistos modestly refused the title, but
playfully added to his name, Gemistos, the equivalent, Plethon,
which approached more nearly to his master's name.[1]

Amidst this admiring circle of Florentine scholars Gemistos
uttered strange sayings for an orthodox theologian of the

---

[1] Ficino, in the preface to his *Plotini Epitome* (Florence, 1492), says:
'Magnus Cosimus, quo tempore concilium inter Graecos et Latinos, sub Eugenio
pontifice, Florentiæ tractabatur, philosophum Græcum, nomine Gemistum
cognomine Plethonem, quasi Platonem alterum de mysteriis Platonicis dis-
putantem frequenter audivit ; e cujus ore ferventi sic afflatus est protinus, sic
animatus, ut inde Academiam quandam alta mente coeceperit, hanc oppor-
tuno primum tempore pariturus.'

Greek Church. He spoke of a new universal religion, which was to absorb all existing systems, Christendom and Islam alike. He pointed for its source to the inspiration of classical antiquity.[1] Most probably the Florentines did not pay much attention to these vague utterances. They were not in search of a religion, they aspired to no scheme of national regeneration; but they longed for a knowledge of Plato's philosophy as the source of greater illumination.

Gemistos Plethon returned from Florence to his school at Mistra, and plunged still further into his scheme of a new religion. As his philosophical ideas awakened so much enthusiasm in Italy, it is worth while examining the religious conceptions to which they led. In 1448 Gemistos wrote a treatise on the question of the Procession of the Holy Ghost, defending the Greek view against that of the Latins. He wrote, however, not as a theologian but as a philosopher, not from the point of view of Scriptural evidence, but from the reasonableness of the thing in itself. He set up what he calls 'the Hellenic theology,' by which he meant his own religious system, in opposition to that of the Church, and then proved the orthodox doctrine from this new theology. He argued that all difficulties about the Procession of the Holy Ghost vanished if, instead of the doctrine of the Church that the Son was equal to the Father, the teaching of the Hellenic theology was accepted, whereby were recognised many children of the Supreme Being, differing in power and other attributes.[2] He sent his book to the Patriarch Gennadios, himself a distinguished scholar under his former name of Georgios Scholarios. Gennadios was in a difficult position. The book supported the orthodox doctrine, and few would care to follow him in inquiring too closely into its method. Gemistos was an old man, of

Religious ideas of Gemistos.

---

[1] George of Trapezus, *Comparatio Platonis et Aristotelis.* 'Audivi ego ipsum Florentiæ, venit enim ad concilium cum Græcis, asserentem unam eamdemque religionem uno animo, una mente, una prædicatione, universum orbem paucis post annis esse suscepturam. Cumque rogassem Christine an Machometi, Neutram, inquit, sed non a gentilitate differentem.'

[2] Πλήθωνος νόμων συγγραφῆς τὰ σώζομενα, ed. Alexandre, Paris, 1858, p. 300: Καὶ ἐντεῦθεν προσλαμβάνοντες καί τι ἀξίωμα τῇ μὲν Ἑλληνικῇ θεολογίᾳ καὶ μάλα φίλον, τῇ δὲ Ἐκκλησίᾳ πολεμιώτατον, ὡς, ὧν μὲν αἱ δυνάμεις διάφοροι καὶ αὐτὰ ἂν εἴη ταῖς οὐσίαις διάφορα. This axiom he applies to the relations of the Persons of the Trinity.

great reputation, and it was not worth while to risk a quarrel with him. Gennadios answered with much tact, approving the object of the treatise, but delicately rebuking its arguments. At the end, however, he uttered words of warning. 'After God's revelation of Himself, how is it possible that there should be men willing to construct new gods, and attempt to rekindle the unreasoning theogonies that have long been quenched? How can they go back to Zoroaster, and Plato, and the Stoics, gathering a crowd of senseless words? If such like writings should ever fall into my hands, I will expose their emptiness, and many others will do likewise. I would subject them to arguments, not to the fire; the fire is more fitting for their authors.'[1] Yet Gennadios was not as good as his word. After the death of Plethon his 'Book of the Laws' fell into the hands of Gennadios, who, after reading it, committed it to the flames, and ordered all copies to be burned. He found it 'full of bitterness against Christians, mocking at our beliefs, not gainsaying them by argument, but setting forth his own.'[2] The efforts of Gennadios were successful, and only fragments of the treatise of Gemistos have survived; but they show a wondrous attempt to revive paganism on a philosophic basis. Gemistos represents himself as seeking the way of truth ignored by men. He took as his guides the law-givers and wise men of antiquity, especially Pythagoras and Plato, and by their help constructed a new theogony, in which Zeus was set up as the supreme god, whose attributes were being, will, activity, and power. From him sprang two orders of inferior deities, one legitimate, the other illegitimate children. The legitimate children of Zeus are the Olympian gods, at whose head stands Poseidon; the bastard children are the Titans. This strange classification was due to Gemistos' desire to construct a theogony which should harmonise with his system of logic. The Olympian gods were the eternal ideas; the Titans were the ideas expressed in form and matter. Below these supra-celestial gods were the legitimate and illegitimate children of Poseidon, who range from planets to demons; below them again were men and beasts and the material world. This new religion Gemistos seriously elaborated into a system by drawing up a calendar, a

---

[1] Alexandre, p. 313.   [2] *Ibid.* p. 439.

liturgy, and a collection of hymns.[1] He gathered round him a band of converts who looked upon their master as inspired by the spirit of Plato. It is a testimony to the influence of Gemistos on Italy that five years after his death his bones were brought from their resting place in the Peloponnesus by the impious Gismundo Malatesta, who placed them in a sarcophagus set in the side arcade of his wondrous Church at Rimini. The inscription calls Gemistos ' the chief philosopher of his time.'[2]

The system of Gemistos was a fantastic revival of Neoplatonism; and never did philosophy make a more futile attempt to provide a religion than in the logical cosmogony of Gemistos, from which the religious element has entirely disappeared. A student of philosophy, imperfectly understanding the system which he professed to follow, clothed his philosophic ideas in the incongruous garments of a religion with which he had long since ceased to sympathise. Gemistos saw that men seemed to need a religion; he threw his opinions into what he supposed to be a religious shape. Yet crude as was his attempt, it pointed to an intellectual question which was of great moment in the future. The theology of the Schoolmen had been built up in accordance with the system of Aristotle, whose philosophy was regarded as entirely orthodox. The discovery of Plato threatened to overthrow the supremacy of Aristotle. How were the opinions of Plato likely to influence the movement of thought? Plato corresponded to the imaginative yearnings with which the new learning filled the minds of its nobler students. It is true that his writings were imperfectly known, and that his system was confounded with that of the later Alexandrian writers. Yet men seized upon the

---

[1] A sample of a hymn to Zeus is worth quoting (Alexandre, p. 202):

Ζεῦ πάτερ, αὐτόπατερ, πρέσβιστέ τε δημιοεργέ,
Παγγενέτορ, βασιλεῦ, πανυπέρτατε, ἔξοχε πάντων,
Παγκρατὲς, αὐτοεόν τε καὶ αὐτοὲν, αὐτό τε ἐσθλὸν,

. . . .

Ἵλαθι, σῶζε, ἄγων σὺν τοῖσιν ὅλοισι καὶ ἄμμε
Σῶν διὰ παίδων αἰὲν ἀγανῶν, οἷς ἐπέτρεψας
Ἡ σοι καὶ τὰ καθ' ἡμέας, οἳ ἄρ' ἔδει, πέπρωται.

[2] It runs: 'Gemistii Byzantini Philosophi suo tempore Principis reliquum Sigismundus Pandulphus Mal. Pan. F. Belli Pelop. adversus Turcor. regum Imp. ob ingentem eruditorum quo flagrat amorem huc afferendum introque mittendum curavit, MCCCCLXV.'

poetical side of his teaching, which they adapted to the dreams of an intellectual childhood. The more religious minds felt the charm of Plato's conception of linking together the material and the immaterial world, and they set themselves to examine how far the doctrines of Christianity were contained implicitly in Plato's teaching. In Italy this process led to a dangerous paring away of the edges of ecclesiastical dogma ; in Germany it animated the rise of a new theology which sought after a direct consciousness of relationship between the soul and God.

Influence of
Bessarion.

The influence of Gemistos Plethon was carried to Rome by his distinguished scholar, Cardinal Bessarion, whose orthodoxy was above suspicion, but who nevertheless was in some degree imbued by his master's spirit. On the death of Gemistos, Bessarion wrote a letter of condolence to his sons. ' I hear,' he says, ' that our common father and guide, laying aside all mortal garments, has removed to heaven and the unsullied land, to take his part in the mystic dance with the Olympian gods.' [1] This is strange language in a Cardinal's mouth, but does not show that Bessarion had any sympathy with the paganism of Gemistos. It shows, however, the double life which the Humanists led : they were ready to talk the language of the Bible or the language of classical antiquity, as occasion needed. They had ceased to be conscious of much antagonism between the two, each of which corresponded to different sides of their nature. The new learning had become an insidious solvent of any definiteness in religious beliefs.

Bessarion did much for the study of Plato. He freed himself from the extravagances of Gemistos, and in the controversy which raged between the partisans of Aristotle and those of Plato he held a moderating position. But George of Trapezus carried his attack upon Plato so far that he drew from Bessarion a work ' Against the Calumniator of Plato ' which raised the knowledge of Plato to a higher level than it had before reached, and established the claim of that philosopher to the attention of the orthodox. Bessarion, moreover, was the centre of a literary circle, and the Academy called by his name was famous throughout

---

[1] Alexandre, 404: Πέπυσμαι τὸν κοινὸν πατέρα τε καὶ καθηγέμονα τὸ γεῶδες πᾶν ἀποθέμενον, ἐς οὐρανὸν καὶ τὸν ἀκραιφνῆ μεταστῆναι χῶρον, τὸν μυστικὸν τοῖς Ὀλυμπίοις θεοῖς συγχορεύσοντα Ἴακχον.

Italy. He formed a large library, which he bequeathed to Venice, where it formed the nucleus of the library of S. Marco.

The system of Academies rapidly spread throughout Italy, and gave the men of the new learning a definite organisation whereby they became influential bodies with a corporate existence. In Rome Bessarion's example furnished a model to the Roman Academy, whose founder was another of those who owed something to the influence of Gemistos. He was a strange man, who loved to shroud his private life in mystery. He called himself Pomponius, as being a good old Roman name, and to this he added Lætus, as a description of the joyousness of his temperament, though at times Lætus was exchanged for Infortunatus. The real name of Pomponius Lætus was Piero: he was a native of Calabria, a bastard of the noble house of the Sanseverini. In early life he came to Rome and was a pupil of Lorenzo Valla, whom he succeeded as the chief teacher among the Roman Humanists. Whether he travelled in Greece or no we cannot say; but he seems to have come in the way of Gemistos,[1] who probably quickened his taste for a revived paganism. Pomponius, however, was not a Platonist, and did not devote his attention to the study of Greek antiquity. He had no interest in inaugurating a new religion, but was content to imbibe the inspiration of the city of Rome, and gave himself unreservedly to its influence. 'No one,' says his friend Sabellicus, 'admired antiquity more; no one spent more pains in its investigation.' He explored every nook and corner of old Rome, and stood gazing with rapt attention on every relic of a bygone age: often, as he looked, his eyes filled with tears, and he wept at the thought of the grand old times. He despised the age in which he lived and did not conceal his contempt for its barbarism. He sneered at religion,[2] openly expressed

---

[1] Plethon quotes against Scholarius Πέτρος ὁ Καλαυρὸς ἀμφοτέρων τε τῶν φωνῶν ἔμπειρος καὶ ἅμα κρίνειν τὰ τοιαῦτα οὐκ ἀδόκιμος. Alexandre, 295. It is difficult to see any other 'Peter the Calabrian' who was sufficiently celebrated to be quoted in a controversy. On the other hand Sabellicus, *Vita Pomponii*, says of him. 'Græca vix attigit.' Probably he early abandoned the study of Greek in favour of Latin antiquity.

[2] 'Fuit ab initio contemptor religionis, sed ingravescente ætate cœpit res ipsa, ut mihi dicitur, curæ esse,' says Sabellicus, who tries to say the utmost that he can.

his dislike of the clergy, and inveighed bitterly amongst his friends against the pride and luxury of the Cardinals. A story is told that one day an enemy asked him publicly if he believed in the existence of God ; ' Yes,' he answered, 'because I believe that there is nothing He hates more than you.'[1] The deity which Pomponius adored was the Genius of the City of Rome. He set an example, which was long followed,[2] of celebrating the city's birthday with high festivities amongst a circle of congenial spirits. In later times men dated from the festivals of Pomponius the beginning of the downfall of faith.

The temper of Pomponius, as shown in the affairs of life, was that of a Stoic. He was poor and sought none of the prizes which literary men in his day so keenly pursued. When his wealthy relatives wished to claim him after he had become famous, and invited him to come and live at Naples, he returned them an answer which has become famous as a model of terseness. ' Pomponius Lætus to his relatives sends greeting. What you ask cannot be. Farewell.' He lived simply in a little house on the Esquiline, and hired a vineyard in the Quirinal, which he cultivated according to the precepts of Varro and Columella. His other amusement was to keep birds, whose habits he carefully observed. He always dressed in the same manner ; though simple in all things he was scrupulously clean and neat. His only interests were in exploring classical antiquity and teaching the students who flocked to his lectures. He rose early in the morning, and often needed the help of a lantern to guide him to his school, where there was scarcely room for the overflowing audience which had already assembled. There was nothing striking in his appearance. He was a small common-looking man, with short curly hair that turned grey before its time, and little eyes deep-set beneath beetling brows ; only when he smiled did his face become expressive.

Pomponius was a genuine teacher, who was interested in his scholars. He did not try to make a name by writings, for

---

[1] Paolo Cortese, *De Cardinalatu*. ' Julius Pom. Lætus cum ei Domitius Calderinus, homo inimicus, dixisset, num ex animi sententia crederet esse Deum, Quidni, inquit, esse credam, cum ei nihil te odiosius esse putem ? '

[2] Burchard, *Diarium*, iii. 131, in the year 1501 : ' Anniversarius Urbis conditæ dies est 20 aprilis ; consuevit singulis annis a poetis Urbis celebrari : quod, si recte memini, Pomponius Lætus, poeta laureatus, primus a paucis annis citra introduxit.'

he said that, like Socrates and Jesus, his scholars should be his books. He gave his attention to his lectures, and delighted in organising revivals of the old Latin comedies. He trained the actors and superintended the smallest details of stage management when any great man opened his house for the representation of a play of Plautus or Terence. He took the young men of Rome under his fatherly care, and would reprove their misdoings by a shake of the head and a remark, 'Your ancestors would not have behaved thus.'

The house of Pomponius was filled with relics of classical art, and the Academy which centred there was the home of very unorthodox opinions.[1] After the dissolution of the College of Abbreviators the Roman Academy became naturally the meeting place of the aggrieved scholars. There they abused the Pope to their hearts' content, while Pomponius sat by and smiled. They vented their spleen by organising a foolish protest against the Church and its ceremonies; and the example of Pomponius suggested to them a plan by which they bound themselves into an esoteric society. Instead of their baptismal names, given them from Christian saints, they chose new names from classical antiquity. Filippo Buonacursi called himself Callimachus Experiens, and we find besides Asclepiades, Glaucus, Petreius, and the like. The festival which Pomponius had instituted for the observance of the foundation day of the city suggested in like manner a parody of pagan rites. As a protest against Paul II., Pomponius Lætus was hailed as Pontifex Maximus, and many of the others took priestly titles. They held meetings in the Catacombs, and parodied the beginnings of the Christian Church.[2] It was an outburst of silly petulance on the part of men whose heads were turned by vanity, till they showed their spite against the Pope by threatening a revival of paganism.

Perhaps no one took these proceedings seriously except Paul II. He had condemned to do public penance some

[1] Canesius in Quirini, 78 : ' Depravatis moribus asserebant nostram fidem orthodoxam potius quibusdam sanctorum astutiis, quam veris rerum testimoniis subsistere.'

[2] Rossi, *Roma Sotterranea*, i., pref. 6, gives some of their inscriptions in the catacombs. One runs : ' Regnante Pomp. Pont. Max. Pantagatus Sacerdos Academiæ Rom.'

Fraticelli who had been sent for trial from Poli; how could he punish heresy and allow profanity to flaunt itself unashamed? Perhaps he was not much affected by the display of animosity towards himself, but he could not be indifferent to the dangers of a republican revival in Rome. The examples of Porcaro and Tiburzio were still warnings to a statesman that Brutus was a hero whom it was perilous to resuscitate. The follies of the Roman Academy might lead to political disturbances.

Paul II. persecutes the Academy. 1468.

We cannot wonder that Paul II. regarded the Roman Academy with suspicion. Its florid classicism, its hostility against the Church, its silly affectation of paganism, were enough to account for his disapproval. But sufficient ground for action was wanting till some vapouring talk of Callimachus Experiens was brought to the Pope's ear. Then Paul II. proceeded to act with promptitude. During the Carnival of 1468 several Roman youths were arrested, and Platina was dragged from the house of Cardinal Gonzaga to the Pope's presence. Paul II. looked on him with scorn, and said, 'So you have conspired against us under the leadership of Callimachus.' In vain Platina pleaded his innocence; he was ordered to be taken to the Castle of S. Angelo and be examined by torture. A letter of Pomponius Lætus, who was absent in Venice, which addressed him as 'Pater Sanctissime,' was regarded as proof of a conspiracy, and Platina was further accused of trying to urge the Emperor to summon a Council and create a new schism.

Pomponius Lætus in prison.

Pomponius was sent back from Venice, 'dragged in chains,' says Platina, 'through Italy like another Jugurtha.' When brought before his inquisitors he showed at first his accustomed spirit. When they asked his reason for assuming the name of Pomponius, he answered, 'What would it matter to you or the Pope if I called myself Hayrick?' But his stoicism rapidly gave way before imprisonment. He set himself to win the good graces of the Castellan of S. Angelo, Rodrigo de Arevalo, a famous theologian, best known by his later title of Bishop of Zamora. At first Pomponius wrote to Rodrigo in terms of scarcely concealed sarcasm; he lauded Paul II. in extravagant terms, and compared his magnanimity with that of Christ, who when he was smitten offered the other cheek: even so the Pope, in a crisis of unexampled danger, had pursued his course unmoved.

Rodrigo showed himself a match for Pomponius in irony. He congratulated him on the lucky chance now offered to a philosopher of showing his constancy and fortitude, which would otherwise have found no field for their display in the trivial concerns of ordinary life. After receiving this answer, Pomponius began to view the matter more seriously, and while admitting the greatness of the opportunity which he enjoyed, pleaded his innocence of any offence, and asked for books to cheer his solitude. Instead, however, of Lactantius and Macrobius, which were the captive's choice, Rodrigo sent a treatise of his own, 'Against the Errors of the Council of Basel,' which he doubtless considered to be a proper remedy for the deplorable unorthodoxy of his prisoner. What Pomponius really said when condemned to this unwonted literary diet we can only guess; what he wrote in reply was a fulsome eulogy of Rodrigo's eloquence, which he preferred to the highest flights of Cicero, because it was animated by a truly Christian spirit. By this letter Pomponius thought that he had cleared the way for a petition. He wrote on the same day in an altered strain; he said that he had been recalling all that the poets sang in praise of solitude; but their solitude, he found, was the solitude of the woods and fields, where they were gladdened by the delights of nature; he, pent in his prison walls, felt the need of kindly friends with whom he might exchange his thoughts. Rodrigo's turn had now come to triumph in this war of wits, and he had an easy task in penetrating the flimsy armour of Stoicism within which Pomponius had professed to stand secure. He dwelt on the pure delights of inward contemplation, treated the complaints of Pomponius as the result of a passing mood, and affectionately besought him not to show himself unworthy of his philosophy. After enjoying his discomfiture for a day or two he took compassion on his prisoners, and allowed them to meet together for talk. Pomponius, in expressing their gratitude, throws his philosophy to the winds. 'Man,' he says, 'always pines for what he does not possess; when weary of society he praises solitude; when in captivity he longs for freedom; if Diogenes had had bounds set, within which only he might roll his tub, he would have neglected philosophy to devise some means of overcoming his limits.'[1]

---

[1] I have printed these interesting letters in the Appendix.

In this frame of mind Pomponius reconciled his former principles to actual conditions. He longed for liberty, and sought it
by writing an abject apology to the Pope, in which he confessed his errors, threw the blame on others, and begged to be
released.[1] Paul II. perhaps felt that such characters as these
were scarcely deserving of serious consideration, and might be
trusted to profit by the lesson which they had received. Pomponius was soon set free, and was allowed to continue his lectures as before.

Platina did not escape so easily. He was kept in prison for
a year and was subjected to many inquisitions. No definite
proofs against him seem to have been forthcoming, but Paul II.
was resolved to teach the Roman Humanists a lesson. If he
had any suspicions of serious designs, Platina's letters from
prison must have convinced him of the futility of any plots
that could be devised by men of such poor spirit. In truth,
there was nothing heroic about Platina, and he wrote abjectly,
once and again, beseeching the Pope to release him. A prison
did not at all suit the luxurious man of letters; he was ready
to promise anything, to gain his release. ' I undertake,' he
writes, ' that if I hear anything, even from the birds as they fly
past, which is directed against your name and safety, I will at
once inform your Holiness by letter or messenger. I entirely
approve your proceedings for restraining and reproving the
license of the scholars; it is the duty of the chief shepherd to
preserve his flock from all infection and disease.' He admits
that in his pecuniary straits when he was dismissed from office
he lamented unworthily against God and man; but he will
never so far forget himself again. If only set at liberty and
freed from poverty he will celebrate with all his friends in prose
and verse the name of Paul. Even when attempting to write
seriously he cannot forget his literary vanity nor his classical
allusions. ' Poets and orators are necessary in all states, that
the memorials of illustrious men may not perish through want
of chroniclers.' He bids the Pope remember that Christ is
known through the writings of the Evangelists, the deeds of
Achilles through the verses of Homer. If the Pope will only

---

[1] Extracts are given by Gregorovius, *Geschichte der Stadt Rom*, vii. 581.
Pomponius signs himself ' Julius Pomponius Infortunatus, gratia tamen vestra,
Fortunatior futurus.'

release him he will promise to turn from his classical studies to
theology, 'where, as in a fertile and flowery meadow I will
gather herbs that are healthful both for body and soul.' If he
erred it was through academic license, the freedom engendered
by universal study. [1] In like strain he wrote to all whom he
thought had any influence with the Pope, Cardinals Bessarion,
Marco Barbo, Borgia, Gonzaga, Ammannati. He repeated to
them all the same protestations; he was accused of irreligion;
but he had always attended confession, gone to church, and
observed God's laws as far as human frailty allowed. Yet in a
letter to Pomponius he confessed that the proceedings of the
Academicians had given ground for suspicion. 'We ought to
bear with equanimity that the Pope took heed for his own
safety and for the Christian religion.' [2] Platina grovelled, but
he did not enjoy the process. He took his revenge in later years
by writing a life of Paul II. Few of those who read his biography have read his letters, or they would hesitate to give
much credence to his ill-natured hints. It is a strong testimony in favour of Paul II. that Platina has so little to say
against him.

On his release from prison Platina hoped that his persistent
grovelling had softened the Pope's heart, and that he would
obtain some mark of favour in return for his sufferings. Paul
II. pardoned him, but gave him no reward. It was enough for
the Pope that he had satisfied himself that Platina and his
friends were only foolish talkers, incapable of doing much
mischief; but Platina was strangely mistaken in thinking that
Paul II. had any need of his pen. He was allowed to go back
to his former obscurity a little crestfallen, and with vengeance
in his heart. Pomponius in like manner resumed his teaching
in Rome, where he died in 1498, and was honoured by a public
funeral. Paul II., however, dissolved the Roman Academy and
declared that all who mentioned its name, even in jest, were
guilty of heresy. Like most of Paul II.'s doings, this decree
was reversed by his successor. Sixtus IV. allowed the Academy

Marginal notes: CHAP. II. — Fortunes of the Roman Academy.

---

[1] Vairani, *Monumenta Cremonensium*, i. 30, &c. Papiensis *Epistolæ*, 230-1.

[2] Vairani, p. 38: 'Justus fuit Pontificis dolor, honesta tanta suspicione quæstio. Proinde et nos ferre æquo animo debemus si saluti suæ, si Christianæ religioni cavit.'

to revive, and it continued till it disappeared in the misery that followed the sack of Rome in 1527.

This persecution of the Roman Academy is a trivial matter in itself, but it has largely influenced the judgment of posterity on Paul II. In Platina's life of Paul II. this incident is raised into the foremost place, and Paul II. is represented as hating and despising literature to such a degree that he branded literary men as heretics.[1] From these words of Platina more recent writers have seen in Paul II.'s proceedings a consciousness of the perils wherewith the Renaissance movement threatened the system of the Church. In truth, however, Paul II. was not hostile to literature, and was himself deeply imbued with the spirit of the Renaissance; nor did he foresee in the revival of learning the precursor of the Reformation. Platina has skilfully succeeded in making himself the type of a martyr to learning, instead of an offensive braggart who trusted that the privileged position of a man of letters would cover any insolence or folly. Paul II. did not persecute scholars, but he put down the Roman Academy as a nuisance, a centre of unseemly buffoonery and sedition, as well as irreligious talk. It would seem that at first the Pope was suspicious of a definite plot against himself. When no evidence was forthcoming on that charge he fell back upon the notorious character of the proceedings of the Academy and decreed its suppression. His precautions may have been exaggerated; his action was certainly high-handed. But the Humanists needed a reminder that they were required to observe the same rules as ordinary citizens, and that no ruler could permit their follies to pass beyond a certain limit.

However, Platina outlived Paul II. and had the opportunity of telling his story in his own fashion. He had tried conclusions with Paul II. and had been worsted: but no one thought very seriously of the matter. Sixtus IV. made Platina his librarian, and in that dignified position Platina's early misdoings were forgotten. He liked to tell the tale of his sufferings, and no doubt the tale grew darker every time that it was told, till Platina verily believed himself to have been a martyr

---

[1] ' Humanitatis autem studia ita oderat et contemnebat ut ejus studiosos uno nomine hæreticos appellaret.'

to literature, and stamped this legend on the mind of the rising generation of scholars.[1]

No doubt such a belief would not have taken root if Paul II. had attached to himself any men of letters. This, however, he showed no desire to do, though Campanus offered to write a history of his pontificate, and Filelfo was desirous to take up his abode in Rome. Paul II. was civil to Filelfo, and received from him a translation of Xenophon's Cyropædia, for which he rewarded the needy old scholar by a present of 400 ducats; but he did not encourage his hope of becoming a regular dependent on the Papal bounty. In fact Paul II. found literary men troublesome; they were foul-mouthed and slanderous, and Paul II. could not endure their license. Even the literary veteran, George of Trapezus, was sent to prison for a month to teach him not to speak evil of previous Popes who had been his patrons.[2] Paul II. took a common-sense view of the venal literature of his age. He did not care for poetry or rhetorical panegyrics, but he was a student of the Scriptures, of canon law, and history. Both in public and private matters Paul II. loved directness. Though he was no orator, he spoke for himself in public business, and did not heed the sneers at his lack of the finished style of Pius II. In private consistories he discarded Latin and spoke in Italian, which no doubt was a severe shock to official propriety.[3]

[1] Paolo Cortese, *De Hominibus Doctis*, 46: ' Ex Platina sæpe sum audire solitus, qui se Campanino comitem in vinculis fuisse dicebat (fuit enim tum litteratis et carceris et exilii subeunda calamitas).' The persecution has already grown to universal dimensions.

[2] Gaspar Veronensis, in Muratori, iii. pt. 2, 103, tells the fact: the reason is gathered from the letters of Rodrigo de Arevalo, Castellan of S. Angelo (MSS. of Corpus Christi College, Cambridge, No. 166). Amongst them is a letter of George of Trapezus, in which he says, ' Teneor in hoc Sancti Angeli Castello, urbis Romæ nobilissimo, jam ultra mensem summi pontificis jussu,' and asks the cause. Rodrigo answers, ' Compertum esse audio in quosdam summos pontifices, quorum gloria summa est et memoria in benedictione erit, quos de te egregie meritos nosti vita functos, aliosque clarissimos maximosque viros, verbo et scriptis maledictis et contumeliis vehementer atque acerrime exarsisse ; quorum famæ et laudibus maculam, quoad te fuit, ut aiunt, addidisti et, ut brevibus agam, os in cœlum posueris lingua tua transeunte super terram.'

[3] Paris de Grassis, Mus. Brit. MSS. Addit. 8440 : ' Paulus ne videretur tumidus in recitando personaliter oravit licet tamen plerumque defecerit ; quinimo ipse in consistoriis secretis et congregationibus et aliis similibus actibus non nisi

Paul II. was not only destitute of literary friends; he had
few friends of any kind and no favourites. The Cardinals
never forgave him for shaking himself loose from the shackles
with which they endeavoured to bind him at his accession,
and Ammannati regarded his sudden death as a judgment upon
him for his want of faith. Paul II. was too sensitive not to
feel the breach that had so been created, and he had not the
qualities which enabled him to repair it. He grew more and
more reserved, and led a somewhat solitary life amidst his outward grandeur. 'He is surrounded by darkness,' wrote Ammannati, 'he is not wont to make rash assertions, but is more
ready to hear than to speak.'[1] This change in his disposition
after his election corresponds to his mental attitude. He felt
that things were amiss, but he did not see how to mend them,
and the Cardinal College had no advice to give. The older
Cardinals were the zealots of the Papal restoration; Carvajal
could advocate warmly the reduction of Bohemia, but pronounced against any reform of the Church. The younger
Cardinals were, like Ammannati, friends of Pius II., or like
Cardinal Gonzaga, men who had been created because their
relatives were politically useful in re-establishing the position
of the Papacy in Italy. Paul II. did not find among them any
counsellors after his own heart; they sufficed for the conduct
of current business, but that was all.

In the course of his pontificate Paul II. created ten Cardinals. He did not, however, increase the College, but merely
filled up the vacancies caused by death. In his selection of
men for this dignity he showed the same mixed motives as is
displayed in the rest of his policy. He did not entirely rise
above personal considerations, as he created three of his
nephews, the Venetians Marco Barbo, Battista Zeno, and
Giovanni Michael; but they were all men of high character,
who proved themselves not unworthy of their office. None of
them became his favourite, or was especially influential with
him, or was unduly enriched. Of the other Cardinals created

vulgari sermone loquebatur. Et cum semel in consistorio voluisset quod unus
advocatus consistorialis, qui tunc erat D. Prosper de Caffarellis, pro seipso
Pontifice loqueretur, et dum loqueretur defecit; contra quem tum Papa
turbatus est et voluit pro eo supplere, qui etiam similiter et plus quam
advocatus defecit; quod magnum ridiculumque scandalum fuit.'
[1] Cardinalis Papiensis *Epistolæ*, No. 202.

by Paul II., two, the Neapolitan Caraffa and Francesco of Savona, were chosen for their learning; and the others, amongst whom were Thomas Bouchier, Archbishop of Canterbury, and the Frenchman La Balue, were intended to add to the representa tive character of the College. When La Balue, in 1469, was imprisoned by Louis XI. for his traitorous correspondence with the Duke of Burgundy, Paul II. did not take his stand on ecclesiastical privilege. La Balue was tried and condemned in France; the Pope contented himself with sending a few judges to assist at the trial.[1]

In the creation of Cardinals Paul II. showed his general impartiality and his good intentions. His fame has suffered because he was impartial and well-intentioned, because he identified himself with no party, and pursued no personal ends. Reserved and sensitive he went upon his way, and where his mind was made up he made all bend to his will. With him, as with many men of a fine nature which has not been disciplined by experience, geniality in a private capacity gave way to coldness in the discharge of public duty. Naturally kindly and sympathetic, he shrank from responsibility, and only assumed it by an effort of self-repression, which he knew that any display of personal feeling would destroy. As a consequence his manner seemed abrupt, and he was misjudged and misrepresented. It pained him to refuse petitions which were presented to him, and he more and more withdrew himself from granting audiences, which was put down to heedlessness and neglect of his duties. It is characteristic of him that he received petitioners as he walked about, that he might not be obliged to see their imploring faces, and might be spared the sight of their disappointment.[2] But when he detected imposture his anger was aroused. One day he turned round sternly and said to one who pleaded, 'You are not speaking the truth'; whereupon a pet parrot who was perched in the room immediately flew upon the object of the Pope's anger, exclaiming 'Turn him out, turn him out, he is not speaking the truth.'[3]

The same shrinking from causing pain made Paul II.

---

[1] Ammannati, *Commentarii*, 448, gives a long account of the deliberations on this point.

[2] Paolo Cortese, *De Cardinalatu*, bk. ii.: 'Quo causa oculorum obtutus fugiendi esset, negandique pudor posset ambulando dilui.'

[3] Canesius in Quirini, 70.

merciful as a ruler of Rome. Whenever he heard the bell of
the Capitol toll for an execution he turned pale and clutched
his breast to check the beating of his heart. This unwilling-
ness to disappoint others led him to live by himself and shun
interviews. He was apparently troubled by asthma and could
not sleep at night ; he took this as an excuse for turning night
into day.[1] Men naturally grumbled and accused him of capri-
ciousness and arrogant disregard of others. Personally Paul II.
was not popular. His stately figure and dignified bearing
commanded respect ; but men feared rather than loved him.
He felt this and was saddened by the feeling. One day a
Cardinal asked him why, when he had all that he could desire,
he was not content. 'A little wormwood,' said the Pope, 'can
pollute a hive of honey.'

Even the points which Paul II. had most in common with
his age were not appreciated. He loved magnificence, and it
was counted as vain glory. He was a patron of architecture ; this
was reckoned to be merely a desire to commemorate his name.
He was an ardent collector of works of art ; because his collection went beyond the prevailing fashion he was accused of
simple avarice. Paul II. had as passionate a love for antique
beauty as had Pomponius Lætus ; because he had the temperament of an artist and not the pedantry of a scholar he was
handed down to posterity as an uncultivated barbarian.

In his love for art Paul II. went far beyond his time, and
may rank as a type of the high minded and large souled
patron and collector. He knew his own tastes and did not
follow the prevailing fashions. The mighty Palazzo di Venezia,
as it is now called, remains as a memorial of the great conceptions of Paul II. and marked the definite triumph of
Renaissance architecture in Rome. It was begun while Paul
II. was a Cardinal, and was finished during his pontificate.
The adjoining basilica of S. Marco was restored, adorned
with frescoes, and its windows were filled with stained glass.
He built three rows of arcades in the first court of the
Vatican, and erected a pulpit from which the Pope might
give the benediction. He resumed the work of Nicolas V.
in building the tribune of S. Peter's. He preserved the

*Architec-
tural works
of Paul II.*

---

[1] The fact is mentioned by Platina and Ammannati. The reason is given
by Canesius, in Quirini, 98 : ' Dormitione nocturna gravius catarro vexabatur.'

ancient monuments of the city, and most of its churches owe something to his care.[1] His chief architect was Giuliano di San Gallo, and he kept in constant employment a number of jewellers and embroiderers who made vestments and ornaments which he bestowed on the Churches in the Patrimony.

The distinguishing feature of the private life of Paul II. was that he was an enthusiastic collector of objects of art. He began the habit in his youth, and when he died he had brought together in his Palace of S. Marco the richest artistic collection that had been formed since the fall of the Roman Empire. As soon as he became Cardinal he commissioned agents to search for him throughout Italy; and many a struggle, such as collectors love, he waged for the possession of some prized object with the Medici, Alfonso of Naples, and Leonello of Este. How skilful he was may be gathered from a letter of Carlo de' Medici, who wrote that he had picked up in Rome from a servant of the great medallist, Pisanello, thirty silver medals. Cardinal Barbo heard of this find, met the unsuspecting Carlo in church one morning, took him graciously by the hand and walked with him to his house, where he contrived to get hold of Carlo's purse containing the medals, relieved it of its treasures and refused to return them.[2] No doubt he paid their full value; for he did not like to be under any obligation, and when he was Pope he wrote to the King of Portugal who sent him a sapphire ring, 'our custom, long and diligently observed, is not to receive gifts.'[3] He showed the same temper about his manuscripts, for it was observed that he was always ready to lend and slow to borrow.

Before he became Pope his museum in the Palace of S. Marco was large and precious; during his pontificate he was always eager to increase it. Cardinal Ammannati wrote to a friend, Helianus Spinula, who was anxious to obtain the Pope's good graces for his son, that he had spoken on his behalf. Paul II. interrupted him, 'I know the man; he has the same tastes as we have, and uses his eyes to discern things that are

---

[1] A full account of Paul II.'s works is given by Müntz, *Les Arts à la Cour des Papes*, ii.; an entire volume is devoted to Paul II.

[2] Gaye, *Carteggio degli Artisti*, i. 163.

[3] Marini, *Archiatri*, ii. 201.

of excellent workmanship. He has treasures which he has gathered from Greece and Asia. He could do me a great favour by letting me have some things from his collection, not, however, as a gift, for our custom has always been to pay, and to pay liberally, for what pleases us.' Ammannati asked what the Pope chiefly desired. 'Images of the saints,' answered Paul II., 'of old workmanship, which the Greeks call Icons, Byzantine tapestries, woven or embroidered, old pictures and sculptures, vases, especially of precious stones, ivory carvings, gold and silver coins, and such like.' Paul II.'s tastes were catholic, and he was not merely content with collecting, but had excellent taste and a great knowledge of archæology. It was remarked with wonder that he knew at a glance the busts of the various Roman Emperors. He caused his collection to be catalogued and every object carefully described. The descriptions show us that mythology was imperfectly understood, and that the knowledge of emblems was still in a rudimentary stage.[1] From this catalogue we learn that Paul II. had gathered together forty-seven antique bronzes, two hundred and twenty-seven cameos, three hundred and twenty intaglios, ninety-seven ancient gold coins, and about a thousand silver coins and medals, besides Byzantine ivories, mosaics, enamels, embroideries, and paintings, as well as jewellery, goldsmith's work, and tapestries of his own age, and a large number of uncut precious stones. This splendid collection was appropriated by Paul II.'s successor. The precious stones were sold to Lorenzo de' Medici, the bronzes probably formed the nucleus of the Capitoline Museum, the rest was gradually dispersed. Even in this point also the achievements of Paul II. were remorselessly swept into oblivion.

The reason why Paul II.'s enjoyment of art was not understood by his contemporaries, was probably because it was merely sensuous and not antiquarian. He loved things for their own preciousness, not for the associations which hung around them. Men in those days had no sympathy with his habit of playing with precious stones and gazing with delight upon their lustre; in such a simple source of pleasure they saw only the gloating of avarice. It must be owned that Paul II. carried his passion to the verge of childish-

[1] It is published by Müntz, *Les Arts à la Cour des Papes*, ii. 181, &c. The first catalogue was made in 1457, but it received many additions.

ness. He took jewels to bed with him; he kept them in hiding-places that he might refresh himself by the sight of them when he had a moment of solitude. After the death of Sixtus IV. Cardinal Barbo recognised in the Pope's private room a writing-desk which had been a favourite piece of furniture of his uncle. On looking into it he found a secret drawer containing seven large sapphires and other stones to the value of 12,000 ducats.

Paul II. was in all things a child of his age; but his fineness of character showed him that his age was in no good way. For himself, he strove to check its worse impulses, and uphold a standard of justice and honour. His only luxury was magnificence; in his private life he was simple and even abstemious. He lacked the force necessary to give decisive effect to his good intentions, and men saw only the outside of his life and character. The beginnings that he made towards better things were so entirely swept away by his impetuous successor that posterity gave him no credit for his fruitless efforts. His pontificate was a time of conscious perplexity in himself, which he was too reserved to confide to others. He acted tentatively, almost despondingly, and led a solitary life. Later times dated from him the decline of the Papacy;[1] it is more true to say that he saw the decline approaching and felt himself powerless to stay it.

[1] Raphael Volterranus, *Commentarium Rerum Urbanarum*, bk. xxii.: ' Res pontificalis magnam ex eo primum fecit inclinationem, ut deinde traditae per manus successiones usque ad hunc diem innumerabilibus malis tempora referserint, dum januis vitiorum omnium reclusis, palam cunctis antiquam disciplinam pastorum pessumdare liceret.'

CHAPTER III.

SIXTUS IV. AND THE REPUBLIC OF FLORENCE.

1471–1480.

BOOK
V.

Conclave
of Sixtus
IV. Au-
gust 6–9,
1471.

THE death of Paul II. was so unexpected that only seventeen
Cardinals out of the twenty-six were present at the Conclave
on August 6. It would seem that there was no decided motive
in choosing a new Pope, and the first voting was very scattered.
In the second voting Cardinals Estouteville, Calandrini, Ca-
pranica, and Ammannati united in favour of Bessarion as the
oldest member of the College, a man of note, and one whose
election was likely to cause a speedy vacancy. But the old
objection to Bessarion as a Greek again revived, and he would
not be politically acceptable to France or to the Italian princes.
Cardinals Borgia, Orsini, and Gonzaga set up against him
Francesco of Savona, whose claims on the ground of learning
and high character might fairly be opposed to those of Bessarion.
It was urged against him that he had only been a Cardinal for
four years, and that his election was a decided slight to many
senior to himself; but his supporters managed to clear away
objections, and Francesco was elected on August 9.[1]

Early life
of Sixtus
IV.

The election of Francesco di Savona awakened great surprise
and showed that the Cardinals still adhered to their policy of
having a Pope who would extend their privileges and rule
according to their will. At the same time it was a testimony
to the influence of Paul II. that they did not venture to choose
an entirely obscure and weak man. Francesco had won his
way to the Cardinalate solely by his reputation for theological
knowledge and for a blameless life. He was of such lowly
origin that he had not a name of his own. His father was a

---

[1] Ammannati, *Epistolæ*, 395, gives some account of this conclave; for the
other details see the Italian translation of the *Conclave* in *Conclavi dei
Pontefici*, i. 115.

poor peasant in a little village near Savona, and at the age of
nine Francesco was handed over to the Franciscans to be
educated. He acted for a time as tutor with the family of
Rovere in Piedmont, and from them he took the name by
which he was afterwards known.[1] His talents and his industry
were great, and he lectured on philosophy and theology at
Bologna, Padua, Pavia, Florence, and Perugia. At Pavia
Bessarion attended Francesco's lectures, and was struck by
his learning.[2] When he rose to the post of General of the
Franciscan Order, and distinguished himself by his reforming
zeal, the recommendations of Bessarion found an echo in the
inclinations of Paul II. and Francesco was elevated to the
Cardinalate. At Rome he was regarded as a profound scholar,
and he increased his reputation by a treatise ' On the Blood of
Christ,' a contribution to the controversy between the Dominicans
and the Franciscans, which Pius II. had vainly striven to appease.
At the time of his election he was fifty-seven years old.

[1] Genealogies were forthcoming for Sixtus IV. in a later time, but contemporaries all agree about the obscurity of his origin. Even in 1517 Garimberto wrote : ' Fu Papa Sixto Quarto nobile di patria, ma di padre ignobilissimo,' *Della Fortuna* (Venice, 1547), 21. The fullest account of his parentage is given in the *Annalisi di Tito*, quoted by Cugnoni, *Archivio della Società Romana*, ii. 225 : ' Franciscus Saonensis juventutis tempore Saone obscuro natus loco nobilibus quibusdam prosapie Roboree in piedmontanis oris servierat ac fuerat familiaris, qui genere suo tantum virtutis conatus est quantum aberat claritatis ut in virum peritissimum evaderet, ita ut insignia roboree nobilitatis, que sunt quercus, acciperet et pro roboreis se reputaret.' A rare Roman edition, *Oratio in funere illustris Dni. Leonhardi de Robore, Alme Urbis prefecti, habita a Rev. P. D. Francisco Episcopo Caariensi S. D. N. Pape Datario*, printed in 1475, shows that even then nothing could be made out of the Pope's family. ' Claret familia ejus hodie honestissima de Robore, totaque in Italia notissima, que et si tempornm curriculis obliterata diuque neglecta sit, non tamen ideo non clara censenda est, cum extent prestantieque nobilitatisque multa vestigia, que nulla temporis oblivio delere unquam potuit. . . Maria Virgo, Domini parens, multo paupertate illustrior quam potuit quantalibet rerum opulentia coruscare, infimo fortune demissa loco fabro nupsit ; erat tamen regio ex sanguine orta Davidice stirpis clara propago. Quippe temporalium inopia rerum humilisque fortuna antique nobilitatis jura obumbrare potest non tollere.'

[2] MS. *Conclare Sixti Quarti* in Yelverton MSS. 74 : ' Antequam Cardinalis crearetur publice legerat philosophiam omnibus Italie studiis et presertim in principalibus ; Pavie autem habuit auditorem inter alios praeclaros viros Cardinalem illm Bessarionem, Latine lingue et Grece doctissimum, quocum insuper vixit familiariter.' An oration of the Venetian Bernardino Giustinian to Sixtus IV. says, ' In Padua moratus es per xx fere annos nobilis alumnus legendo, orando, scribendo.'

BOOK
V.
Coronation
of Sixtus
IV., Au-
gust 25,
1471.

A reputation for learning and a high character would not
have been enough to secure Francesco's election to the Papacy.
The Cardinals were entirely undecided, and there was a good
opportunity for adventurous intrigue.   It would seem that
this was clear to a young Franciscan, Piero Riario, the nephew
and favourite of Cardinal Francesco, who acted as his attendant
in the Conclave.   Piero, seeing the prevailing indecision, had
no scruple in making a bargain with the most influential
Cardinals; and its results were seen immediately after the
election, when Cardinal Orsini was made Chamberlain, Cardinal
Borgia received the rich abbey of Subiaco, and Cardinal Gonzaga
that of S. Gregorio.[1]   The gratitude of the new Pope had been
already discounted by the operations of his nephew Piero, and
with the election of Sixtus IV. began a system of personal intrigue
which rapidly grew into a serious scandal.   The beginning of
his pontificate was tumultuous.   Angered at a crush caused by
a sudden stoppage of the cavalcade, the crowd threw stones at
the Pope's litter, when, on August 25, he was crowned under
the title of Sixtus IV.

The first steps of Sixtus IV. promised a return of the
Papacy to the region of European politics.   The new Pope
resumed the plans of Pius II., and again set forth to Christen-
dom the duty of a Crusade against the Turks.   He issued an
encyclical letter for this purpose, and negotiated with the
Emperor for the summons of a Council to prepare for the Holy
War.   Frederick III. proposed Udine for its meeting-place.
Sixtus IV. replied that the Italian powers would not consent to
Udine, and he himself dared not go so far from the Papal
States; he proposed Rome, but offered to go to Mantua or
Ancona.   The negotiations for a Council came to nothing; but
Sixtus IV. sent out legates, Bessarion to France, Borgia to

---

[1] The *Conclave* says : ' Inter alios Cardinales fuerunt hi tres prælati maximæ
quidem auctoritatis, Latinus Ursinus, Rodericus Borgia Vice Cancellarius,
Franciscus Gonzaga Mantuanus, qui tres capita fuerunt ejusdem electionis, in
se quisquam provinciam assumens difficultates si quæ essent rejiciendo.
Propterea Pontifex factus, ne ingratus ullo modo appareret, Latino Ursino est
elargitus Cameriatum Eccl{ae}, Roderico Vice Cancel{o} dedit Abbatiam de Subiaco,
et Card{ii} alii Mantuano Monasterium Divi Gregorii.' Infessura, in Eccard,
Scriptores, ii., 1789, gives the same account, and adds ' E questo per operatione
di Frate Pietro.'

Spain, Marco Barbo to Germany, and appointed Caraffa admiral of a fleet which, after the example of Calixtus III., he began eagerly to build on the Tiber.

The legates met with no better success than their predecessors in the same business. Bessarion found Louis XI. too busied with his plans against England and the Duke of Burgundy to pay any attention to projects for a Crusade. He succeeded in establishing better relations between the King and the Holy See, but returned without having furthered the object of his mission, and died of fever in Ravenna in November 1472. Borgia went to Spain, delighted to display his magnificence in his native Valencia, where he met with a splendid reception; but the Spanish kingdoms had troubles of their own to occupy their attention, and Borgia was scarcely likely to kindle spiritual zeal by the exhibition of his vanity and self-seeking.[1] It is not surprising that he also accomplished nothing. In Germany Barbo had a more difficult task. Sixtus IV. espoused the cause of Mathias against Ladislas in Bohemia, and threatened the adherents of Ladislas with excommunication. The legate's energies were consumed in fruitless attempts to arrange the strife for Bohemia between the Kings of Poland and Hungary, and to bring about a good understanding between the Emperor and the Electors; he returned in 1474 empty-handed from Germany.

Meanwhile Sixtus IV. had equipped twenty galleys against the Turks, and gave his solemn benediction to the admiral's ship before it set out to Brindisi to join the contingents of Venice and Naples. The combined fleet made a series of plundering raids on the Turkish coast, but caused more terror than damage to the foe. In January 1473 Caraffa returned to Rome and made a triumphal entry with twelve camels and twenty-five Turkish prisoners. It was a novel spectacle, but a scanty return for the expenses of the armament.

Sixtus IV. had now gained sufficient experience of the prospects of a crusading policy. It would seem that he had resolved to give a fair trial to the old political traditions of the

[1] Cardinalis Papiensis *Epistolæ*, 534: 'Multa varietatis et luxus et ambitionis et avaritiæ documenta relinquens, nullo eorum perfecto quod sibi ad nomen legationis prætenderat, odio Principum et populorum renavigat Romam.'

Papacy before entering upon a new sphere of action. He paused to justify in his own eyes the transition from a Franciscan reformer to an Italian prince. He was not prepared to adopt the tentative attitude of Paul II., but was resolved to pursue some definite course of his own. If his energy could be employed in carrying out the plan already marked out by his predecessors, he was willing to devote himself to that work ; but the results of the survey of Europe which was taken by his legates were not encouraging. Everywhere were struggles conducted for national aggrandisement. Religious principles were everywhere weak, morals were corrupt, spiritual agencies were feeble. Before a Crusade was possible, years of conciliatory diplomacy and ecclesiastical reform would be necessary to heal the breaches of Europe and revive the religious basis of its life.

Perhaps Sixtus IV. saw that this was the issue which lay before him ; if so, he rapidly dismissed it as uncongenial to his character. Beneath the frock of the Franciscan, beneath the retiring habits of a student, was concealed the passionate nature of an Italian of the Renaissance. Sixtus IV. was determined to leave his mark upon the events of his pontificate ; he was strong in the strength of an individual character. Already the Italian spirit had invaded the traditions of the papal office ; and since the days of Eugenius IV. each Pope had thought more of signalising his own pontificate than of upholding the continuity of the papal policy. In Sixtus IV. the Italian spirit entirely triumphed, and the Papacy boldly adopted the current aims and methods of the Italian powers which hemmed it in.

If Europe in general was in an evil plight, Italy was even more corrupt than other countries. During the dark days of the Schism and the General Councils, when the papal power was practically in abeyance, Italian politics had developed with marvellous rapidity. Commerce had prospered ; wealth and luxury had increased ; the desire for material comfort had absorbed men's energies ; the culture of the Renaissance had thrown a graceful veil of paganism over self-seeking. Popular liberty had everywhere disappeared before absolutism. The State centred round the person of its individual ruler, who contented his subjects by a display of outward magnificence, and condoned his tyranny by fostering commerce and affording full scope for the particular interests of his people. The stronger rulers made their power still more absolute; the condottieri strove to become independent princes; the smaller lords served the greater, and by their military activity protected themselves against the results of their reckless tyranny.

In the midst of this seething sea of intrigue lay the Papal States, a tempting prize to adventurers small and great. It might well be a question for a sagacious Pope how he was to preserve the temporal sovereignty of the Papacy in the existing movement of Italian politics. The state of Italian thought and feeling left no room for sentiment, and paid no heed to the lofty claims of the papal office. Ladislas of Naples had aimed at secularising the lands of the Church; his plans had been eagerly pursued by Braccio; and only a lucky accident had diverted Francesco Sforza from seeking his fortunes at the expense of the Papacy. Ferrante of Naples was not a neighbour who could be trusted to withstand the temptation of a favourable opportunity. Rome itself was turbulent and was exposed to the constant intrigues of petty tyrants in the neighbourhood. The Counts of Anguillara had long defied the Pope; hordes of bandits made access to Rome difficult and pillaged pilgrims on their way to the tombs of the Apostles. Within Rome itself the Popes could not feel themselves secure. Eugenius IV. had been driven out; the conspiracies of Porcaro and Tiburzio against Popes so excellent as Nicolas V. and Pius II. showed the presence of threatening elements of disaffection, and suggested suspicions of dangerous intrigues on the part of some of the Italian powers.

Position of the Papacy in Italy.

No doubt the Papacy, if it had been strong in its moral hold on Europe, could have disregarded the menacing condition of Italian affairs. But the repeated negotiations about the Crusade showed the Papacy clearly enough that nothing was to be expected from a united Christendom. Italian politics only expressed with greater definiteness the prevalent condition of Europe. Everywhere men were busy with questions that concerned their own material well-being. The hold of the Church was slight over men's affections. The chief ecclesiastics were relatives of kings and princes and were engaged in secular pursuits. The Papacy had not behaved towards Germany in a

Indifference of Europe towards the Papacy.

way to inspire respect; the French crown had laid a firm hand on the Church by means of the Pragmatic Sanction. The great allies of the Papacy in a former age, the Preaching Friars, had forfeited their hold upon the people; and the attempt of Eugenius IV. to galvanise them into renewed vitality had proved a failure. Pius II. had shown the hopelessness of uniting Europe for any common object. Paul II. had swept away the last ecclesiastical problem which faced the Papacy by crushing George Podiebrad in Bohemia.

It is to the credit of Sixtus IV. that he did not begin a new policy till he had convinced himself of the futility of the traditional policy of his office. When that was clearly hopeless he turned to the question which lay immediately at hand. If no loftier aim demanded his energies, they should at least be devoted to a useful purpose, to the organisation of the papal dominions into a compact state. Previous Popes had trusted for the maintenance of their dominions to the respect generally felt towards the Papacy, and to the support of the powers of Europe; Sixtus IV. felt that neither of these was secure. He resolved no longer to shelter himself behind the claims of the Papacy as an institution, but as a man to venture into Italian politics, and establish his temporal sovereignty by means of men, their weapons and their enterprise. When he looked around him he found the Papacy without friends in Italy. The pacific policy and the moderating position of Paul II. had only been maintained by a resolute effort of self-restraint; it was not understood by other powers, and there was no guarantee that it could be safely continued.[1] Sixtus IV. did not think it worth while to give it a trial, but decided that he would use the resources and the authority of his office for the protection and extension of its temporal possessions.

For this purpose he combined natural affection with statecraft, and elevated nepotism into a political principle. If the Pope were to act decisively, he must have lieutenants whom he could entirely trust, whose interests were bound up with his, and who could use for the furtherance of the papal rule the

[1] Sigismondi de' Conti, *Historia*, i. 5: 'Sedes Apostolica nullis in Italia certis amicitiis fulta erat : propterea quod nimia constantia Pauli fere omnibus suspecta erat.'

resources which the Pope could supply. Other Popes had been
nepotists a little, but to Sixtus IV. nepotism stood in the first
place. The schemes of Urban VI. for his nephews' aggrandisement had been wild and crude; Boniface IX. had used his
relatives as trusty henchmen; Martin V. had employed the
existing power of the Colonna family for his own purposes;
Calixtus III. had given his nephews a secure position in Rome;
and Pius II. had gratified his strong feeling of affection
towards his native place by surrounding himself with Sienese
relatives. Sixtus IV. disregarded all considerations of decorum;
he took his nephews, men of no position and little capacity, and
placed at their disposal all the resources of the Roman See. They
were to be magnificent puppets on the stage of Italian politics,
moved by the Pope's hand, executing the Pope's schemes, and
bringing back their spoils to the Pope's feet.

Sixtus IV. had only taken possession of the papal throne, The Car-
dinal
nephews.
when in December 15, 1471, he raised to the Cardinalate two
of his relatives, Giuliano della Rovere, son of his brother Ra-
faelle, and Piero Riario, the orphan son of his sister, whom he
had brought up from early years. Piero was aged twenty-five,
and as yet unknown save for his dexterity in the Conclave; the
other nephew, Giuliano, was also a Franciscan, of the age of
twenty-eight, equally undistinguished. The Cardinals vainly
opposed the creation of two youths, of obscure parentage and of
no experience in affairs: they lamented the disregard shown by
the Pope to the regulations laid down by the Conclave;[1] they
recognised sadly that supreme power meant supreme license, and
they said that Sixtus IV. would heed them no more than Paul
II. On Cardinal Riario the Pope heaped preferment. He first
made him Bishop of Treviso; then the bishoprics of Sinigaglia,
Mende, Spalato, Florence, the patriarchate of Constantinople,
the abbacy of S. Ambrose at Milan, and other dignities rapidly
followed. His revenues exceeded 60,000 gold ducats. He was
omnipotent in Rome, and lived a life of luxury and splendour
such as had never been seen before. 'He gathered,' says a
contemporary, 'vessels of silver and gold, splendid raiment, tapestries and embroideries, and high-mettled horses; he was surrounded by a countless retinue, clad in silks, with curled hair,

---

[1] Card. Papiensis *Epistolæ*, 421.

BOOK
V.

Leonardo
della
Rovere
and the
Neapolitan
alliance.
1472.

Festivities
to Leonora
of Aragon.
June 1473.

rising poets and painters: he delighted in celebrating games, not only the civic games, but tournaments.'[1]

Another nephew, Lionardo della Rovere, brother of Giuliano, was made Prefect of Rome in February 1472, and soon afterwards was married to a bastard daughter of Ferrante of Naples. He was a small man 'and his mind corresponded to his person,' says Infessura;[2] but for his sake the Pope sacrificed the papal claims on Naples, remitted the yearly tribute, and restored the duchy of Sora. Ferrante undertook to guard the shores from pirates, and to send a steed to Rome each year in recognition of the papal suzerainty. Many of the Cardinals murmured at this abandonment of the papal rights; but Sixtus IV. was bent upon a close alliance with Naples as a means of securing himself against the powers of Northern Italy, while he carried out his plans against the aggressors in the neighbourhood of Rome.

This new policy of the Papacy received a splendid, almost a dramatic, embodiment in June 1473, when Leonora, another illegitimate daughter of Ferrante, passed through Rome on her way to Ferrara after her marriage with Duke Ercole d'Este. The magnificence of the papal nephews was employed to certify the firmness of the Pope's friendship to Naples in a way which startled even the luxurious princes of Italy.[3] On Whitsun-eve, June 5, Leonora, with a magnificent suite, entered Rome, and was escorted by the two Cardinal nephews to Riario's palace next the Church of SS. Apostoli, while the streets were thronged with the Cardinals' retinue. The piazza in front of the palace was covered in, and turned into a vast theatre. The palace itself was adorned 'as though S. Peter were descended from heaven to earth again.' The walls were entirely hung with the richest stuffs and tapestries; the splendid hangings of Nicolas V., representing the works of the Creation, formed the curtains of the doors which led into the banqueting-hall. Sideboards groaned with costly plate; couches and chairs were covered with the finest stuffs. Fourteen bedchambers were adorned with equal splendour, and in the most magnificent was an inscription, 'Who would deny that this chamber is worthy of

[1] *Vita Sixti IV.*, in Mur. iii. pt. 2, 1058.

[2] Eccard, ii. 1895.

[3] 'Fu una delle belle cose, che mai fosse fatta in Roma, e ancora fuori di Roma,' says Infessura: Corio calls it 'Stupendissimo onore.'

highest Jupiter? Who would deny that it is inferior to its prince?' Even the smallest articles of use were made of gold and silver.[1]

On Whitsunday the two Cardinals conducted the Duchess to S. Peter's, where the Pope celebrated mass and gave her his benediction. At midday a miracle play of Susanna and the Elders was performed by Florentine actors. Next day the splendour of the entertainment reached its height in a grand banquet at which the two nephews, the Duchess, and three of the most illustrious guests sat at one table; three other members of the Duchess's suite at another. The plate was constantly varied; the attendants were dressed in silk, and the seneschal four times changed his dress during the repast, appearing each time with richer collars of gold and pearls and precious stones. The tables groaned with an endless multitude of dishes, some so vast that they required four squires to bear the gold trays on which they were placed. There was a representation in viands of Atalanta's race, of Perseus, Andromeda, and the dragon. Peacocks were dressed with their feathers, and amongst them sat Orpheus with his lyre. The name of the Duchess's husband gave occasion for confectionaries shaped to represent the labours of Hercules. During the banquet was a concert and masques. The famous lovers of antiquity, Hercules and Deianira, Jason and Medea, Theseus and Phædra, danced in triumph: then centaurs entered and tried to carry off the ladies, and a mimic fight ensued. A mountain of sugar was carried in, from which emerged with gestures of amazement a wild man who recited a few verses. A roast bear in his skin, with a stick in his mouth, was one of the most wonderful dishes in this repast, for which every country had been ransacked.[2] Next day was given a representation of the miracle of Corpus Christi, the day following another of the life of John the Baptist. Finally Leonora departed from Rome with rich presents from the all-powerful nephew, 'who seemed to be son, not brother, of the great Emperor Cæsar, and was honoured

---

[1] Corio, *Storia di Milano*, vi. 2, says: 'Lo stesso luogo ove s' avea a deporre l' inutil peso del ventre eravi una sedia tutta d' argento con un vaso dentro tutto d' oro puro.' Infessura, and even Cardinal Ammannati, *Epistolæ*, 548, bear the same testimony.

[2] Corio has preserved the menu of this repast.

F

more than the real Pope.'[1] No doubt some beholders were struck with amazement at this splendid scene; but more must have exclaimed with Infessura, ' See in what things the treasure of the Church is spent.'

Power of
Piero
Riario.

Cardinal Riario was, in truth, the ruler of Rome, and the Pope sank into secondary importance. Suitors to the Pope first sought the powerful Cardinal, whose audiences thronged by a crowd of sycophants recalled the days of the Roman Empire. When Riario rode through the streets, he was attended by a troop of a hundred horsemen, and visited the Vatican like a prince. Though insolent he was not unkindly, and liked to distribute favours with a lordly hand. Not content with displaying his magnificence in Rome, he made a progress in the autumn of 1473, armed with extraordinary powers as legate of Umbria. He visited Florence, where he went to take possession of the archbishopric, Bologna, Ferrara, and Milan. Everywhere he was received with royal honours; everywhere were splendid festivities, and venal poets poured forth endless verses in the Cardinal's glory. In Milan, the aspiring Duke, Galeazzo Sforza, besought Cardinal Riario to obtain for him from the Pope the title of King of Lombardy; in return, he promised to aid him to the Papacy on the death of Sixtus IV., and even hinted that Sixtus might be compelled to resign in his nephew's favour. From Florence the Cardinal proceeded to Venice, and then retraced his steps to Rome. Soon after his return he died, early in 1474, worn out by his excesses at the age of twenty-eight, a warning that an upstart, ignorant of the virtue of moderation, secures his own destruction.

Death of
Piero
Riario.
1474.

Cardinal Riario was a startling exhibition of the results of nepotism. A lavish expenditure of the wealth of the Church created a prince of the type which Italy could understand. The Pope himself could not enter the lists; but all that he was restrained from doing by virtue of his office, the Cardinal nephew could do in his behalf. The princes of Italy were eclipsed by his grandeur; the resources of the Church were openly exhibited; the political influence of the Papacy was exerted entirely for the glory and advancement of a family. It was clear that the Papacy was a power with which the rulers of Italy would have to reckon. Piero Riario himself had no

[1] Corio, vi. 2.

qualities to commend him save his audacity, and he made no
pretence to decorum. He was as profligate as he was luxurious,
and flaunted his mistresses in attire of surpassing costliness;
even their slippers were embroidered with pearls.[1] So great
was his extravagance that during the two years of his Cardinalate
he spent 200,000 ducats, and left debts to the amount of
60,000 more. When he died, no one regretted him save the
Pope and those who had battened on his follies. Sixtus IV.
commemorated his nephew by a tomb in the Church of SS.
Apostoli; and the recumbent effigy of Piero Riario is one of the
best portrait sculptures in Rome. The strongly marked features and aquiline nose give a sense of power, which is borne out
by the thin compressed lips, the imperious expression, and the
coarse sensual chin. The epitaph which Sixtus IV. set over him
records his grace, liberality, and high-mindedness; 'he had
conceived and gave promise of greater things,' says the Pope,
and we can only hope that his judgment was true.[2]

Sixtus IV. bewailed the loss of his nephew with a depth of
grief that was thought unbecoming: he called him his son, his
only hope. His first thought was one of regret that he had
permitted unrestrained profligacy to cut short the life of his
favourite, and with characteristic impetuosity he proceeded to
frame rules for the regulation of the lives of the Cardinals. A
series of articles was drawn up forbidding Cardinals, when they
went abroad, to have more than thirty attendants, of whom

Sumptuary regulations for the Cardinals. 1474.

---

[1] *Annalisi di Tisi* quoted by Corvisieri, *Il trionfo Romano di Eleanora
d' Aragona* in *Archivio Romano di Storia patria*, i. 478. 'Pellicem Barbaram
facie decoram sed luxu nimio defluentem alebat in propatulo, quæ nulla juris
ratione habita nimio corporis cultui indulgens, sericeis atque purpureis vestibus
exuberans ac lapillis pretiosis, soleas unionibus atque margaritis pretio
aureorum octingentorum pedibus gestabat, ita ut ad summam aureorum viginti
milium hujus misellæ cultus accederet.' Ammannati, *Epistolæ*, 540, says:
'Unam mihi Gebellinæ pellicis cœnanti secum explicuit paratam, ut aiebat,
aureis mille, qualem ejus generis nullam inspexi.'

[2] The epitaph runs: 'Petro Saonensi e gente Riaria nobili ac vetusta ex
ordine Minorum, Card. S. Sixti, Patriarchæ Constantinopolitano, Archiepiscopo
Florentino, Perusii Umbriæque legato, Sixtus IV. Pont. Max. nepoti bene
merenti posuit. Vix. ann. xxvii. men. viii. d. vi. gratia liberalitate ac animi
magnitudine insignis, totius Italiæ legatione functus moritur, magno de se
in tam florida ætate desiderio relicto, quippe qui majora mente conceperat et
pollicebatur, apud ædes miro sumptu apud Apostolos incohatæ ostendunt
MCCCCLXXXIIII.' A terrible epitaph, which shows the popular estimate of
him, is given by Corio, *Storia di Milano*, Bk. vi.

twelve at least were to be clerical. It is a sign how all eccle-siastical discipline had been relaxed, that the Pope goes on to enjoin that these clerical attendants should wear garments reaching as far as the knee, and were not to dress in various colours. The Cardinals were to content themselves with two courses of meats at table, which together with relishes, sweets, and dessert, was judged to be sufficient. They were not to keep dogs, indulge in hunting, or have gold trappings for their horses. They were also bidden to wear the tonsure and cut their hair so that the ears were visible.[1] The Pope wished to warn others from the fate of Piero Riario, and thought that this could be done by regulations about outward things. It is needless to say that these sumptuary enactments were rapidly disregarded.

Rise of Girolamo Riario.

In fact Sixtus IV. soon lost his interest in the good estate of the Cardinals. He soothed his grief for Piero's death, and found comfort by transferring his affections to Piero's brother Girolamo, who was a layman. For him he bought from the Duke of Milan the district of Imola; and the purchase in-cluded the hand of Caterina Sforza, the Duke's illegitimate daughter. By this transaction Girolamo Riario was fairly launched in Italy, and might be trusted to make his way. Besides him there was yet another nephew to be established, Giovanni della Rovere, brother of the Cardinal Giuliano. He was married to the infant daughter of Federigo of Urbino, who in August 1474 was invested by the Pope with the title of duke. To give Giovanni a fair start in life, Sixtus IV. con-ferred on him the district of Sinigaglia and Mondovi, part of the territory which Federigo had with difficulty won for Pius II. from Gismondo Malatesta; in 1475 Lionardo della Rovere died, and the Pope further gave Giovanni his office of Prefect of Rome.

Uneasiness in Italy at the papal policy. 1474.

It was but natural that this openly avowed policy of family aggrandisement on the part of the Pope should awake a certain amount of uneasiness amongst Italian powers which felt that they might be its victims. Sixtus IV. found Italy at peace in virtue of the pacification made in 1470 by Paul II.: but that pacification recognised a separate league between Naples, Florence, and Milan, in reference to the affairs of Rimini.

[1] Corvisieri in *Archivio Romano*, i. 479, from a Vatican MS.

Sixtus IV. was anxious to abolish this separate league as being a hindrance to his schemes. He pleaded that Italy should be entirely united and should offer a firm front against the Turk; he urged that the reasons for a separate league against Paul II. did not apply to himself. The diplomacy of the Curia was, however, ineffectual. When Sixtus IV. succeeded in detaching Ferrante of Naples from the league, the only result was that Venice took his place. In 1474 a league of the northern powers stood watching the Pope and the King of Naples.

So matters stood when the year of jubilee came round in 1475. Few pilgrims visited Rome, where there was indeed little to be found to attract the pious soul. Europe was still ringing with stories of the pagan luxury of Cardinal Riario, and Italy was full of uneasy suspicion. The chief pilgrim was Ferrante of Naples, who gave another proof of his good understanding with the Pope. His visit was interpreted only as a political conference of the two powers, who were bent on breaking up the northern league, whose union prevented Girolamo Riario from extending his dominions towards Tuscany and Ferrante from winning back the towns which Venice held in his kingdom.

It was between the Pope and Florence that the rupture first took place; and the two foremost men in Italy, Sixtus IV. and Lorenzo de' Medici stood suddenly forward in bitter antagonism. Amidst the changes which had befallen the Italian republics, Florence still remained the most truly Italian. Personal government had taken the place of the civic community, and the prince everywhere represented the state. But in Florence the ruler still remained a Florentine burgher, and owed his position to the fact that his family was so closely connected with the fortunes of the city that it had become by mere force of events the city's representative in all that it held most dear. Other cities had been seized by treachery, had fallen before adventurers, or had passed into the hands of condottieri generals; in Florence the family of the Medici slowly absorbed the state by a complete identification of itself with the city's interests. This had not happened without struggles, and the dangerous ascendency of the Medici had not been gained without craft; but affairs had gone so far that Cosimo de' Medici had no alternative save to rule or quit Florence for ever. He made his ascendency complete, but kept it closely veiled. To the outward seeming Florence was governed as before, and Cosimo was but its chiefest and wealthiest citizen; in reality the magistrates were his nominees, and he was counted as an equal by the princes of Europe. Cosimo was succeeded by a weaker son, Piero, whose death in 1469 left the chief position to his two sons Lorenzo and Giuliano. Lorenzo was only twenty-one when the chief men of the city requested him to take care of the state as his grandfather and father had done; and he accepted the task for the preservation of his friends and his substance.[1]

Early
dealings of
Sixtus IV.
and Lo-
renzo de'
Medici.
1471-3.

At first the relations between the young Lorenzo and Sixtus IV. were most cordial. Lorenzo went as ambassador of Florence to congratulate the Pope on his accession. He was received with great honour, and received many valuable presents from the artistic treasures left by Paul II. More-over, as Paul II. left little ready money and a large collection of precious stones, Sixtus IV. sold them to Lorenzo at a moderate price, and Lorenzo made a large profit in retailing them afterwards to other princes.[2] He also made Lorenzo Treasurer to the Papacy, and so gave the papal business to the Medici Bank which was managed in Rome by Giovanni Torna-buoni, Lorenzo's uncle. But Lorenzo expected still more from the Pope: his keen eye saw the advantage which would be gained by the Medici family if it could exercise a permanent influence on the Papacy, and he besought Sixtus IV. to raise his brother Giuliano to the dignity of the cardinalate. The Pope listened, but did not commit himself, though Lorenzo after his return repeatedly urged his wish. The first creation of two nephews gave no sign of the Pope's intention; but the creation in May 1473 of eight Cardinals, amongst whom Giuliano de' Medici was not included, convinced Lorenzo that he reckoned vainly on any hope of influencing the papal policy.

Ill-feelings
between
Lorenzo
and Six-
tus IV.
1474.

Moreover the action of Sixtus IV. grew decidedly antago-nistic to the Medici. In 1474 he appointed as Archbishop of Pisa, Francesco Salviati, a man politically opposed to the Medici,

---

[1] *Riccordi di Lorenzo de' Medici.*

[2] Müntz, *Les Arts à la Cour des Papes*, ii. 154 &c., has collected a number of documents bearing on this transaction, which is a curious instance of the combination of commerce and politics by the Medici.

who vainly tried to have the nomination set aside. Still more did Florence feel aggrieved at the papal purchase of Imola, on which Florence itself had long had designs. Imola had been in the hands of the Manfredi ; but dynastic quarrels had driven them to commit the town to the protection of the Duke of Milan, who had not ventured to sell it to Florence, but could with greater safety hand it over to Girolamo Riario. The Florentines watched with growing anxiety this advance of the papal nephews towards their frontiers, and another occurrence soon increased their suspicions. In the spring of 1474 civic factions in Todi led to a rising against the Pope which spread to Spoleto. Cardinal Giuliano della Rovere showed his military capacity by promptly reducing the rebellious cities ; and Spoleto was savagely sacked by his ill-disciplined forces. Finding that Niccolò Vitelli, lord of Città di Castello, had helped the insurgents, he was not sorry for a pretext to reduce a too powerful vassal of the Holy See. He laid siege to Città di Castello, whereon the Florentines, alarmed at this disturbance so close to their frontiers, sent forces to Borgo San Sepolcro. Federigo of Urbino came to the camp of the legate, and by the terror of his name Vitelli was driven to make peace, though the terms were not so favourable as the Pope desired. Sixtus IV. resented bitterly the attitude of Florence, and complained that it prevented him from becoming master in his own dominions.

At the end of the year 1476 an event occurred which created a profound sensation throughout Italy—the murder of Galeazzo Maria Sforza, Duke of Milan. The impression produced by this assassination was not so much due to the fact in itself as to the motives of the conspirators, which awakened an instinctive sympathy in Italian hearts. Galeazzo Sforza was a typical Italian ruler of his age—splendid in his court, liberal to his subjects, a patron of art and learning, an astute politician, yet oppressive in his taxation, arbitrary in his exactions, and in his private life a lustful tyrant, who behaved with capricious savagery to those who thwarted his will. There was a superfluity of naughtiness in the insolence with which he disregarded all restraints in gratifying his appetites and punishing those whom he suspected. He delighted in the sight of corpses in a tomb ; he punished a poacher who had caught a hare by making him eat his capture, skin, entrails and all, till the unhappy

Murder of Galeazzo Maria Sforza. December 26, 1476.

man died.[1] Many stories were told of his strange ways and reckless cruelty, and he outraged by his conduct the deepest sentiments of the human heart. Some Milanese youths who attended the lectures of one Cola de' Montani, a teacher of classics, were stirred by the examples of classical antiquity which his teaching set before them, till they thirsted to follow in the steps of Harmodius and Aristogeiton, Brutus and the rest, who had freed their country from tyranny.

At last three of them, Olgiati, Lampognano, and Visconti, agreed to assassinate the Duke according to the models of ancient tyrannicide. Yet reminiscences of Christianity strangely mingled with paganism; and the conspirators prayed at the shrine of S. Ambrose each time they met to practise the method of assassination by attacking one another with the sheaths of their daggers. On the morning of S. Stephen's Day the duke went to mass in the Church of S. Stefano: the three conspirators managed to draw near and slew him as he entered. They had taken no steps to secure any results from their deed; they supposed that liberty naturally followed on the death of a tyrant. Lampognano was cut down in the Church; Olgiati was refused shelter by his father, was made prisoner and condemned to death. In prison he wrote a Latin epitaph on the dead tyrant.[2] On the scaffold he summoned up his courage saying: 'Collect yourself, Girolamo; the memory of your deed will endure; death is bitter, fame is everlasting.' The sole result in Milan of this assassination was that Galeazzo Maria was succeeded by his son Giovanni Galeazzo, a child of eight years old, under the guardianship of his mother Bona of Savoy, and a way was thereby opened to the intrigues of his uncle, Ludovico Sforza. When Sixtus IV. heard of the death of Galeazzo Maria, he exclaimed with a truly prophetic spirit: 'To-day is dead the peace of Italy.'

---

[1] The stories told of him by Corio, Bk. VI. ch. 3, cannot be translated, but they all characterise the capricious savagery of a despot.

[2] Corio, l. c.

    'Quem non armatæ potuerunt mille phalanges
    Sternere, privata Galeaz Dux Sfortia dextra
    Concidit; atque illam minime juvere cadentem
    Adstantes famuli nec opes, nec castra, nec urbes:
    Unde patet sœvo tutum nil esse tyranno:
    Hinc patet humanis quæ sit fiducia rebus.'

The murder of the Duke of Milan excited much admiration in Italy. It was so entirely conceived in the antique spirit that it was applauded for its classical motive. A staid Florentine could say that it 'was a worthy, manly, and laudable attempt, deserving of imitation by all who live under a tyrant or one like a tyrant.'[1] The example of the Milanese conspirators found imitators in a case where the tyranny was not so manifest, and where the profits to those engaged in the assassination were likely to be larger. A scheme was planned for upsetting the rule of the Medici in Florence; and however the scheme was constructed to begin with, it ended in a poor imitation of the Milanese patriots, with the patriotism and the classical accessories omitted in favour of self-interested motives.

Florence seemed to rest peaceably under Lorenzo de' Medici's rule, which was exercised quietly, and allowed others to wear the appearance of power while the practical direction of affairs remained in Lorenzo's hands. The government of the Medici secured to the Florentines all that they wished for; commercial prosperity, artistic and literary splendour, and a gay life for the people. Yet Lorenzo was always cautious, and never forgot that the power which his grandfather had secured by craft must be maintained in the same way as it had been acquired. He was careful to keep down possible rivals, and allowed no one's influence to vie with his own. However much he might try to conceal this policy, it was impossible that its objects should not recognise and resent it. The wealthiest and most important family in Florence after the Medici was that of the Pazzi, with whom Cosimo had entered into a close alliance by giving his daughter Bianca in marriage to Guglielmo de' Pazzi. Under Lorenzo the good relationship between the two families somewhat cooled; and the Pazzi Bank at Rome was an obstacle to the designs of Lorenzo, who in his anxiety to prevent the sale of Imola to the Pope's nephew Girolamo, tried to avert it by putting financial difficulties in the Pope's way. The Pope, however, obtained the money by applying to the Pazzi; and as the relations between the Pope and Lorenzo became more unfriendly, he transferred the office of papal receiver from the Medici to the Pazzi Bank. Thenceforth the Pazzi

CHAP. III.

Effect of this example.

Hostility of the Pazzi to the Medici.

[1] Alamanno Rinuccini, *Ricordi Storici*, 125.

Girolamo
Riario
helps the
Pazzi to
conspire
against the
Medici.

were on the Pope's side, and the coolness between them and the Medici increased.

It is, however, improbable that the difference would have been serious had not other interests been involved. Girolamo Riario felt his lordship of Imola endangered by the hostility of Florence. One who owed his position entirely to the Pope was only secure during the Pope's lifetime; and the change of government at Milan left him at the mercy of Florence in case the Pope died. Girolamo was no short-sighted politician; he formed the bold scheme of overthrowing the power of the Medici, and used the Pazzi as his instruments for that purpose. Accordingly, he won over to his plan Francesco de' Pazzi, the head of the Bank at Rome, and the Archbishop of Pisa, Francesco Salviati, who nourished his wrongs against Lorenzo on account of his archbishopric. It soon became obvious to the conspirators that the Medici rule was too securely founded to be upset by any ordinary means; when Francesco de' Pazzi mentioned the matter to his uncle Jacopo at Florence, he found him convinced of the impossibility of success. It was necessary to obtain the Pope's sanction if adherents were to be secured; and Sixtus IV. approved of the overthrow of the Medici if it could be accomplished without bloodshed.

Count Girolamo's first scheme was to invite Lorenzo de' Medici to Rome and there have him assassinated; he could then proceed against Giuliano in Florence. Lorenzo, however, did not show much zeal in accepting Girolamo's invitation; and it was resolved to attack him in his own city. For this purpose confederates were needed, and an army must be in preparation to take advantage of the confusion in Florence. Count Girolamo chose as his agent a general in his employ, Giovan Battista da Montesecco. When the matter was first confided to him, Montesecco remarked that it was a great and difficult undertaking: 'How will it please the Pope?' he asked. 'The Pope,' answered the conspirators, 'will do what we wish: moreover he wishes evil to Lorenzo and desires his fall above all things.' 'Have you spoken to him about it?' 'Yes,' was the answer, 'and we will make him speak to you and tell you his intention.' When the interview with the Pope took place, Sixtus IV. said that he wished for a revolution in Florence, but without the death of any man. 'Holy Father,' said Montesecco, 'it can hardly be done without the death of Lorenzo and Giuliano, and perhaps others.' Sixtus answered, 'I do not wish the death of any man on my account, since it fits not my office to consent to anyone's death ; and though Lorenzo is a rascal, I would not have his death, but only a change of government.' Count Girolamo interposed, 'All will be done that is possible to prevent it; only when it has happened your Holiness will pardon him who has done it.' Sixtus replied to the Count, ' You are a beast : I tell you that I do not wish any man's death, but a change of government.' Count Girolamo and Archbishop Salviati returned to the charge. ' When you have Florence at your disposal you will dictate to half Italy, and all will wish to have you for their friend ; therefore be content that everything be done to arrive at this end.' The Pope ended the interview by saying, ' I tell you I will not have it ; go and do what you will, provided there be no killing.' The Archbishop answered, ' Holy Father, be content that we steer this ship, and that we will steer it well.' The Pope answered 'I am content.' [1]

The attitude of Sixtus IV. in the matter was this; as a statesman he wished for the overthrow of the Medici and gave his countenance to a plan for that object ; as Pope he could not be privy to any scheme of assassination. The plot was not of his making ; he prudently abstained from asking for details ; and the conspirators prudently abstained from confiding them to him. Sixtus IV. cannot be accused of being privy to an assassination ; it may be urged that he expressly stated his objection to any such deed. But he did not demand any assurance that no such thing was contemplated ; he heard it hinted and disavowed it, but he did not make his sanction conditional upon its entire withdrawal from the plan. The utmost that can be said in his behalf is that he saved the honour of his office, but he certainly did so in an ambiguous manner.

Armed with the Pope's sanction, Montesecco visited Florence, viewed the scene of action, and succeeded in winning over to the conspiracy Jacopo de' Pazzi, who was reluctantly

Preparations for the assassination of the Medici.

---

[1] These details come from the confession of Montesecco, as given by the Florentine Chancellor Bartolommeo Scala, in Fabroni ii. 167 ; also in Roscoe, Appendix XXVIII. The statement is that of a blunt soldier who relates truly what happened and draws no inferences of his own.

persuaded. Troops were massed quietly at Imola and confederates were prepared in Florence. Archbishop Salviati found a pretext for visiting Florence, and everything was ready. Count Girolamo thought it well to initiate a young relative into political life under auspicious circumstances, and made a tool of his young nephew, Raffaelle Sansoni, a lad of eighteen, studying at the University of Pisa, whom Sixtus IV. had shamelessly made a cardinal in December 1477. Girolamo caused young Cardinal Raffaelle to pay a visit to Florence in April 1478, as the entertainment of an illustrious guest would offer opportunities to the conspirators. The first plan was to assassinate the brothers at a banquet which was given to the Cardinal in the Medici villa that lies below Fiesole; but Giuliano was unable to be present through sickness and the attempt was put off. The Cardinal then proposed a visit to the Medici at their palace in Florence, and expressed a wish to attend mass in the cathedral on Sunday, April 26. Giuliano sent a message saying that he would not fail to be present in church: and this determined the conspirators to choose that sacred place for their murder. The change of place proved fatal to the success of the plan. The bluff soldier Montesecco, who had undertaken the death of Lorenzo, shrank from the profanation of a church and refused to 'make Christ witness of a crime.' Two priests, Antonio Maffei and Stefano da Bagnone, undertook the work from which the soldier recoiled in horror; but though less scrupulous, they also showed themselves to be less skilful.

On the morning of April 26 Cardinal Raffaelle arrived at Lorenzo's palace and robed himself for the mass. He was accompanied to the Duomo by Lorenzo. At the door Archbishop Salviati made an excuse for going away; he had undertaken to seize the Palazzo Pubblico during the tumult. The Cardinal entered the choir and took his place beside the altar. Mass was begun before the conspirators saw that Giuliano de' Medici was not there. Francesco de' Pazzi and Bernardo Bandini, the two who had undertaken his death, slipped away to bring him; and as they walked with him to the church, Francesco de' Pazzi familiarly put his arm round his victim to discover if he wore any armour of defence. Giuliano advanced into the choir; Lorenzo stood outside; and close by each were the appointed assassins. When the priest had taken the communion,[1] a signal was given and Bandini struck his dagger into the breast of Giuliano, who took a step backwards, tottered and fell; whereon Francesco de' Pazzi rushed upon him and stabbed him again and again with such fury that he wounded himself in the thigh.

The assassins of Lorenzo were not so successful. Maffei aimed at Lorenzo's throat, but only wounded him slightly in the neck. Lorenzo with instant self-possession pulled off his cloak, wrapped it round his left arm for a shield, and sprang into the choir. Bandini, satisfied with his work on Giuliano, dashed at Lorenzo, who was protected by a friend at the cost of his own life. The delay gave time for others of Lorenzo's friends to gather round him and hurry him away to the sacristy, where the doors were shut and bolted against assailants. All was confusion; but though the partisans of the Pazzi were armed, those of Lorenzo quickly assembled and escorted him safely to his palace. Cardinal Raffaelle was left crouching at the altar, and was with difficulty saved from the mob. So great was his terror, that his face wore an ashen hue to the end of his days.

Tumult in Florence.

Archbishop Salviati's attempt to seize the Palazzo Pubblico failed. His stammering speech aroused the suspicions of the Gonfaloniere, who had risen to greet his eminent visitor. The Archbishop's eye wandered to the door, and the Gonfaloniere seeing that others were behind, loudly called the guards and made them prisoners. The cries in the street warned him of danger; the gates of the Palazzo were made fast, and the bands of the Pazzi could gain no entrance. The only man amongst the conspirators who showed any decision was the one who had been slowest to join the plot. Jacopo de' Pazzi boldly raised the cry of 'Liberty;' but the people did not rise; showers of stones were hurled at him and his band, and he was driven to his house, where he found his nephew Francesco so severely wounded by his own hand that he could not flee. Francesco was seized by the crowd, dragged to the Palazzo Pubblico, and hanged. When the news of Giuliano's death reached the magistrates, they hanged out of the palace window Jacopo Bracciolini, son of the famous Poggio, and after him Archbishop Salviati. It is said that

Failure of the conspiracy.

---

[1] There is some difference amongst the accounts about the exact time of the service when the murder was committed. I have followed Poliziano, who was an eyewitness.

Salviati in his death struggle fixed his teeth in a despairing clutch in Jacopo's shoulder. In all the streets the conspirators were cut down by the people, and Florence was filled with slaughter.

Jacopo Pazzi was made prisoner outside Florence and was put to death. The Pazzi family was well nigh annihilated. Montesecco was imprisoned and closely examined about the Pope's complicity in the conspiracy: he was afterwards beheaded. All the chief conspirators were put to death. Bandini, who managed to escape to Constantinople, was delivered up by the Sultan Mohammed II. The failure of the plot was a splendid testimony to the devotion of Florence to Lorenzo, and completed its identification with the Medici family. Lorenzo had no need to take any action against his enemies; the spontaneous outburst of popular feeling wrought vengeance for him.

Lorenzo had escaped the danger which threatened him in Florence: but Count Girolamo's troops were still at Imola. Florence was not prepared for a siege, and no one knew how widely the roots of the conspiracy were spread. Lorenzo was anxious to discover how far the Pope was committed, and hence the careful examination of Montesecco; Sixtus IV., if supported by powerful allies, might plunge Florence into troubles which might shake its allegiance to the Medici. Lorenzo waited eagerly for the first movements of the Pope.

Reception of the news at Rome.

When the news of the failure of his plot reached Rome, Girolamo Riario was beside himself with rage. With three hundred armed men he went to the house of the Florentine ambassador, Donato Acciaiuoli, and in spite of his remonstrances dragged him to the Pope's presence. Sixtus IV. disavowed this violence and dismissed him with an assurance of his safety.[1] Acciaiuoli wrote to Florence urging the immediate release of Cardinal Raffaelle: when this was not immediately granted vengeance was taken on the Florentines resident in Rome, and the Bishop of Perugia was sent to bring back the Cardinal. There was some delay, and not till June 12 did the Cardinal begin his journey from Florence.

It would seem that at first Sixtus IV. wished to exculpate himself from complicity in the attempt at assassination, and even wrote a letter of condolence ot Florence.[2] But the

[1] Vespasiano. *Vita di Donato Acciaiuoli.*
[2] Capponi, *Storia della Repubblica di Firenze,* ii. 123, quotes a MS. letter

examination of Montesecco, the delay in releasing Cardinal
Raffaelle, and the rumours of the menacing attitude of the
Florentines, supplied Count Girolamo with means to kindle the
Pope's wrath. On June 1, Sixtus IV. issued a Bull against
Lorenzo de' Medici and his adherents, the magistrates of
Florence. He called Lorenzo 'a son of iniquity and child of
perdition.' He declared him and his partisans to be anathema-
tised, incapable thenceforth of holding any office ecclesiastical
or civil, or of receiving legacies or performing any legal acts;
their goods were to be confiscated, their houses thrown down
and reduced to ruins for ever; if they were not condignly
punished within a month, Florence was threatened with an
interdict and the deprival of her episcopal dignity. The
grounds for this severe sentence were set forth at length; they
were the hostility of Lorenzo to the Holy See, as shown by his
help to Niccolò Vitelli, his unjust dealings with the Archbishop
of Pisa, his persistent ingratitude and ill-will towards the Pope,
finally the violation of clerical rights by the execution of
Archbishop Salviati and the capture of Cardinal Raffaelle. The
Pope did not say a word about the murder of Giuliano de'
Medici; he merely mentioned scornfully 'some civil and private dissensions amongst the citizens.' The Pope's proceedings
were indeed high-handed. He behaved as though the Holy
See were so entirely above suspicion that it did not require even
a shadow of vindication. His Bull of denunciation was followed
by an interdict before the end of the month.

The proceedings of the Florentines are characteristic of
the Italian method of dealing with the Papacy. Florence
had men who could write as well as the papal secretaries, and
who had the personal knowledge which enabled them to strike
home. Papal thunders could no longer roll on unchecked;
the culture of Humanism had provided weapons of sarcasm
which were powerful against denunciation. On July 21 the
Signoria of Florence sent an answer to the Pope. 'You wish
us,' it ran, 'to cast out of the state Lorenzo de' Medici on
two grounds, because he is our tyrant, and because he opposes
the welfare of the Christian religion. We do not see that by

Margin notes: CHAP. III.

Sixtus IV.'s Bull against the Floren-tines. June 1, 1478.

The Flo-rentine answer. July 21, 1478.

of Sixtus IV. to the Cardinal legate at Bologna in which the Pope says: 'Nos
quoque casum ipsum primum indoluimus et commiserationis nostrae testimonium per literas nostras ad Florentinos dedimus.'

driving out Lorenzo we should recover our liberty, if we acted at your bidding. To save you trouble, we may say that we have learned how to get rid of tyrants and how to manage our state without the advice of others. Collect yourself, we pray you, Holy Father, and return to those sentiments which become the gravity of the Holy See. You call Lorenzo a tyrant: we, speaking in the name of all our citizens, regard him as the defender of our freedom, and are prepared to risk everything for his safety. Your invectives against him provoke our laughter by the emptiness, not to say malignity, of their invention. If Lorenzo had allowed himself to be slaughtered by your emissaries, if your traitors had succeeded in seizing our Palazzo Pubblico, if we had given ourselves up to you for slaughter, we would have had none of this controversy with you.' The letter defends the Medici family, tells of its good deeds towards Christendom and the Papacy, and ends by saying that Florence identified itself with the Medici, and was ready to fight for its religion and its liberty.[1]

Florentine canonists framed an appeal to a future Council, and decided that the force of the interdict was not so great as to forbid public worship. The priests were ordered by the magistrates to perform the Church services as usual, and even if they felt scruples they judged it wiser to obey. It seems that the Archbishop of Florence held a synod, which gave occasion to the publication of a furious invective against the Pope. We cannot suppose that this document was the production of an ecclesiastical assembly: it bears too strongly the marks of being the work of one man. Probably Gentile, Bishop of Arezzo, a staunch friend of the Medici, used the opportunity to issue as a pamphlet an answer to the Bull of Sixtus IV. It was framed on the models of vituperation which the Humanists had employed in their private squabbles, but which had never yet been turned against a Pope. The relations of Sixtus IV. to the Church were assailed in a series of choice metaphors; and the Pope was styled 'pandar,' 'minister of adulterers,' 'Vicar of the devil,' 'pilot of the Church's bark who steered it only to Circe's island.' The writer of the document

---

[1] This letter is printed by Pignotti, *Storia della Toscana.* Appendix to Book IV.

was in possession of information supplied by the magistrates, for he quoted the confession of Montesecco and gave an account of the conspiracy. Then he repelled one by one the charges of the Pope's Bull against Lorenzo; the true cause of the papal interdict was that Florence might be punished for Count Girolamo, the victim for the assassin. 'May God preserve you,' it ends, 'from false shepherds, who come in sheep's clothing, but inwardly are ravening wolves.' [1]

Clerical denunciation overshot the mark on one side as much as on the other. The Florentine bishop met the Pope with insolent abuse. More weighty was the 'Apology for the Florentines' from the pen of the Chancellor Bartolommeo Scala, which was addressed to all and several whom it might meet. [2] Scala strikes a note of true statesmanship by saying that he has an unheard of thing to relate; 'while the enemy of our religion hangs over our necks and threatens Rome, Pope Sixtus and his excellent advisers lend themselves to abandoned acts of treachery, plot against the life and liberty of peoples, harass with anathemas all good men, and wage war against Christians.' He gives in full the confession of Montesecco and a temperate statement of the facts of the assassination of Giuliano. Then he proceeds: 'What treason has failed to do, ecclesiastical censures backed by arms now attempt. We are defending our liberty which is dearer to us than life, while the troops of the Pope attack our territory. God, how long wilt Thou endure such iniquity? We turn to you, Emperor Frederick, believing that in us the welfare of Christendom is at stake. We turn to you, Louis of France, to succour the perils of Christendom. Unless Christian princes and peoples help us, we doubt about the commonwealth of Christ. Haste and consult for its welfare.'

Sixtus IV. answered in a tone of lofty indignation which concealed a crafty policy. In a letter addressed to the Duke of Este he besought the Italian powers to join with him in restoring the peace of Italy by crushing the infamous policy of Lorenzo. He had no ill-will against Florence, but Lorenzo had shown himself persistently hostile to all that was right; taking advantage of an ill-judged conspiracy at Florence he had disregarded the holy canons, had put to death an Arch-

War of
Sixtus IV.
against
Florence.
August
1478.

---

[1] See Appendix. [2] In Fabroni, ii. 173; also in Roscoe, Appendix, 205.

bishop, had treated a Cardinal with indignity, and had be-spattered with abuse the Holy See. In the interests of order, of Italian unity, of a crusade against the Turk, Florence must be rescued, by the joint endeavour of all Catholic princes, from the yoke of such an impious man.[1]

This letter of Sixtus IV. expressed the political issue which Lorenzo well understood. It was of little moment what literary triumphs each side might win. Sixtus IV. had his troops in the field and was allied with the King of Naples. The time for the blow against Florence had been well chosen, as the northern league was dissolved by the death of the Duke of Milan. The attack of Sixtus IV. was directed, not against Florence but against Lorenzo, and Venice had a good excuse for not interfering in a personal quarrel. Florence was not prepared to meet her enemies in the field, and only received slight help from her allies while the papal forces under Federigo of Urbino advanced along the Chiana valley.

Fruitless
mediation
of Louis XI. Lorenzo's greatest hope was in the friendship of Louis XI., who had always been on friendly terms with the Medici, and since his dealings with Pius II. had looked with no great favour on the Papacy. Louis XI. expressed his sympathy with Lorenzo and sent Philip de Commines as his ambassador to Italy. He had a scheme of reducing Florence to admit the suzerainty of France and then establishing the French power over Northern Italy; with this he combined a renewal of the old anti-papal policy of France. He published an ordinance on August 16, forbidding the execution of papal provisions and the export of money to Rome; he urged on Sixtus IV. the summoning of a General Council to be held at Orleans, and sent envoys to the Pope to negotiate for that purpose.

But the papal diplomacy was superior to that of the French king.[2] Sixtus IV. had an answer ready to every proposal made to him, and showed much skill in throwing on the Florentines the blame of refusing to submit to a compromise, though the Emperor and the Kings of Hungary and England united with Louis XI. in urging peace upon the Pope. The position of

---

[1] Sigismondo de' Conti, *Historia*, i. 38 &c.

[2] See Commines, *Mémoires*, Bk. vi. ch. 5, and *Preuves* in Godefroi's edition; also Kervyn de Lettenhove, *Lettres et négociations de Philippe de Commines*, vol. i., and Buser, *Die Beziehungen der Medicaer mit Frankreich*, i. 196, 450, &c.

Sixtus IV. was cleverly chosen; he dissociated Lorenzo de' Medici from Florence, and professed his readiness to make peace with the Republic if Lorenzo would give satisfaction for the wrongs which he had done. Lorenzo, on his side, could not humiliate himself before the Pope without sacrificing his position in Florence, where the ill-success of the arms of the Republic caused growing uneasiness. While Lorenzo's allies threatened the Pope with a Council, the papal and Neapolitan forces ravaged the Florentine territory, and in November 1479, captured Poggibonsi and Certaldo. A truce was made for the winter; but Lorenzo saw clearly that Florence could not endure much longer, and that peace must be made in some more expeditious way than by the negotiations of Louis XI.

Lorenzo had already considered the difficulties which beset him, and saw that if peace was hopeless from the Pope, it might be obtained from the King of Naples. Though Ferrante was desirous of obtaining hold on Tuscany, he dreaded the schemes of Louis XI., and saw the dangers that impended from a continuance of war in Italy. Lorenzo gradually prepared the way for an understanding with Ferrante. On December 5 he called together the chief citizens of Florence and told them that he was resolved to do what he could to procure peace for the city; the King of Naples professed himself the friend of Florence, though the enemy of the Medici; he would put himself in the King's hands and would himself go to Naples to negotiate. On December 18 Lorenzo landed in Naples, and was honourably received by the King.

Lorenzo's visit to Naples. December 1479– February 1480.

It was a bold stroke on Lorenzo's part, and he had staked all on its success. No doubt he had previously assured himself of Ferrante's good intentions; but there were many obstacles to be overcome before these intentions could be carried into effect, as it was a serious matter for Ferrante to break from his league with the Pope. Negotiations were slowly carried on while Ferrante waited to see if Lorenzo's absence from Florence produced any change in the temper of the Florentines. Sixtus IV. objected to Ferrante's intercourse with Lorenzo, and tried by all means to break it off. When he found that terms of peace were being discussed, he insisted that Lorenzo should first go to Rome and make his personal submission. When Lorenzo refused, the Pope asserted that his dignity and honour would not allow him to consent to peace on other terms. He reminded Ferrante that he had spent a fountain of money in the war, and had the victory in his own hands; Lorenzo was in the King's power and might be compelled to act as he chose.[1] Lorenzo had many anxious moments during his stay at Naples, but he made his way by his personal qualities, which commended him to the King and won friends amongst the King's advisers. He succeeded in establishing a basis of peace, and at the end of February 1480 left Naples, and was received

Precarious peace between Florence and Naples, February 1480.

with joy in Florence. The conditions of peace were published in March, and damped the popular rejoicing; they were hard for Florence, but were such as the vanquished might expect. The towns taken in the war were to be restored at the King's pleasure, and the Duke of Calabria was to receive a yearly payment as general of the Republic.

Peace was made with Naples, and Sixtus IV., as the ally of Naples, ratified it; but he was bitterly enraged, and renewed his censures against Florence. Moreover, the alliance with Naples alienated Venice from Florence, and in April Sixtus IV. concluded a separate treaty with Venice. Nor could Florence feel confident of the good intentions of Naples. The Duke of Calabria took up his head-quarters at Siena and behaved as its lord; he seemed to be nourishing a design of making himself master of Tuscany.

Occupation of Otranto by the Turks, July 28, 1480.

A sudden shock compelled the Italian powers to lay aside their ambitious schemes and unite for common defence. While they were plotting against one another they were startled by the news that the Crescent was waving on Italian ground. The Turkish fleet which had been repulsed from Rhodes made a dash upon Italy and occupied Otranto on July 28. The inhabitants were massacred, the fortifications were strengthened, and the new settlers supplied themselves with provisions by ravaging the neighbouring territory. Such was the mutual suspicion of Italian powers that the Venetians were accused of inviting the Turks as a means of avenging themselves on Ferrante, while Lorenzo was suspected of having had a share in

[1] A clear exhibition of the Pope's position is given in his instructions to his envoy in Naples, Antonio Crivelli, printed in Capponi, *Storia della Repubblica di Firenze*, ii., Appendix No. v.

an event which proved advantageous to him in more ways than one.

CHAP.
III.

Absolution
of Florence.
December
1480.

The news of this Turkish invasion called the Duke of Calabria homewards and ended his intrigues at Siena. It drove the Pope to proclaim a truce throughout Italy, and summon all to take up arms against the Infidel. Florence judged the opportunity favourable for making peace with the Pope, who could not with good grace refuse. Twelve of the chief citizens were sent to Rome, with instructions to preserve the honour of the city, but obtain a reconciliation if possible. On the evening of November 25 they entered Rome, but as they were still under excommunication they did not meet with the reception usually accorded to envoys. On the 27th they were admitted to a private consistory, where the Bishop of Volterra asked pardon for the excesses committed against the Pope and the Church. The Pope dismissed them with a few words, saying that he must consult his Cardinals; meanwhile, let them be of good courage and hope for the Pope's mercy. Conferences were held and terms were arranged. At last, on December 3, the formal reconciliation took place. It was the first Sunday in Advent, when the Pope was wont to be present at service in S. Peter's. The Florentine envoys were admitted to the portico where Sixtus IV., surrounded by his Cardinals, was seated on a purple litter in front of the middle door. The Florentines prostrated themselves, and humbly asked pardon for their offences. Luigi Guicciardini spoke on their behalf; but as he was seventy years old his voice was feeble and he was scarcely heard. The Pope ordered one of his notaries to read the terms of peace offered by the Florentines; they promised to obey the Pope, never to wage war against the Church, nor impose taxes on the clergy. The Pope as a penance for their offences ordered them to provide fifteen galleys against the Turks, and the envoys took oath that they would observe these conditions.

Then Sixtus IV. addressed them: ' You have sinned, my sons, grievously; first against our God and Saviour by slaying the Archbishop of Pisa and other priests of God, for it is written, "Touch not mine anointed." You have sinned against the Roman pontiff, who holds on earth the place of our Saviour Jesus Christ, by diffaming him throughout the world. You

have sinned against the sacred order of Cardinals by imprisoning a Cardinal legate of the Holy See. You have sinned
against the whole clerical order, by exacting tribute from the
clergy within your dominions against their will, and by your
disobedience to our apostolical admonitions have caused rapine,
fire, and slaughter. Would that at first you had come to us,
your spiritual father; doubtless then we need not have tried
arms to avenge the injuries done to the Church. We certainly
have done what we have done against our will, but our apostolic office drove us to act. Now, my sons, when you come to
us humbly, we receive you into the bosom of our favour; when
you confess your errors and excesses we forgive you. Sin no
further. You have sufficiently experienced the power of the
arm of the Church; you have found how hard it is to dash
your heads against the shield of God and attempt to break His
breastplate.'[1]

Then taking a rod, as is customary in conferring absolution,
the Pope struck on the head each of the envoys as he knelt
humbly before him, while he and the Cardinals chanted the
penitential strains of the 'Miserere.' Again the Florentines
kissed his feet and received his benediction. The doors of
S. Peter's were opened and mass was said. After the ceremony
the envoys, now free from excommunication, were escorted
home with the honours due to their dignity. A few days
afterwards they left Rome, somewhat heavy in heart on account
of the fifteen galleys, which were a severe tax on the resources
of Florence already drained by the war.

Sixtus IV. might hide his discomfiture by a ceremonial
humiliation of Florence, but the fact remained that his hand
had been forced by Lorenzo de' Medici. He had spent large
sums of money in a war whose object was to overthrow the
power of the Medici, and had not gained his object. He had
shown himself a dangerous leader of Italian politics; and the
only result of his policy had been a temporary change in the
balance of power. Instead of the league of the Pope and
Naples against Florence, Milan, and Venice, he had substituted
a league of the Pope and Venice against Naples, Milan, and
Florence. Moreover, a change in the existing relationships of
Italy was sure to lead to another war.

[1] Jacobi Volaterrani *Diarium Romanum*, in Muratori, xxiii. 114.

CHAPTER IV.

ITALIAN WARS OF SIXTUS IV.

1481–1484.

THE peace which at length prevailed in Italy was not due to the pacific intentions of Sixtus IV., but to the terror caused by the Turkish occupation of Otranto. It was obviously a matter of importance to the whole of Italy that these aliens should be driven from the Italian soil. Sixtus IV. proclaimed a Crusade throughout Christendom, manned galleys for an expedition against Otranto, and gave them his solemn benediction previous to their departure. But it may be doubted whether the arms of the Pope and of Naples would have prevailed against the Turks, had not the death of the great sultan Mahomet II. released Europe from the dread which his name inspired. His death in May 1481 was followed by a civil war between his sons Bajazet and Djem. In this confusion of the Turkish Empire the commander of Otranto judged it prudent to retire, and gave up the city in September to the Duke of Calabria, who had besieged it for some months. On this the papal galleys returned home, though the King of Naples wished to use the opportunity for further expeditions against the Turks; but the Pope's fleet had no supplies, and nothing further was done.

In truth the interest of Sixtus IV. was centred solely in Italy, where his great object was to extend the possessions of Count Girolamo, who had not wasted the opportunities afforded by the Florentine war. He attempted to seize Pesaro, and when this failed succeeded in acquiring Forlì, where the legitimate line of the Ordelaffi came to an end in 1480. The people of Forlì, wearied of the tyranny of the Ordelaffi, put themselves under the protection of the Pope, who sent Girolamo as

CHAP.
IV.

Surrender of Otranto by the Turks. September 1481.

Girolamo Riario seizes Forlì. 1481.

captain of his forces. Girolamo occupied the castle, seized
and put to death an illegitimate son of the late Ordelaffi lord,
and added Forlì to his dominion of Imola.[1] He looked out for
fresh acquisitions, and the new alliance of Sixtus IV. with
Venice gave him grounds for hoping that with Venetian help
more might he won. In September 1481 he visited Venice,
where he was received with great honours and was admitted
into the roll of Venetian nobles. The object of his visit was
soon apparent; Venice had sundry grievances against Duke
Ercole I. of Ferrara, and Sixtus IV. was willing to aid her in
attacking a powerful vassal of the Church, whose dominions
might further enrich the papal nephew.

Pretexts were not wanting for the war which began in
May 1482 and drew all Italy into its vortex. The King of
Naples sent troops in defence of his son-in-law Duke Ercole;
Florence and Milan joined him in opposing the schemes of the
Pope; even Federigo of Urbino exclaimed that it was monstrous that the peace of Italy should be disturbed by the dark
designs of a rash young man. He refused to serve Sixtus IV.,
and Roberto Malatesta of Rimini was made papal general in
his stead.

The time which Sixtus IV. had chosen for the declaration
of war against Ferrara was not fortunate. Rome was disturbed
by a bloody feud which divided it into two opposite factions,
whose struggles gave ample opportunity to the Pope's enemies
to interfere with effect. The Papacy had pursued a policy so
fully in accordance with the traditions of the turbulent Roman
barons, that they naturally hastened to follow the example
which it set. Paul II., by impartiality in Italian politics, was
enabled to govern Rome with justice: the rash designs of
Sixtus IV. awakened the elements of civic discord, and revived
a barbarous past which had only been thrust for a time into the
background. The rise of a blood feud in Rome in the days of
Sixtus IV. stands in marked contrast to the culture of the
Renaissance, and sounds like an echo from a bygone age.

In the tumultuous plundering of the palace of Sixtus IV.
after his election to the papal office, Francesco di Santa Croce
was wounded by a member of the Valle family. He waited
his time, and cut the tendon of his adversary's heel as he was

---

[1] Sigismondo de' Conti, i. 114.

walking one day in the Campo dei Fiori. The Valle in turn went in disguise to the house of Prospero di Santa Croce, his brother-in-law, where he knew that Francesco was at supper. With a stroke of his sword he cleft the head of the unsuspecting man, whose blood spurted over the table. It was now Prospero's turn to take vengeance; but the feud was declared and the Valle were cautious. Prospero vainly sought his foe; at length his patience was exhausted, and he found another victim in Francesco's father-in-law, Piero Margani, an old man of seventy, whom he slew standing at his own door.[1] Margani was a wealthy man and an adherent of Count Girolamo. The feud, intensified by this murder, soon spread through the city, as the Valle were supported by the Colonna, the Santa Croce by the Orsini. For a time the fear of the Turks found occupation for these turbulent spirits in the camp of Alfonso before Otranto; but when they returned to Rome the feud again blazed forth, and grew in violence under the influence of Naples. When Sixtus IV. determined on war against Ferrara, he summoned the Roman barons from the camp of Alfonso. The Orsini obeyed the Pope's summons; the Savelli and Colonna remained; and Alfonso was not sorry to have adherents who might create disturbances in Rome.

Disturbances were not long in arising. On the night of April 3 the Santa Croce, aided by some of the papal guards whom Count Girolamo despatched on this service, attacked the Valle palace and killed in the fray Girolamo Colonna, a natural son of Antonio, prefect of the city. On this Sixtus IV. ordered the house of the Santa Croce to be razed to the ground. This did not much mend matters, as Prospero Colonna, enraged at his brother's death, withdrew from Rome and joined Alfonso, who appeared at the head of his troops and asked leave to pass through the papal dominions on his way to Ferrara. When the Pope refused, Alfonso advanced to the Latin Hills, and the Colonna and Savelli fortified themselves in the strong castle of Marino, whence they ravaged the Campagna and even dashed in a pillaging raid into the city itself. The Neapolitan galleys appeared off Ostia, and Rome was threatened with a siege.

Sixtus IV. retaliated by imprisoning Cardinals Colonna and Savelli on the charge of treasonable correspondence with

The Colonna and Savelli side with Naples.

[1] All this is fully told by Sigismondo de' Conti, i. 134 &c.

Naples. The Romans, meanwhile, murmured at the loss of their harvest from the Neapolitan troops, and Sixtus IV. was so alarmed at their discontent that he dared not send his forces against the foe. He was afraid that if he were left unprotected in Rome the city would rise against him, and judged it more prudent to await the arrival of reinforcements from Venice. Meanwhile, the Vatican was guarded like a fortress, and the Pope's chamber was watched by night and day. Rome, which for some months had been turned into a manufactory of arms, now experienced all the forms of military license. Even the churches were not spared; Count Girolamo took possession of the Lateran and turned the sacristy into a club-room, where he and his friends played cards and draughts upon the reliquaries.[1]

At last, on July 23, Roberto Malatesta arrived before the walls of Rome and was received with the greatest joy by the people as their deliverer. His forces were not numerous at first, and he had to wait for troops which were raised at the cost of Venice. On August 15 a large army was collected and defiled through the Piazza of S. Peter, where the Pope gave them his benediction from a window in the Vatican. On August 18 they marched from the gate of S. Giovanni against the foe, amidst the muttered curses of the Romans whose vineyards had been destroyed and whose city had been rendered pestilential by the soldiers.

On the approach of the papal forces, which outnumbered his own, the Duke of Calabria withdrew from Città Lavigna and took up a strong position in the desolate and unhealthy district of woods and marshes which reaches down to the sea. The spot where he intrenched himself bore the ill-omened name of Campo Morto, a little hill accessible only by two entrances from the neighbouring marsh. According to the courtesies of Italian warfare Malatesta arranged with Duke Alfonso the day and time of battle, and on August 21 the fight began. After the capitulation of Otranto, Alfonso had taken into his pay some of the janissaries, who now appeared in Italian warfare; their valour and the strength of the position repulsed the first onslaught of the papal infantry; but Malatesta, with desperate bravery, reformed his broken lines and meanwhile a

[1] Infessura, in Eccard, ii. 1901.

diversion in the rear threw the Neapolitan camp into confusion. A storm of rain damped their powder and prevented them from using their artillery. Alfonso, fearful for his safety, stole away and made to the seacoast, whence he fled to Terracina; his army was completely routed. The battle was memorable amidst the bloodless contests of Italy; more than 1,000 men were slain and many Neapolitans were made prisoners.

The news of this victory awakened the greatest delight in Rome, which was increased by the surrender of Marino and other strong places held in the neighbourhood by the Neapolitans. The exertion of the battle amid the marshy ground proved fatal to Roberto Malatesta, who returned to Rome and died on September 10, after receiving supreme unction at the hands of Sixtus IV. He was honourably buried in S. Peter's, and the city mourned for its deliverer;[1] but the death of Roberto freed the Pope from a friend who might have become too powerful. His wife received on the same day the news of the death of her husband, and of her father Federigo of Urbino, whose long military career was ended by a fever which he caught in the marshes of Ferrara while leading the troops of the league against Venice.

Death of
Roberto
Malatesta
and Fede-
rigo of
Urbino.
September
1482.

The victory of Campo Morto freed Rome from peril, but did not win anything for the Pope. The Neapolitans still held strong positions in the papal territory; Ferrara was not yet conquered; and Sixtus IV. began to dread the overweening power of Venice. Moreover, a still more serious danger invited Sixtus IV. to greater caution in his rash designs. An attempt was made to raise again the cry for a reforming Council; and the attempt was fostered by foes whom the Italian policy of the Pope had embittered against him. That such a danger should terrify the Pope is a sign of the weakness of the new attitude assumed by the Papacy. If the papal position was to be chiefly political, it was but natural that the Pope's

---

[1] Infessura (Eccard, ii. 1911) tells a good story about Roberto's death. The Sienese owed Roberto a debt of gratitude for helping them in time of need, and met in council to deliberate how it should be repaid. 'To make him lord of their city seemed a scanty recompense: at last one rose and said, "Let us kill him and adore him as a saint, and then we can have him as guardian of our city for ever."' Infessura hints that Sixtus IV. followed the example of the Sienese and rid himself by poison of a too powerful friend, but this is wholly unfounded, and only serves to give point to the story.

BOOK
V.

political opponents should attack him from the ecclesiastical side, and that the question of reformation should be reserved as a convenient weapon against a Pope who threatened to become too powerful. While the papal forces triumphed at Campo Morto the enemies of Sixtus IV. retaliated by the menace of a renewal of the Council of Basel. The threat was empty and its instrument was insignificant, but it nevertheless fulfilled its purpose.

Andrea,
Arch-
bishop of
Krain, in
Rome.
1481.

Andrea Zuccalmaglio, Archbishop of Krain, by birth a Slav, a member of the Dominican Order, was sent to Rome as ambassador by the Emperor Frederick III. in 1479. He seems to have been a simple-minded man, without much knowledge of the world or much experience of affairs. Not unnaturally he was shocked by much that he saw at Rome and ventured to speak his mind plainly to the Pope. Sixtus IV. did not resent his remonstrances, but hinted to the Emperor that he had not chosen a discreet envoy. Frederick III. accordingly recalled Andrea, who meanwhile had waxed bolder and had openly denounced the Pope and his relatives. On the withdrawal of the Emperor's commission he was imprisoned in June 1481 in the Castle of S. Angelo,[1] but was soon released and departed for Germany, smarting under a sense of wrong. He had come to Rome hoping for the cardinalate, and had received imprisonment as the reward of his apostolic frankness. His vanity was wounded; and on his way homeward he published his wrongs till some wily politicians of Northern Italy confirmed him in the belief that he ought to take steps to redress them.

Proclaims
a Council
at Basel.
March
1482.

Accordingly the Archbishop of Krain used his dignity of imperial ambassador as a means of opening a formidable attack upon the Pope. Instead of returning to Vienna, he went to Basel with the intention of reviving the traditions of the last reforming Council. He gave himself the name of cardinal and papal legate, and was lucky enough to find a clever secretary in Peter Numagen, a notary of Trier. On March 25, 1482, he entered the cathedral during the time of service, denounced

---

[1] A letter of Sixtus IV. to Frederick III. is printed in Appendix vii. to Sigismondo de' Conti, *Historia*, i. 410: 'Consueverat ille temeraria quadam audacia de nobis et venerabili Cardinalium Collegio, totaque curia nostra plura et diversa falso obloqui ac palam disseminare; et in ea re callum jam obduxerat neque curabat sese emendare, quamvis saepius cum monuerimus et pristinam benevolentiam nostram illi ostenderimus.'

Pope Sixtus IV., and solemnly proclaimed a Council. He demanded of the city magistrates a safe-conduct in the Emperor's name, and the burghers of Basel had no objection to anything that was likely to bring strangers to their city.

The news of this strange proceeding awakened much anxiety in Rome: it seemed impossible that the Archbishop of Krain should proceed so far without being sure of powerful support. Sixtus IV. suspected that the Emperor was secretly abetting him, and indeed Frederick III., when appealed to by the magistrates of Basel, gave ambiguous answers; he was willing to wait and see if there was anything to be gained from the phantom Council. Everyone laughed at the Archbishop of Krain, whom his own secretary held to be light-headed ;[1] but everyone enjoyed the Pope's discomfiture, and no one was quite sure how matters might turn, whether or no the burlesque might become earnest.

Sixtus IV. was alarmed at the attitude of the Archbishop of Krain, and even amidst the pressure of events in Rome, did not neglect any means to get him into his power. Envoy after envoy was sent to the Emperor and to the citizens of Basel; but Frederick III. did not absolutely order the men of Basel to take the Archbishop prisoner, and without the Emperor's orders the magistrates refused to seize him. Meanwhile Archbishop Andrea thundered forth invectives against the Pope, and summoned him to appear before a Council of which he himself was as yet the sole representative. On July 20 he placarded his summons in Basel: 'Francesco of Savona, son of the devil, you entered your office not through the door but through the window of simony. You are of your father the devil, and labour to do your father's will.' Sixtus IV. excommunicated him, and a Dominican inquisitor in Basel denounced him as a schismatic and heretic. The Archbishop answered by an invective against the Dominicans, though he himself belonged to the Order. It was an unwise step, for it set all the preachers against him: every church rang with their denunciations. The Pope laid Basel under an interdict, but it was not

---

[1] Peter Numagen wrote *Gesta Archiepiscopi Crayneris*, extracts from which are given in Hottinger, *Historia Ecclesiastica*, iv. 347 &c. Numagen says (*l.c.* 355): 'Homo ille cerebro læsus, non sui compos, sed amens in parte, vere amente periculosior nihil sibi prospexit.' Burchard, *Der Erzbischof Andreas von Krain*, quotes from the Basel archives.

observed. The conciliar principle was not yet dead, and the
Curia feared a revival of the Council of Basel. So late as
September, an official of the Pope wrote a letter to the Pro-
vost of the Church of Basel in which he combated the position
that a Council might meet without the Pope's summons. In
so doing he did not venture to impugn the decrees of Constance, but only argued that they had not been carried out and
therefore had lapsed by common consent. The Council of
Basel had been transferred either to Lausanne or to the Lateran,
according as men thought; but in either case it had separated
without fixing a place for meeting again, and it was now impossible to revive the Council of Basel without a new summons.
The treatise throughout is curious, as showing the dread which
the threat of a Council still inspired, and the difficulties of
canonists in arguing against it.[1]

Collapse of
the Arch-
bishop of
Krain.
November
1482.

Matters were now so far serious, that in September Florence
and Milan sent envoys to see what was to be made out of this
new movement. The Florentine envoy reported to Lorenzo de'
Medici, that the Archbishop of Krain was a resolute and
determined man, well adapted to harass the Pope and Count
Girolamo.[2] He promised the men of Basel, that the Italian
League would help them to reform the Church, and he rejoiced
to find the Pope as much hated beyond the Alps as in Florence.
But in spite of this intelligence, the Italian powers did not
care to commit themselves; and the Emperor at last discovered
that he had nothing to gain. On October 20 a letter arrived
in Basel, bidding the magistrates imprison the rebellious Archbishop who was acting contrary to his instructions. After this
the papal legate demanded that the Archbishop be given up
to him as a prisoner, but the magistrates refused for some
time. At last, on December 18, a solemn assembly was held.
Andrea protested his obedience to the Emperor and his fidelity
to the Church, but asserted that he was justified in his attempt
to hold a Council for the reformation of the Church, and
declared that he had not calumniated the Pope, as he had
said nothing but what was notoriously true. He was put in

---

[1] I have given this document in the Appendix No. V. from a very rare print
of Guldinbeck de Sultz, 1482.

[2] Letters in Fabroni, ii. 229. 'Costui è huomo per fare ogni cosa, purchè e
tuffi el Papa, el Conte, e questo basti.'

prison by the magistrates, who refused to give him up to the legate. Their city was laid under the greater excommunication, but they continued steadfast. Andrea remained in prison in Basel, till in November 1484 he hanged himself in his cell. Then a papal legate was sent to seize his papers and give absolution to the city. The corpse of the unhappy man was thrown into the Rhine.

This attempt at a Council was ludicrous enough, and its significance lies only in its influence on the papal policy. If Sixtus IV. had continued in his war against the Italian League, they might have found means to blow up a flame of opposition in Basel.[1] The position of the Pope as Head of Christendom had sunk to be subsidiary to his position as an Italian prince, and was merely a source of weakness to his political plans. Sixtus IV. recognised this fact, and the papal policy underwent a sudden change. The Spanish envoys in Rome negotiated a peace between the Pope and Naples; and on December 11 Sixtus IV. wrote to his ally, the Doge of Venice, bidding him withdraw from the war against Ferrara which was being waged successfully. On December 13 Sixtus IV. celebrated his peace in Rome, by a solemn procession to the Church of S. Maria della Virtù, the name of which he changed to S. Maria della Pace, and resolved to rebuild the church in token of his thankfulness. A few days afterwards the Duke of Calabria paid Rome a visit and was welcomed by the Pope in the Vatican. On December 30 he set out to the aid of Ferrara with the Pope's benediction on his arms. Sixtus IV. suddenly altered his political attitude, but was only waiting to see what new object he might pursue. He had certainly gained nothing by the war in which he had engaged against Ferrara.

Moreover, the Pope's change of attitude was as complete as it was sudden. Not content with leaving Venice in the lurch, he ordered her to make peace with Ferrara immediately. The Venetian senate answered with some dignity, 'You might easily at the beginning have led us to forget our grievances; now, after we have spent more money than Ferrara is worth,

Marginal notes: Sixtus IV. makes peace with Ferrara. December 1482.

Sixtus IV. excommunicates Venice. May 1483.

---

[1] Sixtus IV. admits this in a letter to the Doge of Venice (Sigismondo de' Conti, i. 160): ' Animo metientes quam luctuose rebus Christianis, quam periculose fidei Catholicæ essent hujusmodi perturbationes, maxime propter schisma quod in Ecclesia Dei a nonnullis jam procurabatur.'

and when victory is in our grasp, your exhortation to peace is simply an attempt to wrest from us what we have won, and hold us up to the ridicule of the world. Why do you grudge us our success? We have not summoned a Council, nor promoted a schism.'[1] Venice naturally did not see why her interests should be sacrificed to the Pope's panic. But Sixtus IV. did not do things by halves; he joined the league of Naples, Milan, and Florence against his former ally, and on May 25, 1483, even excommunicated the Venetians for warring against Ferrara, disturbing the peace of Italy, and thereby preventing the pacification of Europe for a Crusade against the Turks. The Venetians answered by appealing to a future Council. Sixtus IV. pronounced their appeal to be *ipso facto* null and void; it could rest only on one of two grounds, either that Christ had not given power on earth to S. Peter and his successors, which was heretical, or that an appeal was possible from Christ's Vicar to Christ himself, which was contrary to the canons, seeing that the two tribunals were identical.[2] At the same time Sixtus IV. was careful to assure himself of the support of Louis XI. of France, the only king who was likely to help Venice in the matter of a Council. He sent an envoy to point out the dangers of Venetian aggression. As Louis XI. had no friendly feeling towards Venice, he permitted the excommunication to be published in his kingdom.

The real reason of the change of the papal policy was a hope of wresting from Venice the towns of Cervia and Ravenna by means of his new allies. Venice was not successful in the campaign of 1483, and tried to make peace with the Pope. Cardinal Costa undertook the office of mediator, and Venice agreed that the papal flag should wave over the towns which she had captured and that papal governors should be admitted. Sixtus IV. demanded that the Venetian garrisons should also be withdrawn, which was equivalent to claiming for himself the Venetian conquests. Cardinal Costa found that he was mocked in his attempts to negotiate, as Count Girolamo showed him a document signed by the Pope, that peace was not to be

---

[1] Sigismondo de' Conti was the Pope's envoy to Venice, and has preserved the letters, *Historia*, i. 158 &c. A still more remarkable letter of the Pope is printed in the Appendix, i. 413, dated Feb. 17, 1483.

[2] Raynaldus, 1483, No. 18 &c.

made till Venice had been driven from Cervia and Ravenna.
No wonder men said that Sixtus IV. preferred war to peace.[1]

Meanwhile, in the city of Rome peace had not put an end
to the disorderly spirit which prevailed. On January 22, 1483,
died Cardinal Estouteville, at the age of eighty. He had been
cardinal for eight-and-thirty years and his possessions were
enormous. His funeral was the occasion of an unseemly
quarrel between the Monks of S. Agostino and the Canons of
S. Maria Maggiore, who both claimed as their perquisites the
rich trappings of the bier. In the tumult that arose the rings
were torn off the fingers of the dead prelate, the disputants
charged one another with their lighted torches, and swords
were drawn by the bystanders. The corpse was only saved
from further indignity by being hurried into the sacristy of S.
Agostino till the fight was over. In February the Carnival was
revived with great splendour after being for seven years in
abeyance ; but a disturbance arose which drove the magistrates
to flee into the Capitol.

If Rome was turbulent, the papal policy did not tend to
pacify it. Sixtus IV. seems to have had an ungovernable
liking for discord. In the peace which had been made with
Naples nothing was said about the Roman allies of King
Ferrante ; so the Cardinals Colonna and Savelli were still kept
in prison, and were not released till November 15. The Colonna
grew more and more suspicious of the Pope, since Count Girolamo Riario was avowedly on the side of the Orsini, and on the
same day as Cardinal Colonna was freed from prison, Gian Battista Orsini was raised to the cardinalate. The avowed animosity
of these two families kept Rome unquiet, and early in 1484
faction fights again burst out so that the festivities of the Carnival could not be celebrated. On February 21 Francesco di
Santa Croce was assassinated by his old enemies the Valle.
On April 28 the head of the Colonna, the protonotary Oddo,
returned to Rome, and the Orsini at once took up arms. The
magistrates appealed to the Pope to save them from civil
war, and Sixtus IV. summoned Oddo to the Vatican. Oddo
sent his excuses to the Pope, declaring that he was in arms
not against the Church but against his personal foes. Sixtus

---

[1] Sigismondo de' Conti, i. 186 : ' Et profecto conventura res esset, et in
magnam pacem Italiæ concessura, ni Sixtus bellum maluisset quam pacem.'

IV. repeated his summons, and Oddo mounted on horseback to obey; but on the way his friends surrounded him, pointed out the danger which he ran, warned him that he would never return alive, and that if he failed them they were all undone. At last some exclaimed that it were better for them to cut him in pieces than leave him to his enemies; his horse was seized and he was dragged back to his palace. Again the Pope repeated his summons; again Oddo was dragged back by his friends. Then Sixtus IV. declared him to be guilty of treason and sent orders for his capture. The Orsini stormed and sacked the Colonna palace, till Oddo, slightly wounded, surrendered to Virginio Orsini, who carried him to the Pope, but had some difficulty in saving his prisoner from Count Girolamo Riario, who made several attempts to stab him by the way.

Oddo Colonna was examined by the Pope and then imprisoned in the Castle of S. Angelo. Meanwhile the Colonna palaces were being plundered; and though the Cardinals urged that they be spared, the Pope issued an order that they be razed to the ground. Pillage and slaughter raged in the city, and every man avenged his private grievances upon his foes. The papal forces were sent against the castle of Marino where Fabrizio Colonna maintained himself. The city magistrates in vain pleaded with Count Girolamo to make a truce—he would with difficulty allow them access to the Pope, who answered that he would neither have truce nor peace till he had the lands of the Colonna in his hands. Count Girolamo was implacable, and even attacked Cardinal Giuliano della Rovere in the Pope's presence for having given refuge in his palace to some barons of the Colonna party; Giuliano answered that the violence of the Count was enough to ruin Pope and Cardinals alike. The Colonna offered to give up to the College of Cardinals Marino, Rocca del Papa, and Ardea; but the Pope answered, at Girolamo's dictation, that he would have their castles by force in their despite. Count Girolamo was master of Rome, and in the Pope's name exacted money from the clergy, even from the papal secretaries, that he might provide artillery for the siege of Marino. On June 23 Sixtus IV. went to inspect the guns before they set out for Marino; raising his eyes to heaven he made the sign of the cross and blessed them, praying that

God would endow them with such virtue, that wherever they
went they might turn to flight the enemies of the Church. It
was a new form of warfare for the Christian faith that Sixtus IV.
invented and set forth with all the forms of ecclesiastical ritual.

To save the life of his brother, Fabrizio Colonna surrendered
to the Pope, on June 25, Marino and Rocca del Papa; but he
trusted to a broken reed if he put any confidence in the Pope's
mercy. Oddo Colonna was subjected to the mockery of a trial
and was sentenced to be executed on June 30. When he came
to the block his confession was read: he turned to those standing by and protested that he had spoken under cruel tortures
what was not true, that he wished to inculpate no man, but
was content to die. Then he commended his spirit to God,
and his head was severed from his body with the name of Jesus
on its lips. His body was placed in a coffin and carried to the
Church of S. Maria in Trastevere, thence to SS. Apostoli, where
his luckless mother received it weeping. Opening the coffin
she gazed on her son's mangled remains, and exclaimed: 'See
the head of my son and the faith of Pope Sixtus, who promised
that if we gave up Marino he would give up my son. He has
Marino and I have my son's corpse; such is his faith.'[1] A week
after, the desolate mother died.

Still Sixtus IV. found, as had several of his predecessors,
that it was a hard matter to destroy a powerful family like the
Colonna. The castle of Cavi held out for three weeks against
Count Girolamo and his artillery. The Colonna then retired to
Palliano, where they made such desperate resistance, and so
harassed the besiegers by constant sallies, that Count Girolamo
wrote mournfully to the Pope asking for reinforcements, and
owning that he had little hopes of success. Sixtus IV. was
greatly depressed at this news: he had hoped for an easy victory
over the Colonna, and was not prepared for their desperate

---

[1] This story is given on the authority of Alegretti, *Diario Sanese*, in Mur.
xxiii. 817. Infessura, who says that he was present at the funeral, does not
mention it, but the Notaio di Nantiporto (Mur. iii. pt. 2, 1087) mentions the
mother's presence: 'In Santo Apostolo aspettò la madre con moltissime
femmine e gli fece gran lamento.' This renders the tale in itself probable.
There is no evidence that the Pope made any promise to release Lorenzo, but
it was natural for a mother to found expectations on the compliance with
the Pope's demand. The story seems to have been sufficiently circulated to
influence popular opinion concerning Sixtus IV.

GENEALOGICAL TABLE OF THE ROVERE FAMILY.

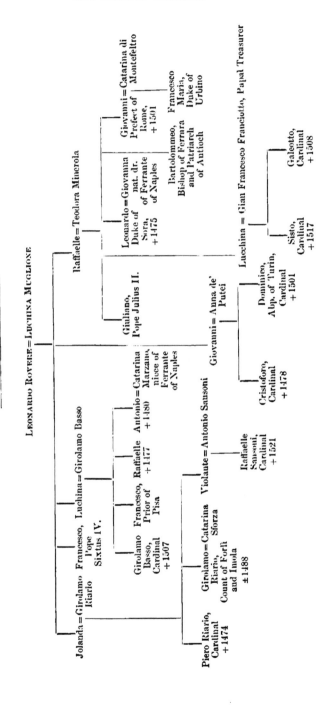

resistance. In the middle of June he had been ill of a fever and his health began to give way. When envoys came on August 11 to announce that his allies had made peace with Venice, Sixtus IV. could hardly speak to express his indignation.[1] ' You bring a peace,' said the dying man, ' full of disgrace and confusion ; I can never accept it.' The legates tried to mollify his wrath, and he dismissed them with a motion of his hand that might be taken either as a blessing or as a command to be gone. His attendants tried to console him, but he grew gradually weaker, and died early next morning, August 12.

Sixtus IV. was a man of strongly marked character, who exercised a powerful influence, both on Italy in his own day and on the future of the Papacy. Machiavelli says of him with truth : ' he was the first Pope who began to show the extent of the papal power, and how things that before were called errors could be hidden behind the papal authority.'[2] The papal power which Machiavelli had before his eyes was not the moral authority of the Head of Christendom, but the power of an Italian prince who was engaged in consolidating his dominions into an important state.

Sixtus IV.
began the
secularisa-
tion of the
Papacy.

However much the formation of the Papal States might be a lawful object of papal endeavour there remains the question of its importance. Sixtus IV. pursued it passionately to the exclusion of the other duties of his office. He paid no heed to the pacification of Christendom, and though sometimes the talk of a Crusade appears in his letters, it is mere hollow pretence. All thought of the policy of Pius II. was entirely abandoned. The affairs of Bohemia and Hungary were left to settle themselves. The sphere of the Pope's political activity was narrowed to Italy only, and Sixtus IV. inaugurated a period of secularisation of the Papacy which continued till the shock of the Reformation startled it again into spiritual activity. Under Sixtus IV. the Papacy became an Italian power, which pursued its own political career with force and dexterity. What Sixtus IV. began Alexander VI. continued, and Julius II. brought to a successful issue. The Papal States were won, but Italy

---

[1] ' Per il catarro essergli ingrossata la lingua in modo che quasi non può formare la parola,' wrote Vespucci to Lorenzo de' Medici on Aug. 12 ; Thuasne, Burchard i. 495.

[2] *Ist. Fiorentine* Bk. vii.

fell under foreign domination, and the Papacy lost its hold on Northern Europe almost as soon as the work was accomplished.

The object which Sixtus IV. set before himself was not a lofty one, nor fitted to absorb all the papal energies. But when Sixtus IV. adopted it he pursued it with all the force and determination of a powerful and resolute character. His strongly marked personality produced a deep impression on Italy and left abiding traces on the Papacy. The vigorous nature that raised the low-born upstart to the papal throne finds its parallel in the condottieri generals who mounted from the cottage to the dukedom, who ruled with munificence and burned to hand down their glory to future ages. Sixtus IV. had an upstart's desire to raise his family and spread the glory of his name. Four of his relatives were made Cardinals, and others were enriched at the expense of the Church. Two were wedded to relations of the King of Naples, and were provided for in the Neapolitan domains. Another was married to the daughter of the Duke of Urbino, and his son substituted the name of Rovere for that of Montefeltro in the ducal seat. These all won their way by peaceful means, supported only by the Pope's influence; but Girolamo Riario was reserved to be the instrument of the Pope's policy in winning back and organising the possessions of the Church. For him the Pope plunged into one war after another and lavished all the resources of his temporal and spiritual authority.

Yet Girolamo Riario had nothing to commend him except his readiness to accept the part which the Pope wished him to play. If Sixtus IV. was resolute and unscrupulous, Girolamo surpassed him in his determination to let nothing slip that might promote his own advancement. We have seen how his zeal outsped that of Sixtus IV. in his desire to overthrow Lorenzo de' Medici; and in all other matters he acted with equal disregard to morality. Arrogant, uncultivated, and brutal, he took pleasure in nothing but the chase, which he raised to a magnificence never equalled since the days of the Roman Circus. Under the shadow of the Pope's protection he carried all before him in Rome, and those who were not prepared to become his creatures were exposed to his vengeance. His violence shocked even his relatives, and Cardinal Giuliano openly reproved him. His cousin, Antonio Basso, on his deathbed denounced the crimes of Count Girolamo, who came to bid him farewell. 'Whether his mind was deranged or he wished to ease himself of the venom which had long been retained,' says an eye-witness,[1] 'he inveighed vehemently against the Count. He told him of deeds of his that were everywhere condemned, of his character everywhere reprobated. We who stood by the bedside blushed for shame, and some quietly withdrew.' The dying man ventured to speak out the truth to the favourite who enjoyed the entire confidence of the Pope.

Indeed it is impossible not to feel that the low savagery and brutal resoluteness of Count Girolamo were echoes of the natural man of Sixtus IV., which had been in some measure tempered by early training and the habits of self-restraint. The policy of Sixtus IV. is marked by wild energy rather than by any greatness of conception. He set an object definitely before himself, and pursued it by any means that offered. The existing generation of Italian statesmen were polished and prudent diplomatists: they had won their position by fraud or force, but aimed at retaining it by wisdom and caution. Sixtus IV. went back to the traditions of the more barbarous age of condottieri adventurers. Hence he spread dismay amongst the politicians of Italy, because he revived a past which they were striving to forget. The diplomatic webs of Lorenzo de' Medici and Ludovico Sforza were useless to enchain Sixtus IV., who remained an incalculable element in their schemes. It was through his restless energy, not through his wisdom, that Sixtus IV. caused dread. His plans, such as they were, never succeeded; yet none the less he raised the Papacy to the level of a great power. He failed to overthrow Lorenzo de' Medici; he failed to win anything from Ferrara, or from Naples, or from Venice; he failed to overcome the Colonna faction in Rome. Yet all whom he attacked felt that he might have succeeded, and acknowledged the power of their foe.

Great as was the political energy of Sixtus IV. it did not hinder his activity in other directions. He was a mighty organiser and builder, as well as a patron of art and literature. If his policy left an abiding impress on the Papacy, no less did his

---

[1] Jacobo Volterrano, *Diarium Romanum*, in Muratori, xxiii. 109.

care leave a permanent mark on the outward aspect of the
city of Rome. It is at first sight astonishing to find a violent
politician like Sixtus IV. busied with art and architecture;
but Italy in that age was full of contradictions, and Sixtus IV.
was above all things an Italian. If he borrowed his policy
from his neighbours, he borrowed with equal readiness their
patronage of art; or rather in both points he developed the
exclusively Italian elements which the Papacy, as an Italian
power, necessarily contained. Yet here, as well as in politics,
we see the traces of overpowering energy rather than of individual feeling or clear conception. Sixtus IV. did not understand the splendid dream of Nicolas V., the conversion of
Rome into the literary and artistic capital of Christendom;
still less had he the fine taste which made Paul II. a
passionate amateur, with all an amateur's exclusiveness and
selfish delight in amassing delicate treasures full of fascination
to himself.

In spite of its apparent culture the period of the Renaissance was wofully one-sided in its interests and its appreciation.
A student of ancient art cared nothing for the works of his own
age; few could regard sculpture and painting as sister arts;
builders made no scruple in pulling down the precious remains
of antiquity to provide materials for their new edifices. Every
man was engaged in some one pursuit to the exclusion of all
others; and if the men of the Renaissance saved some of the
treasures of antiquity with one hand, they destroyed almost as
much with the other. Sixtus IV. regarded Paul II.'s cameos
and medals as baubles of little consequence; the larger
objects he kept, and with them formed the nucleus of the
Capitoline Museum. It is characteristic of Sixtus IV. that he
was heedless of things whose size did not fit them for public
display.

The same want of appreciation was shown by Sixtus IV. in
his treatment of the remains of antiquity. He restored the
celebrated equestrian statue of Marcus Aurelius which now stands
in front of the Capitol, and he forbade the destruction of ancient
monuments; but he empowered his architects to quarry where
they pleased to obtain stones for his new works. The Sistine
Bridge was built from the blocks of the Coliseum: the temple
of Hercules was entirely swept away. In estimating what

Sixtus IV. did for the city of Rome we can appraise his achievements, but we can only guess what he destroyed.[1]

Still the practical sense and energy of Sixtus IV. enabled him to work more lasting results than were accomplished by the finer taste of his predecessors. He had no plan of transforming Rome into a magnificent city, but for that very reason he did much towards making it more habitable. Rome in the Middle Ages was far below other Italian cities in the outward accompaniments of civilised life. It was a wild, desolate, uncared-for place. The streets were crooked and narrow, destitute of pavement, and encumbered with porticoes which harboured dirt. Infessura says that Ferrante of Naples on his visit to the Pope in 1475 pointed out the strategical disadvantages of such irregular streets; he told Sixtus IV. that he could never be master of a city where barricades could be so easily constructed, and where a few women from the top of the overhanging balconies could keep a troop of soldiers at bay.[2] Whether in consequence of this advice or no cannot be said, but Sixtus IV. took in hand the work of rearranging the chief streets of his capital. He straightened their labyrinthine turns, swept away the projecting porches, and paved the streets with tiles.[3] The works were begun in 1480 under the direction of commissioners, and were carried out with promptitude. The Romans at first murmured, but gradually saw the advantages of the Pope's proceedings. Moreover, Sixtus IV. had a summary manner of dealing with objectors. One day, when he went to view the works in progress, he found a burgher who refused to allow the papal workmen to widen the approach to the Bridge of S. Angelo by throwing down the booths which he had built to contain his wares. The Pope ordered the man to

Improvement of the city of Rome.

---

[1] An epigram of Fausto Maddaleno de' Capi di Ferro, quoted by Gregorovius, *Geschichte der Stadt Rom*, vii. 659, ends

Quæ neque vis cæli neque fulmine Jupiter ullo
　　Obruit, et fuerant religiosa diis,
Æquat humi Lygurum natus, proh Jupiter, arvis,
　　Substinet et tantum Martia Roma nefas.

[2] Infessura, in Mur. iii. pt. 2, 1145.

[3] Bartolomæus Senegara, in Mur. xxiv. 532: 'Illo jubente stratæ sunt viæ Urbis latere cocto: et quæ tortuosæ et deformes erant porticibus cænosis et obscuris, dirutæ et in apertam formam et rectam reductæ sunt.

prison, and stood by till he saw his house as well as his booths demolished.[1]

By such vigorous measures Sixtus IV. succeeded in working some reforms in the Roman streets. He secured a clear communication between the Vatican and the Bridge of S. Angelo, thence through the Campus Martius to the Capitol. Moreover, in preparation for the Jubilee of 1475, he built the bridge across the Tiber which still bears his name, the Ponte Sisto. He was mindful of the disaster which had occurred in the Jubilee of 1450, through the crowding on the Bridge of S. Angelo, which was the only available means of communication with S. Peter's. The new bridge was strongly built of blocks of travertine, and its architect aimed at a solid rather than a graceful structure. In another matter Sixtus IV. deserved well of the Romans: he cared for the water supply and brought down the Acqua Vergine from the Quirinal to the Trevi fountain. In everything that could improve and beautify Rome, Sixtus IV. took a keen and active interest. He did much to give the city its modern aspect, and if he had lived long enough he would have transformed it entirely.[2] He did his best to encourage others to follow his example by giving right of ownership to all who built houses in the district of Rome. The Cardinals, especially Estouteville, were incited to build, and many palaces owe their foundation to the energy of the Rovere family and their imitators.

The monumental works of Sixtus IV. have borne the impress

---

[1] Jacopus Volterranus, *Diarium*, in Mur. xxiii. 166.

[2] *Vita Sixti IV.* in Mur. x. pt. 2, 1664 : 'Adeo ubique per Urbem ædificatur ut brevi novam formam omnino sit habitura si Sixto vivere contigerit.' Ciaconius, iii. 32 &c., gives a collection of inscriptions in Rome which record the works of Sixtus IV. Noticeable is one which still remains near to the Campo dei Fiori in the Vicolo dei Balestrari :

> Quæ modo putris eras et olenti sordida cæno
> Plenaque deformis Martia terra situ,
> Exuis hanc turpem Xysto sub Principe formam ;
> Omnia sunt nitidis conspicienda locis.
> Digna salutifero debentur præmia Xysto.
> O quantum est summo debita Roma Luci.

Via Florea

ANNO SALUTIS

MCCCCLXXXIII.

Baptista Archioneus et) curatores
Ludovicus Marganeus ∫ viarum.

of his activity to the present day more distinctly than have the buildings of his predecessors. In the Vatican he erected a block containing a Library on the ground floor, and above it the famous Sistine Chapel which still bears the Pope's name. The requirements of the Vatican library have long outsped the modest provision made by Sixtus IV., and this building now serves as offices. The Chapel owes its fame to the mighty pencil of Michel Angelo and not to any architectural merits. It is nothing more than a large room, coldly ornamented with pilasters along the sides, with a flatly vaulted roof. There is nothing in the construction of the Chapel that bespeaks its purposes, yet its very bareness and simplicity seem to have fitted it for papal ceremonies; its structure has remained unchanged, and it has owed its dignity to the master's hand which has made the blank walls vocal with his genius.

So was it with the other buildings of Sixtus IV. None of them are great architectural creations. Vasari assigns them to the Florentine Baccio Pontelli; but they seem to have been chiefly the work of smaller men, Meo del Caprina, Giacomo di Pietra Santa, and others whose names only survive.[1] Sixtus IV. wanted his work done, and cared more for its rapid execution than for its fine design. Moreover, his age was not distinguished by any great architect. The stars of Brunelleschi and of Leo Battista Alberti had set, and their great conceptions were reproduced by timid copyists. The works of Sixtus IV. are interesting as showing the modest beginnings in Rome of the triumph of the Renaissance, opposed as it was to the sentiment of the city's past, over the Gothic architecture. In S. Maria della Pace and S. Maria del Popolo we find traces of Gothic influence in the rose windows, the clustered pillars, and the vaulted nave; but the octagonal dome, the simple treatment of the façade, and the pilasters of the portico mark them as works of the Renaissance. Poor as they are in details, they form the link between Brunelleschi and Bramante. The ideas of Brunelleschi are being applied experimentally till the free hand of Bramante can give them full expression.

The Church of S. Maria del Popolo became the favourite

[1] See Müntz, *Les Arts à la Cour des Papes,* iii. 69 &c. I am largely indebted to M Müntz for all that concerns the artistic side of the pontificate of Sixtus IV.

Church of the Rovere family, and its monuments make it a museum of Renaissance art. The Church of S. Maria della Pace was not finished by Sixtus IV., but his successor continued the work. Besides these chief buildings of Sixtus IV., the Churches of S. Pietro in Vincoli, S. Balbina, SS. Nereo ed Achilleo, S. Quirico, S. Susanna and others were restored; and the tribune of SS. Apostoli was rebuilt. Still more characteristic is the building of the great hospital of S. Spirito which Sixtus IV. began immediately on his accession. The octagonal cupola with pointed windows, and the tower of the neighbouring Church of S. Spirito, are perhaps the happiest remains of the architecture of Sixtus IV. The restoration of this ruined hospital is a memorial that Sixtus IV. was not so entirely engrossed in worldly schemes as to forget altogether his mission as a Christian priest.

In painting, Sixtus IV. had a larger choice of artists, and summoned to Rome almost all the great masters of his day. The large room of the hospital of S. Spirito was adorned with a series of frescoes, now much ruined, representing the life of the Pope. They set forth the dream of her child's greatness which his mother dreamed; the miracles that accompanied his childhood; the foundation of the hospital; the restoration of the Roman churches; the ceremonial receptions given to sovereigns; the canonisation of S. Bonaventura and the like.[1] There is no mention of the wars of Sixtus IV.: the only allusion to martial exploits is the victory of the papal fleet over the Turks. If the history of Sixtus IV. were read by the aid of the record which he himself has left, we should picture a kindly and devout old man entirely devoted to the discharge of his spiritual duties.

For the decoration of his buildings Sixtus IV. summoned to Rome Perugino, Sandro Botticelli, Domenico, Ghirlandaio, Cosimo Roselli, Melozzo da Forlì, Filippino Lippi, Luca Signorelli, Piero da Cosimo, Fra Diamante, and others of less note. Even in his dealings with painters we see his practical spirit, for he united them into a confraternity under the patronage of S. Luke;[2] and the confraternity was afterwards raised by

---

[1] The subjects are described at length by a contemporary in Muratori, iii. pt. 2, 1065.

[2] The statutes of this corporation, dated 1478, are given by Müntz, l.c. 101.

Gregory XIII. in 1577 to the dignity of a corporate academy for the painters of Rome. Yet though Sixtus IV. protected artists, they had to be careful how they offended him. During the siege of Cavi, a young Roman painted the scene with such exactness that it filled Rome with admiration. The tents and standards of the besiegers, the guns, and the troops engaged in conflict were portrayed with spirit. The Pope sent for the picture and at first was pleased with it; but he grew angry as he saw that it represented the defeat of the soldiers of the Church, and the discovery of an episode which seemed to mock at Count Girolamo filled up the measure of his wrath. He ordered the luckless painter to be imprisoned, to receive ten stripes, and on the next day to be hanged and his house to be pulled down. The Pope's wrath was only mitigated by the plea that the man was light-headed; his life was spared but he was banished from Rome.[1]

Perhaps the feeling that they served an uncertain master weighed on the spirits of the great painters who came to Rome; perhaps they were fettered by the Pope's directions; perhaps the atmosphere of the place was still strange to their art, and there was nothing to inspire them. At all events, none of them produced a masterpiece in their decoration of the Sistine Chapel, and few rose to their ordinary level. Yet the conception of the twelve pictures which adorn the side walls is dignified. On one side are six episodes from the life of Moses; on the other side six corresponding events in the life of Jesus, showing his fulfilment of the types set forth by the lawgiver of the Old Dispensation. The art of the painter has been too much bound down by the didactic nature of the task assigned him. Each picture contains several distinct motives; thus Botticelli represents, in one picture, Moses slaying the Egyptian, fleeing to Midian, driving away the shepherds from the fountain, watering Zipporah's sheep, kneeling before the burning bush, and finally returning to Egypt. The eye wanders vainly amid this multitude of details, which are not separated by any formal division; nor is the size of the picture large enough to admit of the treatment of any one of these subjects. Ghirlandaio and Perugino have succeeded best because their chief pictures, the call of S. Andrew and S. Peter, and the delivery of

[1] Infessura, in Mur. iii. pt. 2, 1178

the keys to S. Peter, were naturally of sufficient importance to occupy the entire space. Most probably the great artists of the Sistine Chapel, Perugino, Botticelli, Rosselli, Signorelli, and Ghirlandaio, had their subjects assigned by the Pope and were bound to put into their pictures as much as he wanted. We have seen that Sixtus IV. took a quantitative view of artistic excellence, and there are traces of an opinion that the Pope's taste was sadly uncultivated. Vasari tells the story that Sixtus IV. offered a prize to the artist who should acquit himself best. Cosimo Roselli, feeling that he had no chance on other grounds, set himself to captivate the Pope by the brilliancy of his colouring. His rivals laughed at his gaudy colours, his profusion of gold and ultramarine; but Cosimo knew his man and turned the laugh against the scoffers; when Sixtus IV. came to judge he was caught by Cosimo's trap, and awarded him the prize.

Besides these great painters, Melozzo da Forlì enjoyed the patronage of the Pope and his nephews. Much of his work in Rome has been destroyed; but the picture in the Vatican gallery is of great historical interest. Originally it was a fresco which adorned the walls of the library, but it has been transferred to canvas. It represents Sixtus IV. founding the Vatican Library. The Pope, with a face characterised by mingled strength and coarseness, his hands grasping the arms of his chair, sits looking at Platina, who kneels before him—a man whose face is that of a scholar, with square jaw, thin lips, finely-cut mouth, and keen glancing eye. Cardinal Giuliano stands like an official who is about to give a message to the Pope, by whose side is Piero Riario, with aquiline nose and sensual chin, red-cheeked and supercilious. Behind Platina is Count Girolamo with a shock of black hair falling over large black eyes, his look contemptuous and his mien imperious.[1]

This picture of Melozzo represents Sixtus IV. in his rela-

---

[1] The inscription below runs:

Templa, domum expositis, vicos, fora, mœnia, pontes,
　Virgineam Trivii quod repararis aquam,
Prisca licet nautis statuas dare commoda portus
　Et Vaticanum cingere, Sixte, jugum,
Plus tamen urbs debet, nam quæ squalore latebat
　Cernitur in celebri Bibliotheca loco.

tion to literature, which also he prided himself on patronising.
The cloud which hung over men of letters in the days of Paul II.
was rolled away and they again basked in the sunshine of papal
patronage.   The unlucky Platina was again taken into favour,
the lectures of Pomponius Lætus were again thronged with
students.   The Vatican Library, which was committed to Platina's charge, contained 2,500 volumes, of which the greater
part were theological works and the remainder Greek and Latin
classics. Platina had four assistants, with whose help he began
the important labour of cataloguing the papal archives, and had
advanced so far as to fill three large volumes at the time of his
death in 1481.[1]   Under Sixtus IV. there was no doubt of the
triumph of Humanism at the papal court.   Greek literature
had flourished under the protection of Bessarion ; Theodore
Gaza and George of Trebizond lived and quarrelled in Rome. But
these three scholars died soon after the accession of Sixtus IV.,
and their place was taken by John Argyropoulos, who counted
among his hearers in his lectures on Thucydides the learned
German, Johann Reuchlin.   Sixtus IV. endeavoured to attract
to Rome the Florentine, Marsiglio Ficino, but he was too closely
bound to the Medici to quit Florence.   Failing him, the Pope
welcomed the veteran Filelfo, who after venting his spite against
Pius II. and Paul II. for their want of appreciation of his
merits, still hankered after the sweets of papal patronage.   He
came to Rome in 1475, with the promise of an annual salary of
600 florins ; and though then seventy-seven years of age, lectured with vigour for four hours a day.   Rome pleased him in
many ways, especially for ' the incredible liberty which there
existed.'[2]   In this judgment Filelfo's experience renders him
a great authority ; probably nowhere could a man who enjoyed
the Pope's protection speak or behave more freely than in Rome ;
if the Pope was tolerant so was everyone else.   Filelfo, however, did not stay long in Rome, where his only published work
was a translation of a Greek treatise ' About the Priesthood of
Christ amongst the Jews,' which showed by quotations from
the Greek fathers, that Christ exercised amongst the Jews the
office of priest.   Even this was a work done many years before

[1] Raynaldus, *Annales*, 1478, § 48.
[2] Ep. lx. in Rosmini, *Vita di Filelfo.* ' Et quod maximi omnium faciendu
videtur mihi, incredibilis quædam hic libertas est.

and hastily revised as suitable for dedication to the Pope.
Filelfo did not stay long at Rome, where his salary was irregularly paid by the papal treasurer. Sixtus IV. was better in promises than in the careful administration which is necessary to
secure their fulfilment. Filelfo, who was poor, began with
supplications and remonstrances, which soon passed into violent
abuse.[1] He went to Milan to visit his ailing wife in 1476, and
never returned to Rome, but died at Florence in 1481, at the
age of eighty-three.[2]

Sixtus IV. himself had been in early days famous as a theologian, and had taken part in the controversies in which the
Franciscans were engaged against the Dominicans. Besides
his treatise, 'About the Blood of Christ,' he wrote also a work
in behalf of the Immaculate Conception of the Virgin, and a
logical work, 'De Futuris Contingentibus.' Nor did he, in the
midst of his political projects, forget his theological interests.
At first sight it would seem that there was as little in common
between Pope Sixtus IV. and Fra Francesco di Savona as there
was between the magnificent restorer of Rome and the poor friar
who, when he came to Rome as Cardinal, had to borrow money
to make his dwelling habitable. Yet the pontificate of
Sixtus IV. stands in marked contrast to that of his successors
through the fact that it left a great impress on the doctrine
and organisation of the Church. Sixtus IV. did not forget his
debt to the Franciscan Order, and showed his wonted energy
in repaying it. He confirmed and enlarged the privileges of
the Mendicants, and he decisively favoured those tenets of
the Franciscans which were winning their way in popular
theology.

Two Bulls issued in 1474 and 1479[3] mark the highest
advance of the Mendicant Orders, which are termed the two
rivers which flow from Paradise, the Seraphim raised on wings
of heavenly contemplation above all earthly things. Their
exemption from the jurisdiction of ordinaries, the privileges
of their churches, their power of hearing confessions and

---

[1] Rosmini, *Vita di Filelfo*, ii. no. lxviii.

[2] He was the father of twenty-four children, twelve boys and twelve girls.
When he died his youngest daughter was ten years old; only five of this
numerous family survived him.

[3] *Bullarium Romanum*, i. 395 and 418.

administering the sacraments against the will of parish priests
—all that they strove for and claimed was acknowledged in
the most ample terms. Moreover, Sixtus IV. strongly adhered
to the favourite belief of the Franciscans in the immaculate
conception of the Virgin, who was to him a special object of
veneration. To her were dedicated his two great churches
in Rome—S. Maria del Popolo and S. Maria della Pace. He
issued in 1477 a special office for the festival of the Conception
of the Virgin, and granted indulgences to those who used it.
He carefully observed all the festivals of the Virgin, and prayed
so fervently before her image that it was observed he never
even moved his eyes for the space of an hour.[1] When this
avowed partisanship of the Pope gave rise to bitter controversies,
he interfered in 1483 by a decree which recognised the belief
in the immaculate conception as an open question not yet
decided by the Apostolic See, and forbade the disputants on
either side to accuse their adversaries of heresy.[2]

Moreover, the pontificate of Sixtus IV. was marked by the
institution of the tribunal known as the Spanish Inquisition.
Since the beginning of the thirteenth century the office of
extirpating heresy had been committed to the Dominican Order,
and their zeal had been sufficient to protect the purity of the
Christian faith. But as the Spanish kingdoms gained in cohe-
rence, and could look forward to the day when the Moors would
be driven out of the land, the old fervour of the crusading
spirit grew strong among the people. There rose a national
jealousy against the numerous Jews, some of whom had em-
braced Christianity, but their prosperity awakened cupidity,
and their lives suspicion. To protect the Christian faith and
maintain the purity of Spanish blood, Ferdinand and Isabella
applied in 1478 for the Pope's authority to appoint inquisitions
for the suppression of heresy throughout their realms. Permission was granted; but the real work of the Spanish Inquisition was not begun till 1483 by Thomas of Torquemada, whom
Sixtus IV. empowered to constitute the Holy Office, and Spain
unfortunately proved a fruitful soil for its activity. This institution, however, did not proceed from Rome, but was of native

[1] Sigismondo de' Conti, i. 205 : 'Cujus ante imaginem ita intentis et mente
et oculis orare solitus erat, ut horæ spatio nunquam connivere sit visus.'
[2] Raynaldus, 1483, § 64.

growth. It is unfair to brand Sixtus IV. as a persecutor because as head of the Church he granted to princes the powers which they considered necessary for the maintenance of the faith within their dominions.

It was not by neglect of his priestly duties, but by his frank acceptance of the world as it was, that Sixtus IV. is to be regarded as the beginner of the secularisation of the Papacy. Other popes had been keen politicians; but none had openly ventured to play the same game as their neighbours and for the same stakes. Sixtus IV. came forward as an Italian prince, who was relieved from ordinary considerations of decency, consistency, or prudence, because his position as Pope saved him from serious disaster. His theology was a survival of his early training; his new interest in politics stood in the foreground and was immediately influential. During his pontificate the Cardinal College was hopelessly debased and the whole course of life in Rome was changed for the worse. The old Cardinals who represented the traditions of Nicholas V. and Pius II. died out, and were succeeded by others who bore the impress of an age of luxury and intrigue unredeemed by serious effort. Sixtus IV. created thirty-five new cardinals, and at his death there were only five members of the College who did not owe their dignity to his choice. Amongst the creations of Sixtus IV. there were some members of the Franciscan Order who were men of merit; but they were old and soon died. The Cardinals who lived at Rome and were the Pope's companions were either his relatives or men appointed solely on political grounds: Giovanni of Aragon, son of Ferrante of Naples, Ascanio Sforza, Cardinals Colonna, Orsini, Savelli, de' Conti, and the like. Few were chosen for learning or capacity. The papal court became a centre of luxury and magnificence: it represented and reflected the contemporary life of Italy. The older Cardinals looked with dismay on the beginnings of this new system, and strove to avert it. In June 1473 Cardinal Ammannati wrote to Cardinal Borgia: 'In May eight cardinals were created; in June there would have been as many more had not God's mercy intervened. But the matter is only put off, not abandoned; and others will tell you what sort of men are prepared for our disgrace. Such was the violence of him who has the power, that how we escaped this peril I still wonder. His reputation established for so many years, the entreaties of many Cardinals, my testimony to the facts, had no weight with his impetuous mind.'[1]

Sixtus IV. changed the course of life in Rome because his outspoken recklessness was heedless of decorum. Hitherto the Roman court had worn a semblance of ecclesiastical gravity, which the extravagances of Cardinal Piero Riario overthrew in a moment. Conventional propriety is of slow growth; it is easily destroyed and is restored with difficulty. Perhaps Sixtus IV. thought that the papal dignity might be maintained by himself and a few of the older Cardinals, while the young bloods might be of service by making a display in a world which was singularly impressionable. Perhaps he wished to make the papal court a microcosm in which men of all sorts might go their own way. The result was that the worse elements rose to the top, and Rome became more famous for pleasure than for piety. It is true that Paul II. had advanced in this direction by encouraging the festivities of the Carnival; but Paul II.'s attitude was that of a kindly patron who wished to promote the amusement of his people. The banquets, the hunting parties, the gambling bouts, the nightly revels of Cardinal Riario and Count Girolamo were a new departure in the social traditions of the court. Neither Pius II. nor Paul II. was overburdened with scruples; but conduct which they would not have tolerated for a moment became common in the days of Sixtus IV. Sixtus IV. meant nothing by his tolerance; but the Rovere stock was hard to civilise.

A stern, imperious, passionate, resolute man, Sixtus IV. did not inspire much attachment, and we hear of few traits of his personal life. Yet he inspired deep hatred; and Infessura, who was an adherent of the Colonna family and had the spirit of a republican, has blackened his memory with accusations of the foulest crimes. These charges, made by a partisan who writes with undisguised animosity, must be dismissed as

---

[1] Papiensis *Epistolæ*, 514. The particular case which exercised Ammannati's mind was the proposal to create a bastard, and he implores Cardinal Borgia to help him in this endeavour. I wonder that none of the apologists of Alexander VI. have used this letter as an argument in favour of Cardinal Borgia's reputation for purity. It would have been a stronger argument than many which they have used.

unproved.[1] Sixtus IV. impressed his contemporaries as a great and vigorous personality, as a skilful organiser, a munificent patron, and a man of indomitable resolution. On a survey of the results of his doings we must admit that his energy was crude and misdirected; that he was deficient in elevation of mind and largeness of view; that his force too much resembled unreflecting brutality; and that in all his magnificence there is the trace of a vulgar upstart.

The serious charge against Sixtus IV. is that he hopelessly lowered the moral standard of the Papacy. Other Popes had pursued secular ends; had fought for their temporal dominions, and had pursued a purely selfish policy; but while doing so they regarded the dignity of their office, and sought for decent pretexts for their actions. Sixtus IV. had not been Cardinal long enough for the traditions of the Curia to curb the violence of a strong and coarse nature. His nepotism was unblushing, and he did not conceal the fact that he meant to use his nephew as a means of establishing his temporal power while he reserved himself for the functions of ecclesiastical head of Christendom. He allowed himself to become an accomplice in a scheme for assassination which shocked even the blunted conscience of Italy; when it failed he visited with the severest penalties of the Church the irregularities which its victims not unnaturally committed. Hitherto the Papacy had on the whole maintained a moral standard; for some time to come it tended to sink even below the ordinary level. The loss that was thus inflicted upon Europe was incalculable. In an age when faith was weak, when the old ideals had vanished and nothing had taken their place, it was a serious matter that self-seeking, intrigue, and effrontery should be too plainly visible to be overlooked in the acknowledged head of Western Christendom. Under Sixtus IV. the Papacy ceased to offer any resistance to the corruption of the age. It was not a strong bulwark before; but at least it upheld the forms of better things. Henceforth, not only do the lowest motives prevail, but they are unblushingly avowed. Sixtus IV. made possible the cynicism of Machiavelli; he lowered the moral tone of Europe and prepared the way for still unworthier successors in the chair of S. Peter.

---

[1] The most offensive remarks of Infessura are not given in Muratori, but may be found in Eccard, ii. 1939 &c.

CHAPTER V.

INNOCENT VIII.

1484–1492.

THE death of Sixtus IV. plunged Rome into confusion. The barons armed themselves; the palace of Count Girolamo was attacked, its garden destroyed, its doors and windows broken; the corn magazines on the Ripa were sacked; the Genoese banks were plundered: everywhere was pillage and disorder.[1] The camp before Palliano was broken up; and the besieged, hearing of the Pope's death, made a sally and seized the artillery which the besiegers were preparing to carry off. On August 14 Count Girolamo came hurriedly with his troops to Rome, where his wife, Caterina, held the Castle of S. Angelo and the Vatican. The Colonna followed Girolamo and took possession of their palace, whereon Girolamo withdrew to Isola. Barricades were erected in the streets, and Rome was turned upside down. The Orsini on Monte Giordano, the Colonna in the palace of SS. Apostoli, stood under arms. The citizens in alarm built up the entrances to the bridges so that horsemen might not pass; and the magistrates besought the Cardinals to hasten the election as the only means of averting civil war. Meanwhile the funeral rites of Sixtus IV. were hastily performed. So quickly was the Vatican stripped of its furniture that Burchard could scarcely find the necessary vessels for washing the corpse. At the funeral many of the Cardinals of the Colonna party were not present, on the ground that they did not think it safe to pass the Castle of S. Angelo.

At length a truce was arranged, and on August 25 the Castle of S. Angelo was surrendered to the Cardinals by Count

CHAP.
V.

Disturbance in Rome.
August 1484.

[1] Letters of the Florentine Vespucci, August 14–18, in Thuasne's Burchard, i. 498.

BOOK
V.

Girolamo in exchange for 7,000 ducats. Thereon the Orsini agreed to withdraw for a month to Viterbo, provided the Colonna also left the city. When this was done the Cardinals, on August 26, entered the Conclave.

Preparations for the Conclave, August 20–26, 1484.

During this period many negotiations had passed about the election, which was a very open question. Ferrante of Naples urged the claims of his son Giovanni, but this was too obviously a political measure; and Cardinals Barbo and Costa were discussed as the two men of highest character amongst the Cardinals. On August 23 Ascanio Sforza entered Rome and laid down a principle which the other Cardinals accepted, that it was necessary to elect a Pope who would not be offensive to the League. When Giovanni of Aragon saw that his chance was thus destroyed, he approached Ascanio, and on the eve of the Conclave they agreed whom they would exclude, but could not determine whom they would elect; Ascanio favoured the Novarese Arcimboldo; the Cardinal of Aragon wished for the Neapolitan Caraffa. Meanwhile Cardinal Borgia did his utmost to put himself forward; he offered money, benefices, offices, even his own palace, in return for votes. But corrupt as the Cardinals were, they still retained some prudence, and their fears of the pride and perfidy of Borgia outweighed their cupidity.[1]

Conclave of Innocent VIII., August 26–29, 1484.

The first proceeding of the twenty-five Cardinals in Conclave was to repeat the useless formality of drawing up elaborate regulations to bind the future Pope. Their chief object was to secure the privileges of the Cardinals, but one of the provisions is noticeable as a protest against the nepotism of Sixtus IV.; the new Pope was made to promise that he would not confer any important office or administration on any layman whatsoever.[2] In the matter of the election Cardinal Borgia was so confident of his own success that he had his palace barricaded to preserve it against the pillage that was sure to ensue. But the first scrutiny showed Borgia that his party was not so strong as he imagined. The candidate who obtained most votes was the Venetian Cardinal Barbo, for whom

[1] Letters of Vespucci, August 21, in Thuasne's Burchard, i. 507: 'Il vice-cancelliere fa grande forza con prometter danari, uficii, la casa sua, beneficii; ma è tenuto si superbo et di mala fide che non se ne ha paura.'

[2] See Burchard, *Diarium*, i. 332, &c.

ten gave their voices, induced, it would seem, by a desire to return to the decorous days of his uncle Paul II. Cardinal Rovere now took the lead and worked for the election of a Pope under whom he might himself be powerful. The chief supporter of Borgia against Barbo was the Cardinal of Aragon; Rovere offered to negotiate with Barbo the transference of three additional votes to his side if he would give up to the Cardinal of Aragon the Palazzo of S. Marco. Barbo did not fall into the snare, but answered that it would destroy the peace of the city if so strong a fortress were in the hands of Naples. Cardinal Rovere had now set the Cardinal of Aragon against Barbo: he next turned to Borgia and proposed to him that they two should unite their parties against Barbo and so secure a Pope in their common interest; and Borgia consented to sink his own claims in order to prevent Barbo's election. They agreed on the Genoese Cardinal Cibò; and during the night of August 28, after the Cardinals had retired to rest, Borgia and Rovere visited them privately and secured by promises of papal favours the necessary majority for their new candidate. Legations, rich abbeys, palaces, castles, were promised in Cibò's behalf, and Cardinal Rovere despoiled himself of some of his own possessions to win the necessary votes. Before the morning all the Cardinals, except six of the eldest and most respectable, had been won over and nineteen votes were secured. The six who had been deemed incorruptible were awakened. 'Come and let us make a Pope.' 'Whom?' they asked. 'Cardinal Cibò.' 'How is that?' they inquired in amazement. 'While you slept,' they were told, 'we gathered all the votes except those of you drowsy ones.' They felt that nothing was to be done, and when the scrutiny was held they also gave their votes for Cardinal Cibò, whose unanimous election was announced on August 29.[1]

Giovanni Battista Cibò was born in Genoa in 1432. His father was a statesman who held the office of Viceroy in Naples for René of Anjou, and was made Senator of Rome by Calixtus III. in 1453. The son was a favourite of Cardinal

Early life of Cardinal Cibò.

---

[1] The account of the Conclave is taken from Infessura (Mur. iii. part 2. 1189). I should have hesitated to follow Infessura on a matter of hearsay, were he not supported by two Florentine reports to Lorenzo de' Medici, dated August 29 and 30, printed in Fabroni, *Vita Laurentii*, ii. 56, and in Thuasne's edition of Burchard, i. 497–520.

Calandrini, who initiated him into the manners of the Curia. He was made Bishop of Savona by Paul II., and was elevated by Sixtus IV. to the bishopric of Molfetta, and in 1473 to the cardinalate. He was not remarkable in any way, save for kindliness and geniality. He had little experience of politics, and was not famous for learning. He was a tall, stalwart man, fifty-five years old, and was chiefly notorious for his open avowal of an illegitimate family.[1] How many sons and daughters he had cannot be said with certainty; but a daughter, Teodorina, was married to a Genoese merchant, Gerardo Usodimare; and a son, Franceschetto Cibò, took his place at the papal court, where he was called the Pope's nephew.

On September 12, Cardinal Cibò was crowned under the name of Innocent VIII. As he owed his election to the influence of Cardinal Rovere he was at first entirely in his hands. Rovere lived in the Vatican, dictated the Pope's actions, and made him revoke things done without his consent. The Pope's position was indeed a difficult one. The policy of

---

[1] We only know the names of Franceschetto and Teodorina. Teodorina had a daughter old enough to marry in 1488, and Franceschetto was thirty-five at his father's election. It is therefore probable that these children were born before their father was in orders; but they were not born in wedlock, for Burchard, i. 321, says: 'Franciscus filius Papæ bastardus, prout domina Theodorina' (see the authorities quoted in Thuasne's note); more explicitly Sigismondo de' Conti, ii. 33, says: 'Habuit Innocentius Francischettum et Theodorinam filios ante sacerdotium, non ex uxore susceptos, qui ejus nomini magnas maculas asperserunt.' Rumour attributed to him many more children. Infessura says: 'Ex pluribus mulieribus septem filios inter mares et fœminas habet.' The epigram of Marullus gave him sixteen:

'Octo nocens pueros genuit, totidemque puellas:
Hunc merito potuit dicere Roma patrem.'

The Florentine Vespucci writes on his election: 'Ha figliuolo maschio bastardo, e figliuole maritate qui;' and Loeti: 'Ha figliuoli et figliuole.' Thuasne, Burchard, i. 517–519. These discrepancies leave us in doubt if they are not rhetorical exaggerations of the basis of fact supplied by Franceschetto and Teodorina. However, Sigismondo de' Conti, ii. 37, says of Innocent VIII.: 'In Venerem natura admodum pronus, licet quantum humana fragilitas patiebatur appetitum rationi obedientem præberet.' As the apologists for Alexander VI. have made capital out of the fact that Cesare Borgia is often styled the Pope's nephew, it is worth while to notice how Burchard speaks of Franceschetto Cibò, i. 278, 'S. S. D. N. papæ filio, nepoti nuncupato,' and in i. 262 he gives him his official title 'nepos Papæ ex fratre sororis Papæ natus'; there is obviously a mistake here in the text; Generelli suggests 'seniore' for 'sororis.'

Sixtus IV. had been so entirely personal that it was impossible to gather together its threads. Cardinal Rovere was in the confidence of Sixtus IV., but had by no means unreservedly approved of his actions. He was the best man to unravel the tangled skein of confusion.

The power and greed of the Cardinals and the Curia had developed with great rapidity under the rule of Sixtus IV., and the new Pope was helpless, even if he had wished, to put any barrier to their demands. The city of Rome was the first to suffer. It strove to defend itself by exacting from the Pope a promise that all offices within the city, benefices, abbeys, and the like, should be conferred only on Roman citizens. But this was soon set aside; the Cardinals seized the chief dignities in the city; citizens who had bought posts for life from Sixtus IV. were dismissed without receiving compensation, and Innocent VIII. maintained that Cardinals were reckoned amongst the citizens of Rome. He gave an office to his Genoese son-in-law, and when the magistrates objected that he was not a citizen, he ordered his name to be entered on the burgess-roll so as to do away with the technical objection. All expectations of reform from the new Pope were rapidly dashed to the ground. Men said that he would follow in the steps of Sixtus IV. 'He was elected in darkness,' said the Augustinian general, 'he lives in darkness, and in darkness he will die.'[1]

Greed of the Cardinals.

The factions of the Roman nobles had been too successfully aroused under Sixtus IV. to sink at once into quietness. In March 1485, Innocent VIII. was seriously ill and there were rumours of his death. The Orsini attempted to seize the city gates. The Colonna at once took up arms, and there was war in the Campagna. The Colonna recovered the castles of Città Lavigna, Nemi, Genazzano, and Frascati. At last, in July, the Pope managed to interfere in this contest. He summoned both parties before him, and demanded that their quarrels should be submitted to his decision. The Colonna obeyed and agreed to place in the hands of the Pope the disputed castles: the Orsini refused the Pope's mediation.

Quarrels of the Roman barons. March–July, 1485

But the quarrels of the Roman barons soon widened into a broader issue. Innocent VIII. had inherited a dislike to the

The Neapolitan barons.

[1] Infessura, Mur. iii., part 2, 1192.

Aragonese power in Naples, and Cardinal Rovere considered that Sixtus IV. had parted with the rights of the Church in his desire to win Ferrante to his side. The tribute due from the vassal kingdom of Naples had been commuted into the yearly gift of a white palfrey as a recognition of the papal suzerainty. Innocent VIII. refused to accept this commutation, and demanded the payment of the former tribute. He counted on the growing discontent of the Neapolitan barons against Ferrante's strong rule. Ferrante had learned in his early days the dangerous power which the protracted struggle between the houses of Anjou and Aragon had given to the barons of Naples. He steadily pursued a policy of diminishing the baronial privileges; and as the barons became conscious of his meaning they were anxious to rise before it was too late. The changed attitude of the Papacy towards Naples gave them the encouragement which they required.

Beginning of the Barons' War in Naples. Ferrante, though a capable ruler, was oppressive in his financial exactions, and was regarded as false and treacherous. But his eldest son, Alfonso, Duke of Calabria, threw his father's unpopularity into the shade; violent, cruel, and perfidious, he had all the instincts of a despot. He did not conceal his hatred of the barons, and his growing influence over his aged father increased their alarm. In the summer of 1485, a treacherous act of Alfonso fired the smouldering discontent. He managed to inveigle into his hands the Count of Montorio, lord of Aquila, in the Abruzzi, a free city which recognised the supremacy of the Neapolitan crown. The imprisonment of the Count of Montorio and his family was a menace to the Neapolitan barons, and alarmed the Colonna whose lands adjoined the territory of Aquila. On October 17, the men of Aquila put themselves under the Pope's protection. War was imminent, but neither side was ready. Ferrante strove to gain time and summoned his barons to a parliament, but only three obeyed his summons. He sent his son, the Cardinal of Aragon, to negotiate with the Pope; but on October 16 he died in Rome, immediately after his arrival. The first allies whom Ferrante succeeded in gaining were the Orsini, who ravaged the Campagna and threatened Rome with a famine.

The obvious form for war with Naples to assume was to set up an Angevin claimant to the crown. But the luckless René of

Anjou outlived his son Jean, and on his death, in 1481, bequeathed to Louis XI. of France his lands and rights. The
only representative of his line was the son of his daughter
Iolante, wife of Count Frederick of Baudremont. Innocent
VIII. offered to invest this son, René II., Duke of Lorraine, with
the kingdom of Naples; but Charles VIII. of France hesitated
to recognise his claims on Naples or give him any support. Still
the dread of French interference prompted Florence and Milan
to side with Ferrante; while the Pope and the Neapolitan barons
appealed for help to Venice. But Venice did not wish to
involve itself in war, and did no more than detach for the
Pope's service the condottieri general Roberto di Sanseverino,
who proceeded leisurely to gather troops. Meanwhile Ferrante enlisted on his side the discontented barons of Rome;
and Virginio Orsini was enough to reduce the Pope to great
straits. He seized the Porta Nomentana and reduced the Rome be-
city to a state of siege. Innocent VIII. was terrified and sat sieged by
Virginio
barricaded within the Vatican. In his terror he ordered all Orsini.
malefactors banished for their offences to return to Rome and December
1485.
guard the city; they obeyed his summons, but only added
crime and violence to the general confusion. Cardinals Rovere,
Savelli, and Colonna took charge of affairs; they visited the
walls and set the watch, and inflamed to the utmost the
wrath of Virginio by ordering his palace on Monte Giordano to
be burned down. Virginio retaliated by scattering in the city
documents exhorting the people to rise against the Pope and
drive him and his Cardinals from the city: he was no true
Pope, for he was not canonically elected; it was unworthy of the
Roman people to be ruled by a Genoese skipper;[1] let them
make a true Pope and true Cardinals. Especially did his
anger blaze against Cardinal Rovere; he exhorted all men
to destroy him as a man steeped in unnatural vices; he threatened, if God gave him the victory, to carry his head on a
lance through the city. He even sent a message to the Pope
that he would throw him into the Tiber. It was long since
Rome and the Pope had suffered such indignities, and the
arrival of Sanseverino with a force of thirty-three squadrons of
horse on Christmas Day was hailed with heartfelt joy by all in
Rome.

[1] 'Naviculatori servire.'—Sigismondo de' Conti, i. 241.

BOOK
V.

Rome re-
lieved by
Roberto
Sanseve-
rino, De-
cember
25, 1485.

Sanseverino drove the Orsini from the Ponte Nomentano, but won no decisive victory. His soldiers plundered friend and foe alike, and the imperial ambassadors who wished to come to Rome under his escort were stripped to their shirts by his lawless troops. Rome was not much encouraged by his presence. On January 21, 1486, a rumour of the Pope's death threw the city into a panic. The members of the Curia gathered what they could and prepared to flee ; the Cardinals fortified their houses. As regards the war, neither Alfonso of Calabria nor Roberto of Sanseverino showed any military capacity. Innocent VIII. began to suspect the good faith of his general, and shrank before the dangers which beset him. In March he sent Cardinal Rovere to Genoa, that he might summon René and negotiate with the French king for help. On his part Ferrante had nothing to gain from the war ; he could not restore order within his kingdom till he had peace abroad. Florence and Milan were anxious to stop the Pope's dealings with France, which might bring a dangerous foe into Italy. Thus everyone wished for peace, and the Florentines are said to have added to the Pope's terrors by contriving that letters should be intercepted which spoke of Roberto of Sanseverino as intriguing with his enemies.[1]

Dread of French intervention banded many of the Cardinals together. Ascanio Sforza expressed his opinions strongly against its dangers ; and the Spanish party in the Curia, headed by Cardinal Borgia, seconded him.[2] In the beginning of June a majority of the Cardinals besought the Pope to make peace ; they offered on Ferrante's part the payment of the accustomed tribute by Naples and the surrender of Aquila to the Church. The French Cardinal La Balue opposed the peace as dishonourable to the Church, and there was a stormy scene between him and Cardinal Borgia ; Borgia called La Balue a drunkard, and La Balue answered with still coarser taunts ;[3] they almost came to blows in the Pope's presence.

---

[1] Acciaiuoli's *Vita di Piero Capponi*, in *Archivio Storico Italiano* (first series), vol. iv. part ii. p. 24.

[2] l. c. p. 67–71, there is an account of a meeting of a private consistory given by Cardinal Sforza to the Duke of Milan, dated March 6.

[3] Infessura, p. 1205 : 'Dictus Abalius retulit verba vituperosa, videlicet eum esse maranum, et filium meretricis et vitam suam inhonestam ; propter

Innocent VIII., bereft of the counsel of Cardinal Rovere, was
helpless.   He had no money ; he did not trust his general
Sanseverino ; Rome was in confusion ; Cardinals Borgia and
Sforza openly negotiated with the Orsini.   In June the approach of the Duke of Calabria increased the Pope's alarm, and
the pressure of the Cardinals soon prevailed over his feeble
will.   On August 11 peace was made with Naples through the
intervention of the Milanese general Gian Giacopo Trivulzio.[1]
Ferrante agreed to pay the tribute of 8,000 ducats, to respect
the rights of the Church, to leave Aquila at liberty, and pardon
his rebellious barons.

This peace was dishonourable to the Pope, who abandoned his
allies to the mercy of Ferrante, and gained no advantage from
the war.   Roberto Sanseverino was dismissed, but the Orsini
did not lay down their arms and continued their raids against
the Colonna.   The city of Aquila was occupied by Neapolitan
troops and the papal governor was put to death.   Roberto di
Sanseverino was pursued on his departure from Rome by the
Duke of Calabria, and with difficulty managed to escape into
the Venetian territory; the Neapolitan barons found themselves
left at the mercy of Ferrante.   The chief leader of the revolt,
the Prince of Salerno, judged it wiser to flee to France than
return to Naples; and the event proved that he judged rightly,
as the other rebels were seized by Ferrante and thrown into
prison, whence they never reappeared.   Nor did the Pope
gain even the purely ecclesiastical points which his treaty with
Ferrante guaranteed.   When he sent next year to ask for the
promised tribute, Ferrante answered that he had spent so
much money for the Church that he could not pay.   When
the Pope complained that Ferrante wrongfully conferred benefices within his kingdom, he was told that the King knew best
who were worthy of office, and that it was enough for the Pope
to confirm his nominations.   When he complained of the imprisonment of the Neapolitan barons he was referred to the
example of Sixtus IV., who dealt with the Colonna as he

Peace with
Ferrante,
August 11,
1486.

quod maximus tumultus factus fuit in dicto Consistorio, ita quod unusquisque
credebat eos venturos ad manus.'   'Maranus' was the name given to the Jews
expelled from Spain.

[1] His letters to the Duke of Milan are printed by Rosmini, *Vita di
Trivulzio,* ii. 130 &c.

BOOK
V.

Disorders
in Rome.
1486.

Lives of the
Cardinals.

thought fit. Having thus answered the Pope's legate, Fer-
raute mounted his horse and went out hunting.[1]

The peace with Naples covered Innocent VIII. with ridicule
as a statesman. Yet it was welcomed gladly by the Roman
people, whom the war had reduced to misery, while the lawless
spirit which it encouraged led to entire anarchy within the city.
Innocent VIII. issued Bulls against evil-doers; but law was
powerless. Women were carried off by night: each morning brought its tale of murders and of riots; the wild justice
of armed revenge was the only one which prevailed.[2] Men did
not even abstain from sacrilege; a piece of the true Cross,
enshrined in silver, was stolen from the sacristy of S. Maria in
Trastevere, and the holy relic was found denuded of its setting,
thrown away in a vineyard. It was said that the Pope con-
nived at the flight of malefactors who paid him money, and
granted pardons for sins before their commission. No public
executions testified to the power of the law; sometimes men
were found hanged in the morning from the Torre del Nono,
but their names and their crimes were unknown. Men imprisoned on the most fearful charges were released on payment.[3]
When the Vice-Chancellor Borgia was asked why justice was
not done, he answered, 'God desires not the death of a sinner,
but rather that he should pay and live.'

The Cardinals were the chief abettors of this lawlessness.
Their palaces were fortified and strengthened with towers.
Their spacious courtyards housed great numbers of retainers,
and each household maintained the quarrels of its members or
interfered in a body in any passing fray. Such justice as
there was was powerless against these combinations. Often also
these households came into collision. One day the captain of
the court of Cardinal Savelli was arresting a debtor near the
palace of Cardinal La Balue. There was a tumult, and Cardinal
La Balue from a window forbade the arrest of any one within
the precincts of his palace. The arrest, however, was made,

---

[1] Infessura, 1218.

[2] Infessura, 1212, gives a vivid account of a tumult which arose about the
possession of a prostitute; eight men were killed and a house burned down.

[3] Infessura, 1226, tells of a man who committed incest with his two
daughters, and then murdered them, but escaped punishment by paying 800
ducats.

whereon La Balue ordered his retainers to attack the Savelli, and Cardinals Savelli and Colonna called out their men to retaliate. The Pope summoned them all to the Vatican, where the Cardinals heaped abuse on one another in the Pope's presence, till a sulky reconciliation was brought about. These quarrels of the Cardinals descended amongst the people and were identified with the feuds of the Roman barons. The last days of the Roman Republic were restored, when the city was filled with magnates and their dependents. The example of Popes like Sixtus IV. and Innocent VIII. was easily followed, and the Cardinals imitated their master in a career of personal aggrandisement and the foundation of a princely family; they had sons or nephews whom they strove to enrich, and each surrounded himself with a court composed of parasites and bravoes.

CHAP. V.

Politically, Innocent VIII. showed all the waywardness of a weak and irresolute man. He had foolishly entered the Neapolitan war at the bidding of Cardinal Giuliano della Rovere, who at an early period of his career displayed his willingness to work his own ways by means of foreign help. But when Cardinal Rovere was gone to negotiate with France, Innocent VIII.'s resolution failed him and he could not await his return. When he came back he found the Pope wincing under his ignominious treatment by Ferrante, and tried to resume his former influence, and induce him to renew the war against Naples. But Innocent VIII. was afraid of his former master and wanted to try his own hand in politics. He found employment for Rovere by sending him to besiege Osimo, where a private citizen, Boccalino Gozzone, had made himself master of the city, driven out the papal governor, and when the peace with Naples left him helpless had even made overtures to the Turkish Sultan. In April 1487 Rovere set out for Osimo; but the Pope mistrusted his zeal and recalled him in June, whereon he returned to Rome in disgrace. Cardinal La Balue succeeded him, and with help from Trivulzio reduced Boccalino to surrender on August 1. Even then the mediation of Lorenzo de' Medici was needed and Boccalino received 7,000 ducats with which he took refuge in Florence.[1]

Siege of Osimo. 1486–7.

[1] Many documents relating to these events are printed by Rosmini, *Vita di Trivulzio*, ii. 158 &c.

BOOK
V.

Alliance of
Innocent
VIII. with
Lorenzo de'
Medici.
1487.

Free from Cardinal Rovere, Innocent VIII. tried to discover a policy of his own. Venice had shown itself well-disposed towards the Pope in the Neapolitan war, and had a common interest in putting down a freebooter such as Boccalino at Osimo. Innocent VIII. accordingly formed a league with Venice, which was published early in 1487; he hoped that his new alliance would keep Ferrante of Naples in check, regardless of the fact that it awakened the distrust of Florence and Milan. When Lorenzo de' Medici heard of it, he poured out his wrath to the Ferrarese ambassador. 'I can believe anything bad,' he said, ' of this Pope; the States of the Church have always been the ruin of Italy, for their rulers are ignorant of the art of government, and so bring danger on every side.'[1] But Lorenzo set himself to guide the incapable ruler of the Church ; he offered his help in the troublesome matter of Osimo, and insinuated that an alliance with Florence was preferable to an alliance with Venice. Lorenzo had personal aims to serve and personal advantages to offer. He felt that the power of his house was declining in Florence, and resolved to secure himself by family connexions. He played upon the Pope's parental feelings by proposing a marriage between his daughter Maddelena and the Pope's son Franceschetto. The bait was too tempting for the political consistency of Innocent VIII.; his alliance with Venice was scarcely concluded before it gave way to an alliance with Florence. No wonder that such feeble self-seeking awakened the scorn of all. The bluff soldier Trivulzio, who went to Rome after the capture of Osimo, bluntly expressed his opinion of Innocent VIII. 'The Pope is full of greed, cowardice, and baseness, like a common knave ; were there not men about him who inspired him with some spirit he would crawl away like a rabbit, and grovel like any dastard.' Perhaps Italy was not sorry when Innocent VIII. fell into the hands of Lorenzo de' Medici.

The alliance of Lorenzo with the Pope gave him the position of mediator between Rome and Naples, and thereby secured for a time the peace of Italy and averted the danger of foreign intervention.[2] In Rome itself it altered the attitude of the

---

[1] *Notizie Estensi* in *Atti e Memorie per le provincie Modenesi,* i. 291, quoted by Brosch, *Papst Julius II.* 39.

[2] The labours of Lorenzo to induce Innocent VIII. to adopt a pacific policy

Pope towards the baronial factions. Hitherto, under the influence of Cardinal Rovere, he had favoured the Colonna; but
the marriage of his son Franceschetto brought him into alliance
with the Orsini; for Maddelena de' Medici's mother was Clarice,
sister of Virginio Orsini. Innocent VIII. at once accepted this
result of his family arrangements, made peace with Virginio in
June 1487, and admitted him to his favour. This was a blow to
Cardinal Rovere, whose brother the Prefect was imprisoned,
and the Castellan of S. Angelo was removed as being a staunch
adherent of the Rovere. On this the Cardinal withdrew for a
while from Rome.

Thus the policy of Sixtus IV. was entirely reversed. Lorenzo Murder of
Girolamo
Riario.
April 14,
1488.
de' Medici, whom he had laboured to overthrow, was installed
as the Pope's chief adviser; the persecuted Orsini were recalled
to favour; the Rovere family lost its influence, and fortune still
further declared against it. On April 14, 1488, Girolamo Riario,
for whom Sixtus IV. had laboured so strenuously, was murdered
by three of his bodyguard, who wished to rid the world of a
second Nero. They entered the room where Girolamo was sitting after supper, and fell upon him unawares; his naked corpse
was thrown out of the palace window, and the people at once
rose with the cry of 'Liberty,' sacked the palace, and took
prisoner Girolamo's wife, Caterina Sforza, who was far advanced
in pregnancy. But the castle of Forlì still held out and
threatened to make a stubborn resistance. Caterina offered to
negotiate for its surrender, and went to confer with the governor,
leaving her children behind as hostages. When she reached
the castle she caused the gates to be shut, and told the rebels
that they might kill her children if they would; she had one
son safe at Imola and bore another in her womb. Her courage
inspired the garrison of the castle to resist. That Innocent VIII.
was privy to the plot is doubtful;[1] but the rebels looked to him

may be seen from the letters of Jacopo Volterrano in *Archivio Storico Italiano*,
3rd series, vii. 3 &c.

[1] We have an account of the proceedings in a letter from the assassins, and
also of a Medicean agent to Lorenzo, dated April 18 and 19, printed in Fabroni,
Vita Laurentii, Appendix, 318, and also in Thuasne's Burchard, i. 520 &c.
The agent writes: 'Checho [the chief of the conspirators] dice lo ha facto,
conscio Pontifice, con farli altra volta intendere che non potevano più tolerare
la signoria del Conte per essere troppo impia.' But no particular weight can
be attached to the statement of a man who was seeking allies by all means in
his power.

for help and their envoys were graciously received at Rome.
Forlì was taken under the protection of the Church, and the
governor of Cesena went to its aid. But the Duke of Milan
sent troops to defend his relative, Caterina ; the papal garrison
were made prisoners, the assassins were put to death, and Caterina's young son, Ottaviano Riario, was set up as lord of Forlì.
Caterina, as regent, could wreak her vengeance upon the rebellious people, and Innocent VIII. did not attempt to interfere
further. Men said that he allowed his sheep to be devoured by
wolves, and did to Forlì as he did to Aquila.[1]

Really Innocent VIII. was incapable of any policy, and
could not persevere in any intention which disturbed his com-
placent indolence. He was incompetent, and his incompetence
was hereditary. None of his relatives showed any taste for
statesmanship, and there was no one at hand to direct the Pope.
Early in 1488, Cardinal Rovere returned to Rome and began again
to assume his former influence over the yielding Innocent VIII.
The only matter that interested the Pope was the marriage of
his granddaughter, Peretta, daughter of the Genoese merchant,
Gerardo Usodimare, who had married the Pope's daughter,
Teodorina. The marriage feast of Peretta and Alfonso del
Caretto, Marquis of Finale, was celebrated in the Vatican on
November 16. It caused great stir in Rome ; for it was contrary
to all custom that women should sit at table with the Pope.[2]
Most men would at least have respected the traditional decorum
of their office ; but Innocent VIII. aimed at nothing more
than the pleasures of a father of a family.

Creation of
Cardinals.
March
1489. One act of papal authority, however, Innocent VIII. was
ready to perform ; the creation of new Cardinals. Though he
had promised at his election not to increase the number of
Cardinals beyond twenty-four, he paid no heed to his promise.
On March 9, 1489, he created five new Cardinals, and nominated
three others secretly, reserving their actual appointment for the
present. One of the Cardinals created was Lorenzo Cibò, a son
of the Pope's brother, whose nomination caused some scandal as
he was a bastard.[3] One of those created *in petto* was Giovanni

---

[1] Infessura, 1220.   [2] Burchard, i. 323.

[3] Sigismondo de' Conti, i. 326, says that he was the son of a Spanish lady
whom his father had married in Spain, though he had already a wife at
Genoa. The opinion of canonists was 'eum cuivis dignitati idoneum esse, nec

de' Medici, youngest son of Lorenzo, a boy of fourteen. Lorenzo thought it well to use his opportunity as a cautious Florentine merchant, and secure his son's accession to the cardinalate while he had the power. But Innocent VIII. refused to publish the creation of so young a Cardinal till a period of three years had elapsed; and Lorenzo watched with anxiety the Pope's uncertain health, which threatened to throw obstacles in the way of his design of establishing the Medici in the Curia.

The remainder of the new Cardinals were insignificant men, save one who earned his creation by a service which marks a disgraceful episode in the history of Europe. This was Pierre d'Aubusson, Grand Master of the Knights of S. John, who had distinguished himself by his brave defence of Rhodes against the Turks in 1480. Mahomet II. was preparing to renew the siege when his death, in 1481, was the signal for a civil war between his two sons, Bajazet and Djem. Djem was defeated at Broussa, and hopeless of his cause, sought refuge among the Knights of Rhodes, by whom he was courteously received in July 1482. He soon found, however, that though he came as a guest he was detained as a prisoner. He was treated as a valuable hostage for the good behaviour of Bajazet II., who trembled at the thought of a rival backed by Christian arms. The Sultan made peace with the Knights of S. John and agreed to pay them a yearly tribute of 45,000 ducats, ostensibly for the expenses of his brother's maintenance.[1] The conduct of the Knights of Rhodes was bad enough, but they were not allowed to enjoy the fruits of their breach of faith. The sum of 45,000 ducats yearly awakened universal cupidity, and the Knights of S. John found it more prudent to remove their lucrative captive to the mainland for safer keeping. He was carried to the Commandery of Bourgneuf in Poitou, where he was under the protection of the King of France. There were many claimants for the honour and profit of entertaining him. The Sultan of Egypt was willing to make war in his behalf; the Spanish sovereigns were engaged in war against the infidel; Mathias of

---

fraudem paternam proli obesse, quando mater credula et fraudis inscia bona fide et publice contraxisset.'

[1] The contemporary account of Djem is by Gulielmus Caoursin, *Obsidionis Rhodii Urbis Descriptio* (Ulm, 1496), of which the chief parts are reprinted by Thuasne, Burchard, i. 528.

Hungary desired to have Djem's help to drive the Turks from the Danube valley; Ferrante of Naples pleaded that he was the natural protector of the Mediterranean waters; Innocent VIII. claimed as Pope to be the proper head of all crusading movements.[1] The Regent of France, Anne of Bourbon, put Djem up to auction amongst these eager competitors, and delayed any decision that she might reap a richer harvest.

The Pope, however, had means at his command which the others lacked. Djem could not be disposed of without the consent of the Knights of S. John, and Innocent VIII. promised their Grand Master a Cardinal's hat if Djem were handed over to himself. Moreover France had need of the Pope's good offices. The marriage of Anne, heiress of Brittany, was a matter of the greatest moment to the French monarchy. A strong party in Brittany wished to give Anne in marriage to Alain d'Albret of Béarn, to whom she had been promised by her father. This marriage, however, required a papal dispensation on the ground of consanguinity, and the price of the Pope's refusal to grant it was the surrender of Djem. Feeble as Innocent VIII. might be in other ways, he showed himself clever at striking a bargain, and would not pay till the goods were ready for delivery; D'Aubusson was not made Cardinal till Djem was nearly at the walls of Rome. Nor did this miserable huckstering end here. Others felt that they might follow in the steps of Pope and Kings. Franceschetto Cibò, before Djem's arrival, tried to curry favour with Venice by promising to deliver over to the Republic the Turkish prince as soon as Innocent VIII. were dead. Some of those who stood closest to the Pope went further, and offered Sultan Bajazet to poison Djem if he would pay a sufficient price. No incident displays in a more lurid light the cynical corruption of the time in every nation.[2]

The entry of Djem into Rome, on March 13, was a wondrous sight for the citizens. Djem, accompanied by the Prior of Auvergne, was escorted by Cardinal La Balue and Franceschetto Cibò. The other Cardinals sent their house-

[1] The Venetian letters which trace the progress of the intrigues about Djem are printed by Lamansky, Secrets d'Etat de Venise, 201 &c.

[2] See Brosch, Papst Julius II. 45, and his quotations from Venetian letters 310-11.

holds to greet him, and a white horse, a present from the Pope, was waiting for him at the city gate. Djem showed the unmoved bearing of an Oriental; he wore a turban, and his face was shrouded by a veil. The ambassador of the Sultan of Egypt, who was in Rome at the time, came to meet him at the gate. He dismounted, and with profound reverences threw himself on the ground, kissed the horse's foot, then Djem's foot and knee, while tears filled his eyes. Djem in a word bade him mount his horse again, and the mingled cavalcade of Moslems and Christians swept onward through the chief streets of Rome to the Vatican.[1] It was a strange spectacle, the coming of one who claimed to be the head of the Mohammedan world to the palace of the chief priest of Christendom.

The significance of such an event did not trouble Innocent VIII. To him Djem was a princely guest, to be received with befitting ceremony. Charles VIII. of France was too good a Christian to admit the infidel prince to an interview; but Innocent VIII. had no such scruples. Fanaticism had no place in Rome, nor did the papal court trouble itself about trifles. Next day Djem was received by the Pope in a Consistory. He was carefully instructed in the proper ceremonial, but entirely declined to follow it. Short, corpulent and broad-chested, with an aquiline nose and blind in one eye, while the other flashed uneasy glances on every side, he strode up to the Pope, with his turban on his head, after making an almost imperceptible inclination of his body. He did not kneel nor kiss the Pope's foot, but standing upright kissed his shoulder; then by means of an interpreter conveyed his greetings to the Pope. The Pope assured him his of friendliness, and Djem at his departure wished to kiss the Pope on the face; but Innocent VIII. drew back his head and offered him his shoulder.[2] He sent Djem many presents, but the haughty Turk did not even honour them with a look. He stayed in his rooms, watched by a few knights of Rhodes, and treated like a prince. His only dread was lest he should be poisoned by some emissaries of his brother. Sometimes he indulged in sport, music, and banquets. He was a cultivated man, fond of literature; but he felt the hopelessness of his

---

[1] Burchard, i. 336 &c.

[2] Letter of Matteo Bosso, in Thuasne's Burchard, i. 527, gives the same account as Burchard himself.

fortunes, and most of his time was passed in sleep or in apathetic indolence.

The captivity of Djem in Rome was a means of extending the relations between Christendom and Islam. Bajazet was willing to pay a large sum to have Djem put to death, or to pay a yearly tribute to have him kept safely in prison where he could do no mischief. Rome soon saw the testimony of the Sultan's wishes in both these ways. In May 1490 an attempt to poison Djem and the Pope was discovered. A baron of Castel Leone, Cristoforo Castanea, who had been dispossessed of his lands, went to Constantinople and offered himself as an agent to the Sultan. He came to Rome with a poison which he was to put into the well whence the water for the use of the Vatican was ordinarily drawn. When he was taken prisoner he breathed dark hints of a vast number of men engaged in the same design. He was dragged naked through the city and torn with pincers; finally he was killed with a blow from a wooden mallet and was quartered. At the end of November came an embassy from Bajazet bringing the Pope three years' salary for the maintenance of Djem, and promising peace with Christendom so long as he was kept in security. The ambassador, however, was cautious enough to demand an interview with Djem to assure himself that he was really alive. Djem refused to receive the ambassador otherwise than as a sultan. The approach to the Vatican was hung with splendid tapestry, and Djem surrounded by his attendants and two prelates was seated on a lofty throne. Every precaution against poisoning was taken; before being admitted the ambassador was rubbed down with a towel and was made to kiss it. Thrice he prostrated himself before Djem and presented to him a letter from his brother; he was called upon to lick it all over before it was received. Then an attendant read it, and the ambassador proffered gifts on which Djem did not cast his eyes.

It is no wonder that men were startled at these heathenish doings in the Vatican, that they saw portents in the sky and listened to prophesyings. In 1491 a man of unknown nation, dressed in beggar's rags, wandered through Rome and preached in the streets: 'I tell you Romans, that in this year ye will weep much and suffer many tribulations. Next year the woe will extend through Italy. Florence, Milan, and the other states will be deprived of their liberty and placed under the yoke of another, while Venice will be deprived of her possessions on land. In the third year the clergy will lose their temporal power; there will be an Angelical Shepherd who will care only for the life of souls and spiritual things. I tell you the truth; believe me. The time will come when you will not call me foolish.' Then he passed on, bearing in his hands a wooden cross.[1] We hear in Rome a forecast of the spirit which was growing in the breast of a Dominican friar, Girolamo Savonarola, in Florence. But Rome was hardened and few listened to the preacher's words; he passed away unnoticed as he came. Yet there was an uneasy feeling of disquiet. Men sought a cause for the decay of faith, and found it in the corruption brought by foreign influences. There was a great influx into Italy of Jews and Moors from Spain who fled before the Inquisition and the conquering arms of Ferdinand and Isabella. They brought the plague, and it was thought that they also brought heresy in their train. An attempt was made to mend matters by an investigation into the orthodoxy of the members of the Curia, amongst whom was found a priest who in the mass service substituted words of derision for the solemn words of consecration.[2] More than fifteen hundred households in Rome were condemned to pay fines for heretical opinions; and we cannot think that Roman inquisitors were likely to err on the side of severity.

Already the heedless secularity of the Papacy was beginning to afford a means of political attack. Innocent VIII. had good cause to be dissatisfied with Ferrante of Naples, who refused to pay the promised tribute and set at naught the papal authority. In vain the Pope remonstrated; Ferrante counted on the Pope's weakness and entered upon the career of cynical indifference to others which precipitated the fall of his kingdom and of the independence of Italy. Innocent VIII. made some show of undertaking war against Naples; and in June 1489 he invested Niccolò Orsini, Count of Pitigliano, as Captain General of the Church, as the negotiations with France about

Innocent VIII. and Naples. 1489-90.

----

[1] Infessura, 1236.

[2] Sigismondo de' Conti, i. 352: 'Sacerdos quidam inventus est . . . qui cum ferme quotidie sacrificaret, pro illis sacramentalibus verbis . . . diceret in derisum: "O fatuos Christianos, qui cibum et potum ut Deum adorant."'

the surrender of Djem gave him hopes of foreign aid. On September 11, 1489, he declared in a Consistory that the kingdom of Naples had lapsed to the Holy See through the non-payment of the tribute. The Neapolitan ambassador appealed to a future Council, and offered to prove that the tribute was not rightfully due. In this critical state of affairs Lorenzo de' Medici interposed to keep the peace. With the genius of a true statesman he pointed out to the Pope that Naples could not be conquered unless Venice and Milan remained neutral and either France or Spain joined in the attack. He went on to consider the chances of effective help from France or Spain, and ended with the warning that 'whoever became king of Naples would settle his own accounts.'[1] Innocent VIII. hesitated before the dangers of either French or Spanish intervention, and satisfied himself with complaining of Ferrante's conduct. Ferrante on his side thought that France was sufficiently occupied at home and paid no heed to the gathering storm. In May 1490, on the occasion of one of the interminable disputes about precedence amongst ambassadors at the papal court, the Neapolitan envoy prepared to force his way by violence into the papal chapel; and to prevent a scandal the other envoys were requested to absent themselves till the matter was settled. Soon afterwards the Pope was disturbed by hearing that Ferrante had written to Maximilian, King of the Romans, telling him of the life and morals of the Pope and Cardinals, their sons and daughters, their simony, luxury, and avarice, beseeching him to provide according to God's precept for the tottering Church.[2] Italy was beginning to use the scandal of the papal court as a political engine of attack, and cried to Germany to undertake the task of reform which was beyond her own moral capacity.

Rumour of
Innocent
VIII's
death.
September
1490

The instability of the papal rule was soon exhibited with startling clearness. In September 1490 Innocent VIII. was ill, and on the 27th there was a rumour that he was dead. Immediately the shops were shut and men armed themselves in expectation of a tumult. Franceschetto Cibò left his father's

[1] Letter to the Florentine envoy in Rome, in Roscoe, *Life of Lorenzo*, Appendix XLVII, with the envoy's answer in *Archivio Storico Italiano*, Series III., xv. 296.

[2] Infessura, 1232.

deathbed to make a swoop on the papal treasury. When he
was frustrated in his attempt, he tried to get hold of Djem as
an opening for financial speculations. Next day the Cardinals
thought it well to secure the Pope's treasure against Franceschetto's designs; they went in a body to the Vatican and proceeded to make an inventory, after which they left Cardinal
Savelli in charge. Though it was suspected that much of the
Pope's treasure was already deposited in Florence, yet the
Cardinals found in one chest 800,000 ducats, and in another
300,000. When Innocent VIII. recovered, he was very angry
at this investigation into his possessions; he said that he hoped
to outlive all the Cardinals, though they plotted against his
life.

While Innocent VIII. sat inactively on the papal throne, Marriage of
Charles
VIII. and
Anne of
Brittany,
December
6, 1491.
engaged only in feeble bickerings with the King of Naples,
events of momentous importance were occurring in Europe.
The consolidation of the French kingdom, which had been
skilfully pursued by Louis XI., became an accomplished fact;
and the marriage of Charles VIII. with Anne of Brittany was
the last step in the incorporation of the provinces under the
crown of France. This marriage, however, was brought about
in a way dishonourable to all concerned. Innocent VIII. had
been willing to prevent the marriage of Anne to Alain d'Albret;
but another suitor came forward in the person of Maximilian.
With the utmost secresy Anne, a girl of thirteen, was affianced
to the future Emperor, who, however, took no steps to succour
his bride against the arms of France. At last it seemed the
shortest way to annex Brittany to the French crown by marry-
ing Anne to Charles VIII., though she was betrothed to Maximilian and Charles VIII. was betrothed to Margaret, Maximilian's daughter, a child of ten years old already at the
French court. The papal dispensation was required both on
the ground of previous contracts and because Anne stood
within the prohibited degrees to Charles. Anne's consent was
wrung from her by the dread of the French arms, and
Charles VIII. so far presumed on the Pope's complaisance
that he did not await his formal dispensation for an act which
shocked even the low sense of decorum of the day. The
marriage was celebrated on December 6, and the French ambassadors demanding the Bulls only entered Rome on December 5;

BOOK
V.
the Bulls themselves were issued ten days after the marriage had taken place.[1]

There could be no doubt of the political importance of this event. It warned Ferrante of Naples that France was likely to seek occupation for her energies abroad. The desire for a good understanding with the French king was the cause of the Pope's complaisance, and the effect of the good understanding was soon obvious on Neapolitan diplomacy. Ferrante listened more heedfully to the advice of Lorenzo de' Medici; he agreed to pay the tribute for Naples which the Pope demanded, and in the middle of February 1492 peace was made between Ferrante and Innocent VIII.

Capture of
Grenada.
January
1492.
A second great event occurred about the same time. On January 2, 1492, Grenada, the last stronghold of the Moors in Spain, surrendered to King Ferdinand the Catholic. The union of the crowns of Aragon and Castile, by the marriage of Ferdinand and Isabella, had led to a vigorous crusade which ended in the expulsion of the Moors from the peninsula. The effect of a great enterprise, founded on an appeal to Christian sentiment, was to weaken provincial jealousies and combine the Spanish peoples into a nation. The crusading spirit, which could not be kindled in Eastern Europe, was strong in the West, and Spain rose at once to be a great power in Europe. But Italy did not understand the mighty change that was being wrought by the creation of powerful kingdoms, and there was no statesman in the Roman court who could perceive the signs of the times. Rome celebrated the triumph of Christian arms after her wonted fashion. There were processions and bonfires, races of men and boys and buffaloes. Bread and wine were distributed to the populace. The Spanish ambassadors gave a representation of the capture of Grenada by erecting a wooden tower in the Piazza Navona and offering prizes to those who could first climb up its walls. Cardinal Borgia entertained the people by a bull-fight in which five bulls were killed.[2]

Arrival in
Rome of
Cardinal
Medici,
March 22,
1492.
Rome was a city of festivals, and was enlivened on November 22 by the magnificent entry of the young Florentine Cardinal, Giovanni de' Medici. The three years' term which Innocent VIII. had imposed when first he secretly created Giovanni Cardinal was at an end, and Lorenzo at last enjoyed

---

[1] Burchard, i. 136.   [2] Burchard, 139.

the realisation of his most cherished scheme. Lorenzo had carefully prepared Giovanni to be an ecclesiastical personage. He used his influence with Louis XI. of France to obtain for him in his childhood an abbey in France: the Pope declared him capable of holding benefices, and conferred on him the dignity of a protonotary. Shortly afterwards Louis XI. made him Archbishop of Aix; but the Pope refused his confirmation to this monstrous nomination.[1] Still, at the age of fifteen Giovanni was promised the Cardinalate, and at the age of eighteen was thought of mature years to take his place amongst the Pope's counsellors. He was invested with the insignia of his dignity at Fiesole, and Florence celebrated with unwonted rejoicings the honour conferred upon her chief family. When the young Cardinal set out for Rome, he was escorted two miles out of Florence by the chief citizens. At Siena he was received with as much honour as if he had been the Pope himself. At Viterbo he was met by Franceschetto Cibò, who escorted him to Rome, where the whole city came out to meet him in spite of torrents of rain. He went through the ceremonial of presentation to the Pope with dignity and with address, and paid the accustomed visits to his brother Cardinals. Amongst them was Raffaelle Riario, who had played such a suspicious part in the conspiracy of the Pazzi. He felt the awkwardness of the situation and reinforced himself for the visit by the presence of Cardinal Orsini. It is said that he and Giovanni de' Medici turned deadly pale at their meeting, and could scarcely stammer out a few formal sentences.

Soon after his arrival in Rome the young Cardinal received from his father a letter of advice. The letter is honourable to Lorenzo, and shows that he was by no means destitute of principle. He urges upon Giovanni gratitude to God for His mercies—gratitude to be shown by a holy, exemplary, and upright life. He beseeches him not to forget the lessons of his early training, not to neglect the means of grace afforded by Confession and Communion. 'I know that by going to Rome, which is a sink of all iniquities, you encounter greater difficulties than hitherto. Not only is there the danger of bad example, but many will endeavour to allure and corrupt you. Your elevation at your age to the Cardinalate caused much

[1] *Ricordi di Lorenzo*, in Roscoe, Appendix LXII.

envy, and many who could not prevent your dignity will endeavour to diminish it by blackening your life and casting you into the ditch where they have fallen themselves. Your youth will encourage them to hope for an easy success. You must withstand these dangers with greater firmness, as there is at present less virtue in the College of Cardinals. Yet there are some men in the College, learned and good and of holy life. Follow their example, and you will be the more esteemed as you are the more distinguished from the rest.'

So far Lorenzo has spoken as a moralist, his concluding remarks are those of a statesman and observer of life. He warns his son to avoid hypocrisy, to observe a mean in all things, to shun austerity and severity, to give no offence. He dwells on the difficulty of life amid men of different characters, and urges geniality, reasonableness, and care not to make enemies. On this first visit to Rome it were better to use his ears than his tongue. 'You are devoted to God and the Church; yet you will find many ways to help your city and your house. You are the chain that binds this city with the Church, and your house goes with the city. You are the youngest Cardinal; be the most zealous and the most humble. Let no one have to wait for you. Encourage as little intimacy as may be with the less reputable of your brethren, but in public converse with all. In all matters of display, be under rather than over the mean. Let your establishment be refined and well ordered rather than rich and splendid. Silks and jewels are not becoming; collect rather a few elegant antiques and rare books.[1] Let your attendants be well conducted and learned, rather than numerous. In entertainments, do nothing superfluous, but invite more often than you are invited. Let your food be plain and take plenty of exercise; for men of your cloth easily contract infirmities if they are not careful. The dignity of Cardinal is as secure as it is great; let not this security beguile you into negligence, as it has done many. Rise in good time in the morning; this habit is not only good for your health but gives you time to arrange what you have to do in the day. Every evening think over the morrow's business that you be not taken unawares. In consistory, submit your opinion to that of the Pope on the ground of your

---

[1] 'Qualche gentilezza di cose antiche e belli libri.'

youth. Beware of carrying petitions to the Pope or of troubling him, for his character is to give most to those who ask him least.'[1] Surely it was from Italy that Polonius learned his saws.

This letter of Lorenzo's was his last testament to his son. On April 7, 1492, he died at the age of forty-four, and Italy lost its one great statesman. Lorenzo had striven to identify the Medici family with Florence, and had been himself the representative and expression of the desires and aspirations of Florentine life and culture. He had also learned that the existence of Italy depended upon the maintenance of internal peace, and his efforts for that end had for the last ten years of his life been unceasing. His early experience had taught him how difficult was the position which he had to maintain, that of the chief citizen of a free city, whose fortunes and whose very existence depended on exercising absolute power without seeming to do so. It is easy to accuse him of insidiously destroying Florentine liberty; but the policy of Sixtus IV. left him no choice between such a course and retirement from Florence, and he may be pardoned if he doubted whether his abdication would conduce to the welfare of the city. He has been accused of abetting the moral enervation and corruption of his people; but the causes of this corruption are to be found in the general character of Italian life, and Lorenzo did no more than follow the prevailing fashion in lending his refinement to give expression to the popular taste. Lorenzo did what all Italian statesmen were doing; he identified his city for good and ill with his own house. He worked craftily and insidiously, not by open violence, and in the midst of his self-seeking he retained the large views of a statesman and embodied the culture of his age.

Death of Lorenzo de' Medici. April 7, 1492.

Florence was the most eminently Italian of all Italian cities, and had long shown herself to be the brain of Italy. It was there that the culture of the Renaissance found its highest and most serious expression, and there the first attempt was made to bring the ideas of the new learning into relation with the old system of thought on which the life of Christendom was founded. The Aristotelian logic had furnished the phraseology and the method of the teaching of the Schoolmen;

Marsilio Ficino.

[1] Roscoe, *Lorenzo de' Medici*, Appendix LXVI.

the scholars of the Renaissance sought in Plato a larger expression of their widening views. At Florence this was done deliberately by the patronage of Cosimo de' Medici, who founded a Platonic Academy and chose as its first head the son of his physician Marsilio Ficino, who was carefully educated in the Greek language. Marsilio was a scholar of fine mind and keen susceptibilities, who entered with fervour upon the study of Plato, and established a religious cult of his great master. A shrine was built to Plato, and a lamp burned before it; his bust was crowned with laurels, and his birthday was celebrated with a high festival. The Florentine Academy met and discussed the writings of Plato, and Marsilio spent his life in their translation and exposition. Though a philosopher, Marsilio was also a sincere Christian. At the age of forty he took orders after serious deliberation, but he did not seek high office or large revenues from the Church. He lived and died a poor man, and his works were published at the expense of Lorenzo de' Medici and other wealthy Florentines.

Ficino's knowledge of Plato was neither accurate nor profound. He lacked the critical faculty which was necessary to understand the Platonic system. He did not distinguish between the writings of Plato and those of the Alexandrian mystics of later times; to him Plotinus was a true interpreter of his master. Ficino seized on the mystical side of Plato, and found in it a means of reconciling Christianity with the new philosophy. He saw in Plato an Attic-speaking Moses; he compared the life of Socrates with that of Jesus; he discovered in the doctrines of Plato a forecast of Christian dogma. He did this with all sincerity and earnestness. It was the first attempt to unify the intellectual world, to weave into a system the old and new beliefs.

Pico della
Mirandola.

This intellectual movement, which Ficino expressed, was carried further by his scholar, Giovanni Pico della Mirandola. Son of the Count of Mirandola, he early devoted himself to study and at the age of twenty came to Florence where he showed himself a zealous disciple of Ficino. He went to Paris in quest of more learning, and set himself to supplement Ficino's system by researches into Jewish tradition. The teaching of the Alexandrian school had largely affected the Jews, and a body of tradition, called the Cabbalah, had gradually grown up which expanded the teaching of Moses into a theosophy. From the Cabbalah, from astrology, from magic, Pico obtained proofs of the truth of Christian doctrine, and carried into the more obscure regions of mediæval knowledge the unifying process which Ficino had begun. In 1486 Pico visited Rome, and in a fit of youthful self-sufficiency promulgated nine hundred theses which he was ready to maintain in public disputation. His theses dealt with theology, philosophy, in fact all human knowledge down to magic and the Cabbalah. This audacity awakened enemies who were not slow in pointing out heresies which lay lurking in some of Pico's propositions. Innocent VIII. issued a brief against the more dangerous theses, and Pico, foreseeing a storm, left Rome, published an apology protesting his orthodoxy, and took refuge in France. Pico dreaded a citation to Rome and possible imprisonment; and the influence of Lorenzo de' Medici was needed to induce the Pope to suspend proceedings. Pico returned to Florence after a while, but only Lorenzo's exertions prevailed on the Pope to stay his hand.

The Florentine neoplatonism was an attempt to bring the new learning into connexion with Christian doctrine. It aspired to a restoration of the unity of human thought, and was aimed against the prevalent materialism and indifference to religion. It was a protest against the ignorance of the clergy, who were rapidly being left stranded by the advance of men's interests and the development of an intelligent and critical curiosity about all speculative matters. According to Ficino, the priest and the philosopher were identical; religion was to be rescued from ignorance and philosophy from godlessness. The soul came from God, and yearned after the consciousness of its union with Him. All religions were the expression of this desire; the Christian religion alone was true, and showed its truth by the completeness of the union between God and man which it revealed. Ficino and Pico alike aimed at a complete identification of wisdom and piety, as only being different aspects of the same quality. Hence they took up an attitude of large intellectual tolerance. The truth to them was one and indivisible; all that was good and noble was but a reflection of the complete truth which was fully revealed in Christ. Ficino and Pico were men of undoubted piety, but their teaching did not produce any deep impression. On the one side it did not prove an effective barrier against the growing material-ism of the Aristotelian school; on the other side it easily passed into a vague philosophic theism which attracted a character like that of Lorenzo de' Medici. In no way was it fitted to impress the mass of mankind and turn them back to piety.[1]

Lorenzo's
literary
circle.

Lorenzo was the centre of a literary circle which some-times listened to the Platonic philosophy of Ficino and Pico, sometimes to the moral disputations of Cristoforo Landino, and sometimes to the burlesques of Luigi Pulci. The first force of the classical revival was spent, and men brought back the knowledge they had gained from the study of style to deck their native literature. Pulci's ' Morgante Maggiore' was the beginning of a revived romanticism. The legends of chivalry were again told in the vulgar tongue, with no serious purpose and with a strong infusion of popular buffonery. Pulci refined the literature of the market-place, and introduced it into culti-vated society. His poem contains a strange mixture of piety and mocking scepticism. He jests with Scripture, with miracles, with sacred words, without any sense of incongruity. He is under the humour of the moment; his seriousness and his laughter are alike transient; his piety and his profanity rest equally on no basis of firm conviction.

Angelo
Poliziano.

The greatest man in this Florentine circle was Angelo Poliziano, so called from his birth-place of Monte Pulciano. He was the foremost scholar in Italy, and his lectures were thronged by an eager audience. He was so far master of Latin that he wrote Latin poems with an ease of style and mastery of expression which entitled him to rank as an original Latin poet. He stands, moreover, first among the poets of the revived Italian tongue. The passion, the fire of true poetry rings through his songs; but his greatest poems are only graceful trifles, and he wasted his powers on such themes as a tourna-ment at which Giuliano de' Medici bore away the prize. There were mastery of language and gifts of genius, but there was no depth of feeling, no grasp of reality. Italy was enjoying a dream of beauty and lived only for the day.

[1] For Marsilio Ficino see Galeotti in *Archivio Storico Italiano*, Nuova Serie, vols. ix. and x.

Amongst these literary men Lorenzo moved, not merely as a
patron, but as one who himself had won a foremost place. His
Italian poems are careful and pleasing, though they lack the
spontaneity of Poliziano. Florence was proud of its literary
chief and Lorenzo gratified every taste; he wrote sonnets for
the cultivated, a coarse satire on drunkenness for the rude, and
a collection of sacred lauds for the pious. Moreover, he turned
his artistic gifts to the organisation of the festivals which the
Florentines loved so well. At Carnival time the young men used
to ramble through the city in masques, singing and dancing.
Lorenzo aimed at giving greater variety to these songs and
dances. He wrote *Canzoni a ballo*, and had them set to
music. He arranged costumes for the masqueraders, and
designed for them chariots filled with mythological figures
which they drew through the streets. They sallied forth after
dinner, sometimes to the number of three hundred, and
traversed the city with their songs and dances till the stars
began to fade.[1]

These Carnival songs give us a surprising insight into
Lorenzo's mind and the tone of thought in his days. They
openly incite to breaches of the moral law; they clothe profligacy with the veil of gallantry; they take the ordinary
occupations of life and turn them into elaborate innuendoes
of obscenity. The ruler of Florence himself devised and encouraged this means of corrupting what remained of moral
sentiment among the Florentine youth. Lorenzo's example
might not be edifying, his tone of thought might not be noble,
but these only directly affected those who were in his immediate circle. By his Carnival songs, he carried to all ranks
and classes the incitement to abandon self-restraint and
adopt as a rule of life the pursuit of self-indulgence. He gave
them as their motto:

> Quant' è bella giovinezza,
> Che si fugge tuttavia!
> Chi vuol esser lieto, sia;
> Di doman non c' è certezza.[2]

Even Poliziano was amazed at Lorenzo's versatility, at the ease

CHAP.
V.

Poetry of
Lorenzo.

---

[1] Lasca's Preface to *Tutti i Trionfi, Carri, Canti Carnescialeschi* (1559).
[2] *Trionfo di Bacco ed Arianna.*

with which he changed his tone from his songs for the mas-
querades to his lauds for the pious penitents.[1]

Amongst the memorials of the Medici in Florence, few are
more interesting than the Convent of S. Marco, which Cosimo
rebuilt with splendid magnificence. Michelozzo Michelozzi
laboured for six years to make a worthy monument of Cosimo's
liberality; and in it Cosimo established a branch of the Dominicans of Lombardy, to whose care he committed the first
public library of Italy, of which the collection of Niccolò Niccoli
formed the nucleus. Everything favoured Cosimo's desire to
make the Convent of S. Marco a monumental building. Fra
Angelico came from Fiesole and adorned its walls with fresco;
the holy Archbishop of Florence, S. Antonino, shed round it
the memories of his sanctity.

To this Convent of S. Marco, thus richly endowed by the
patronage of the Medici, came in 1482 a young brother, Girolamo
Savonarola. He was a native of Ferrara, born in 1452; his
father wished to educate him as a classical scholar, but Girolamo
showed a decided preference for the works of S. Thomas Aquinas.
A disappointment in love is said to have done much to wean
his mind from the world, but his own reading and reflection did
more. At the age of twenty-two he left his parents and found
a refuge for his weary soul amongst the Dominicans of Bologna.
On his departure from home he left behind him, to console his
father, a short treatise 'On Contempt of the World,' which
shows how deeply he felt the wickedness around him.
'Everything is full of impiety, of usury and robbery, foul and
wicked blasphemies, fornication, adultery, sodomy, and all uncleanness, murder and envy, ambition and pride, hypocrisy
and falseness, crime and iniquity. Virtues are turned into
vices and vices into virtues. There is none that doeth good,
no not one. Men are summoned to penitence by disasters,
earthquakes, hailstones, and storms of wind; but they do not
hearken. They are summoned by floods, diseases, famines;

---

[1] *Nutricia*, sub fine:

> 'Non vacat argutosque sales satyraque bibaces
> Descriptos memorare senes: non carmina festis
> Excipienda choris querulasve animantia chordas.
> Idem etiam tacitæ referens pastoria vitæ
> Otia et urbanos thyrso extimulante labores
> Mox fugis in cælum, non ceu per lubrica nisus,
> Extremamque boni gaudes contingere metam.'

but they do not hearken. They are summoned by the impious deeds of the overweening Turks; but they do not hearken. They are summoned by the affectionate voice of preachers and servants of God; but they do not hearken. All, in fine, are summoned by the natural pricks of conscience; but they do not hearken.'[1]

With these feelings in his heart Savonarola quietly performed his noviciate at Bologna, whence in 1482 he was sent by order of his superiors to preach at Ferrara. He found that he had no honour in his own country; but the outbreak of the war into which Sixtus IV. plunged Ferrara soon drove him to seek another refuge and he entered the Convent of S. Marco at Florence. In 1483 he began to preach and testify against the prevalent corruptions. He was not, however, successful; his rugged oratory, his passionate appeals, did not attract the cultivated Florentines, who looked upon sermons as rhetorical exercises. Savonarola was left to preach to empty benches in S. Lorenzo while everyone flocked to S. Spirito to hear the favourite preacher of Lorenzo de' Medici, Mariano de Genazzano. They admired his voice, his management of his breath, his graceful action. Their critical sense was satisfied by his periods, his dexterous transitions, his pathos, his command of his main argument while seemingly wandering at his pleasure.[2] They were delighted at his artificial simplicity, entirely destitute of dignity. They applauded the orator all the more because he had not the bad taste to aim at convincing their minds or carrying truth to their hearts.[3]

Savonarola grieved over his own want of success, but it only convinced him of the hardness of men's hearts. He read with greater fervour the writings of the Hebrew prophets, till their spirit took possession of his soul. He felt that to him too had come a mission from on high, a mission to announce God's coming judgment to an unrepentant world; and his fiery

[1] In Villari, *Storia di Savonarola*, vol. ii. *Documenti* II.
[2] See a letter of Poliziano to Tristano Chalcho, in Lib. V. of *Politiani Epistolæ*. Poliziano does not say a word about the subject of the preacher.
[3] Paolo Cortese, *De Cardinalatu*: 'Nec nimis illa genera reprehendi solent quibus inest fucatus sine dignitate candor; qualis nobis pueris Mariani Ghinazanensis est locutio quotidiana visa; quæ ita nimii artificii diligentia nimioque calamistrorum usu compta fuerat ut et rei auctoritatem adimeret et sermonis expositioni fidem.'

zeal made him realise the imminence of the impending doom. In his Lenten sermons, preached at S. Gemignano in 1484 and 1485, he foretold that the scourge of God's wrath would rapidly fall upon the Church, which should be purified and revived by punishment. These sermons were eagerly listened to, and Savonarola acquired confidence by seeing that his ideas could awaken the sympathy of others. He returned to Florence, strengthened in his own beliefs and with growing faith in his own mission. In 1486 he was ordered to preach at Brescia. There he expounded the Apocalypse with terrible vividness, so that his fame as a preacher of righteousness was spread abroad in Northern Italy, where he continued to preach till 1490, when he was ordered by his superiors to return to Florence.[1]

In Florence he undertook the work of teaching the novices in S. Marco ; but many people sought him out and besought him to give expository lectures on the Apocalypse. At first he spoke in the cloister, but his audience increased so rapidly that he had to transfer himself to the church. There he produced a marked impression on his hearers and became a ruling power in Florence. In the Lent of 1491 he preached to a crowded congregation in the cathedral, and his triumph as a preacher was assured.

Savona-rola's preaching.

The object of Savonarola's teaching was to awaken men to a sense of righteousness, temperance, and judgment to come. He called them back from the study of Plato and Plotinus to the study of the Scriptures. He bade them renounce their life of pleasure for a life of communion with God. He besought them to turn their eyes from the newly discovered glories of this world to the eternal splendour of the world to come. In this he did not differ from the earnest spiritual teachers of all times. But he did not appeal to men only as a teacher ; he warned them as a prophet. The prevailing cor-

---

[1] The accounts given by the biographers of Savonarola, Pico, Burlamacchi, and Barsanti all say that he was recalled by Lorenzo at the request of Pico della Mirandola, who was struck by his eloquence at a Dominican Chapter held in Reggio. As this Chapter was supposed to be held in 1486, the story was suspicious, because it required a long while for Pico to influence Lorenzo and Lorenzo to recall Savonarola. Gherardi, *Nuori Documenti intorno a Savonarola*, 250 &c , shows that the Chapter at Reggio was held in 1482, which disposes of the story conclusively.

ruption was so vividly present to his mind that he saw with equal
vividness and certainty the scourge of God's vengeance. He
called upon his hearers not merely to flee from God's wrath
hereafter, but to prepare for a speedy manifestation of His
judgment upon earth. The deep sense of universal wickedness
was combined in his mind with an ideal of a pure and holy
Church. He saw God's hand already stretched out to work
through suffering and woe a mighty process of purification, and
he expressed the results of his insight with the imperiousness
and certainty of the Hebrew prophets. He found the pleadings
of reason, the arguments of experience, cold and inconclusive ;
overmastered by his sense of prophetic insight, he was driven
to rest his admonitions on the certainty of immediate punishment. His preaching rested upon prophecy; and an age whose
enlightenment had not advanced beyond the realm of unfettered
imagination needed a prophet. Men who with all their culture
believed in astrology and magic were riveted by the fire of
Savonarola's denunciations, though they would have paid little
heed to his reasonings.

Between the spiritual movement set on foot by Savonarola
and the ideas of Lorenzo de' Medici there could be little sympathy. Savonarola justly regarded Lorenzo's government as
one great source of Florentine corruption ; he held aloof from
the Medicean circle, and assumed an independent attitude.
Five of the chief citizens went to him and advised him to be
more moderate in his language. ' I see that you are sent to
me by Lorenzo,' said Savonarola. ' Tell him to repent of his
sins, for the Lord spares no one and fears not the princes of the
earth.' They spoke to him of the probability of exile. ' I fear
not your exile,' he answered, ' for this city of yours is like a
grain of lentil on the earth. Nevertheless, though I am a
stranger and Lorenzo the first citizen in your city, I must remain and he must depart.' When in July 1491 Savonarola
was elected Prior of S. Marco, he refused to pay the usual visit
of ceremony to Lorenzo. ' I owe my election to God only,' he
said, ' and to Him will I pay my obedience.' Lorenzo, when
this speech was told him said, in jest, ' You see, a stranger has
come into my house and does not even think fit to visit me.'
It was the passing rebuke of a statesman to what he considered
the discourtesy of ecclesiastical pretentiousness.

Lorenzo on his part could not sympathise with the exalted enthusiasm of Savonarola's preaching. He could not fail to recognise that it contained elements of political danger, and he looked to the popular Franciscan, Mariano of Genazzano, to outdo Savonarola's eloquence. But Mariano overshot the mark in a sermon on the text, 'It is not for you to know the times and seasons.' His invective was so violent that it failed to carry conviction, and Mariano's failure left Savonarola more popular than before. Lorenzo treated Savonarola with kindly tolerance; he visited the Convent of S. Marco as before, though Savonarola studiously kept out of his way. In his behaviour towards Lorenzo, Savonarola's zeal led him to take up the position of a partisan. As a preacher of repentance he might have laboured to influence Lorenzo amongst other sinners. As it was, he did not strive to bring Lorenzo to better ways, but aimed at a reformation in his despite.

Lorenzo bore no animosity against Savonarola, but respected him for his good intentions and was willing that the Florentines should enjoy a preacher of their own choice. In the beginning of 1492 he suffered greatly from gout; and already on the departure of his son Giovanni for Rome, there were but slight hopes of his recovery. His disease grew worse and he prepared to die like a Christian. On April 7 he sent for a priest to administer to him the Holy Communion. He dragged himself from his sick bed, supported by his attendants, to go and meet the host, before which he knelt with expressions of devout contrition. The priest seeing his weakness, besought him to lie down in bed, where he received the last solemn rites of religion. He then summoned his son Piero and gave him his last advice. He looked with a smile on Poliziano, who was at his bedside; 'Ah! Angelo,' he said, and pressed his old friend's hands. He asked for Pico, and bade him farewell, saying pleasantly, 'I wish that death had left me time to finish your library.' When Pico had gone another visitor appeared, Fra Girolamo Savonarola. He came at the request of Lorenzo, who wished to die in charity with all men. Savonarola addressed a few words of exhortation to the dying man. He admonished him to hold the faith: Lorenzo replied that he held it firmly. He exhorted him to amend his life, and Lorenzo promised to do so diligently. Finally he urged him to endure death, if need be, with constancy. 'Nothing could please me more,' said Lorenzo, 'if it were God's will.' Savonarola prepared to depart. 'Give me your blessing, father, before you go,' Lorenzo asked. He bowed his head and with pious mien joined in Savonarola's prayers, while all around gave way to uncontrolled grief. After this, Lorenzo rapidly sank. He bade farewell to his servants and asked their forgiveness if he had in aught offended them. He desired to have read to him the Passion of our Lord, and his lips moved as he followed the reader. A crucifix was held before him; he raised himself to kiss it, fell back and died.[1]

The death of Lorenzo was of grave moment to the politics of Italy, and bereft Innocent VIII. of his adviser. Innocent VIII. did not survive Lorenzo many months, and their record is that of a succession of festivals. On May 27, Don Ferrantino, Prince of Capua, son of Alfonso of Calabria, entered Rome in pomp, to celebrate the reconciliation of Naples with the Pope. He was entertained by Cardinal Ascanio Sforza at a banquet of incredible splendour, so that the chronicler Infessura declares himself unequal to the task of describing it.[2] His retinue of nine hundred horsemen and two hundred and sixty mules laden with luggage proved troublesome guests; they sold in the market much of the food with which the Pope supplied them, and at their departure they despoiled their quarters of all their furniture.

Ferrantino of Naples in Rome. May–June, 1492.

The arrival of Ferrantino was rapidly succeeded by an imposing ecclesiastical ceremony. The Sultan Bajazet, in his desire to ingratiate himself with his brother's gaoler, sent the Pope a valuable present, the head of the lance with which the Saviour was pierced. There was some discussion among the Cardinals about the reception of this holy relic. It was pointed out that already both Paris and Nürnberg claimed to possess the same thing: it was urged that the Sultan, an enemy of the Christian faith, might be sending this gift in derision. The majority of the Cardinals were in favour of receiving it without any solemnity and waiting to make inquiries about its genuineness. But the Pope thought otherwise, and sent a Cardinal to receive it at Ancona and bring it reverently to Rome.[3] On

Reception of the Holy Lance. May 31, 1492.

---

[1] See Appendix, No. VII, The Death of Lorenzo de' Medici.
[2] Mur. iii. pt. ii. 1240.   [3] Burchard, i. 473 &c.

May 29 the Sultan's ambassador arrived and was conducted in state to his lodgings. It was thought well that he should come in advance of the prelates who bore the relic, so as not to mix an incongruous figure in the solemnity, which was fixed for Ascension Day, May 31. Meanwhile the question was raised how the next day should be spent. The vigil of the Ascension was a fast day; but Burchard, the papal Master of Ceremonies, gave it as his opinion that under present circumstances a fast, instead of inspiring devotion, might cause many to blaspheme. He suggested as an amendment to the fast that fountains of wine should play in the street through which the procession was to pass. The Pope so far followed his opinion as to say nothing about the fast in his proclamation of the ceremonies.[1]

On May 31 Innocent VII. advanced to the Porta del Popolo and received the Holy Lance which was borne in procession to the Vatican. The Pope was too feeble to attend the mass, but gave his benediction to the people from the loggia of the portico, while Cardinal Borgia standing by his side held aloft the relic. He then received the Sultan's ambassador and returned to his room, leaving the Cardinals to finish the ecclesiastical part of the ceremony.

Family alliance with Naples, June 3, 1492.

Yet the ailing Pope could still nerve himself for a family festival. Ferrante of Naples, in his desire to detach the Pope from France, was willing to cement his political alliance by a marriage. He asked the hand of the Pope's granddaughter, Battistina Cibò, daughter of Gerardo Usodimare, for his grandson Don Luigi, Marquis of Gerace; and the marriage took place on June 3 in the Vatican, amidst a brilliant throng of lords and ladies. After this token of friendship the Prince of Capua received the investiture of Naples, which Innocent VIII. in 1489 had declared to have reverted to the Holy See.

Death of Innocent VIII., July 25, 1492.

From this time the health of Innocent VIII. grew worse, till in the beginning of July there were small hopes of his recovery. The Cardinals began to prepare against any tumults that might arise on his death. They placed Djem in a safe place over the Sistine Chapel, as they were afraid that an attempt might be made to seize so lucrative a prisoner. They gathered troops to protect the Vatican, and proceeded to make an inventory of the property of the Church. The dying Pope asked their permission

[1] Burchard, i. 483.

to distribute 48,000 ducats amongst his relatives; they acceded to his request, and he made provision for his grandchildren. A fever seized him, and he sank slowly. At the last, he became so feeble that he could take no nourishment except woman's milk. It is said that a Jew doctor offered to cure the Pope by transfusion of blood. Three boys of ten years old were chosen for this purpose, and were paid a ducat each; they died in the experiment, and the Pope obtained no benefit.[1] On the night of July 25 Innocent VIII. died; he was buried on August 5 in S. Peter's, where his grave is adorned by a brazen monument of Pollaiuolo, which represents the Pope seated, and in the act of giving the benediction.

The inscription on the tomb of Innocent VIII., 'Italicæ pacis perpetuo custodi,' 'the constant guardian of the peace of Italy,' records his one claim to respect. Coming between Sixtus IV. and Alexander VI., Innocent VIII. seemed to play a harmless part in Italian politics. His easy good nature was a quality which all men appreciated, and which made Innocent VIII. an involuntary benefactor to Italy. He was incapable of any great design and willingly yielded himself to others. At first he was in the hands of Giuliano della Rovere, who urged him to follow the bold career of Sixtus IV. But Innocent VIII. had no capacity for facing difficulties, and shrank back at the approach of danger. He withdrew from his fiery adviser and placed himself in the hands of Lorenzo de' Medici, who skilfully used the Papacy as a great factor in the Italian balance of power which he strove to bring about. Moreover, Lorenzo used his opportunity to connect the interests of Rome and Florence, and establish the Medici family in the Curia, which thus became more widely representative of Italian politics.

Character of Innocent VIII.

In other matters also, he was helped by his incompetence. He enriched his family, but he had not the energy or capacity

---

[1] The circumstances of the death of Innocent VIII. are told in a series of letters written from day to day by the Florentine envoy Valori, in Thuasne's Burchard, Appendix, 567 &c. Valori says nothing about the transfusion of blood, which is recorded by Infessura, Mur. iii. pt. ii. 1241. Unfortunately the diary of Burchard is a blank from June 14 to December 2. Raynaldus, *Annales*, sub anno, No. 21, repeats the story, and adds that Innocent VIII., who was unconscious at the time, was indignant when he knew of it. It would seem that he had some other authority for the statement.

to do so by far-reaching schemes. He made his son Frances-chetto, Count of Cervetri and Anguillara; but Franceschetto had no ambition beyond an easy life and on his father's death he sold his territory to Virginio Orsini. One of his nephews, Lorenzo Cibò, he created Cardinal; a dignity which Lorenzo worthily filled. But it was clear that the Cibò family was in no way remarkable. Innocent VIII. seems most at his ease when engaged in family festivals in the Vatican, which during his pontificate began to wear a homelike aspect. It was often graced with the presence of ladies, and Innocent VIII. set the example of an estimable father of a family.[1]

There were, however, affairs in which the easy good nature of Innocent VIII. did not stand him in such good stead. He was incapable of dealing with the turbulence of Rome, and his administration varied between outbursts of severity and periods of neglect. Generally the Vice Chancellor Borgia and Franceschetto Cibò divided between them the fees that could be obtained from the administration of justice; and a lawless spirit of revenge prevailed amongst the dwellers in Rome. Innocent VIII. was in sore need of money; he was not a good manager, and the troubles of the early part of his reign left him in great straits. To recruit his finances he followed the example of Sixtus IV. and created new offices in the Curia, which he sold to aspiring candidates. He increased the number of papal secretaries to twenty-six, and sold these posts for 62,400 ducats. The new officials multiplied the general business of the Curia and exacted taxes on all appointments to offices in the Papal States; even from the officers who superintended the Roman markets. Moreover Innocent VIII. appointed fifty-two Plumbatores, whose duty was to seal the Bulls; each of them paid the Pope 2,500 ducats on their appointment.[2] This multiplication of needless offices as

---

[1] Raphael Volterranus, *Commentarii*, bk. xxii: 'Pontificum etiam primus qui novum et ipse exemplum introduceret palam liberos nothos jactandi ac soluta omni antiqua disciplina divitiis eos omnibus cumulandi.' Ægidius of Viterbo, MS. in *Bibliotheca Angelica*: 'Primus pontificum filios filiasque palam ostentavit; primus eorum apertas fecit nuptias; primus domesticos hymenæos celebravit.'

[2] Ciaconius, iii. 95. Ægidius of Viterbo, MS.: 'Innocentius culpæ predecessoris sectator quam emendator esse maluit, ac spem dedit eo usque hæc sordium onera processura, ut migrandum quocunque ex obsessa his morbis urbe Roma sit.'

a means of raising money, not only increased the extortions of the Curia, but also lowered the character of its officials. In September 1489, two papal secretaries and four subordinates were seized and imprisoned on the charge of forging papal Bulls. These two secretaries confessed that during the preceding two years they had forged and sold upwards of fifty Bulls, giving dispensations of various kinds. One of them adopted the ingenious process of obliterating portions of Bulls granted for small matters, and filling in the blank with matters of weightier moment. The Pope was naturally incensed at this discovery, and the criminals were burnt to death in spite of the efforts of wealthier relatives to buy them off.[1] There were other irregularities in the Curia; many Jews and Marrani made their way to high places, and held the posts of scribes and protonotaries.[2] But the general condition of the Curia was such that it was useless to be scrupulous about the lesser officials. The Cardinals lived lives of luxury ill-befitting the princes of the Church. It was said that in two nights' gambling, at the palace of Raffaelle Riario, Franceschetto Cibò lost 14,000 ducats, and Cardinal La Balue 800. Riario was famous for his good luck, and Franceschetto, with characteristic feebleness, complained to the Pope of foul play. Innocent VIII. ordered Riario to restore the money, but was answered that it was already spent in paying for the new palace which he was engaged in building.[3] It is no wonder that Cardinal Ardicino della Porta, a learned theologian, found Rome a dangerous place for one who had aspirations after a spiritual life. He laid aside his robes and left Rome secretly by night, with the intention of entering the monastery of Camaldoli. But he had only advanced to Roncilione when a messenger from the Pope commanded his return, as he had acted irregularly in laying aside his cardinalate without the Pope's permission. The Cardinals objected to this bad example of seeking after saintliness; but Ardicino did not trouble them long; soon after his return to Rome he sickened and died.[4]

[1] Burchard, i. 365, &c.; Infessura, 1229; Sigismondo de' Conti, ii. 38 &c.
[2] Infessura, 1217. 'In ecclesia Dei cepisse multa officia, prout vidi, aliquos Protonotarios, scriptores, Janizzeros et similia officia habentes; contra quos Papa non multum ferventer, ut res ipsa postulabat, processit.'
[3] Ibid. 1230.
[4] Infessura, 1236, tells the story morosely; compare the letter of Ardicino to the Pope in Ciaconius, iii. 126.

Innocent VIII. was not a man of learning or of culture, though he welcomed Poliziano at Rome and received the dedication of his translation of Herodotus. Pomponius Lætus contrived to be the literary dictator of the city, and the classical revival took deeper and deeper hold of men's minds. In 1485 the Renaissance even discovered its saint. Some workmen engaged in excavations at the Via Appia found a marble sarcophagus, which when opened showed the body of a Roman girl who had been embalmed. Men's excited imaginations found in this mummy unsurpassed beauty; the maiden lay in all the loveliness of youth, her golden hair encircled with a fillet of gold; her eyes and mouth were partly open, and the roseate hue of health was on her cheek.[1] Pilgrims from all parts of Italy flocked to Rome, amongst them many painters who wished to make sketches of this classic model. But the corpse gradually began to decompose through exposure to the air, and one night it was quietly buried on the Appian road in the tomb believed to be that of Cicero's Tullia: nothing save the empty sarcophagus was left for the disappointed votaries. Of course the body was identified, and the general opinion was in favour of Julia, daughter of Claudius; though others claimed her as Priscilla, wife of Abascantius, Domitian's minister, whose burial is sung by Statius.[2]

Innocent VIII. continued the architectural decoration of Rome. He adorned the piazza of S. Peter's with a marble fountain, in the form of two vases one above the other, so finely wrought that it was reckoned to be the fairest work of the kind in Italy.[3] He made some additions to the Vatican and to S. Peter's; but his chief work was the Villa Belvedere, designed by Antonio Pollaiuolo, which was erected in the Vatican gardens, and still stands joined by a cortile to the central block of buildings. A small chapel, dedicated to S. John, adjoined the Belvedere, and Andrea Mantegna was employed by the

---

[1] Infessura, 1192, is most enthusiastic. The Notary of Nantiporto (Mur. iii. pt. iii. 1094) is more reserved, and says: 'Molti credono sia stato morto degli anni 170.' He differs from Infessura in giving the girl black hair, not golden; but he says: 'Andava tante genti a vederlo che pareva vi f. sse la perdonanza.' Matarazzo, 180.

[2] This is the opinion of Sigismondo de' Conti, who quotes the passage from Statius, Sylvæ, v. 223 &c.; Historia, ii. 45.

[3] Infessura, 1232.

Pope to adorn it. This he did with so much care that the walls and ceiling seemed painted in miniature rather than fresco. A picture of the Baptism of Christ above the altar was remarkable for the realism shown in depicting the efforts of the crowd to divest themselves of their garments before entering the water. Innocent VIII. was an irregular paymaster, and one day when he visited the chapel he found Mantegna at work on an allegorical figure. He inquired the subject, and the painter with a meaning smile answered 'Discretion.' 'Set Patience beside her,' was Innocent VIII.'s answer. When the works were finished the Pope paid Mantegna liberally and dismissed him contented.[1] These works of Mantegna were destroyed by Pius VI., who pulled down the chapel that he might enlarge the Vatican Museum.

Eight miles out of Rome in the direction of the sea Innocent VIII. built a country house, La Magliana, which was a favourite resort of his successors; but the advance of the malaria rendered it unhealthy and it now lies in ruins. It is still a massive pile of buildings and the name of Innocent VIII. may still be seen inscribed above the windows. In the city of Rome Innocent VIII.'s great work was the rebuilding of the ancient Church of S. Maria in Via Lata. For this purpose he removed the arch of Diocletian which stood on the site. Only the main building, as the church is at present, belongs to the time of Innocent VIII.; its façade and the decoration of the interior date from 1660.

The pontificate of Innocent VIII. was ignoble. He drifted with the stream, and his example was disastrous to the discipline of the Church. The general corruption of morals in Italy advanced unchecked during his pontificate. A Pope whose son and daughter were openly recognised in the Vatican could do nothing towards stemming the irregularity of the clergy. The Papacy under Innocent VIII. was merely a factor in Italian politics of which Lorenzo de' Medici made a prudent use; in the affairs of Christendom its voice was scarcely heard. The best that can be said of Innocent VIII. is that in politics he was too indolent to do anything mischievous, and he was pacific

---

[1] Vasari, *Vita di Andrea Mantegna*, is the authority for these works of Mantegna. The story was known by Paolo Cortese, *De Cardinalatu*, published in 1510, and is therefore better attested than most of the kind.

because he shrank from effort. In minor matters he was generally complaisant, and England owed him some gratitude for a Bull which helped to re-establish peace, by securing the succession of the crown to the children born of Henry VII. and Elizabeth of York or any future wife. Henry VII. further obtained from him a Bull which diminished the rights of sanctuary, an important concession to a king who was troubled by persistent rebellions. Bacon gives a true picture of Innocent VIII. when he says that this Bull was granted in return for a complimentary oration delivered by the English ambassadors: 'The Pope knowing himself to be lazy and unprofitable to the Christian world was wonderfully glad to hear that there were such echoes of him sounding in so distant parts.' He was willing to barter eccclesiastical immunities for a little judicious flattery.[1]

[1] See Balzani, *Una Ambasciata inglese a Roma*, in *Archivio Romano*, iii. 174.

CHAPTER VI.

BEGINNINGS OF ALEXANDER VI.

1492–94.

ON August 6, 1492, the twenty-three Cardinals in Rome entered the Conclave. The death of Innocent VIII. had been long foreseen, and the probabilities of the future election had been discussed. Innocent VIII.'s nephew, Lorenzo Cibò, was anxious for the election of some one bound to his house by ties of gratitude. His candidate was the Genoese Cardinal Pallavicini; but Cardinal Cibò shared the incompetence of his family, and when he saw that his first proposal was unacceptable he had no one else to propose. Charles VIII. of France was anxious to secure the election of Cardinal Rovere, and sent 200,000 ducats to a Roman bank as a means of furthering his desire.[1] A Pope in the French interest was dreaded by Milan; and Cardinal Ascanio Sforza was resolutely opposed to Rovere. Sforza did not judge it wise to put himself forward as a candidate; he rather wished to have a Pope who would owe everything to him, and he joined with Raffaelle Riario in pressing the election of Cardinal Borgia. There were many reasons why Borgia should be acceptable. As a Spaniard he would hold a neutral position towards political parties in Italy, and the recent successes of the Spanish monarchs had turned men's eyes to Spain as a power which was rising to importance in the affairs of Christendom. Moreover Borgia was the richest Cardinal in Rome; his election would vacate many important offices, for which there were eager candidates. The former objections to his personal character disappeared in the low tone of morality which was now almost universal.

CHAP.
VI.

Election of Rodrigo Borgia, August 10, 1492.

---

[1] Despatch of Cavalieri in *Atti e Memorie per le provincie Modenesi e Parmesi*, i. 429.

The first days of the Conclave were spent in the futile proceeding of making regulations to bind the future Pope. Ascanio Sforza, seconded by Orsini, was working hard to secure the election of Borgia, who debased himself to make the most humble entreaties. Borgia's wealth was a useful argument to confirm the minds of waverers; Ascanio Sforza's zeal was increased by the promise of the office of Vice Chancellor and Borgia's palace; Orsini, Colonna, Savelli, Sanseverino, Riario, Pallavicini, even the nonagenarian Gherardo of Venice, all received promises of benefices or gifts of money.[1] So matters proceeded smoothly in the Conclave, and late in the evening of August 10 the election of Rodrigo Borgia was unanimously accomplished.

We are told that the first utterance of the newly-elected Pope was a cry of joy, 'I am Pope and Vicar of Christ.' Cardinal Sforza said that the election was the work of God, and that 'great things were expected of the new Pope for the good of the Church.' Borgia replied that he felt his own weakness, but trusted to God's Holy Spirit. He showed great haste in clothing himself with the pontifical vestments, and ordered the Master of the Ceremonies to write the fact of his election on pieces of paper and throw them out of the window. It was late in the evening when the election was made, and not till the early dawn did the crowd assemble outside the Vatican and hear the customary proclamation from the window; then the bells rung and Rome was filled with rejoicing. When Borgia was asked what name he would take, and 'Calixtus' was suggested in remembrance of his uncle, he answered, 'We desire the name of the invincible Alexander.' Cardinal Medici, alarmed at the demeanour of the new Pope, whispered in the ear of Cardinal Cibò, 'We are in the jaws of a rapacious wolf; if we do not flee he will devour us.' Alexander VI. was enthroned

---

[1] The testimony of Infessura, 1244, who says ironically of the new Pope, 'dispersit et dedit pauperibus bona sua,' would of itself be doubtful. But it is confirmed by the despatches of Manfredi, the Ferrarese ambassador at Florence, who passes on the contents of the despatches from the Florentine envoy at Rome; *Atti e Memorie*, iv. 322, &c. A letter of the Florentine Valori, in Thuasne's Burchard, ii. 610, specifies what each cardinal received. He says significantly of the election : ' Per buono rispecto non è bene scriverlo, et ancora molti particulari non si possono cosi bene dire per lettere come a bocha.' Corio, *Storia di Milano*, parte iii. cap. 1, gives some details omitted ' per buono rispecto.'

in S. Peter's, where Cardinal Sanseverino, a man of huge sta-
ture, lifted the new Pope in his arms and placed him on the
high altar.[1]

Rodrigo Borgia was born at Xativa, in the diocese of
Valencia, on January 1, 1431.[2] His parents, Jofre and Isabella
Borgia, were cousins, and belonged to a family which may have
had far-off claims to nobility, but was poor and of small
account.[3] The young Rodrigo was early destined to a clerical
career, in which his uncle Alfonso, Bishop of Valencia, could
help him to preferment. The elevation of Alfonso Borgia to the
pontificate brought Rodrigo a cardinalate at the age of twenty-
five, and soon afterwards the lucrative office of Vice Chancellor.
At the time of his election to the Papacy, he had had thirty-
six years' experience of the Curia, and had served under five
Popes. He went with Pius II. to the Congress of Mantua, and
had been the legate of Sixtus IV. to Spain in the first fervour
of his crusading zeal. He had seen the old ideals of the
Papacy die away, and had gracefully accommodated himself to
changes as they came. He was always influential but never
powerful, and cultivated useful friends. He was capable in
business and used his opportunities to amass money, so that no
Cardinal, except Estouteville, ever established so great a reputation for wealth.

On great occasions he displayed a becoming magnificence,
as at the festival of Pius II. at Viterbo, and the celebration in
Rome of the fall of Grenada; but he was not given to prodi-
gality or luxury. He lived with careful economy, and when
he was Pope preferred to make his meal of one dish only, so

---

[1] These details are taken from the documents printed by Generelli in his
edition of Burchard, 208 &c., from the *Conclari de' Pontefici*, Cologne, 1691,
and from the letters in Thuasne's Burchard, ii. Appendix 172.

[2] We know this for certain, as Burchard, ii. 425, notes under date Jan. 1.
1498, that he heard Alexander VI. tell his cardinals 'sese complevisse heri
sexagesimum septimum annum ætatis suæ.'

[3] L'Espinois, *Le Pape Alexandre VI*, in *Revue des Questions Historiques*
for April 1, 1881, calls attention to a passage in Villanueva, *Viage literario á
las iglesias de España*, ii. 213, who quotes from the archives of San Felipe at
Xativa a deposition made by thirteen witnesses on Alexander VI.'s accession
to the Papacy: 'Dixeron que el Pontefice era natural de Xativa, que era hijo
de los nobles Jofre de Borja y Isabel de Borja . . . que su padre tenia quatro
caballos . . . que muerto su padre, siendo el ya da edad de diez años, se fue
su madre con el y con toda sua casa a la ciutad de Valencia.'

that lovers of good fare found it an infliction to dine with him.[1] 'He built himself a splendid palace near the river;[2] but in so doing he only followed the fashion of his time. He was kindly, and showed active benevolence to those who were in want. But the most striking thing about him was his fascinating appearance and attractive manners. 'He is handsome,' says a contemporary, 'with a pleasant look, and honeyed tongue; he attracts ladies to love him, and draws them to him in a wondrous way more than a magnet draws iron.'[3]

Children of Alexander VI.

Cardinal Borgia's fascinations for women were not always kept in check by rigorous self-restraint. When he was at Siena in 1460, Pius II. reproved him for unseemly gallantry.[4] Cardinal Ammannati at a later date wrote and exhorted him to a change of life.[5] Indeed, there were evidences enough that Cardinal Borgia was not true to his priestly vow of chastity. He had a daughter Girolama who was old enough to be married in 1482.[6] A son, Pedro Luis, lived in Spain, and Cardinal Borgia used some of his wealth to buy for him the duchy of Gandia; he died, however, in 1488, before his father's accession to the Papacy. Besides these children, whose mother we do not know, Cardinal Borgia had four others, Giovanni, Cesare, Lucrezia,[7] and Giofrè, whose mother's name was Vanozza dei Catanei, a Roman. The testimonies that we have of Vanozza speak of her as an excellent

---

[1] Ferrarese ambassador, in May 1495, quoted by Leonetti, i. 159: 'Il Papa si ciba di una vivanda sola, abbenchè questa debba essere abbondante. È quindi una pena desinare con lui.'

[2] Now the Palazzo Sforza Cesarini; but it was altered in later days, and has lost its original features.

[3] Gaspar Veronensis, Mur. iii. pt. 2, 1036: 'quas tamen intactas dimittere sane putatur,' he adds.

[4] The authenticity of this document has been impugned without any grounds, by Leonetti, i. 162, &c. See L'Espinois in *Revue des Questions Historiques*, April 1881, p. 367.

[5] Card. Papiensis *Epistolæ*, No. 660.

[6] Gregorovius, *Lucrezia Borgia*, Appendix I., gives the marriage contract, in which the Cardinal is said 'intendens ipsam Jeronimam puellam, quæ de sua domo et familia existit, veluti filiam recognoscere.' She is called the sister of Pier Luigi and Juan.

[7] Gregorovius, *Id.* No. 4. Marriage contract of Lucrezia Borgia with Don Cherubin. Joan de Centelles speaks of Lucrezia as 'filla carnal de dit R^mo Car^l,' and then says: 'Don l'elois de Borja quondam Duc de Gandia en son testament a dita dona Lucretia germana sua.' See also the letters of Sixtus IV. in Thuasne's Burchard, iii. 3 and 4. Juan is called 'infans' in 1482.

woman, and the inscription on her tomb calls her upright, pious and charitable. Her youngest son Giofrè was born in 1480 or 1481; and either immediately before or after his birth she was married to a scribe, Giorgio della Croce, and after his death in 1485, she married a second husband, Carlo Canale, a secretary of the Penitentiary.[1] Vanozza lived a quiet and secluded life; we never hear of her presence at the Vatican, or of any recognition shown her by the Pope. She signs a letter to her daughter Lucrezia 'La Felice et Infelice Madre Vanozza Borgia.'[2] 'The happy and unhappy mother'—that was the summary of her chequered life. She was happy in her children, their worldly success, their splendid opportunities; she was unhappy because there was a bar between them and her, and she could only witness their triumphs from a distance. She lived to the age of seventy-six, and died respected in 1518.

These facts about the private life of Cardinal Borgia must have been known to the majority of his electors. But the election of Innocent VIII. had already shown that the current feeling, even amongst Churchmen, was not rigorous in judging breaches of the priestly vow. Cardinal Borgia was a loving and tender father, who took care betimes for the advancement of his children. They were probably all brought up by relatives of his at Rome. Girolama was comfortably married at an early age; Giovanni succeeded to his brother's duchy of Gandia in Spain; Cesare was destined for a clerical career, and in 1488 Sixtus IV. granted him a dispensation from proving the legality of his birth, and allowed him to receive minor orders at the age of seven. In 1482 another act of Sixtus IV. appointed Cardinal Borgia administrator of the revenues of any ecclesiastical benefices which might be conferred upon this young clerk before he

---

[1] The inscription on Vanozza's tomb has been preserved by Forcella, *Inscrizioni delle Chiese di Roma*, i. 335:

Vanotiæ Cathanæ Cæsare Valentiæ Joanne Candiæ
Jufredo Scylattii et Lucretia Ferrariæ ducib. filiis nobili
Probitate insigni religioni eximia pari et ætate et
Prudentia optime de Xenodochio Lateran. meritæ
Hieronymus Picus fideicommis. procur. ex test. pos.
Vix. Ann. lxxvi. M. iv. D, xiii. Obiit anno MDXVIII. xxvi. nov.

[2] Gregorovius, *Lucrezia Borgia*, Appendix, No. LVI.

reached the age of fourteen.[1] The tolerance of Sixtus IV. and the example of Innocent VIII. had relaxed the bonds of ecclesiastical discipline into accordance with prevalent morality. Cardinal Borgia was a kindly man and likely to make a capable ruler : his elevation to the Papacy suited the self-interest of the Cardinal College. They looked no further into his private life ; and Italy in general was quite satisfied with the choice which they made.

The Romans rejoiced in the election of Alexander VI., which opened to them the prospect of a splendid pontificate. On the night of his enthronement the magistrates rode in procession by torchlight to the Vatican to do him honour. For a mile the streets and squares gleamed with the brightness of mid-day. 'Even Mark Antony,' exclaims a spectator, 'did not receive Cleopatra with such splendour. I thought of the nocturnal sacrifices of the ancients, or the Bacchanals bearing torches in honour of their god.'[2] The Pope received them graciously, and gave his benediction from the top of the Vatican.

On August 26 the coronation of Alexander VI. was celebrated with unwonted magnificence. The Cardinals vied with one another in the splendour of the dresses of their equipage for the procession which accompanied the Pope in his progress to the Lateran. The streets were adorned with triumphal arches, with tapestries, flowers and paintings which celebrated the glories of Cardinal Borgia in the past and foretold his successes in the future. There were processions of allegorical figures and addresses in profusion.[3] The inscriptions in the streets were framed in terms of extravagant adulation ; and the Borgia arms, a grazing bull on a gold field, lent itself to mythological interpretations of surpassing ingenuity. By the Palazzo of S. Marco was a gigantic figure of a bull, from whose horns, eyes, nostrils and ears flowed water, and from its fore-

[1] These documents from the archives of the Duke d'Ossuna ed Infantado are printed by Thuasne in the appendix to vol. iii. of his edition of Burchard. In both of them it is said : 'defectum natalium pateris, de episcopo cardinali genitus et conjugata.'

[2] The account is given by Michele Ferno, *Legationes Italicæ*, of which a translation is given by Generelli, Burchard, 206.

[3] The fullest description is given by Corio, *Storia di Milano*, part 7, ch. i. The most startling inscription ran :

> Cæsare magna fuit, nunc Roma est maxima : Sextus
> Regnat Alexander ; ille vir, iste deus.

head a stream of wine. The procession moved slowly, and the intense heat of an August sun was so oppressive to the Pope, who sweltered beneath the weight of his magnificent apparel, that when he reached the Lateran he could scarcely stand. He had to be propped up by two Cardinals; and when he sat down at last on the papal throne he fainted, and was supported by Cardinal Riario till he recovered consciousness.[1]

Alexander VI. repaid the loyalty of the Roman citizens by taking steps for the restoration of order within Rome. It was computed that in the interval between the death of Innocent VIII. and the coronation of Alexander VI. no fewer than 220 men had been assassinated in the streets. Alexander VI. made an example of the first assassin whom he could discover. He sent the magistrates to pull down his house; he hanged the culprit and his brother. It was so long since Rome had seen such vigour in the administration of justice, that the citizens ascribed it to the direct disposition of God.[2] Alexander VI. further established commissioners for the trial of disputes, and appointed days of public audience in which he himself decided quarrels. He gave every sign of vigour and good intentions and even undertook the reform in the Curia. 'He has promised,' wrote the Ferrarese ambassador on August 17, 'to make many reforms in the Curia, to dismiss the secretaries and many tyrannical officials, to keep his sons far from Rome, and make worthy appointments. It is said that he will be a glorious pontiff and will have no need of guardians.'[3] We have no reason for thinking that Alexander VI.'s intentions were not sincere; but the love of his relatives was strong within him, and his good intentions fell before his regard for his own kin. On September 1 he raised to the cardinalate a nephew, Juan Borgia, Bishop of Monreale, and issued a Bull in which, 'by the consent of the Cardinals, and the plenitude of the Apostolic power,' he absolved himself from keeping the restrictions imposed by the regulations of the conclave on the nomination of Cardinals.[4]

Alexander VI. restores order in Rome.

If Rome was well content with the new Pope, so also were

---

[1] Petrus Delfinus, *Epistolæ*, iii. 38: 'Et tanti faciunt isti pontificatum,' he exclaims, 'qui tanti constat, tanto periculo comparatur.'

[2] Infessura, 2009.

[3] Capelli in *Atti e Memorie per le Provincie Parmesi e Modenesi*, iv. 823.

[4] It is given in Raynaldus, 1492, § 30.

BOOK
V.

Italy's ex-
pectations
from the
new Pope.

the Italian powers. Congratulatory embassies poured into the
city, and vied with one another in praising the majestic appearance, the tried capacity, and large experience of Alexander
VI.[1] Italy was sincere in its good wishes; it felt the need of
a guiding hand in its political perplexities. Men were enjoying prosperity to the full, and only longed for peace in which
to reap the harvest of pleasure. But a vague presentiment
of coming misfortune mingled with their satisfaction; and
the prophecies of Savonarola owed their force to the fact that
they corresponded to a concealed uneasiness. The death of
Lorenzo de' Medici removed a powerful influence for peace;
Italy looked for guidance to the new Pope.

Affairs of
Milan.
1476–1492.

The chief source of danger to the peace of Italy lay in the
condition of affairs at Milan. The assassination of Galeazzo
Maria Sforza, in 1476, left the duchy of Milan in the hands of
his infant son, Gian Galeazzo. His mother, Bona of Savoy,
undertook the regency, and managed to hold it in spite of the
machinations of the four brothers of the deceased duke. But
Bona's government was feeble, and the eldest of these brothers,
Ludovico Sforza, surnamed Il Moro, succeeded in 1479 in
wresting the power from her hands. Ludovico ruled as regent
of Milan, and was helped at Rome by his brother, the Cardinal
Ascanio. In 1482 Bona appealed to King Louis XI. of France,
but the death of Louis XI. delivered Ludovico from danger.
The young Gian Galeazzo was kept in retirement at Pavia and
Ludovico reigned supreme. But Gian Galeazzo had been affi-
anced by his mother to Isabella, daughter of Alfonso Duke of
Calabria, and when in 1489 he reached the age of twenty,
Ludovico had no pretext for refusing to fulfil the contract.
Gian Galeazzo was married with all due festivity, and then
returned with his wife to Pavia. In 1490 Isabella gave birth to
a son, and it became increasingly difficult for Ludovico to keep
his nephew any longer in tutelage. In 1491 Ludovico married
Beatrice d' Este, daughter of the Duke of Ferrara, and the indignation of Isabella was increased by seeing another receive the
homage and enjoy the splendour which she justly considered to
be her own. She appealed to her father Alfonso, for help to
restore her husband to his rightful station, and Alfonso was

[1] Many of them have been printed, Hieronymi Porcii *Orationes ad Alex-
andrum VI.* (Rome, 1493).

willing to attend her summons. The old age of Ferrante made him cautious, and the influence of Lorenzo de' Medici had preserved peace hitherto; but war was imminent unless Ludovico Sforza withdrew from his usurped authority. Both sides waited anxiously to see the policy of the new Pope; and Italy generally hoped that he might play the part of mediator. The death of Innocent VIII. left the Papacy at peace with Naples; but Alexander VI. owed his election to Ascanio Sforza, brother of Ludovico Il Moro. The political position of the new Pope was delicate, and the consequences of his action were likely to be momentous.

On December 11, Don Federigo, Prince of Altamura, second son of Ferrante, arrived in Rome to congratulate the new Pope and offer him the obedience of Naples. He was magnificently entertained by Cardinal Giuliano della Rovere during his stay. There was every outward manifestation of good-will between the Pope and Don Federigo; but difficulties had already begun to arise. Federigo besought the Pope to side with Naples in a family matter. Mathias Corvinus, King of Hungary, had married Beatrice, an illegitimate daughter of King Ferrante. On the death of Mathias in 1490, Beatrice lent her influence to procure the Hungarian succession for Wladislaf, King of Bohemia, on condition that he married her in return. Wladislaf succeeded to the Hungarian crown, but sought a dispensation from his promise of marriage. Don Federigo begged the Pope to refuse this dispensation, and when Alexander VI. refused to make any promise in the matter, Federigo was aggrieved.

It is not surprising that Alexander VI. was not over anxious to please the King of Naples. He had received the news of a transaction which he could not look upon without alarm, and which was clearly due to Neapolitan intrigues. On the death of Innocent VIII. his son Franceschetto Cibò had withdrawn to Florence, to live under the protection of his brother-in-law, Piero de' Medici. Franceschetto had no ambition beyond that of leading a comfortable life, and did not care for the responsibilities attaching to a baron in the States of the Church. He had not aspired to found a principality, and at his father's death he hastened to dispose of lands which Innocent VIII. had conferred upon him, the lordships of Cervetri and Anguillara.

As early as September 3, he sold them for 40,000 ducats to
Virginio Orsini; and Piero de' Medici negotiated the bargain
between his two brothers-in-law.[1] As Virginio Orsini was a
firm adherent of Ferrante of Naples, it was clear that Ferrante
had supplied the money for this purchase. Alexander VI. was
justified in objecting to this unauthorised transfer of lands held
under the Pope; and Ludovico Il Moro regarded with suspicion
a transaction which opened up the road from Naples to Tuscany,
and which showed a good understanding between Piero de'
Medici and Ferrante.

In the delicate equilibrium of Italian politics a small matter sufficed to bring powerful parties into antagonism. Alexander VI., urged by Cardinal Ascanio Sforza, protested against
the transfer of Cervetri and Anguillara. The cause of Naples
was espoused by Cardinal Giuliano della Rovere, who had been
the Neapolitan candidate for the Papacy, and who was supported
by the Colonna and the Orsini. Giuliano was opposed to
Ascanio Sforza, and was resolved that one or other of them
should quit the Curia. Hostile feeling went so far between
them, and Alexander VI. was so clearly allied with Ascanio,
that Giuliano suspected the Pope of forging some plot to ruin
his reputation and deprive him of his dignities,[2] and did
not consider Rome a safe place of residence. At the end of
January 1493 he withdrew to his bishopric of Ostia, where he
surrounded himself with armed men. This was a direct menace,
as Ostia commanded the mouth of the Tiber and might cut
off supplies from Rome; and Alexander VI. was alarmed at
this hostile demonstration. One day, when he was going to
picnic at Innocent VIII.'s villa of La Magliana, he was so terrified by the sound of some cannon which were fired in honour
of his approach, that he returned in haste to Rome, amid the
murmurs of his attendants, who were disappointed of their
dinner.[3] He suspected a landing of Neapolitan troops at Ostia,
and an attempt to seize his person.

[1] Franceschetto Cibò had married Maddelena de' Medici, and Piero de'
Medici had married Alfonsina degli Orsini.

[2] So writes the Florentine Valori Jan. 20, 1493: ' el Papa da alchuni è stato
confortato che a volere potere disponere del Collegio liberamente. Era necessario che sua Sanctità pigliassi qualche forma di torre riputazione a Vincola.'
Thuasne's Burchard, ii. 644.

[3] Infessura, 1245.

Ludovico Il Moro, on his side, was alarmed at the alliance between Florence and Naples, and sought to meet it by a league between the Pope, Milan, and Venice. Ferrante of Naples saw, with the wisdom of long experience, the dangers which would follow a breach of the peace of Italy. He was willing to gather together a party which might make him formidable to the Pope; but he hastened to adopt the position of mediator and do away all causes of dispute. He sent envoys to Alexander VI., urging the cause of peace. He sent envoys to Florence, even to Milan, to plead for pacific counsels, and to make proposals for a peaceful settlement of the question of Anguillara.[1] Alexander VI. so far listened to Ferrante as to propose a marriage of his young son Giofrè with Donna Lucrezia, a granddaughter of Ferrante. But either Alexander VI. did not trust Ferrante, or he wished to terrify him further, or the influence of Milan was still too strong in Rome. He gathered troops and prepared for war; he fortified the walls between the Vatican and the Castle of S. Angelo. Ludovico Sforza pursued his negotiations for a league; and Venice was won over by the dread of a predominance of the power of Naples in North Italy, it Ferrante succeeded in ousting Ludovico in favour of Gian Galeazzo, who would be entirely dependent on Naples. On April 25 Alexander VI., accompanied by an armed escort, celebrated mass in the church of S. Marco, and after mass published his league with Venice, the Duke of Milan, Siena, Mantua, and Ferrara. The bells of the Roman churches were rung in sign of joy, and Rome wore a military aspect.

When the news reached Naples, the king's eldest son, Alfonso wished to unite at once with Piero de' Medici, arouse the Orsini and Colonna, and attack Rome. The more cautious Ferrante checked a plan which would have plunged Italy into confusion. Yet he saw only too clearly the dangers of an alliance between Ludovico Sforza and France, and in his alarm he turned for help to the Spanish king. He wrote a long invective against the Pope, who so terrorised his Cardinals that they dared not speak the truth, and dreaded lest they should be driven away from Rome like Cardinal Rovere; Alexander VI. had found Italy in profound peace, and had already created .

[1] The details of these negotiations are given in Trinchera, *Codice Aragonese*, ii. 251 &c.

discord. Ferrante gave his own account of the Pope's policy and then proceeded, 'He leads a life that is abhorred by all, without respect to the seat which he holds. He cares for nothing else save to aggrandise his children by fair means or foul. From the beginning of his pontificate he has done nothing else than plunge us into disquietude.'[1] Ferrante showed his foresight; he had penetrated the Pope's policy of regaining the possessions of the Holy See, and of promoting the interests of his children. He saw that Alexander VI. was resolute and unscrupulous, and he found out the weak point in his position when he urged against him the disorders of his private life.

Award of
Alexander
VI. about
the New
World.
May, 1493.
Spain was at this time connected with the Pope about a most momentous matter. The Genoese, Cristoforo Colombo, arrived at the Spanish court in March 1493, with the astounding news of the discovery of a new continent. The mediæval love of adventure, which found its expression in the crusading spirit, had taken a new shape under the inspiration of the awakening curiosity of the Renaissance; and Colombo had gone forth in quest of new regions which might be added to Christendom. The ardour of the explorer, strengthened by the fervour of religious zeal, had led to a great discovery. The idea of the New World filled men's minds with strange excitement, and Colombo set out again to extend the field of knowledge.

Meanwhile Ferdinand and Isabella thought it wise to secure a title to all that might ensue from their new discovery. The Pope, as Vicar of Christ, was held to have authority to dispose of lands inhabited by the heathen; and by papal Bulls the discoveries of Portugal along the African coast had been secured. The Portuguese showed signs of urging claims to the New World, as being already conveyed to them by the papal grants previously issued in their favour. To remove all cause of dispute the Spanish monarchs at once had recourse to Alexander VI., who issued two Bulls on May 4 and 5 to determine the respective rights of Spain and Portugal.[2] In the first, the Pope granted to the Spanish monarchs and their heirs all lands discovered or hereafter to be discovered in the western ocean. In the second,

---

[1] Trinchera, *Cod. Aragon.* ii. pt. 241, dated June 9, 1493.

[2] Raynaldus, 1493, § 18, &c. An interesting description of the original map illustrating the division, now preserved in the College of the Propaganda, is given in the *Times* of Oct. 14, 1885.

he defined his grant to mean all lands that might be discovered west and south of an imaginary line, drawn from the North to the South Pole, at the distance of a hundred leagues westward of the Azores and Cape de Verd Islands. In the light of our present knowledge we are amazed at this simple means of disposing of a vast extent of the earth's surface. We have to remind ourselves that no one grasped the importance of the new impulse which Europe had received; and the Pope's solution of the difficulties likely to arise between Spain and Portugal was sufficiently accurate for the knowledge of his age.

A Pope who had shown himself so ready to reward the Christian zeal of Spain had no cause to dread any untoward results to himself from Spanish intervention, though the Spanish rulers looked on him with no good will. 'They fear,' writes Peter Martyr, 'lest his cupidity, his ambition, or, what is more serious, his tenderness towards his children, should expose the Christian religion to peril.'[1] Their fears were not without good grounds. Alexander VI. was occupied in using the position which he held in Italian politics as a means of furthering the interests of his children. He had already striven to provide for his daughter Lucrezia, by betrothing her in 1491, at the age of thirteen, to a Spaniard, Don Cherubin de Centelles. Scarcely was the betrothal accomplished before Cardinal Borgia found a better husband in another Spaniard, Don Gasparo da Procida, to whom she was contracted in the same year. But his elevation to the papal dignity enabled Alexander VI. to look still higher for a son-in-law; the contract with Don Gasparo was dissolved, and Alexander VI. used his alliance with the Sforza to wed his daughter to Giovanni Sforza, lord of Pesaro. The marriage was celebrated in the Vatican on June 12, in the presence of the Pope, ten Cardinals, and the chief nobles of Rome, whose wives, to the number of a hundred and fifty, were also invited. The marriage feast was magnificent; the Roman ladies were presented by the Pope with silver cups full of sweetmeats, which were in many cases thrown into their bosoms;[2] magnificent gifts were offered to the bridal pair. After the banquet there was a ball, and

Marriage of Lucrezia Borgia to Giovanni Sforza, June 12, 1493.

---

[1] To Ascanio Sforza, Sep. 26, 1492; *Ep.* v. 119.

[2] 'Et hoc ad honorem et laudem omnipotentis Dei et ecclesiæ Romanæ,' adds Infessura, 1246.

the Pope and his companions spent the whole night in this splendid entertainment, which was varied by comedies of a questionable character.[1] The Pope married his daughter with the splendour becoming his secular greatness; but he gave, at the same time, an open manifestation of disregard for ecclesiastical discipline, and certainly set the tongues of men wagging with hints of graver irregularities.[2]

A Spanish ambassador in Rome. June, 1493.

Three days after this festivity the Spanish envoy, Don Diego Lopez de Haro, arrived in Rome to offer the obedience of the Spanish monarchs. He had many questions to discuss with the Pope. There were points to be settled about the discovery of the New World and the steps to be taken for its evangelisation; and Ferdinand the Catholic needed grants of Church revenues to enable him to carry on his crusading projects, which he hoped to extend as far as the recovery of the Holy Land. Moreover, Spain was aggrieved at the reception into the Papal States of the refugee Jews or Moors who were driven from Spain by the stringency of the Inquisition. The Spaniards, in the assertion of their nationality, were desirous to rid themselves of all foreign elements, and employed the Inquisition for that purpose. The crowds of luckless Marrani, as they were called, awakened the compassion of the Italians who saw them arrive on their coasts;[3] and many of them came to Rome, where they were subjected to no persecution. A crowd encamped outside the Appian Gate, and were the means of bringing an outbreak of plague into the city. The papal tolerance was displeasing to the Spanish rulers, and the ambassador expressed his wonder that the Pope, who was the head of the Christian faith, should receive into his city those who had been driven from Spain as enemies of the Christian faith. We do not find that Alexander VI. paid much heed to these remonstrances; the Papacy in its spirit of tolerance was far in advance of public opinion.[4]

---

[1] The account of Infessura is corroborated and supplemented by the despatch of the Ferrarese envoy Boccaccio to the Duke, dated Rome, June 13, in Gregorovius, *Lucrezia Borgia*, Appendix No. 10.

[2] Infessura, in Eccard, ii. 2012, says : 'et multa alia dicta sunt quae hic non scribo, vel si sunt incredibilia sunt.'

[3] See Senegara, Muratori, xxiv. 531–32.

[4] Writers who themselves regard toleration as a virtue, sneer at the papal treatment of Prince Djem and the Marrani, as proofs of papal indifference to

The most important object, however, of the Spanish ambassador was to urge on Alexander VI. the maintenance of the peace of Italy, as the means of preventing French interference. To make his intervention more powerful the envoy set forth ecclesiastical grievances which needed remedy at the hands of the Pope. He pointed out the extortions of the Curia, the abuse of dispensations for pluralities, the heedlessness shown in ecclesiastical appointments and such like matters, which since the days of the Council of Constance had been standing complaints against the Papacy, to be urged in all negotiations for other purposes.[1] The real point which Spain wished to press on the Pope was peace with Naples. Ludovico Il Moro, though strong in his league with the Pope and Venice, did not trust much to the sincerity of his allies. He carried on a double policy, and negotiated with Charles VIII., whose fancy was so fired by the Milanese ambassador, Belgioso, that he entered into a secret agreement with Ludovico, who, though warned of the dangers of his course, trusted that a disturbance in Italian affairs would turn out to his own profit. He wished to be prepared against all risks.

The pleadings of the Spanish ambassador were enforced by a hostile demonstration on the part of Naples. Don Federigo of Altamura came to Ostia with eleven galleys, and was welcomed by Cardinal Rovere, Virginio Orsini, and the Colonna. Alexander VI. agreed to negotiate, and a truce was made. Don Federigo came to Rome, and was followed on July 24 by Cardinal Rovere and Virginio Orsini. Rome rejoiced at the expectations of peace which the representations of the Spanish envoy at length succeeded in making. Virginio Orsini was allowed to keep the castles which he had bought from Franceschetto Cibò on condition that he again paid the purchase money, 40,000 ducats, to the Pope; and peace with Naples was cemented by a marriage between the Pope's son Giofrè and Sancia, a daughter of Alfonso. As Giofrè was only thirteen years old, the marriage could not take place immediately; but it was agreed that he should go to Naples and receive his wife's dowry, the principality of Squillace. This agreement with Naples was

religion, following in this Infessura. I do not consider this fair, as the Papacy in the Middle Ages always showed a tolerant spirit in matters of opinion.

[1] The authority for this is Infessura, *Eccard*, ii. 2013.

only concluded when the ambassador of Charles VIII., Perron de Basche, who had been sent to try the dispositions of the Italian powers towards the French invasion of Naples, arrived in Rome. He came too late to win over Alexander VI., and was dismissed with vague admonitions.

Creation of
twelve
Cardinals,
September
20, 1493.

Ferrante of Naples rejoiced that by his alliance with the Pope all difficulties were now at an end, and the schemes of France were baffled; but he wished to be sure of the Pope's good intentions, and urged the withdrawal of papal favour from Cardinal Ascanio Sforza. In this he was seconded by Cardinal Rovere, who showed all his uncle's resoluteness in prosecuting his animosities. Alexander VI. adopted a policy of conciliation; he did not dismiss Ascanio, but he showed signs of favour to Rovere. He wished to unite the Cardinal College that he might decorously accomplish a creation of new Cardinals. Accordingly he used his opportunity when both parties had much to hope from his favour in the future, and on September 20 created twelve new Cardinals without encountering any decided opposition to his choice, though it is said that only seven of the old Cardinals gave their assent.[1]

Cesare
Borgia.

The new Cardinals were fairly chosen from various parts of Christendom. Amongst them was an Englishman, John Morton, Archbishop of Canterbury, a Frenchman, a Spaniard, Raymund Perrault, Bishop of Gurk, a favourite of Maximilian, Ippolito d' Este, son of Duke Ercole of Ferrara and of Leonora, daughter of Ferrante of Naples; and the rest represented various Italian powers. But two of the new Cardinals owed their position to the personal favour of the Pope. One was the Pope's son, Cesare Borgia,[2] a youth of eighteen, who had been carefully educated at Rome, and afterwards had studied at the Universities of Perugia and Pisa. Innocent VIII. conferred upon him the bishopric of Pampluna, and Alexander VI. that

---

[1] This is on the authority of Infessura. Mariana, *Hist. Hispana*, xxvi. says: 'Contra hiscere nemo cardinalium, cum quibus rem communicavit, ausus est.'

[2] Infessura and Mariana both say that Cesare was legitimatised as the son of Domenico Arignano, to whom Vanozza had been married. But Cesare never bore the name of Arignano, nor do we find elsewhere any notice of the marriage of Vanozza to this supposed parent. Moreover the dispensation of Sixtus IV., quoted p. 161 n. 1, was sufficient without any farther act on the Pope's part.

of Valencia which he had held himself before his pontificate. Cesare was regarded as a young man of great promise, the rising hope of the Borgia family.

Another creation which gave rise to greater scandal was that of Alessandro Farnese, who afterwards became Pope Paul III. The Farnese family had not hitherto been of much importance in Rome. They took their name from the Isola Farnese, a castle built on the ruins of the ancient Veii, but had not made themselves important amongst the dynasties of small barons who held the Tuscan Campagna. Alessandro Farnese was, however, a man of some capacity, and was Protonotary of the Church. He owed his good fortune under Alexander VI. to his sister Giulia, who in 1489 married Orsino Orsini, whose mother Adriana was a relative of Alexander VI., and brought up his daughter Lucrezia. Giulia was a great favourite with the Pope, and her influence founded the fortunes of the Farnese family in Rome, so that Alessandro was mockingly called 'Il Cardinale della gonella,' the petticoat Cardinal. The relations of Alexander VI. to Giulia were a matter of common rumour, and men openly spoke of her as the Pope's mistress.[1] We might hesitate to believe the voice of rumour on such a matter, in an age when men's tongues were unrestrained by any thoughts of decency. But a letter written by the Pope's own hand to his daughter Lucrezia, in July 1494, expresses the greatest concern at Giulia's departure from Rome without his express permission, and rebukes Lucrezia for her want of consideration to himself in having allowed this departure to

---

[1] Infessura, *Eccard*, ii. 2015, calls her 'ejus concubina,' as does Matarazzo, *Cronica di Perugia* in *Archivio Storico*, xvi. (1ᵐᵃ serie) pt. 2, p. 3. A Florentine notice, 'Avvisi del tempo di Papa Alessandro VI.' of the date 1494, quoted by Gregorovius, *Geschichte der Stadt Rom*, vii. 340, calls her 'sposa di Cristo.' A curious document, *Dyalogus Mortis et pontificis laborantis febre*, 1500, preserved by Marin Sanuto, in Gregorovius, *Lucrezia Borgia*, has the following doggrel lines:

> *P.* Julia, me miserum cur non defendis, amavi
> Si te corde magis ? *M.* Digna lenone satis.
> Nunc morere et te non defendet Julia, neque (namque ?)
> Enixa est utero terque quaterque tibi.

The cause of the creation of Alessandro Farnese was so currently believed in later times that it was quoted as a reason for his policy, when he succeeded to the Papacy as Paul III. Thus the Venetian envoy Soriano in 1535 gives it as a reason why Paul III. was averse to summoning a Council: 'Nè anco sua Santità manca di opposizione; chè la sua promozione al cardinalato non fu

take place during his absence.[1] Moreover, the new Cardinal Alessandro, and the Florentine Lorenzo Pucci, his brother-in-law, who also became a Cardinal later, certainly believed in the connexion between Giulia and the Pope. They recognised a daughter of Giulia, born in 1492, as the Pope's child, and speculated as early as 1493 on matrimonial projects for this infant. Pucci paid Giulia a visit and was struck by the resemblance which her daughter bore to the strongly-marked features of the Pope; Giulia's husband was, in his opinion, amply compensated for his equivocal position by a few castles near Basanello.[2] It is difficult to doubt this evidence. Alexander VI., though now of the age of sixty-two, still possessed the power of 'drawing women to him as a magnet draws iron.' Giulia Farnese lived under his protection, and used her influence to promote the interests of her family. It was regarded as natural by the Cardinals that such should be the case, and no one in Italy was particularly scandalised at this state of things. It was universally recognised that the Pope was an Italian prince, and that his policy largely depended on arrangements for his domestic comfort.

The political condition of Italy received a further shock by

molto onesta, essendo proceduta per causa oscena; ciò è dall' amore e dalla familiarità che aveva papa Alessandro VI. con la signora Giulia sua sorella.' Alberi, *Relazioni Venete*, 2nd ser. vol. iii. 314. In the *Rivista Cristiana*, ii. p. 261, is a letter of Fra Berardino to Paul III.: 'Di poi tu dei ricordare con che arti pervenisti alla dignità di cardinalato dal quale il Collegio de' Cardinali ti ributtò tre volte, ma havendo di poi la tua sorella madama Julia mandato un piatto di maccheroni alla Romanesca a l'apa Alessandro et mandatoli a dire che proprio era un *maccherone* [Roman for 'a silly fellow '] a lassarti in ciò contradire da Cardinali, giurando non voler andare mai più dove egli fusse, nel concistorio venente, possendo più l'appetito che la raggione in lui, indebitamente ti creò Cardinale.'

[1] The letter is printed by Ugolini, *Storia dei Conti e Duchi d'Urbino*, ii. Doc. n. 13: 'Veramente in questa faccenda della partenza di madama Adriana e di Giulia, il signor Giovanni e tu avete avuto poco rispetto e considerazione verso di noi. Le lasciate partire senza espressa licenza nostra; mentre avreste dovuto pensare che un repentino allontanamento, senza nostra saputa, non ci poteva che sommamente dispiacere.'

[2] Letter of Lorenzo Pucci to his brother Gianozzo, from Rome, Dec. 24, 1493: 'Chostei è pure figliuola del Papa, nipote di Cardinale e figliuola putativa del Sig^re Orsini al quale nostro Sig^re darà anchora 3 o 4 chastella sono presso a Basanello;' 'volse ch' io vedessi la fanciulla la quale è gia grande et, ut mihi videtur, est similis Pontifici, adeo ut vere ex ejus semine orta dici possit.' Gregorovius, *Lucrezia Borgia*, Doc. No. 11.

the death of Ferrante of Naples on January 25, 1494. He was seventy years old and had reigned for thirty-five years. Cruel and treacherous as Ferrante had shown himself, he was not a harsh ruler to the people, though he ruthlessly crushed the barons. He had great political experience and had learned caution in his long and tortuous career; he was profoundly impressed with the evils likely to follow on French intervention in Italy, and his last efforts had been directed to prevent it. Since the death of Lorenzo de' Medici he was the only Italian who deserved the name of statesman. He died regretted, not so much for any merits of his own as from dread of his successor Alfonso II., whose violent and brutal character had created universal terror.

CHAP. VI.

Death of Ferrante of Naples, January 25, 1494.

The death of Ferrante gave Charles VIII. an opportunity to advance formally his claims on the Neapolitan kingdom, and Alexander VI. at first made a show of drawing to the French side. On February 1, he issued a brief taking Charles VIII. under his protection and authorising him to come with an army to Rome on his way to a Crusade against the Turks.[1] No mention was made of Naples; but Charles VIII.'s claims were notorious. The French ambassadors, supported by a strong party among the Cardinals, protested against Alfonso II.'s investiture with the Neapolitan kingdom; but Alexander VI. had much to gain from Alfonso's gratitude, and perhaps saw the dangers of a French invasion, though he was willing to use it as a threat when his own purposes required. He agreed to recognise Alfonso II., and appointed a legate to confer on him the Neapolitan crown, whereon the French ambassador appealed to a future Council. Cardinal Rovère now abandoned the cause of Naples, when Naples was allied with the Pope; filled with distrust and hatred of Alexander VI. he again retired to Ostia.[2] In April he took ship to Genoa and thence made his way to the French king, who received him with respect. He bitterly complained of Alexander VI., and his personal animosity led him to aid the foreigners to enter Italy,

Alexander VI. recognises Alfonso II.

---

[1] It is given in Malipiero's *Annali Veneti*, p. 404.

[2] Sanuto, *La Spedizione di Carlo VIII.* 42, says that Rovere fled in consequence of a plot of the Pope against his life, but this is not mentioned elsewhere.

a step the evil effects of which he afterwards vainly strove to counteract.

Alfonso II. was crowned in Naples on May 7, and his daughter's marriage with Giofrè Borgia was celebrated with pomp and rejoicings. Giofrè was made Prince of Squillace, with a revenue of 40,000 ducats; his eldest brother, the Duke of Gandia, was made Prince of Tricarico; and Cardinal Cesare was enriched by Neapolitan benefices. Ostia, the stronghold of the rebellious Cardinal Rovere, was captured by the papal forces. Thus Alexander VI. had reduced his enemies and enriched his family. But his arrangements had no permanent foundation; while he developed his plans Charles VIII. was gathering his army.

Alexander VI. and Ludovico Sforza had been willing to use the French invasion as a threat; it was rapidly becoming a reality. Yet Alexander VI. cannot fairly be accused of having caused this beginning of the ruin of Italy, and when it actually came to pass he did his best to stay it. But he was no wiser and no more disinterested than the other Italian princes of the time; he alternately invoked and dissuaded to suit his own purposes. A resolute attitude, a moderating spirit at the beginning of his pontificate, might have averted the impending disaster. Italy had been only too successful in enchaining the Papacy and bringing it entirely within the sphere of its moral and political ideas. The secularisation of the Papacy had become so complete that, at a crisis in the fate of Italy, the Pope had no higher ideas than the aggrandisement of his own family, and no greater political influence than a secondary Italian power.

CHAPTER VII.

CHARLES VIII. IN ITALY.

1494–95.

THE Italian expedition of Charles VIII. marks a new epoch in the politics of Europe. While Italy was busied with the emancipation of men's minds and the organisation of intellectual life, a great political change was passing over Europe. France and England, after a long period of destructive warfare and internal troubles, had attained a national unity which they had never known before. Spain, by united action against the Infidels, had gained the elements of a strong national life. Even in distracted Germany the long reign of Frederick III. had made the Austrian house the centre of German affairs ; and Frederick's son Maximilian was spreading into outlying regions the claims and influence of the House of Austria. Everywhere there were signs of new and powerful political organisations centring round a monarchy. As Italy found that the intellectual forms of the Middle Ages were no longer fit to contain the new wine of man's spirit, so other lands drifted away from the mediæval conception of politics. Feudalism was crumbling ; and the different classes in the State were being brought into more direct connexion with the Crown. There was a growing consciousness of national unity, which was the sure forerunner of a wish for national aggrandisement.

France was the first nation which realised her new strength. Charles VII. reconquered France from the English ; but he owed his conquest greatly to the help of the Dukes of Brittany and Burgundy. Louis XI. was aided by fortune as much as by his own cleverness in his endeavours to make himself really King of France. The Dukes of Berry, Burgundy, Anjou, and Brittany died without male heirs ; Louis XI. inherited Berry

BOOK
V.

from his brother, and managed to gain from the Burgundian
heritage the towns on the Somme and the Duchy of Burgundy.
René of Anjou died in 1480 and left Anjou to the French
crown; his other possessions, Provence and the Angevin
claim to Naples, he bequeathed to his nephew Charles of
Maine, who died next year, after having instituted Louis XI.
his universal legatee. At the accession of Charles VIII. Brittany only remained as a bulwark of feudalism against the might
of the Crown. The young King's nearest relative, the Duke
of Orleans, made common cause with the Duke of Brittany;
but the royal army was successful; the Duke of Orleans was
imprisoned, and the Duke of Brittany died of chagrin. There
were still elements of discord, as England threatened to interfere in Brittany, and Maximilian was betrothed to its heiress.
But the young king Charles VIII. in 1491 assured the internal
peace and accomplished the unity of France by freeing Louis of
Orleans from his prison and treating him as a friend, while by
marriage with Anne of Brittany he united the last great fief to
the French crown. France entered upon a period of prosperity
unknown before, and its King was eager to find a field for his
energies.

French
designs on
Naples.

The assertion of the old claims of the House of Anjou on
Naples opened up a prospect which might well have turned a
wiser head than that of Charles VIII. With them was united
the title to the kingdom of Jerusalem; Naples was the stepping-
stone to a great crusading expedition, in which the French
king, strong in his national forces, might stand at the head of
Europe and strike a deadly blow at the common enemy of
Christendom. The old spirit of adventure joined with the new
desire for national aggrandisement, and still strove to accommo-
date itself to the religious ideal of the past. The policy of
France rested on a visionary basis.

Charles VIII., however, would never have been able to
realise his dream if Italy had not invited him. The views
of Italian statesmen were bounded by the artificial equilibrium of Italian politics. They were accustomed to a system
of constantly changing combinations depending on the interests of the moment. They played a game of ceaseless check
and counter check till they lost all sense of the reality of
political forces. They had used the threat of French inter-

vention as a weapon in extremities till they had forgotten its actual meaning. Ludovico Sforza regarded it as a means of producing new combinations of political forces in Italy, and did not scruple to use it for his own purposes. But none of the other powers offered any decided resistance when the project began to take definite form. Venice was coldly cautious; Alexander VI. dallied with the idea as a means of driving Naples into close alliance; Cardinal Rovere, in his hatred of the Pope, fled to France, and added his entreaties to those of Ludovico Sforza. Italy was devoid of national feeling, and its statesmen, in spite of their boasted astuteness, knew nothing of the real forces which lay beyond the borders of Italy. The substitution of cleverness for principle was Italy's ruin.

CHAP. VII.

Before undertaking his expedition to Italy, Charles VIII. was careful to protect himself against a coalition of his enemies. In 1492 he made peace with Henry VII. of England, and undertook to pay him for all his claims. In 1493 he made peace with Spain, and ceded the frontier provinces of Roussillon and Cerdogne which were matters of dispute. He even mollified Maximilian, whom he had robbed of his bride, by giving up the claims of France to parts of the Burgundian heritage. He made large sacrifices of the interests of France that he might feel himself free to prosecute the splendid enterprise on which his heart was set. In March 1494 Charles VIII. went to Lyons, where he spent his money in festivities and lived a life of pleasure that seemed a strange prelude to a warlike expedition. His counsellors strove to dissuade him from his purpose, and his envoys in Italy reported that the alliance between the Pope, Naples, and Piero de' Medici was firm; Venice remained neutral; only the Duke of Savoy, the Marquis of Montserrat, the Marquis of Saluzzo, and Duke Ercole of Ferrara, declared themselves friendly to France. The rest of Italy was cautiously waiting to join the winning side. Even Ludovico Sforza hesitated, till the military preparations of Alfonso II. showed him that his ruin was at hand unless he gained the help of France.

Preparations of Charles VIII.

When the danger from France was imminent Alexander VI. and Alfonso II. cemented their alliance by an interview on July 14, at Vicovaro, where they resolved on the measures to be taken for their common protection. Alexander VI.

Alfonso II.'s measures of defence. July 1494.

was anxious for the safety of his own dominions; and it was agreed that Alfonso II. should wait with his troops on the border of the Abruzzi, while Virginio Orsini should defend the Papal States; Alfonso's son, Ferrantino, was to advance through the Romagna towards Milan, drive out Ludovico, and occupy the French in Lombardy; meanwhile the Neapolitan fleet was to surprise Genoa and command the northern coast. The plan was good enough in itself, but it ought to have been devised sooner and carried out with promptitude. As it was, the French fleet assembled to defend Genoa, and the French army crossed the Alps to succour Milan, before Naples had struck a blow.

Don Federigo, Alfonso's brother, finding Genoa too strong to be surprised, began an onslaught on the towns along the Riviera. His first attempt on Porto Venere, which commands the promontory of the Gulf of Spezia, was an entire failure. The inhabitants made a resolute resistance, hurled down stones on their assailants and repulsed them with great loss; so that Federigo was driven to retire to Livorno to repair his fleet. Charles VIII. sent Louis Duke of Orleans with some Swiss troops to Genoa, where a French fleet was assembling. Not till September 8 did Federigo again advance. He took Rapallo, a little town about twenty miles from Genoa, where a body of Genoese exiles landed and took up a strong position. The Duke of Orleans attacked them by land and sea and completely routed them, while Federigo's fleet lay idle at Sestri di Levante. A hundred of the vanquished were left dead on the field, and Rapallo was sacked and pillaged by the Swiss. Italy was amazed at warfare conducted on these bloodthirsty principles. The battles of condottieri had been exercises of strategy, in which prisoners were taken for ransom, and no one was slain unless he had the misfortune to be trampled to death as he lay on the ground. The sack of Rapallo convinced Italy that she had to do with assailants who meant to carry on war in earnest. The immediate result of this engagement was that Federigo returned with his fleet to Naples, leaving the sea open to the French.

On September 8 Charles VIII. crossed the Alps and next day arrived at Asti, where he was welcomed by Ludovico Sforza, and received the news of the victory at Rapallo. Charles VIII.

was young, inexperienced, badly educated, and destitute of
military talents. He scarcely knew what were his plans, and
he had no money to pay his troops. Ludovico Sforza advised
a rapid advance southwards as a means of withdrawing the
Neapolitan forces from the Romagna, and furnished money to
the King for this purpose. An attack of small-pox rendered
Charles VIII. unable to move for a while ; but early in October
he advanced to Pavia and paid a visit to the luckless Duke Gian
Galeazzo. The sight of his helplessness, his bodily weakness,
and his entreaties that the King would take care of his infant
son, moved the compassion of the French ; and Ludovico Sforza
saw with terror that he was regarded with little favour by the
French nobles. He hurried the King from Pavia to Piacenza,
whither, on October 21, came the news that Gian Galeazzo
was dead. Everyone accused Ludovico of having poisoned his
nephew ; he hurried to Milan, and by a packed assembly of
his own partisans was requested to assume the ducal sceptre.
He had now gained all that he had schemed for ; he was Duke
of Milan, and Naples was occupied with France. So soon as
France had terrified Naples sufficiently, Ludovico had no further
interest in his ally.

The French successes soon found an echo in Rome, and
troubled Alexander VI. The barons of the French party, the
Colonna and Savelli, prompted by Ascanio Sforza, gathered
their troops and threatened the city. On September 18 Fabrizio
Colonna seized Ostia in the name of Cardinal Rovere and
hoisted the French flag, while French galleys from Genoa brought
reinforcements and anchored off the mouth of the Tiber. This
was a serious menace to Rome, and crippled the Neapolitan
forces in the Romagna, as they dared not advance against Milan
through fear of leaving Rome unprotected. It was not long
before Caterina, the widow of Girolamo Riario, declared for France
at Imola, and so made the position of the army in the Romagna
doubly insecure. Alexander VI. was seriously alarmed, but
tried to put on a bold face, and on October 6 issued a proclamation against those who had seized Ostia and demanded its
restitution under pain of excommunication.[1] However, he
showed his terror by removing Djem into the Castle of S. Angelo
for safe keeping, and sent Cardinal Piccolomini as an envoy to

---

[1] Burchard, ii. 189 &c.

Charles VIII., who refused to receive him, saying that he hoped
to meet the Pope himself in Rome.

If Alexander VI. trembled at the occupation of Ostia, he
was still more terrified at the unexpected movements of the
French army. The Duke of Calabria had taken up a strong
position at Cesena to check the French advance; but Charles
VIII., by the advice of Ludovico Sforza, who wished that a
blow should be struck against his enemy, Florence, chose the
more difficult road over the Apennines in preference to the
easier road by Bologna. By this means he kept near his fleet.

The state of affairs in Florence was critical, and Piero de'
Medici showed none of his father's sagacity. He forgot
Lorenzo's advice: 'Remember that you are nothing more than
a Florentine citizen as I am.' Lorenzo was conscious that he
had created a position which was difficult for his successor to
fill. He himself had concealed the extent of his power and
wore the semblance of an influential citizen; but his marriage
with Clarice Orsini, his connexion with the Roman nobles, the
dignity of the cardinalate which he had won for his son Giovanni, and his own far-reaching influence, combined to create
in Piero's mind an undue sense of the greatness of the Medicean
house; so that he pursued his own policy without identifying
Florence with it. The alliance of Florence with France was of
long standing and could not easily be set aside. When Piero
refused to abandon the cause of Naples, Charles VIII. banished
the Florentine merchants from his kingdom and thereby struck
a blow at the material interests of the city. The old republican
party began to revive; the enemies of the Medici held up their
heads. Even Piero's cousins, Giovanni and Lorenzino de' Medici,
made their way to Charles VIII. at Piacenza and besought him
to free Florence from Piero's yoke; they affirmed that the
Florentine people were on the side of France, and that Piero
alone was the King's enemy.

Perhaps the strongest support of the French cause in
Florence was to be found in the preaching of Fra Girolamo
Savonarola. After Lorenzo's death Savonarola became more
and more convinced that his mission lay in Florence; as the
heart was the centre of man, so, he said, was Florence the
centre of Italy, and in Florence he resolved to stay. The
Convent of S. Marco was subject to the Dominican Congrega-

tion of Lombardy; and Savonarola, as its prior, was subordinate
to the commands of the superiors of the Congregation and so
might easily be silenced. Wishing to obtain an independent
position, he urged the separation of the Tuscan Congregation
from that of Lombardy, and in this he was aided by Piero de'
Medici. Piero did not foresee any evil results from Savonarola's
preaching, and thought that the existence of a separate Congregation of Tuscany would add to the dignity of Florence;
perhaps, too, he was willing to further any scheme which might
mark his opposition to Ludovico Sforza. The question was
referred to Alexander VI. early in 1493, when the Pope was
entirely on the side of Milan; and at first the application of
Florence, being opposed by Ludovico Sforza, had little success.
But it was warmly favoured by Cardinal Caraffa, who prevailed
on Alexander VI. to sign, on May 22, a Bull which accomplished
the separation. Savonarola had himself transferred to the
Tuscan Congregation, was re-elected Prior of S. Marco, and
was afterwards chosen Vicar-General of the Tuscan Congregation. By this means he was subject to no ecclesiastical authority
save that of the Pope and the General of the Dominican Order.
This free position Savonarola used to work a reform in the
discipline of the Convent of S. Marco, so as to bring it back
to the original rule of S. Dominic. In this reform he carried
the brethren with him, and his convent became the centre of a
genuine religious life.

In the Advent season of 1493 Savonarola resumed his preaching in Florence, with increased reputation amongst the people
and increased confidence in his own mission. In Lent 1494 he
continued a series of expository lectures on the Book of Genesis
which he had begun in 1492. He reached the history of the
building of the Ark by Noah, and lingered over it; each plank
and nail had its mystic meaning; but the general purpose of
his discourses was to urge all men to enter the Ark of the Lord,
that they might save themselves from the coming tribulation.
Already Florence was disturbed by the expectation of the army
of Charles VIII., and Savonarola recognised in the French army
the scourge of God which was to afflict but purify the Church.
In September he resumed his preaching. At first he put forth
his visions as parables; then he tried to drop the subject,
but was haunted by sleepless nights of remorse till he felt

that he was bound to speak in obedience to God's commands. More and more he spoke like a prophet, and introduced his utterances with the phrase, 'Thus saith the Lord.' On September 21, St. Matthew's Day, he reached the text, 'Behold I bring a flood of waters upon the earth.' His hearers, excited by the news that the French had entered Italy, recognised a miraculous guidance in the preacher's subject. Amazed they listened to the preacher's denunciations, and Savonarola himself was overpowered with the sense of his own inspiration. The congregation dispersed half dead with terror.

When it was too late, Piero de' Medici perceived the perilous position in which he stood. He had drawn upon his head the animosity of the French king; he had no forces to oppose him, and the Florentines were not united. Still there was an opportunity for a vigorous resistance, as the Florentine frontier was guarded by the strong castles of Sarzanella and Pietra Santa; and the road through Lunigiana was difficult, so that a few resolute men could have held the passes and checked the advance of the French. In the uncertain state of feeling that prevailed, a check to the French army would have ruined its prestige, and the elements of a strong opposition would rapidly have gathered. At first Piero thought of resistance, and sent his brother-in-law, Paolo Orsini, to reinforce Sarzana. But he was alarmed at the sullen discontent of the Florentines, and suddenly resolved to make peace with Charles VIII. He bethought himself of the example of his father, Lorenzo, who in the crisis of his life re-established his position by a bold journey to his chief foe, Ferrante of Naples. Piero determined to imitate his father's courage, without possessing his father's wisdom. He set out from Florence, and at Pietra Santa asked Charles VIII. for a safe-conduct to his presence. When he arrived in the French camp his courage entirely deserted him; he fell on his knees before the King and besought his pardon—he professed himself ready to make amends for his errors. He was asked to recall the Florentine troops from the army in the Romagna; to give up to the King the fortresses of Sarzana, Sarzanella, Pietra Santa, Pisa, and Livorno, to be returned when the French were masters of Naples; and finally to lend the King 200,000 ducats. To these conditions Piero at once assented, though he saw before his eyes Sarzanella offering a stubborn resistance. The French in proposing these conditions never expected that they would be accepted, and were amazed at Piero's ready agreement. Though the treaty was to be signed in Florence, they demanded that the fortresses should be given up at once. Sarzana and Sarzanella were delivered to the French, and the road was now open before them. It is no wonder that the French began to consider their success as miraculous, and looked upon themselves as the instruments of God.

In Florence the news of Piero's proceedings filled the city with dismay. The Signori summoned the chief citizens to a consultation. Piero Capponi, a man whose political experience and sterling worth commanded universal esteem, rose and gave expression to the feeling which was in all men's minds. He was no orator, but went straight to the point, and one sentence in his speech became the motto of Florence. 'It is time,' he exclaimed, ' to have done with the government of children, and to recover our liberty.'[1] The Signori, moved by the popular feeling, agreed to send ambassadors to Charles VIII. to undo, if possible, the mischievous results of Piero's activity. Amongst the five were Piero Capponi and Fra Girolamo Savonarola, who was chosen because he had all the love of the people. They set out on November 6 with instructions which left it to their discretion to modify in any way the conditions which Piero had so basely accepted.[2] Next day they found Charles VIII. at Lucca, and followed him to Pisa, where with difficulty they obtained admittance to his presence; the King received them coldly and said that he would arrange the terms of peace in Florence. Savonarola stood forth, and spoke words of prophetic warning: ' Know that you are an instrument in the hands of the Lord, who has sent you to heal the woes of Italy and to reform the prostrate Church. But if you do not show yourself just and pitiful, if you do not respect the city of Florence and its people, if you forget the work for which the Lord has sent you, He will choose another in your place, and will pour upon you his wrath. I speak in the name of the Lord.'[3] These

Florentine
embassy to
Charles
VIII.,
November
6, 1491.

---

[1] Acciaiuoli, *Vita di Piero Capponi* in *Archivio Storico Italiano*, 2ª serie, vol. iv. pt. 2, 30 : ' Essere ormai tempo di uscire di governo di fanciulli e di ricuperare la libertà.'

[2] Desjardins, *Négociations de France avec la Tuscane*, i. 600.

[3] In Savonarola's *Compendium Revelationum.*

Expulsion
of the
Medici
from Flo-
rence,
November
9, 1494.

warnings harmonised with the prevailing temper of the French, who regarded their success as miraculous, and Charles VIII. was impressed by Savonarola's words, though impressions did not produce any enduring results on his feeble mind.

When Piero de' Medici heard of the despatch of this embassy he thought that it was time for him to return and watch over affairs at Florence. He returned to the city on November 8, and men believed that he meant to summon the people and compel them by his armed forces to declare him absolute lord of Florence. It was known that Paolo Orsini had advanced with his troops and was close by the Porta di San Gallo; so Florence was full of suspicion, and when Piero next morning proceeded with a large company of attendants to the Palazzo of the Signori he found the door shut, and was told that he alone would be admitted by the postern gate. Piero replied by a gesture of contempt and turned away. One of his partisans among the Signori sent a messenger to recall him. Again Piero stood at the gate; but some of the Signori descended in anger, and after a scuffle took possession of the entrance. After a wordy altercation between the Signori and Piero, the door was shut in his face. These unwonted proceedings caused a crowd to gather rapidly; there were cries to Piero, 'Go away and do not disturb the Signori;' hisses were heard, and stones began to fly. Piero stood irresolute with his drawn sword in his hand till his attendants hurried him away. He withdrew to his palace and armed himself; meanwhile his brother Cardinal Giovanni tried to raise the people with the Medicean cry of ' Palle, Palle:' no one answered, and Giovanni was obliged to return home. Piero and his brother Giuliano meanwhile made their way to the Porta di San Gallo and tried to rally the people of that suburb, who had always been partisans of the Medici. Here, also, he was unsuccessful, and lost all courage. His terror infected the troops of Paolo Orsini and they began a rapid flight towards Bologna. Cardinal Giovanni, disguised as a Franciscan friar, managed to make his escape from Florence. The three Medici brothers were coldly received at Bologna, and passed on to Venice, the home of Italian exiles. In Florence the Medici palace was sacked by the mob; the Signori set a price on Piero and Giovanni, alive or dead; every trace of the Medicean rule was rapidly abolished, and Florence exulted in the recovery of its liberty.[1]

CHAP. VII.

Causes of this revolution.

The overthrow of the Medicean rule in Florence was an event of momentous importance to Italy; yet in the prevailing excitement it attracted little notice. For sixty years Florence had been identified with the Medici house, and they had been years of great prosperity and glory. Cosimo and Lorenzo had made Florence the centre of all that was most eminently Italian, and from Florence had radiated the artistic and literary energy of Italy. Moreover, Lorenzo had established Florence as the mediating power in Italian politics, and had spread her influence in every Italian state. The overthrow of the Medicean house was a dislocation of the state-system of Italy, and the influences which produced it aimed at remodelling the Italian conceptions of life and action. The blundering of Piero was the occasion of the Florentine revolution; but the sentiment which caused it was the expression of the popular desire for a sounder and nobler life. The general uneasiness created a revival of the old republican feeling, and the preaching of Savonarola awakened moral aspirations which the rule of the Medici had lulled to sleep.

The new republic of Florence had soon to face the fact that revolutions do not come singly. The news was brought that, on the same day on which Florence expelled the Medici, Pisa had revolted from the Florentine yoke. The luckless city of Pisa since its conquest by Florence had seen its commerce decay and its glory disappear. With sullen resignation the Pisans submitted to the rule of Florence, but they regarded themselves as slaves rather than subjects. 'The Florentines,' says Machiavelli, 'were not wise enough to follow the example of the ancient Romans. They forgot that if they wished to hold Pisa they must either associate her with themselves or destroy her.'[2] Pisa, plundered and humiliated, but neither reconciled nor destroyed, only longed for an opportunity to rise against her masters. On the evening of November 9 a deputation of

Revolution at Pisa, November 10, 1494.

---

[1] See Nardi, *Storia di Firenze*, lib. i., who gives the most exact account. The *Diario* of Luca Landucci is interesting, as giving the confused impressions of an eyewitness. Many details are found in other contemporaries.

[2] *Discorsi sopra Tito Livio*, Lib. II. ch. xxiv.: 'Era necessario, volendola tenere, osservare il modo Romano: o farsela compagna, o disfarla.'

Pisan citizens approached the French king. Their spokesman, who spoke in French, set forth with passionate energy the wrongs of Pisa; he flung himself before Charles VIII. and adjured him to remember his lofty calling of liberator of Italy. A sympathetic murmur arose from the French nobles who were present; Charles VIII. was moved, and answered that he was content. He spoke without much reflection, 'understanding little what the word liberty signified,' says Commines.[1] But the Pisans knew what they meant by liberty; raising the cry ' Viva Francia!' they rushed through the city, cast into the Arno the Florentine emblem of the Marzocco, a lion on a marble column, killed the Florentine merchants who were not lucky enough to escape by flight, and seized the fortresses. The Pisan revolution was rapidly accomplished, before Charles VIII. had learned what liberty meant; he did not trouble himself about matters farther, but left a garrison of 300 French-men and passed on next day to Empoli.

Charles
VIII.
enters
Florence,
November
17, 1494.

The Florentines were too alarmed for themselves to pay much attention to the revolt of Pisa. They sent ambassadors to Charles VIII. to make terms with him; but Charles VIII. gave his usual answer that he would arrange matters in the ' gran villa,' as he called Florence with a mixture of French and Italian.[2] Florence did her best to receive with fitting honour her dangerous visitor; with ill-concealed anxiety the magistrates went forth to meet a guest whom they feared to be a foe. On the evening of November 17 the French army entered the city, and created mixed feelings of wonder and terror. First came the musicians; then thirty-six cannon drawn by sturdy horses; next the Swiss infantry with short coats of different colours, carrying their halberts of hammered iron. The Gascons followed, small and active, armed with bows and swords, and dressed in white and violet. Then came the archers, followed by 800 men-at-arms, the flower of the French nobles, mounted on powerful horses, attired in rich cloaks of silk with collars of gold. The light cavalry came

[1] Commines, livre vii. ch. 9. The proceedings of Charles VIII. in Pisa are given in Paulus Jovius, book i., and by the eyewitness, Giovanni Portoveneri, *Memoriale* in *Archivio Storico Italiano* (1ᵐᵃ serie), vi. part 2, 287, &c.

[2] Nardi, lib. i.: ' A quali rispose che dentro alla gran villa s' assetterebbero in buona forma tutte le cose.'

next; then the archers of the guard dressed in cloth of gold; and, finally, a hundred bodyguards preceded the king.

Charles VIII., mounted on a war-horse, the gift of Ludovico Sforza, advanced beneath a rich baldachino. He was armed, save his helmet, in gilt armour enriched with precious stones; over this he wore a cloak of cloth of gold, and on a white cap he wore his crown. He bore himself in military fashion, carrying his lance in rest as a token that he came as conqueror. But Charles VIII. was not a man to adorn a triumph or inspire awe by the majesty of his presence. The liberator of Italy made but an insignificant figure. A little man, with a very large head, aquiline nose, big protruding eyes and huge mouth, he had little slender legs which ended in large and deformed feet.[1] If he disappointed the Florentines when they saw him on horseback, they were still more amazed when they saw his full deformity, as he dismounted at the door of the cathedral where he went to give thanks.

Now that Charles VIII. had entered the 'gran villa' the Florentine magistrates pressed for a definite understanding. Charles considered that he had come as a conqueror; but the Florentines were not so much impressed by the exact position of his lance as to accept that view of the case. They were ready to accept Charles VIII. as a friend and ally of the Republic, but not to submit to his dictation. It soon became clear that the views of the King and the Florentine magistrates differed. Charles VIII. pressed for the restoration of Piero de' Medici, who would thus be rendered absolutely dependent on France. The Signori summoned the chief citizens to

---

[1] There are many Italian descriptions of Charles VIII. Andrea Mantegna, in Gaye, *Carteggio*, i. 326, says: 'Avere grande difformità si degli occhi grossi et sporti in fuori, si etiam peccare nel naso grande aquilino, et difforme con pochi capilli e rari in capo: la immaginazione et admirazione da tanto homo piccolo et gobo fece in me sognandomi caso.' Portoveneri, p. 288, says: 'È uomo di piccola statura, piccolissimo, con poca barba quasi rossetta, con gran faccia, magro in viso.' Cerretani adds: 'Le scarpe o pantolle di velluto nero e in modo tonde che parevano il piede d' un bue o cavallo.' 'Vedutolo a piede parve al popolo un poco diminuita la fama; perchè in vero era molto piccolo uomo,' says Landucci, p. 80. The Venetian Contarini, in Romanin, *Storia Documentata di Venezia*, v. 15: 'Piccolo e mal composto della persona, brutto di volto, . . . i labbri eziandio grossi, i quali continuamente tien aperti ed ha alcuni movimenti di mano spasmodici che paiono molto brutti a vederli, ed è tardissimo nella locuzione.'

deliberate. All answered that they would never consent to the
return of the Medici; anything might be granted rather than
that. The city was full of alarm and suspicion; shops were
shut and a threatening crowd gathered in the Piazza. The
sight of some Italian prisoners led in chains by their Swiss
captors caused a riot which threatened to become serious.
Houses were barricaded; stones were flung from windows and
housetops; and peace was only restored by the intervention of
many French nobles and of the magistrates. The French saw
that warfare in the streets of Florence would be no easy matter.
If the French army in Florence numbered 20,000 men, the
Florentines could raise 50,000. Though the French could
easily have defeated them in the open field, they might be
excused for shrinking from a combat in a labyrinth of narrow
lanes. Charles VIII. judged it wise to abandon his attitude of
treating Florence as a conquered city to which he might dictate
terms, and consented to make an alliance. Negotiations proceeded with difficulty; Charles VIII. wavered in his demands
and the suspicions of the Florentines increased. The King's
request for money seemed to them unreasonable; his proposal
to leave a deputy who should be present at all their discussions
and whose assent should be necessary to their proceedings was
an outrage to Florentine independence.[1] The Florentine commissioners remonstrated; Charles VIII. insisted and bade his
secretary read the conditions which he would accept. Again
the commissioners refused; 'Then we will blow our trumpets,'
said the King in an angry voice. Piero Capponi seized the
paper from the secretary's hand and tore it in pieces, saying,
'And we will ring our bells.' It was a rash act on Capponi's
part, and the next moment was decisive for the fate of Florence.
But Charles VIII. knew and respected Capponi, who had been
an ambassador in France; he was a resolute man, whose active
mind had driven him to serve Lorenzo de' Medici, but who was
now leader of the Republican party in Florence. Charles VIII.
felt that it was unwise to provoke a breach with Florence; he
recalled the departing commissioners; 'Ah, Capponi, Capponi,'
he said; 'you are a bad capon.' The King smiled at his poor

[1] Parenti, quoted in Gelli's edition of Nardi, p. 39: 'Si fermarono loro a
volere che un presidente ci restassi il quale a tutte nostre pratiche intervenisse,
e senza del quale terminatione alcuna fare non potessimo.'

joke and the conference was renewed. The daring act of Capponi was the only memory of the French invasion on which Italy could look back with pride.[1] It was the sole display of the old Italian spirit, and its rashness was justified by its success. Capponi had beliefs and spoke out manfully; he and Savonarola are the only prominent Italians of the time of whom this can be said.

The terms of the agreement between Florence and Charles VIII. were at length drawn up in twenty-seven articles. Their general purport was that Florence recognised Charles VIII. as protector of its liberties, left in his hands till the end of the French expedition against Naples the fortresses already occupied by the French, and undertook to pay him 120,000 ducats. Pisa was to be restored to Florence, which agreed to pardon the Pisans for their revolt; Piero de' Medici and his brothers were to be exiled from Florence, but their goods were to be restored to them.[2] The agreement was substantially the same as had been made by Piero de' Medici. When it had been signed on November 24 the city rang its bells and lit bonfires in token of rejoicing. But the joy of the citizens was short-lived, when they saw that Charles VIII. gave no signs of departing. Again they feared that he meditated the sack of the city: again Florence wore a sombre aspect of suspicion. Savonarola, true to his prophetic mission, approached the King with words of warning. 'The people,' he said, 'are afflicted by your stay in Florence and you waste your time. God has called you to renew His Church. Go forth to your high calling lest God visit you with His wrath and choose another instrument in your stead to carry out His designs.' Charles VIII. received Savonarola with respect and listened to his admonitions.[3] On November 28 the French army left Florence.

Alexander VI., meanwhile, was in sore perplexity, and appealed to Ascanio Sforza to come to his aid. He wrote to

---

[1] Machiavelli's lines in the *Decennali* extend Charles VIII.'s witticism:

'Lo strepito dell' armi e de' cavalli
Non potè far che non fosse sentita
La voce d' un Cappon fra cento Galli.'

[2] The agreement is given in *Archivio Storico Italiano*, vol. i. (1ma serie) 362 &c.

[3] This account is given in Nardi, lib. i., in Landucci, *Diario*, p. 85, and is referred to by Savonarola in his sermons more than once.

him with his own hand, beseeching him by his old friendship, and by his oath as a Cardinal, to come and put his shoulders as a pillar to support the tottering fabric of the papal power. Ascanio did not refuse to do his office as a good Cardinal, but demanded that, as hostage for his security, Cesare Borgia should go to Marino and be in the custody of the Colonna. When this was done Ascanio went to Rome with Prospero Colonna on November 2 and had a long conference with the Pope, who told his Cardinals afterwards that Ascanio had advised him to make terms with the French king. 'But,' he went on, 'I am assured of the justice of my cause and would lose my mitre, my lands, and my life, rather than fail Alfonso in his need.' Ascanio, after receiving this answer, rode cheerfully away to Ostia; and men conjectured that the Pope, for all his brave words, had sent him to make overtures to Charles VIII.[1]

While Charles VIII. was at Florence a discovery was made which threw a still darker light upon the Pope's character, and which was calculated to become a serious weapon against him in the hands of the French king. In his anxiety for his own safety Alexander VI. determined to leave no stone unturned and besought even the Sultan to help him against France. The captivity of Djem and the payment of a yearly allowance to his gaoler had opened up diplomatic intercourse between Rome and Constantinople. Soon after his accession to the pontificate Alexander VI. sent one of his secretaries, Giorgio Buzardo, to demand the customary payment; Buzardo returned in January 1493 with the report that Bajazet II. had refused to pay any more and had dismissed him with empty hands.[2] The French invasion gave Alexander VI. a reason for closer communication with the Sultan. In July 1494 he again sent Buzardo to inform Bajazet II. that the French king was marching against Rome with the intention of seizing Djem, and using him as a pretext for making war against Constantinople; if he succeeded he would be joined by Spain, Eng-

---

[1] The letter of Alexander VI. is given by Sigismondo de' Conti, ii. 83; and a description of Ascanio's visit is given in two letters of Guidotti de Colle, the Florentine envoy, in Thuasne's Burchard, ii. 191, 646.

[2] Letter of Valori from Rome, dated Jan. 16, 1493, in Thuasne's Burchard, ii. 622.

land, and Maximilian, and would give the Sultan much trouble.
The Pope, therefore, begged Bajazet to pay him the money
due, to use his influence to induce Venice to withstand the
French, and further to make common cause with himself and
Alfonso. Bajazet II. received Buzardo graciously, paid him
the 40,000 ducats which the Pope demanded, and sent him
back accompanied by an envoy of his own, who should confer
further with the Pope. Unfortunately for Alexander VI.
Buzardo fell into the hands of Giovanni della Rovere, brother
of the Cardinal, at Sinigaglia, on his homeward journey. The
40,000 ducats were taken from him, and, what was still more
serious, the Pope's instructions, and the Sultan's letters in
reply, were discovered and were forwarded at once to Cardinal
Rovere at Florence. The Pope's instructions to Buzardo were
sufficiently startling; but the Sultan's answer was still more
amazing. It was contained in four letters written in Turkish
characters and one written in Latin. The Turkish documents
praised Buzardo, commended to the Pope the Turkish envoy,
and, strangely enough, asked him to confer the cardinalate on
Niccolò Cibò, Archbishop of Arles, whom Bajazet II. had known
in the days of Innocent VIII. The Latin letter suggested to
Alexander VI. a short way of dealing with Djem : let the Pope
put him to death and so defeat the plans of the French king:
if the Pope would send his dead body to Constantinople,
Bajazet II. would give in exchange for it 300,000 ducats,
' wherewith your highness may buy some dominions for your
children.' This monstrous proposal was made, the Sultan says,
after full deliberation with the Pope's envoy Buzardo.[1] It cannot, therefore, be dismissed as the wild dream of an oriental
who did not know the insult which such a proposition contained.
It is not surprising that Cardinal Rovere thought the contents
of these letters to be ' a stupendous matter, fraught with danger
to Christendom.'[2] He had the Turkish documents translated,
and put copies of them into the hands of the chief counsellors
of the French king.[3]

[1] The letters are given in full by Burchard, ii. 202, to whom they were
given by the Cardinal of Gurk.
[2] So he told Manfredi, the Ferrarese ambassador at Florence, on Nov. 24 :
' Che erano di qualità che era stupenda cosa et pericolosa alla christianitade.'
Atti e Memorie per le provincie Parmesi e Modenesi, iv. 334.
[3] On the authenticity of these letters, see Appendix.

It was but natural that Alexander VI. in later years should deny these dealings with the Sultan, and declare that they were inventions of his enemy, Giovanni della Rovere.[1] He could not avoid the knowledge that his conduct had seriously shocked even the low sentiment of Europe, and he could not defend it. But it was not unnatural for a man like Alexander VI. to seek for help where he could find it, and to recognise community of interest as the most binding tie. Venice and Naples had set the example of negotiating with the Turk; and Alexander VI. was rather an Italian prince than the head of Christendom. He was free from prejudice and was not restrained by the traditions of his office. He and his family treated Djem with kindness. The Turkish prince rode out in public with the Pope, going in front of the cross which was carried in the procession. The Duke of Gandia was seen in Turkish attire riding by the side of Djem; he even took the Turkish prince into the Lateran Church and showed him its curiosities.[2] There was no intolerance about the court of Alexander VI., and his tolerant spirit easily extended itself into politics. If the Emperor was unwilling or unable to come to his aid, it seemed natural to apply to the Sultan. When he disavowed the fact he probably disavowed the extreme inferences which his enemies drew from it. Alexander VI. was eminently versatile and light-hearted; he probably wondered why people attached so much importance to a trifle; and after a little while Europe took his view of the matter.

Declara-
tion of
Charles
VIII., No-
vember 22,
1494.

At the time, however, the possession of these documents enabled the Pope's enemies to produce an impression on the mind of Charles VIII. On November 22, probably the very day on which the news of the capture of the Pope's envoy reached Florence, Charles VIII. issued a general statement of his intentions. In high-sounding language he announced his object to be war against the Turk and the restoration of Christendom: to carry out this design more surely he purposed first to assert his hereditary claim to the kingdom of Naples; he

---

[1] Instructions to his envoys to Louis XII. on his accession, Thuasne's Burchard, ii. 675, speaking of Giovanni della Rovere: 'Quod magis moleste tulimus, falsis machinationibus famam nostram maculare conatus est, contra nos fingens quod cum Turcis sentiremus.'

[2] Burchard, ii. 69.

required Alexander VI. to give him safe passage through the
lands of the Church; if this were refused the blame of untoward consequences would rest on those who through perfidy
and iniquity attempted to hinder this pious plan. He protested
beforehand that he would lay all injuries which he might suffer
before the universal Church and the princes of Europe, whom
he purposed to summon for the accomplishment of his crusading scheme.[1] It was a warning to Alexander VI. that he might
be impeached before a General Council as a traitor to the interests of Europe if he persisted in his opposition to the French
king.

After this declaration the French army rapidly advanced,
and on December 2 was at Siena. Alexander VI. still hoped
to defend the papal frontier, and sent troops to Viterbo, where
they were refused admittance. He protested to the German
ambassador at Rome and called the Emperor to his aid; he
ordered the Romans to defend their city; he provisioned the
Castle of S. Angelo, which shortly before had been connected
by a covered corridor with the Vatican. Above all, he revoked
his troops to Rome; now that Florence was lost, the army in
the Romagna served no useful purpose. On December 9 the
Duke of Calabria, at the head of 5,000 infantry and 1,500
cavalry, entered Rome.

Yet the Pope's position was hopelessly insecure. Ostia was
open to the French; there was a strong party in their favour
among the Cardinals; the Colonna were ready to make common
cause with them. Encouraged by the Neapolitan troops,
Alexander VI. determined to strike terror into his foes. On
the evening of December 9 he ordered four of the Cardinals to
be arrested as they left a Consistory. Ascanio Sforza, who had
just returned to Rome, and Sanseverino were confined in the
Vatican; Prospero Colonna and Estouteville were shut up in
the Castle of S. Angelo.

This resolute attitude of the Pope did not long continue.
Alexander VI. was like a drowning man catching at a straw.
He was encouraged for a moment by the Neapolitan forces,
though those forces were quite inadequate to offer any real
resistance to the French. On December 10 he told the French
envoys that he would not give the King passage through his

[1] Burchard, ii. 196.

territories. On the same day Charles VIII. entered Viterbo,
and everywhere the towns opened their gates to him. The
Pope was sorely perplexed, and on December 14 used the
opportunity of Ascanio Sforza's presence at mass to open up
communications with his prisoner. ' During the whole mass,'
says Burchard, 'the Pope talked with him, even after the
elevation of the holy sacrament ; when it was time for standing
he sat, that he might talk more conveniently.' [1] The colloquy
with Ascanio did not reassure him, but he still hoped to hold
out. He sent for some of the chief Germans resident in Rome
and besought them to form a troop of their compatriots for
the defence of the city. After some consultation amongst themselves, they answered that they were under the commands of
the city magistrates and could not renounce their proper
officers. The Pope's allies saw that resistance was hopeless.
On December 15 Charles VIII. was at Nepi, and Virginio Orsini
sent to offer him admission to his castles, so that on December
19 Charles VIII.'s head-quarters were in the Orsini castle of
Bracciano. This defection of the Orsini was the last blow to
the hopes of the Pope and of Naples alike ; Virginio Orsini
was Constable of Naples, was connected by marriage with the
Neapolitan king, and his family had an hereditary alliance with
the Aragonese house.

Alexander VI. was now seriously alarmed. He released his
captive Cardinals and sent his possessions into the Castle of S.
Angelo, while his more precious goods were packed in readiness
for flight ; horses stood always ready for his departure. But
flight meant almost certain ruin. If the French king came to
Rome he needed a responsible ruler with whom he could treat.
If Alexander VI. were to flee, he must for his own security
take with him all his Cardinals ; but already many had openly
joined Charles VIII. ; probably there were few who would follow
the Pope of their own free will. There would certainly gather
round the French king a large majority of the College, who
would be willing to declare Alexander VI. deposed and proceed
to a new election. Alexander VI. had not the moral character
which alone enables a man to act resolutely in a crisis. He
prepared to retreat from his position, and sent envoys to

---

[1] Burchard, ii. 201. 'Alia observata more solito,' is Burchard's next
remark.

Charles VIII. at Bracciano. They besought the French king to remember his ancestors and do no hurt to Rome; the Pope had wished him to submit his claims on Naples to arbitration; since, however, he had seen fit to proceed by arms, let him choose another road and not disturb the Pope; if he wished to visit the holy places of Rome let him come without his troops. Finally, the Pope exhorted him to pay no heed to his detractors, who were restless and unquiet men whom no kindness could satisfy.[1] This was not a happy stroke of papal diplomacy, as it awakened the wrath of Cardinals Rovere, Sforza, Perraud, Savelli, and Sanseverino, who were with Charles VIII. The envoys, by their advice, were dismissed with scanty courtesy; and the French advanced, uncertain whether they were to enter Rome as friends or foes. On December 23 Cardinal Perraud wrote to the Germans in Rome that their lives and goods would be respected in case of an attack on the city.[2] At last, on December 24, the Pope assembled a Consistory and announced his intention of making terms with Charles VIII. He sent his nephew, the Cardinal of Monreale, to the French camp at Bracciano. Charles VIII. demanded that the Pope should at least declare himself neutral, and give free passage to the French troops; in return, he promised a safe-conduct to the Duke of Calabria, and professed his reverence for the Pope as the head of Christendom. Still Alexander VI. wavered. Next day he made an agreement with the Duke of Calabria that he might be received in Naples in case of need; he stipulated that he should have possession of Gaeta and receive a yearly allowance during his stay;[3] he celebrated mass in his chapel and gave his benediction to the Duke, saying, 'God will help us.' On December 31 the Neapolitan troops retired from Rome, and Alexander VI. sent Burchard, his Master of the Ceremonies, to meet Charles VIII. Burchard was desirous of instructing Charles VIII. in matters of ceremonial; but the King answered that he meant to enter Rome without pomp. He kept Burchard by his side, and asked him many questions about the Pope's

Alexander
VI. makes
terms with
Charles
VIII.,
December
24, 1494.

---

[1] Sigismondo de' Conti, *Historia*, ii. 84. See also Marin Sanuto, *La Spedizione di Carlo, VIII.* 148 &c., for an account of the Pope's proceedings.

[2] Burchard, ii. 212.

[3] In Theiner, *Codex Diplomaticus Dominii Temporalis*, iii. n. 426.

personal character and about Cesare Borgia; unfortunately Burchard has not told us his answers.

The same evening the French army entered Rome by the Porta del Popolo. From three o'clock till nine the procession lasted before the astonished eyes of the Romans, and the wavering light of torches added to the terrible aspect of the soldiers. As on entering Florence, Charles VIII. was clad in armour and bore his lance by his side. With him were the Cardinals della Rovere, Sforza, Savelli, and Colonna, who mixed strangely with the martial throng. The French artillery awakened the greatest wonder amongst the Romans, who had never seen such guns before.[1] Amid cries of 'Francia,' 'Colonna,' and 'Vincula,'[2] the King moved along the Corso to the Palazzo of S. Marco, where he took up his abode. Cannon were posted round the Palazzo, and two thousand men were posted in the Campo dei Fiori, where they kept watch all night.

Only the Tiber separated the King from the Pope, and Alexander VI. was ill at ease. Centuries had passed since a king with a hostile army had entered the walls of Rome, and a more sensitive mind than that of Alexander VI. would have deeply felt his humiliating position. But Alexander VI. had no thought of the dignity of his office: he cared only for his personal safety. Really the French king could ill afford to provoke the determined hostility of the Pope, as complications with the head of Christendom would have given an opportunity for the interference of Germany and Spain, which were watching with ill-concealed jealousy the astounding successes of France. Charles VIII.'s counsellors were eager for the plunder of Naples, and wished to accomplish rapidly the main object of their expedition. His special favourite Briçonnet, Bishop of S. Malo, longed for the dignity of the cardinalate, which would be endangered by an open breach with the Pope. On the other hand, Cardinals Rovere and Sforza urged Charles VIII. to call the Pope to account, to summon a Council, and depose him as simoniacally elected. Ascanio Sforza had been the chief agent in this election, and had earned his share of the money spent in simony; but this did not restrain him from urging the

[1] Paulus Jovius, *Historia*, lib. ii., gives a vivid account of this scene.
[2] In honour of Cardinal Rovere, whose title was Cardinal of S. Peter ad Vincula.

charge against Alexander VI. when it suited his own purposes.
Charles VIII. may be pardoned if he doubted his own fitness
to superintend the work of reforming the Church. He had
neither the intellectual nor the moral qualities for such a task.
Feeble in mind, contemptible in appearance, sunk in profligacy,
and incapable of serious purpose, he was wise in not undertaking a labour far beyond his strength. Alexander VI. might
be unfit to be Pope, but Charles VIII. was equally unfit to say
so. Charles VIII. showed some political wisdom when he said
that he wished for a reformation of the Church, but not the
deposition of the Pope.[1]

Charles VIII., however, was in Rome, and Alexander VI.
was driven to come to terms. Quarrels between the French
soldiers and the Roman citizens were inevitable. Frenchmen
were murdered by night, and their comrades retaliated by
plunder. The house of Vanozza, the mother of Alexander's
children, was sacked:[2] the Bank was pillaged, and it required
all the efforts of Cardinal Colonna to prevent graver disorders.
On January 2 Alexander VI. sent several of his Cardinals,
amongst them Cesare Borgia, Carvajal, and Raffaelle Riario, to
the King, who received them coldly. They addressed him in a
speech of much cleverness, which took occasion to refute the
charges brought against the Pope, and entreated Charles VIII.
to follow the example of his predecessors, Pippin and Charles
the Great. They regretted that he had shown ill-will towards
the Pope, who was only labouring for the peace of Christendom.
'What,' they proceeded significantly, 'do you think that other
Christian princes will say if it be bruited abroad that you
besiege the Pope and claim to judge him, to whom God has
committed the judgment of all men?' The Pope had urged
that the French claim to Naples should be decided by arbitration, not by arms, because he feared lest Alfonso in his fear
might call the Turk to his aid and so bring the Infidels into
Italy. They retorted with crushing logic on the rebellious

Negotia-
tions be-
tween
Charles
VIII. and
Alexander
VI., Janu-
ary 2-15,
1495.

[1] Letter of Briçonnet to the Queen, in Pillorgerie, *Campagnes et bulletins*,
134. Ludovico Sforza expressed the opinion of most people when he said to
the Venetians: 'Se dice voler andar per riformare la chiesa, questo non spetta
a lui, perchè a dirlo con le Mag.^lie V^re, e' ha piu bisogno lui di riformazione
che di riformar loro.' Romanin, *Storia Documentata di Venezia*, v. 56.

[2] Burchard, ii. 220: 'Similiter et (spoliata et depredata est) domus domine
Rose matris R^mi. D. Cardinalis Valentini.'

Cardinals: 'Alexander VI. has his detractors; but he knows that Jesus was accused as a wine-bibber and a friend of publicans and sinners. Let slanderers tell what tales they will, Alexander VI. is holier, or at least as holy, as he was at the time of his election. He did not impose on his electors by hypocrisy, or win their good-will by any new pretence. For thirty-seven years he approved himself in high office, so that his doings and sayings were not hid from them. The very men who now withdraw their votes were the chief in procuring his election.'[1] The argument was true and cogent. Alexander VI. was no hypocrite; his electors had been rewarded for their trouble, and had no just ground for complaining of the man whom they had chosen.

This speech produced some effect, as Alexander VI. had prepared the way by bribes judiciously administered to the French counsellors of the King.[2] The Italians did not sympathise with the party move of Alexander VI.'s enemies to use against him the irregularities of his private life. In their opinion it was a low trick; it was an attempt to throw dust in the eyes of the ignorant Frenchmen and apply to the Pope a standard of holiness which had long ago been pronounced impossible in Italy. 'The French,' says Sigismondo de' Conti, 'and those who dwell in the remoter parts of Christendom, think that the Pope is not made like other men, but is like one sent down from heaven, who cannot be moved by human feelings and has not, as S. Paul says, a law in his members contrary to the law in his mind.'[3] Sigismondo pronounces the charges against the Pope to be trifling, and the French learned to take the Italian view of moral considerations. One of the results of the French invasion of Italy was that the nations beyond the Alps lost their superstitious respect for the Pope's sanctity. The counsellors of Charles VIII. soon convinced him that Alexander VI.'s personal character had nothing to do with his own political ends.

So Charles VIII. dismissed his reforming schemes, and

---

[1] Sigismondo de' Conti, *Historia*, ii. 88. Leonetti (ii. 362) quotes as much of this speech as suits his purpose, as a testimony to the high character of Alexander VI. A professed apologist can have no sense of humour.

[2] Sigismondo, ii. 91: 'Inflexit animum regis sapiens et vera oratio, sed multo magis largitio Alexandri, qui penitiores regis amicos corruperat.'

[3] *Historia*, ii. 86.

answered that he was ready to render obedience to the Pope and enter into strait alliance with him on three conditions: that the Castle of S. Angelo be occupied by a French garrison; that Cesare Borgia accompany the French army to Naples as legate; and that Prince Djem be handed over to the King.[1] Alexander VI. objected strongly to these conditions, and Charles VIII. gave him six days for consideration. On January 5 so many French nobles came to kiss the Pope's foot and receive his benediction, that Alexander VI. fainted. After deliberating with his Cardinals he answered the French king that he could not consent to give up the Castle of S. Angelo for fear of Cardinal Rovere, who would occupy it and be master of Rome; if it were besieged he would expose on its walls the holiest relics.[2] After sending this answer Alexander VI. was seized with terror, and fled into the Castle of S. Angelo accompanied by six Cardinals. A piece of the wall of the castle had fallen on the day when Charles VIII. entered Rome. It was repaired hastily and fell again. Men looked on this as an evil omen; Alexander VI. regarded it as a sign that the castle was not a secure refuge. Twice the French artillery was pointed against the walls; twice it was withdrawn. At last, on January 11, a compromise was made, and terms of peace were arranged. The Pope agreed to give up to the King Cività Vecchia, to appoint governors whom the King chose in the cities of the Patrimony, to receive into his favour the Cardinals and nobles who had favoured the French cause, to deliver up Prince Djem, and send Cardinal Cesare Borgia as legate with the French army for four months. Charles VIII. withdrew his demand for the Castle of S. Angelo.

When peace had thus been made Charles VIII. ventured for the first time to traverse the streets of Rome and visit its churches and antiquities. On January 15 the treaty was signed by the King, and Rome rejoiced at being free from danger. Next day Charles VIII. took up his abode in the Vatican, and a meeting between him and the Pope was arranged. Charles VIII. was walking in the Vatican garden when Alexander VI. issued from the corridor which led to the Castle of S. Angelo. Twice the King, uncovering his head, bowed to the Pope; but Alexander VI. professed not to see

Meeting of
Charles
VIII. and
Alexander
VI., January 16,
1495.

---

[1] Pillorgerie, *Campagnes et bulletins*, p. 147.

[2] Idem; and Malipiero, *Annali Veneti*, 331; Sanuto, 170.

him. On the third genuflexion Alexander also uncovered his
head, and taking the King's hand prevented him from kissing
his feet. Then he walked by his side and expressed his joy at
this meeting. They passed together into the hall of the Consistory, where the King set forth his reverence for the Pope,
and asked as a favour the elevation of the Bishop of S. Malo
to the cardinalate. Alexander VI. assented, and led the way
to the room where the creation of Cardinals was declared.
On the way he fainted; Burchard regarded it as a pretence
that he might demand the attentions of the King.[1] When he
recovered he nominated Briçonnet a Cardinal, conferred on
him the insignia of his dignity, and assigned him rooms in the
Vatican. Alexander VI. had now recovered his self-possession.
So long as he had a serious political problem to solve he was
helpless and allowed matters to drift; now that it was a
question of managing men, his subtlety and astuteness returned. He was ready to make the most of Charles VIII., and
lived with him on terms of the most complete friendliness.
The Cardinals who had joined the party of Charles VIII. saw
themselves entirely abandoned. Ascanio Sforza and Lunate
fled from Rome; Prospero Colonna, Savelli, and Perraud reconciled themselves with the Pope. Perraud afterwards boasted
that he had spoken his mind to Alexander VI. and had reproved
him for his evil life, his simony, and his dealings with the Turk.
Probably the loquacious Cardinal told his friends what was in
his mind rather than on his tongue.[2] Cardinal Rovere alone
remained steadfast in his hostility, and preferred to accompany
Charles VIII. rather than remain in Rome.

Alexander
VI. re-
ceives the
obedience of
France,
January 19,
1495.
On January 19 Alexander VI. had the satisfaction of receiving from Charles VIII. the obedience of France. The conqueror of Italy entered the capital of the Pope who opposed
him, and formally recognised his authority without obtaining
a withdrawal of his opposition. It is true that he showed
some signs of using pressure, and kept the Consistory waiting
for an hour before he appeared. Then his orator demanded
the investiture of Naples, which Alexander VI. refused, saying

---

[1] 'Finxit se pontifex syncopa turbari.' Burchard, ii. 222: Pillorgerie, 154,
gives a French account of the interview; Sanuto, 185.

[2] Burchard, to whom this was told, seems to have doubted; 'si sui verum
mihi retulerunt,' ii. 233.

that he could not prejudice the rights of another without due deliberation with the Cardinals; he vaguely added that he wished in all things to please his dear son, the King of France. If Charles VIII.'s advisers wished to overawe the Pope, the King threw away the opportunity; he rose at once and said in French, 'Holy Father, I have come to do obedience and reverence in the same way as my predecessors.' During the ceremonial speeches which followed, the French who were present broke out into such loud expressions of disgust that the Cardinals crowded round the Pope's throne for protection. If Alexander VI. showed his incapacity before Charles VIII. entered Rome, Charles VIII. showed still greater want of capacity when he was master of the situation. It might be unwise to attempt the Pope's overthrow; but to offer him the obedience of France was to strengthen the position of an enemy who had only been driven by superior force to dissemble his hostility for the moment.

A few more days were spent by Charles VIII. in Rome, and were largely given to ecclesiastical ceremonial, till at last Alexander VI. saw with relief that Charles VIII. prepared to take his departure. Prince Djem was handed over to him and was received with courtesy and marks of respect. The Pope bestowed pardons on the numerous nobles who thronged to ask for them, and Cesare Borgia presented the King with six magnificent horses. Then, on January 28, Charles VIII., with Djem on his left and Cesare Borgia on his right, rode out of Rome, in full confidence that he had won the lasting friendship of the Pope. But this belief was soon dispelled; on the evening of January 30, Cardinal Cesare, disguised as a groom, fled from the French quarters at Velletri. He rode rapidly to Rome and took refuge in the house of a papal official. The Roman magistrates came trembling to the Pope, and begged him to order Cesare's departure, lest the King return to take vengeance. Cesare was safely conveyed to Spoleto, and Alexander VI. was well contented to know that Charles VIII. no longer had in his power a hostage for his fidelity. When Charles VIII. sent to demand Cesare's return, the Pope declared that he knew nothing of his flight nor of his hiding-place. Charles VIII. saw, when it was too late, that he had been the Pope's dupe.

Departure of the French army, January 25, 1495.

BOOK
V.
Alarm of
Spain at
the French
successes.

The reason of Cesare's bold step is not difficult to find. On the day of his flight two Spanish ambassadors presented themselves before Charles VIII. at Velletri, and demanded that he should desist from his attempt against Naples. Ferdinand of Spain considered that he had done enough to deserve the grant of Roussillon; he bethought himself of his old alliance with Naples, and his envoys urged that if Naples did not belong to Alfonso II., it belonged to Ferdinand of Aragon as the legitimate heir of Alfonso I. They proposed that the question be referred to the arbitration of the Pope; Charles VIII. answered, 'Alexander VI. is a Spaniard,' and dismissed them. Still he received an unpleasant intimation of the jealousy which his success was causing. Cesare Borgia saw that France had dangerous enemies, and that the Papacy was still a useful centre round which they might rally. Feeling satisfied that Charles VIII. would hesitate to return to Rome in search of new hostages, he judged that the time had come for flight.

Abdication
of Alfonso
II., January 23,
1495.

Naples, however, itself offered no opposition to the French advance. Alfonso II. was as cowardly as he was cruel,[1] and saw expressed in the faces of his subjects the hatred which his conduct had inspired; men said that he was haunted at nights by the ghosts of the barons whom he had treacherously put to death. He had not the courage to defend himself, and judged that the sole chance of saving his dynasty was to abdicate in favour of his innocent son Ferrantino. On January 23 he resigned his crown and prepared to flee to Sicily. The weather was too stormy to set sail at once and he spent some days in terror, crying out that he heard the French advancing, that the very trees and stones cried 'France;' at last he escaped to Sicily, and took refuge in the Olivetan monastery of Mazara.

Charles
VIII.
enters
Naples,
February
22, 1495.

Ferrante II. was crowned amidst ominous silence from the crowd. He did what he could to win the affections of his subjects. He implored help from Ludovico Sforza, even from the Sultan Bajazet; then he set out for the camp at San Germano, resolved to merit the glory of a worthy prince. But the news that the French had stormed Monte San Giovanni and mas-

---

[1] Commines' remark has almost passed into a proverb: 'Jamais homme cruel ne fut hardy' (vii. ch. 11)

sacred all its inhabitants [1] filled the Neapolitan army with terror, so that it hastily abandoned the strong position of San Germano, which was the key to Naples, and fell back on Capua. Ferrante II. hastened to Naples to gather reinforcements; during his absence his general, Trivulzio, made terms with Charles VIII. and Capua was opened to the French. Naples rose in tumultuous confusion and Ferrante II. bade his subjects a dignified farewell. 'Fortune has declared against me, and I withdraw. I absolve you from your homage and counsel you by obedience to mitigate the natural pride of the French. If their barbarity awaken your hatred and make you wish for my return, I will be ready at your call to risk my life in your service. If you are satisfied with their rule I will never disturb the peace of the realm. I have wronged no man; the sins of my fathers, not my own, are visited on my head.' [2] On February 21 he sailed for Ischia, and next day Charles VIII. entered Naples amidst the joyous greetings of the people, who had already sent to tell him that they awaited his coming as did the Jews that of the Messiah. Only the two castles of Naples held out for Ferrante, and they were reduced to submission on March 20.

The success of Charles VIII. was marvellous. The states of Italy had fallen before him at the first touch. They had no root of patriotism or national sentiment; each lived for itself and for the immediate present, and the expediency of the moment was the sole element in each man's calculations. Those who had been most strongly attached to the House of Aragon in Naples, and who owed everything to its favour, were the first to prostrate themselves before the victorious King of France. A saying was put into the mouth of Alexander VI. that 'the French came into Italy with wooden spurs, carrying in their hands chalk to mark their billets.' Indeed, they scarcely needed any other appliances, for where they came to conquer they were welcomed as friends. It is no wonder that Charles VIII. struck a medal in Naples with the inscription *Missus a Deo*, 'sent by God.' [3]

---

[1] 'Le carnage fut un des plus horribles qu'on vit jamais, lequel dura huit heures entières,' says André de la Vigne, in Godefroi, p. 130.

[2] Guicciardini, lib. i.; and more briefly in Sigismondo de' Conti (ii. 106), whom very probably Guicciardini has expanded.

[3] Malipiero, *Annali Veneti*, 333.

Now that Charles VIII. was master of Naples it was in his power to carry out his great design of warring against the Turk. Bajazet II. was a feeble ruler; Commines was of opinion that he might have been dispossessed of his throne as easily as Alfonso of Naples,[1] since the Greeks were ready to rebel at the first news of the French advance. But Charles VIII. does not seem to have been much more in earnest about a Crusade than those who had professed their zeal in previous days, and such intentions as he had were dispelled by the death of Prince Djem on February 25. On the journey Djem caught a cold which developed into bronchitis, under which he sank. Men said that the Pope had poisoned him before he left Rome; but we must doubt the operation of a poison which worked so slowly as to produce death only after a month's interval. Yet this version of the cause of Djem's death was believed on all sides by Alexander VI.'s contemporaries, who clearly thought that the Pope would shrink from no crime which might bring him advantage. Alexander VI. throughout his whole career had to pay the penalty for the known disorders of his life, and no accusation against him was incredible. However, the death of Djem seems to have arisen from natural causes. It was not singular that one who had led for many years a sedentary life should succumb before a winter journey, during which his regular habits of life were disregarded. Alexander VI. may fairly be acquitted of the charge of poisoning Djem.[2]

[1] 'Le Turc eust esté aussi aisé à troubler qu'avoit esté le Roy Alfonse, car il estoit homme de nulle valeur' (Liv. vii. ch. 14).

[2] About the prevalence of the belief, there can be no question. Commines, vii. 14, says: 'disoit on qu'il fut baillé empoisonné'; Malipiero, 145, 'si dice che l' è tossicato'; Priuli, 'Francesi diceva che il papa gli aveva dato attossicato.' Paulus Jovius and Guicciardini repeat a like rumour. On the other hand, Burchard, i. 242, says: 'ex esu seu potu statui suo non convenienti vita est functus.' A Venetian despatch to Gritti at Constantinople gives the account which the Venetian envoy at Naples had heard from Djem's physician; he died of a cold, which settled on his chest, and produced great irritation of the throat; for this he was bled: 'quantunque li fosse sta tracto sangue, non ricevete però rimedio.' Romanin, *Storia Documentata di Venezia*, v. 61; also Cherrier, *Histoire de Charles VIII.* ii. 137. Sanuto, *Spedizione di Carlo VIII.*, 243, gives a like account. Ludovico Sforza, when he heard of Djem's death, said that Charles VIII. had killed him by taking him from Rome: 'e fatolo mutar aere senz' alcun rispeto.' Romanin, *ut supra*. Sigismondo de' Conti, ii. 92, tells us that Alexander VI. had feared the same result: 'Verebatur ne ille qui annis circiter octo in conclavibus asservatus fuerat,

Djem's death and the delights of Naples dispelled the crusading schemes of Charles VIII. His vanity was fully satisfied by his triumphal procession through Italy, and his inglorious campaign required its meed of enjoyment. Charles VIII. was contented to compare himself with Charles the Great [1] without incurring any farther risks. The French nobles were bent only on apportioning among themselves the spoils of the Neapolitan kingdom. There was no statesman to point out that the commanding position which Charles VIII. assumed could only be maintained by some further exploit which would silence jealousy. Charles VIII. revelled in the delights of the Neapolitan gardens which seemed to him 'a terrestrial paradise save for the absence of Adam and Eve.' [2] His troops followed his example in their way, and indulged in the strong cheap wine of Naples till their drunken licentiousness filled the Neapolitans with hatred and terror. Commines admits that the French did not regard the Italians as men; [3] they had had only too much justification for their contempt and did not scruple to show it. The offices of the state were all given to needy Frenchmen, and though Charles VIII. promised large remissions of taxation, the luxury of his court prevented his promises being carried into effect. The Neapolitans soon regretted their faithlessness to Ferrante II.

Meanwhile all the powers of Europe felt themselves menaced by this accession of power to France. Ferdinand of Spain feared for Sicily; Maximilian was alarmed at the preponderance which France had won in Europe; Ludovico Sforza saw that by opening Italy to France he had taken a dangerous step. The Duke of Orleans was the descendant of Valentino Visconti, the last representative of the Visconti line, and could produce as good a title to Milan as Charles VIII. had urged successfully on Naples. Venice and the Pope were both alarmed. There

insolentia liberioris cœli lethalem morbum, prout contraxit, contraheret.' Indeed the result of taking a Djem, after eight years of seclusion in hot rooms, to face an Italian winter on horseback might have been foretold by anyone.

[1] Maximilian was informed that Charles took the title 'Carolus Octavus, secundus Magnus': Cherrier, vol. ii. 147, from Florentine Archives.

[2] 'Il semble qu'il n'y faille que Adam et Eve pour en faire un paradis terrestre': Pillorgerie, 216.

[3] 'Entressent en telle gloire qu'il ne sembloit point à nostres que les Italiens fussent hommes' (liv. vii. ch. 14).

were many negotiations amongst these powers during the progress of the French invasion; the conquest of Naples led to decisive steps. On March 31 a league was concluded at Venice between Maximilian, Ferdinand, Ludovico Sforza, the Pope, and Venice. Its ostensible objects were, war against the Turks, the preservation of peace in Italy, and the mutual defence of the territories of the allies; its real object was the expulsion of the French from Naples.[1]

Retreat of
Charles
VIII.
May, 1495.

Prudence dictated to Charles VIII. a speedy departure from Naples before his enemies had time to collect their forces; but vanity made him desirous of a formal coronation, and he wasted time in fruitless negotiations with the Pope. He still hoped by fair promises to detach Alexander VI. from the League, and obtain from him the investiture of the Neapolitan kingdom. But Alexander VI. was promised help from Venice and refused the King's proposals.[2] On May 12 Charles VIII. was crowned by the Archbishop of Naples, and on May 20 set out on his return to France. Alexander VI. fled before his coming and took refuge in Orvieto; as Charles VIII. advanced and invited him to a conference, he removed for greater safety to Perugia.

Everywhere as Charles VIII. returned he was confronted by complications which his previous want of foresight had created. When he arrived at Poggibonsi he had to choose between the roads through Florence or through Pisa. He had given the Pisans freedom from Florence; he had promised the Florentines to restore Pisa to their rule; so that both regarded him with suspicion. Florence sent envoys to Poggibonsi, amongst whom was Savonarola. Again Charles VIII. listened to the words of the prophet; 'You have provoked the anger of the Lord because you have not kept faith with Florence, and have abandoned the reform of the Church, for which purpose you were sent.' Charles VIII. showed his usual inconsistency; he promised at first to restore Pisa to Florence, but afterwards said that his engagement to Pisa was made before that with Florence. Then he pursued his road to Pisa, where the citizens

---

[1] Commines, liv. vii. ch. xv., gives his experience, as French ambassador at Venice, of the diplomatic subterfuges to which he was exposed.

[2] The Pope's behaviour at this time is described by Sanuto, *Spedizione*, 277 &c.

received him with joy, and next day with lamentable cries besought him not to hand them over to Florence. As usual he answered that he would do what they wished. Charles VIII. was incapable of forming any policy or deciding any question.

The French were not to leave Italy so easily as they entered it. The troops of the League were called into the field by Ludovico Sforza, who had been the chief agent in summoning the French into Italy, and was now the most eager to drive them from it. Louis Duke of Orleans had through sickness been left behind at Asti, where a small force was posted to keep open communications with France. The neighbourhood of Louis disquieted Ludovico. The Duke of Orleans claimed the title of Duke of Milan; Ludovico felt that his subjects were discontented with his rule, and feared that the presence of Louis might give the opportunity for a rising against himself. No sooner was the League concluded than he summoned the Duke of Orleans to evacuate Asti, and proceeded to gather troops. Contrary to the orders of Charles VIII., Orleans obtained succours from France and resolved to act on the offensive. On June 13 he seized Novara, and this act of aggression was enough to absolve the Italian powers from their promises of neutrality to Charles VIII. Venice gathered an army under the command of Francesco Gonzaga, Marquis of Mantua. Novara was besieged, and Gonzaga prepared to intercept Charles VIII. near Fornovo on the little river Taro.

The battle was fought on July 5, a battle big with the destinies of Italy. An invader had broken into her cities and had disturbed her peace. Internal dissensions had favoured him, and men had not seen at first the danger his presence brought. But now Italy had recovered from her first stupor. She was united in a way that she had not been for centuries. It was too late to retrieve the past; but she might so chastise the rash intruder as to make his fate a warning for the future. Italian independence had been threatened of old, but had been nobly vindicated. Fornovo might be in the annals of Italy as glorious a memory as Legnano.

The army of the League had every advantage. It was twice as numerous as the French, which had been weakened

by leaving garrisons in Naples and elsewhere. It was fresh
and had plenty of provisions, while the French were wearied
with a laborious march and were suffering from hunger. It
had the choice of position, while the French emerging from
the gorge amongst the mountains had perforce to cross the
Taro and make their way towards Piacenza. Charles VIII.
judged it wiser not to fight a battle, but to pursue his route.
For this purpose he exposed his flank to the enemy and
marched along the skirts of the mountains. Francesco Gonzaga
endeavoured to intercept him. There was some confused
fighting and much bloodshed. But some of Gonzaga's soldiers
fell to plundering; he himself charged at the head of a
division and left no orders for his reserves, who stood idly by
their tents, passive spectators of the fight. Charles VIII.
pursued his way, leaving much booty in the enemy's hands.
The Italians rejoiced over their victory; but the French had
better reason for rejoicing. The battle of Fornovo displayed the
military incapacity of Italy.[1]

The French
leave Italy.
November,
1495.

When Charles VIII. reached Asti he had to consider if he
intended to pursue the war in Lombardy where the Duke of
Orleans was still besieged in Novara. Alexander VI., who had
recovered from his fright and returned to Rome on June 27,
issued on August 5 a papal admonition to Charles VIII., bidding
him cross the Alps and no longer disturb the peace of Italy;
in case of disobedience he summoned the King to Rome to
show cause why he should not be excommunicated. Even
Charles VIII. had wit enough to reply: 'I wonder that the
Pope is so desirous to see me at Rome, as he did not wait for
me when I was there last. I hope to obey him by opening the
road again, and must beg him to wait a little while.'[2] At first
Charles VIII. thought of bringing Swiss soldiers and relieving
Novara. But Ludovico Sforza was anxious to be rid of the
French, and offered to make terms with the King. Novara

---

[1] The letters sent to Venice are given by Malipiero, 356 &c, and Sanuto,
473 &c. Further, the battle is described by Corio, Guicciardini, Paulus
Jovius; on the French side by André de Vignée and Commines. The French
despatches are in Pillorgerie, *Campagnes et Bulletins*, 349 &c.

[2] This is from Guicciardini, whose speeches are not always to be trusted,
but Malipiero (who gives the Pope's admonition in full, p. 383) says, p. 409:
'El Papa se duol d' haver mandà in Fraza l' interditto, perche glie n' è successo
vergogna e danno.'

was restored to him, and he undertook to give free passage through his territories to the French troops when they marched to Naples. Venice, aggrieved at this desertion of the League, regarded Ludovico as a traitor, and his own subjects joined in the same opinion. Ludovico, who had been the cause of the French invasion, was the man who most rejoiced to see the French safely out of Italy; like most clever schemers he had rid himself of one danger only to incur another.

Before he had returned to France Charles VIII. had lost Naples. Ferrante II. returned on July 7, aided by Spanish troops from Sicily under the command of Gonzalvo de Cordova. The Neapolitans rose against the French, and welcomed back their former king with frantic joy. Place after place was lost to the French, who still gallantly defended themselves. Charles VIII. talked of sending reinforcements and of making another expedition, but while he talked his troops in Calabria wasted away. In November 1496 the last remnants of the French occupation had disappeared.

There is something fantastic, almost grotesque, in this French invasion of Italy. The rashness of the attempt, its instantaneous success, and its absence of result are equally amazing. Still more amazing is it to find in the contemporary records of Italy no sense of the importance of the events that were happening. The Italian had no sense of national unity: he regarded the French as 'barbarians,' but felt no shame that the barbarians should dispose of Italy at their pleasure. He reckoned them to be only a temporary factor in the changing combinations of political parties to which he had been so long accustomed. The idea of national honour, the dread of national danger, never occurred to his mind. Even the most sincere man amongst the Italians of the time, Girolamo Savonarola, regarded the French king as the scourge of God who was to chastise and purify the Church. Italy, enervated by prosperity, corrupted by over-rapid mental enfranchisement, was limited by narrow conceptions of self-interest. The papal restoration had succeeded in checking the adventurous schemes of an Italian kingdom which had floated before the eyes of Giovanni Visconti, of Ladislas of Naples, of the condottiere Braccio. It had made possible the artificial balance of Italian states which had given Italy half a century of luxurious enjoyment and now left it helpless when danger was at hand. Never was a time when resoluteness was more required, and the only Italian capable of political courage was Giuliano della Rovere, whom passionate resentment carried into the camp of France.

Yet the Italian expedition of Charles VIII. was a turning-point of the intellectual and political life of Europe. It revealed at once the glory and the helplessness of Italy. The peoples of the North had just reached the point of intellectual development when they could understand, if they were incapable of creating, the beauties and the refinement of Italian life and thought. The earthly paradise once discovered was never again free from the foot of the invader. Charles VIII. pointed out the splendid prey which lay before the strongest, and Italy became the battlefield of the newly-organised nations of Europe. From the beginning she enthralled her captors. The spoils of Naples were carried back to France, where Charles VIII. began to remodel the Castle of Amboise. The French nobles, weary with their gloomy castles, which since the development of artillery had ceased to be impregnable, followed the fashion of Italy and changed their castles into luxurious country houses. The printing press gave a ready means for the multiplication of books. French literature, which was beginning to wear a courtly dress under Clément Marot, received a new impulse from Italy. Charles VIII. carried beyond the Alps a vague yet powerful fragrance of the spirit of the Italian Renaissance. The result was not entirely good. If French manners had been rude before they rapidly became dissolute. The sojourn of the French in Naples called into existence a plague which went by the name of 'the French evil,' the product of the physical and moral uncleanness of the age.

In another way, also, Italy spread her influence over Europe. The League which was formed against Charles VIII. was an extension into European politics of the principles which had been developed in Italy. A deliberate check was planned against French aggrandisement, and the artificial balance which prevailed in Italian politics was introduced into a larger sphere. Round Italy gathered dynastic jealousies, which were strongly interwoven with national aspirations, and in the struggles for the possession of Italy a new system of European states slowly emerged.

CHAPTER VIII.

ALEXANDER VI. AND FRA GIROLAMO SAVONAROLA.

1495–1498.

THE end of the year 1495 was most disastrous for the city of Rome. The waters of the Tiber rose suddenly to a height unknown before, and inflicted irreparable damage. The flood almost reached the top of the arches of the Ponte di Sisto. The waters spread through the streets, drowned many, ruined property, and undermined houses. The churches and public buildings especially suffered; tombs and altars were swept away, mosaic pavements were destroyed, and many precious memorials of the early Renaissance art were obliterated. The loss was estimated at 300,000 ducats, and it was computed that Rome would not recover from the damage for a quarter of a century.[1]

Alexander VI. was occupied at home by attempting to repair the ravages of this terrible inundation. But he was equally in earnest in his desire to strengthen the League against France, which was joined by Henry VII. of England in the end of July. Though the League was imposing in appearance, Alexander VI. found it no easy matter to stir it to take any definite action. Negotiations were carried on with Maximilian to discuss the details of a joint expedition; and the Pope's legate made the modest request that all cities and castles taken by the French in the Neapolitan kingdom should be placed in the Pope's hands as supreme lord.[2] There was much talk about the division of spoil, much flattering of his

CHAP.
VIII.

Inundation of Rome. December, 1495.

Projects of the League. 1496.

---

[1] The effects of this inundation are graphically described in two letters of Venetians in Rome, in Malipiero, *Annali Veneti*, 409 &c.

[2] Letters of the Venetian Foscari in *Archivio Storico Italiano*, 1ᵐᵃ serie, vii. pt. 2, 770.

imperial majesty, and a sincere desire that Maximilian would
do the bidding of Italy against the French king. But Germany felt no interest in Maximilian's imperial policy, and the
Italian members of the League were not prepared for any great
undertaking.

In truth Italy had been profoundly shaken by the French
invasion, and her statesmen had not recovered their nerve.
They felt that ruin had been terribly near; they dimly saw their
individual mistakes, but each threw the greater part of the
blame on his neighbour. Ludovico Sforza said to the Venetian
Foscari: 'I confess that I have done great mischief to Italy,
but I did it to keep myself in my place, and I did it against
my will. The fault lay with King Ferrante, and also in some
degree with Venice, because it would not interpose. But afterwards, have you not seen my continuous efforts for the freedom
of Italy? Rest assured that if I had delayed any longer in
making the peace of Novara, Italy would have been undone,
for our affairs were in the most desperate condition.'[1] Ludovico
was driven to admit his fault, but had no better policy for the
future than a franker recognition by everyone of the instability
of Italian politics. Italy was to be protected by a cautious
protection of her fragility, not by an endeavour to establish a
sounder foundation. So the allies shrank from any definite
action. The French were gone for the present, and it was
better to wait. When Venice heard of continued reverses of
the French in Naples she secretly tried to dissuade Maximilian
from his expedition.[2]

Position of
Florence.
1496.
However, if something was to be done, there was one object
which seemed to be within the power of the League. The
sole Italian state which still maintained its alliance with France
was Florence. The French invasion had brought to Florence
the expulsion of the Medici and the loss of Pisa. The Florentines were bent on preventing a Medicean restoration and on
recovering Pisa; and they thought that these objects could
best be obtained by an alliance with France. The aim of the
League was a pacification of Italy against France; and this
principle, as applied to Florence, would have meant the restora-

---

[1] Letter of Foscari, under date September 7, 1496; *Archivio Storico
Italiano*, 1ᵐᵃ serie, vii. pt. 2, 843.

[2] *Ibid.* p. 807.

tion of the Medici and the recognition of the independence of
Pisa. Florence on political grounds was not prepared to make
such a sacrifice to secure the unity of Italy. The preaching of
Savonarola had led a large number of her citizens to regard
Charles VIII. as the scourge of God who should purify the
Church; and Florentine vanity was gratified by the thought
that she was to serve as a model to the regenerate world. The
influence of Savonarola was a strange mixture of good and evil.
It awakened a higher sense of Christian zeal and of moral
effort; but it also rested on a definite scheme of politics,
according to which Charles VIII. was a heaven-sent deliverer,
and the rights which Florence recognised as inherent in her
own citizens were denied to the citizens of Pisa. As a moral
and religious teacher Savonarola deserves all praise; as a
politician he taught Florence to take up a position adverse to
the interests of Italy, to trust to France blindly in spite of
all disappointments, and to war against Pisa for casting off the
Florentine yoke in the same way as Florence herself had cast
off the yoke of the Medici. We cannot wonder that this attitude awakened no sympathy in Italy, and that the efforts of
the League were directed to the subjugation of Florence.

After the expulsion of the Medici the Florentines found
some difficulty in arranging a new government. Some wished
to keep the existing system, and to inspire it with the old
vigour of the Florentine republic. Others wished to establish
a more popular form, and turned their eyes to Venice for an
example. Just as the Spartan constitution was the ideal of
Athenian philosophers, so Venice was regarded by Italians as
the state which had solved the problem of attaining political
stability. The Consiglio Grande, of which every Venetian
noble was a member, formed the basis of the Venetian constitution; the popular party at Florence demanded that a great
council of the chiefest citizens should be set in a similar position in Florence. Feeling ran high, and men were sorely
divided between these proposals when Savonarola interposed.
He summoned to the Duomo the magistrates and all the
citizens, excluding women and children. Before them he stood
as a Christian teacher who believed that Christianity had power
to regenerate society, and that its principles were applicable to
political organisation. The prophet who saw in Charles VIII.

CHAP.
VIII

New con-
stitution of
Florence.
December,
1494.

the instrument of God to deliver, yet chastise Florence, felt himself called to set the Government in a path where it might advance to the accomplishment of its mighty destiny. He spoke with the zeal of a Christian moralist, and enforced his words by the lofty assurance of a prophet. He defined the requisites of good government and applied his principles to the existing needs of Florence. He put before his hearers four great objects to be followed—the fear of God as the foundation of moral reform, love for the common welfare as superior to private interests, universal peace and amnesty to the partisans of the Medici, finally a form of government which should comprise all eligible citizens, so as to prevent factions and the consequent rise of individuals to domination.[1] Savonarola's advice prevailed. On December 23 the Consiglio Grande was adopted by a large majority, and the democratic principle became the basis of the new constitution of Florence.

In thus venturing into the field of party politics, Savonarola took a step which drew upon him many enemies. Those who were opposed to the democratic constitution saw in Savonarola its great upholder, and worked to overthrow his influence. They found little difficulty in enlisting on their side the jealousy of the Franciscans against the Dominicans, and an attempt was made to get rid of Savonarola from Florence, by an order from his superior that he should preach at Lucca. The Florentine magistrates with some difficulty obtained from Alexander VI. a suspension of this order.[2] It would, indeed, have been difficult to withdraw Savonarola from Florence, where he stood as the head of the dominant political party and was striving to direct the energies of the city towards a revival of religious and moral life. He professed that he did not meddle with the affairs of the state, and he believed that he was labouring to establish a kingdom of Christ on earth. But, to an outside view, he had encouraged Florence to set up an independent form of government, resting on principles difficult to understand, and to pursue a policy which was not in accordance with the interest of the rest of Italy. Moreover, however

---

[1] *Compendium Rerelationum*, which was published in August 1495, and sent to the Pope.

[2] The difficulties relating to this transaction are discussed by Cosci in an article on Savonarola in the *Archirio Storico Italiano* for 1879, vol. ii. p. 300.

much he might desire a united Florence, it was inevitable that the new constitution should have some opponents. Savonarola linked his fortunes with those of a political party. His friends were contemptuously known as the Piagnoni, because they wept at the eloquence of their master; his foes were called the Arrabiati, because of the fury of their attacks upon him. Watching these two parties were the partisans of the Medici, who only awaited an opportunity to raise their heads.

Savonarola was not ignorant of the dangers which beset him. In a sermon preached on December 21, 1494, he compared himself to one who has gone out fishing, and has been carried from sight of the shore while intent on his occupation. 'Oh, my Florence, I am that man! I was in a safe haven, the life of a friar; I looked at the waves of the world and saw therein much fish; with my hook I caught some, that is, by my preaching I led a few into the way of salvation. As I took pleasure therein the Lord drave my bark into the open sea. Before me on the vast ocean I see terrible tempests brewing. Behind I have lost sight of my haven: the wind drives me forward, and the Lord forbids my return. On my right the elect of God demand my help; on my left demons and wicked men lie in ambush. On high I see eternal life, and my soul rising on the wings of desire seeks its heavenly home, but falls helpless and overwhelmed with sadness because it must yet wait long time. Below I see hell, which fills me with terror. I communed last night with the Lord, and said, " Pity me, Lord ; lead me back to my haven." "It is impossible; see you not that the wind is contrary?" "I will preach, if so I must; but why need I meddle with the government of Florence?" "If thou wouldst make Florence a holy city thou must establish her on firm foundations, and give her a government which favours virtue." "But, Lord, I am not sufficient for these things." "Knowest thou not that God chooses the weak of this world to confound the mighty? Thou art the instrument, I am the doer." Then I was convinced, and cried, "Lord, I will do Thy will; but tell me, what shall be my reward?" "Eye hath not seen nor ear heard." "But in this life, Lord?" "My son, the servant is not above his master. The Jews made Me die on the Cross: a like lot awaits thee." "Yea, Lord, let me die as Thou didst die for me." Then He said, "Wait yet

a while; let that be done which must be done, then arm thy-
self with courage." [1]

These predictions of troubles were soon realised. It was
inevitable that the political attitude of Florence should be
challenged, and that Savonarola's responsibility should be
brought to light. When the league against France was being
formed Alexander VI. strove to draw Florence into it, but his
envoy reported that the city was entirely under the power of
Savonarola. In July 1495 the Pope invited him to come to
Rome and explain his claims to a divine commission. Savonarola excused himself on the ground of ill-health, and for a time
his excuses were admitted. He referred the Pope to his book,
'Compendium Revelationum,' which was just on the point of
appearing, and which contained a simple account of the growth
of his belief in his own mission. In this book he recognises the
arguments against this belief; they had sorely tried his own
mind till he saw in them temptations of the devil to lead him
away from his duty. The tempter suggested to him that he
was misled by his moral enthusiasm to seek a sanction for his
words, and urged that prophets ought to prove their commission
by performing miracles. Against him Savonarola quoted the
examples of Jonah and John the Baptist, who were prophets
sent from God to call men to repentance, but who had no
power beyond that of their words. The book ends with a pre-
diction of the Virgin that Florence after trials and tribulations
would come forth more glorious than before.

Savonarola
suspended
from
preaching.
September,
1495.

We may doubt if Alexander VI. read Savonarola's book.
He had no objection to Savonarola preaching or prophesying as
he chose, but he could not understand the political attitude of
Florence. Charles VIII. had left Italy without restoring Pisa,
and the Florentines had nothing to hope from French help, yet
they showed no disposition to enter the League. Alexander VI.
on September 8 addressed to them a letter, in which he professed his desire for peace, declared his intention of excommunicating Charles VIII. if he again attempted to invade
Italy, and threatened all who aided him with like penalties.
He exhorted the Florentines not to endure the reproach of

---

[1] Sermon xix., Advent, 1494; quoted by Bayonne, *Etude sur Jérôme
Savonarola*, 61 &c.

being the only men who sought the ruin of Italy.[1] Besides
this general admonition the Pope issued a brief, specially
addressed to Savonarola, declaring that he had been led astray
by novel and perverse doctrine, had spoken rashly, and despite
his warnings had published his sermons. Till the case was
further investigated he suspended Savonarola from preaching.[2]
Savonarola replied by entreating the Pope to inform himself
better before deciding. Meanwhile, as an attempt at the
restoration of the Medici caused a ferment in the popular mind
at Florence, he again preached on October 11. On October 16
came a second letter from the Pope, reproaching him with disturbing the peace of the city and again ordering him to be
silent.

Savonarola bowed to the Pope's command, and during
Advent his voice was not heard in the pulpit. The Florentine
people were discontented at his silence. In truth Savonarola
occupied a position seldom gained by a preacher, for he was the
centre of a great revival of religious zeal, of a moral reformation,
and of a new system of government which strove to carry out
his principles. The feverish ardour of his followers needed
the stimulus of his exhortations. Florence believed in his
prophetic gift and longed for his consolations to support her in
the repeated disappointments of the recovery of Pisa. The
magistrates were urgent that the Pope should recall his suspension, as the city had with difficulty endured Savonarola's
silence during Advent. On February 11, 1496, the Signori
decreed that Savonarola should preach in Lent, or earlier if
he chose, under pain of their severe displeasure.[3] It would
seem that Alexander VI., pressed to recall his suspension, made
some vague remark that Savonarola might preach as he pleased
provided he did not speak evil of the Pope or the Court
of Rome. This remark was communicated to Savonarola by
his friend Cardinal Caraffa, and Savonarola regarded it as sufficient permission.[4]

*Savonarola
resumes
preaching.
February,
1496.*

---

[1] Sanuto, *Spedizione di Carlo*, viii. 584.

[2] I have followed Gherardi, *Nuori Documenti intorno a Savonarola*, 256,
and Bayonne, *Etude sur Jérôme Savonarola*, 75, in transferring the letters
given in Quetef, ii. 130, and there dated October 16, 1497, to the dates of
September 8 and October 14, 1495.

[3] Gherardi, *Nuori Documenti*, 65.

[4] This permission of the Pope is somewhat obscure. Pandolfini, Bishop

BOOK
V.

Florentine
Carnival of
1496.

The Carnival of 1496 gave a striking exhibition of Savonarola's moral influence over the city. Instead of the licentious masques wherewith Lorenzo de' Medici had gratified the popular taste, Savonarola organised religious processions. Instead of the Carnival songs the streets of Florence echoed with the music of lauds. Savonarola had always attracted the young. He had arranged raised seats for them in the cathedral where they might listen without disturbing the crowd below. He had enrolled them into guilds for the promotion of moral reform, and to the great consolation of sober citizens had checked 'the silly and brutal custom of stone-throwing,' whereby the youth of the city disturbed the peace of respectable elders.[1] He now produced a deep impression on the popular imagination by processions of children, varying in age from six to sixteen, who bore olive branches in their hands and chanted lauds with cries of 'Viva Cristo e la Vergine Maria nostra regina.' Their parents were moved by the memory of Christ's entry into Jerusalem, and felt the meaning of the words 'out of the mouths of babes and sucklings hast thou perfected praise.' Such was the zeal of these youthful enthusiasts that their mothers could not keep them in bed on the mornings when the Friar preached, so eager were they to be in their places in the cathedral. No wonder that this childish zeal was contagious. Pious hearts were deeply touched and said 'This is the Lord's doing.'[2]

Savonarola
criticises
the papal
inhibition.
February,
1496.

It was natural that Savonarola should be stirred by this testimony to his moral power. It is inevitable that the preacher and the social reformer should be nurtured on the enthusiasm which he excites, and should forget the strength of opposing forces which are hidden from his eyes. To Savonarola Italy was centred in Florence, and Florence was swayed by his words. The papal inhibition did not remind him

---

of Pistoia (Marchese, *Archivio Storico*, Appendix, viii. 151), writing from Rome, March 24, speaks of 'permessa per la relazione di uno Cardinale.' But Savonarola, in resuming his preaching, makes no allusion to any papal permission, nor does the decree of the Signori. Perhaps it was judged expedient to make use of a vague intimation which could not be publicly alleged.

[1] 'Fu dimessa quella stolta e bestiale consuetudine del giuoco de' sassi,' says Nardi. Luca Landucci, p. 124, says the same.

[2] So thought Luca Landucci (125-26), whose children were amongst the 'blessed bands.'

that there were larger interests beyond, and that his conception
of the mission of Florence was opposed to the current views of
the stability of Italian affairs. He appeared before the Florentines with unabated confidence in his own prophetic mission, and
declared his loyalty to the Catholic Church, by which he meant
the Church of Rome ; to its decision he was always ready to
submit himself and his teaching. But, he went on to say, no
papal prohibition could move him from the path of duty. 'We
are not bound to obey all commands. If they come through
false information, they are not valid. If they contradict the
law of love set forth in the Gospel, we must withstand them as
S. Paul withstood S. Peter. We cannot suppose such a possibility : but if it were so, we must answer our superior, "You
err ; you are not the Roman Church, you are a man and a
sinner."'[1]

These were bold words; but if they were reported to
Alexander VI. he does not seem to have paid any heed to them
on personal or ecclesiastical grounds. He had suffered enough
from one French invasion and was resolved to run no risk of a
second. He was bent upon banding Italy against the invader,
and Florence must be won over to the Italian League. He had
no quarrel against Florence, no ill-will against Savonarola ;
but Florence must abandon its alliance with France, and
Savonarola was the leader of the French party in Florence.
Alexander VI. wished to settle matters quietly, and, as a man
of the world, was amazed at the infatuation of Florence for a
' chattering friar.'[2] He had allowed Savonarola to preach on
the tacit understanding that he should keep away from politics
and confine himself to religion. He was indignant when he
heard that Savonarola had shown himself more obstinate than
before in his political ideas and even dared to brave the Pope's
displeasure. So long as Savonarola confined himself to the
things of the kingdom of Heaven, the Pope was content that
he should go his own way ; but he could not be allowed to
interfere longer with the Pope's views about the affairs of his
earthly kingdom.[3]

---

[1] Predica del 17 Febbraio, 1496.

[2] Alexander VI. said to the Florentine envoy that their obstinacy lay ' nella
prophetia di quello vostro *parabolano* ': Gherardi, *Nuovi Documenti*, 82.

[3] 'Molto si duole di Fra Geronimo,' writes the Florentine envoy from

Alexander VI. was too much of a practical statesman to push matters to extremity. The words of Savonarola provoked a passing anger; but Alexander VI. was not intolerant of plain speaking. He thought it beneath the papal dignity to quarrel with a friar. The enemies of Savonarola were numerous, and they filled the Pope's ear with complaints against him. They magnified his influence in Florence, they distorted his words, they forged letters from him to Charles VIII. urging a new French invasion of Italy. But Alexander VI. was not greatly moved by any of these things. From time to time he warned Savonarola; but he had no wish to proceed severely against him. He bent all his efforts to induce Florence to break off its alliance with France and enter the Italian League. He knew that Savonarola was the chief obstacle to his wish; but he was willing to try all other means before attacking Savonarola himself.

So matters stood when Maximilian proposed to enter Italy. The League was powerful and Florence was weak. It was suffering from a long famine; its people were impoverished by the long war; its castles were badly fortified and ill prepared to endure a siege; help from France was no longer to be expected. The envoys of the Pope and of the League made fair promises of the restoration of Pisa, if only the French alliance were abandoned. Florence was in great straits and for a moment its citizens wavered. But they valued their newly won liberty; they dreaded that the triumph of the League would mean the restoration of the Medici; they could not put much faith in promises made by a body of allies whose separate interests were so diverse. They resolved that they would not try a new fortune, whatever risks their resolution might bring.

Maximilian and his allies came to teach Florence a lesson. They were joyously received at Pisa, and in the middle of October undertook the siege of Livorno. The Venetian ships blockaded it by sea and cut off supplies from the famished Florentines. Attempts to bring provisions were frustrated by a storm which scattered the ships laden with corn from

Rome, 'per intendere quel dice, et che da Monsignore reverendissimo di Napoli et molti altri gli era stato promesso non s' impaccerebbe *delle cose di quà.*' The phrase 'cose di quà' smacks of the directness of expression which characterised Alexander VI.

Marseilles. Florence was in great distress and men turned to Savonarola for comfort. On October 28 he preached a stirring sermon and promised them speedy help. On October 30 the miraculous image of the Virgin of S. Maria della Impruneta was carried in procession through the city; and the strains of the penitential litany were suddenly broken by a shout of joy. A messenger came from Livorno bringing the news that some ships from Marseilles, taking advantage of a storm which scattered the Venetian squadron, had entered the harbour of Livorno with supplies.

This transient success would have availed the Florentines little if the allies had resolutely pushed the siege. But the Venetians and Milanese were suspicious of one another, and neither of them really wished to see Maximilian obtain a foothold in Italy. The storms of autumn wrecked the Venetian fleet, and Maximilian himself was in peril of his life. The ships were disabled, and Maximilian, weary of his profitless enterprise, left Pisa on November 21, and hastened into Lombardy. There he bitterly reproached the Milanese and Venetians for their conduct; then he returned ingloriously across the Alps. Savonarola's predictions were fulfilled; Florence was saved, and looked with greater confidence upon its prophet.

It would seem that Alexander VI. had not put great confidence in the success of this expedition as a means of solving the Florentine difficulty. He negotiated privately with Savonarola that he might win him to his own side. He sent to Florence the Proctor-General of the Dominicans, Luigi of Ferrara, who for three days reasoned with the prophet. At last, when he had exhausted his arguments, he said: 'The Pope, confident in your virtue and wisdom, will raise you to the cardinalate if you will cease to foretell the future.' 'I cannot abandon the embassy of the King, my master,' replied Savonarola, 'Come to my sermon to-morrow, and I will answer you.' Next day Savonarola asserted anew his belief in his prophecies, then he went on: 'I seek no earthly glory; far be it from me. It is enough, my God, that Thy blood was shed through love for me. I only wish to be glorified in Thee. I seek neither hat nor mitre, I desire only what Thou hast given to Thy saints—death. Give me a hat, a red hat, but red with

CHAP. VIII.

Retreat of Maximilian. November, 1496.

Alexander VI. negotiates with Savonarola. 1496.

BOOK
V.

Alexander
VI. founds
a new Con-
gregation
of Domini-
cans. No-
vember,
1496.

blood; that is my desire.' Fra Luigi had his answer and returned to Rome.[1]

Savonarola's bitterest and most skilful enemies were those of the Dominican Order, who were jealous of his reputation and viewed his reforms with alarm. One of them, Francesco Mei, suggested to the Pope a plan by which this inconvenient politician might be silenced. Savonarola was strong in Florence by virtue of his independent position as head of the Tuscan Congregation of the Dominican Order. That position had been conferred on him by a papal brief; inasmuch as he misused his power, let the Pope take it away. This could easily be done by a redistribution of the Dominican convents. Savonarola had induced the Pope to separate the Tuscan Congregation from the Congregation of Lombardy. Plausible reasons could be adduced for a further change, for the formation of a new Congregation which should unite the Convent of S. Marco at Florence with some convents detached from the Congregations of Lombardy and of Rome. Grounds of convenience in ecclesiastical organisation could easily be found for the creation of this Tusco-Roman Congregation, which would destroy Savonarola's independent position and subject him to the orders of an ecclesiastical superior.

No doubt this was an unworthy manœuvre; but it was a skilful one. Savonarola could not urge much against it; for he himself had used the Pope's authority to arrange for his own purposes the distribution of the Dominican convents. It was true that his plan was founded upon a sound principle and had met with success. It was equally true that the new scheme set forth by the Pope's brief was opposed to all sound principles, was almost impracticable, and had no other end than the removal of Savonarola from Florence. But men not versed in details could not so clearly see the issue. Even the Florentine envoy at Rome wrote home that Savonarola was bound to obey the Pope, whose plan was not directed against himself, but was solely for the honour of God.[2]

[1] I have accepted this story on the ground of the concurrent testimony of Savonarola's biographers, who, however, give no precise date to this offer of a cardinal's hat. I have followed Bayonne, *Nouvelles Etudes sur Savonarole*, 90, in assigning it to this period, on the ground that the words quoted occur in a sermon preached August 20, 1496.

[2] Gherardi, *Nuovi Documenti*, p. 84, n. 5, under date of March 19, 1497.

The papal brief was issued on November 7, 1496, ordering
the priors and monks of the convents named to join the new
Congregation under penalty of excommunication. Savonarola
did not disguise from himself the weight of the blow which
had fallen upon him; 'The children of my mother,' he exclaimed, 'have fought against me.' He resolved to offer a
resolute but moderate resistance. It would be unfair to say that
he was moved thereto solely by personal considerations. Great
as was his influence in Florence, much as he believed in his
mission to the city, he was above all things true to his convent.
He lived amongst his brethren; he fired them with his own zeal
for righteousness; he cared for their souls. If the proposed
change were made, his work in S. Marco would be undone,
his reforms would be swept away, his devoted band of brethren
would be dispersed. For their sake, for God's sake, he felt it
to be his duty to resist.

His first steps showed his straightforwardness. He gathered
together the parents of his monks, who were mostly members
of noble families, and asked their opinion. They answered
unanimously that they were opposed to the new scheme, and if
it were carried out, would remove their sons. Then Savonarola
gathered together his brethren, who to the number of two hundred and fifty set their hands to a letter to the Pope in which
they declared that they would suffer any hardship rather than
consent to the proposed union.[1]

Here this matter rested for a time. The failure of Maximilian and his allies at Livorno was hailed by the Florentines
as a great deliverance. The republican party was strengthened,
and Savonarola's influence in Florence was secure. But he
felt that the plots against him were gradually producing an
effect. Each attack might be repulsed, but it involved some
loss. Savonarola was more and more driven to stand on the defensive, and a false step at any moment was sure to be fatal.
He was more and more diligent in his work as a moral reformer,
and found an enthusiastic helper in Fra Domenico da Pescia, to
whom he especially committed the training of the young. The
Carnival of 1497 was signalised by the puritan efforts of Savonarola's boys. They went from door to door asking for 'vanities,'

[1] See Savonarola's *Apologeticum Fratrum Congregationis Sancti Marci*, in
Quetif, ii. 74.

and gathered a huge pile of miscellaneous objects which the consciences of the people prompted them to give up. Immodest books, pictures, ornaments, frivolous articles of attire, whatever was thought to stand in the way of godliness, all were heaped up in the Piazza de' Signori and were solemnly burned. It was the most striking and the most dramatic testimony to Savonarola's influence over the luxurious and artistic Florentines.

Meanwhile Alexander VI. was steadily pursuing his policy of detaching Florence from France. He appealed to the self-interest of the Florentines by offering on behalf of the Italian League to restore Pisa, provided the Florentines would show themselves 'good Italians' by breaking their alliance with France and joining the League. The promise was fair; but the Florentines asked themselves how it was to be fulfilled. If they could not win back Pisa for themselves, they doubted if the Pope and the League could win it for them. The Florentine envoy in Rome, Bracci, was instructed to tell the Pope that Florence would not abandon its French alliance. He did so, adding that nevertheless the Florentines were 'excellent Italians,' and that their alliance with France involved no obligation to injure in any way any Italian power. Alexander VI.'s answer was characteristic of his resoluteness and plain speaking. 'Sir secretary,' he said, 'you are as fat as we are, but you have come with a thin commission; and if you have nothing else to say you may begone. We see that your masters stand on their customary fair speeches and excuses; we tell you that if you do not wish our blessing, it shall be far from you. We shall be blameless before God and man if, after having done our duty as a good shepherd towards your city, you yourselves wish to be the cause of your own ill, which, we tell you, is closer than you think. You will find that, since you do not choose to come to our side through goodwill, you will have to come of necessity, through force and through means whereby we can make a great revolution in your affairs. We do not know whence springs this obstinacy of yours.' He paused and went on in a still more angry voice, 'We believe that it has its root in the prophecies of your chattering friar.' Then he went on to complain that the government of Florence allowed Savonarola to speak evil of himself.[1]

[1] Bracci's *Relazione* in Gherardi, *Nuovi Documenti*, pp. 82-3.

The immediate result of the Pope's menace was an attempt by Piero de' Medici to surprise Florence. Piero was driven from its gates on April 28, and the Medicean party in Florence was consequently discredited. The Arrabbiati gained political ascendency, and the new magistrates were not so warmly in Savonarola's favour. This encouraged his opponents, who seized the opportunity of his next appearance to make a demonstration against him. He was to preach on Ascension Day, May 4, and the previous night some young men managed to enter the Duomo and fill the pulpit with filth. The news of this outrage produced great excitement amongst Savonarola's congregation. Men listened with excited feelings, and when during the sermon the chest for receiving alms was pushed over and fell with a clang, there was a general uproar. A body of Savonarola's friends gathered round the pulpit and drew their swords. Savonarola in vain tried to quiet the disturbance. He knelt a while in silent prayer; then he left the Duomo, and was escorted home by a band of armed adherents.

CHAP. VIII.

Demonstration against Savonarola. May 4, 1497.

This scandalous scene caused much talk throughout Italy. The Florentine magistrates issued an order prohibiting friars of any order to preach without their permission, and the benches which had been erected in the Duomo for Savonarola's congregation were all removed. Though they hastened to inform the Pope what they had done, and at the same time spoke slightingly of the disturbance which had taken place, their apologies came too late. On May 13 the Pope signed a brief excommunicating Savonarola, on the grounds that he was suspected of preaching dangerous doctrines, that he had refused the Pope's summons to come to Rome and clear himself, had continued preaching in spite of the Pope's prohibitions, and refused to obey the Pope's orders to unite the Convent of S. Marco to a newly-instituted Congregation.

Excommunication of Savonarola. May 13, 1497.

Still, though the brief was signed, it was not published till June 18. Alexander VI. did not wish to quarrel with the Florentine people, but wished to strike Savonarola only. The brief was not addressed to the people and clergy of Florence; but briefs were sent to the several convents, and were published by the brethren at their discretion.[1] Savonarola replied by a

[1] There is a difference of date in the publication of the excommunication; but Luca Landucci, *Diario*. p. 153, gives the date June 18, as an eyewitness in

letter addressed to all Christians, in which he argued that an unjust excommunication was invalid. He quoted Gerson as an authority for resisting a Pope who misused his power. He quoted the decrees of Constance and Basel as to the limitation of excommunications. But the arguments of a letter sounded cold to those who had hung on the prophet's lips. There was nothing to kindle the enthusiasm of Savonarola's followers, and they mourned that they were 'deprived of the Word of God.'[1] A reaction against puritanism set in. The taverns were again filled with customers, and the games at the street corners were resumed. Savonarola's friends were put on the defensive. They were assailed with ridicule, and were driven to defend themselves by argument in which they did not always get the best.

Still the magistrates of Florence strove to induce the Pope to withdraw his brief of excommunication. Alexander VI. was much grieved by the death of his son the Duke of Gandia, who was found murdered on June 15. He spoke of reforming the Church and instituted a commission of six Cardinals to whom he committed Savonarola's case. Savonarola wrote a letter of condolence to the Pope, in which he urged that zeal for the faith was the one consolation for sorrow.[2] Alexander VI. was not displeased at this frankness, but he soon recovered from his distress and returned to his political interests. Letters expressing confidence in Savonarola were sent to the Pope, one signed by all the brethren of S. Marco, another signed by three hundred and seventy of the chief citizens of Florence. On June 27 Alexander VI. told the Florentine envoy that the publication of the brief of excommunication was contrary to his wishes. But the zeal of Savonarola's friends stirred up a corresponding zeal on the part of his enemies, whose letters accusing Savonarola poured in upon the Pope; and Alexander VI. took no steps to recall his excommunication.

Savonarola remained quietly in his cell at S. Marco, while Florence in the month of August was convulsed by a great

---

Santo Spirito. The publication in the Duomo may have taken place on June 22.

[1] Luca Landucci, 151 : 'Eravamo privati del verbo di Dio. Non lasciavano predicare in chiesa veruna.'

[2] The letter is published by Perrens, *Jérôme Savonarole*, Appendix ix.

strife. Evidence came to light which fixed the blame of the Medicean rising in April on five of the chief citizens of Florence, whose complicity had hitherto been unsuspected. There was great excitement and much discussion what was to be done. Ultimately the conspirators were put to death without the chance of appeal. The result of this firmness was the supremacy in Florence of Savonarola's friends, the Piagnoni. Savonarola himself took no part in this affair; he was engaged in publishing his great theological work, 'Il Trionfo della Croce.' He had good hopes that the Pope would revoke his censure, and was content to wait quietly, and allow the arguments of his friends to sink into the minds of the people. He did not wish to scandalise his weaker brethren, though he did not hope to justify himself to his opponents.[1] He was prepared to maintain that the excommunication was issued on erroneous grounds, and that the Pope had overstepped the limits of justice; but he waited for a time before taking any definite action.

At last Savonarola stood forward in opposition to the Pope's excommunication. On Christmas Day he celebrated the mass in S. Marco. The Florentine magistrates declared themselves on his side by going on the Epiphany to make offerings in S. Marco, where they kissed Savonarola's hand as he stood by the high altar. He was invited to resume his preaching, and the seats were again erected in the Duomo. The vicar of the Archbishop of Florence attempted to prevent this; but the Signori threatened to declare him a rebel unless he withdrew his opposition. On February 11, 1498, Savonarola again entered the pulpit and preached to an anxious crowd. Regarding the excommunication he said: 'God governs the world by secondary agents, which are instruments in His hand. When the agent withdraws himself from God, he is no longer an instrument; he is a broken iron. But, you will ask how I am to know when the agent fails. I answer: compare his commands with the root of all wisdom, that is, good living and charity: if they are contrary thereto the instrument is a broken iron, and you are no longer bound to obey. Those who by false reports have sought my excommunication wished to do away with good

---

[1] Bayonne, *Nouvelle Etude*, 127, quotes Piero de la Salice, who seems to show Savonarola's policy at this time: 'Quo facto amplius non est scandalum pusillorum, sed Pharisæorum, unde contemnendum.'

living and good government, to open the door to every vice.'
Savonarola appealed from the Pope to the better informed conscience of his hearers. He explained his position more fully
to the envoy of the Duke of Ferrara, to whom he said: 'I
could not take any commission to preach from the Signori, nor
even from the Pope, seeing that he continues in his present
manner of life. I await my commission from One superior to
the Pope and to every other creature.' When the envoy represented the possible scandal that might arise, Savonarola
answered: 'If I knew that the excommunication was justified
I would have respected it. Moreover, I am more than certain
that my preaching will cause no scandal nor disorder in the
city.'[1]

*Division in
his party.*

Savonarola overestimated the weight attaching to good
intentions when they lead to a course opposed to recognised
order. 'Many,' says one of his Florentine followers, 'refused
to go to his preaching through fear of the excommunication,
saying, "Just or unjust, it is to be feared." I myself was one
of those who did not go.'[2] Men of this cautious turn of mind
did not make their voices heard, but their attitude was
dangerous. Savonarola listened only to the eager disciples
who crowded round him, saying 'When will you preach again?
We are dying of hunger.'[3] He satisfied their desires. His
sermons followed thick and fast during the month of February.
In the Carnival, on February 27, Savonarola said mass in S.
Marco, and with his own hand communicated all the brethren of
the convent and several thousands of men and women. Then
he advanced to a pulpit outside the church, bearing in his hand
the consecrated host, and adjured God to strike him dead if he
had spoken anything false, if he deserved the excommunication.
Popular excitement ran high, and many expected to see signs
and wonders. There was another ' Burning of Vanities ' in the
Piazza. His opponents mocked and said, ' He is excommunicated himself and communicates others.' Sober citizens who
believed in his commission thought that he was making

---

[1] Manfreddi to Ercole of Ferrara, February 1, 1498, in Capelli, *Documenti*
in *Atti e Memorie per le Provincie Modenesi*, iv. 398.

[2] Luca Landucci, *Diario*, 162.

[3] *Processo di Savonarola*, in Villari, ii. 266: ' Alchuni di quelli che usavan
in San Marco mi dicevano, Quando si predica? noi ci moiamo di fame.'

a mistake, and abstained from showing themselves on his side.[1]

Savonarola's first sermon was circulated throughout Italy and produced much comment. Alexander VI. could scarcely enjoy being called 'a broken iron;' but he was not a man to attach importance to hasty words. He showed no resentment against Savonarola, and listened to the Florentine envoys who pleaded in his favour. He was anxious only for the success of his political plans, and on February 22 again pressed the envoys to know if Florence would lay aside its alliance with France. When they held out no hopes he rose in anger and left the room. At the door he paused and said, 'Go on and set Fra Girolamo to preach. I could never have believed that you would have treated me thus.'[2] In vain the envoys tried to calm him. On February 25 he threatened to lay Florence under an interdict. Next day he issued two briefs, one to the Canons of the Duomo ordering them to prevent Savonarola from preaching in their church, the other to the Signori bidding them send Savonarola to Rome. Still he showed himself placable to the Florentine envoys. He was still ready to work for the restoration of Pisa, if Florence would join the League: if Savonarola would cease from preaching he was willing to absolve him. On March 1 he assembled the ambassadors of the League and proposed to them the restitution of Pisa to Florence. All agreed except the Venetian envoy, who expressed distrust of Florence and tried to irritate the Pope against her by quoting Savonarola's sermons and exaggerating their expressions against the Pope. Alexander VI. answered with calmness, exhorting the Venetians to agree to a step which was for the common good of Italy: he himself would not allow any private injury to stand in the way of that end.[3]

But Alexander VI. was now resolved to reduce Savonarola to silence. He commissioned Savonarola's old enemy, Fra Mariano da Genazzano, to preach against his doctrines at Rome. Fra Mariano lost himself in unworthy and scurrilous abuse, to the disgust of his audience.[4] Yet the Florentine ambassador

---

[1] Luca Landucci, *Diario*, 163: 'E benche a me e' pareva errore, ancora che gli credessi: ma non volli mettermi mai a pericolo andare a udirlo, poichè fu scommunicato.'

[2] Gherardi, *Nuovi Documenti*, 104.   [3] *Id.* 109, 110.

[4] Villari, Appendix No. xli., gives a letter from Rome describing his sermon.

regarded his sermon as an ominous sign of the Pope's displeasure. Piero de' Medici was frequently seen at the Vatican,
and the Pope showed him manifest signs of his favour. The
Florentine merchants in Rome were threatened with the withdrawal of the Pope's protection and the confiscation of their
goods; they petitioned the Florentine magistrates to act in
their behalf. The scheme for the restoration of Pisa was held
before the Florentine envoy, and the Pope declared that he
would no longer favour Florence unless Savonarola were silenced.
The envoy wrote anxious letters home. The majority of the magistrates who had come into office did not belong to Savonarola's
party, but they would not at once abandon him. They wrote,
on March 3, a dignified defence of his wonderful influence as a
moral reformer; and said that they could not obey the Pope's
commands without causing serious disturbances in Florence.
When this letter was laid before the Pope he expressed his surprise. 'No attention has been paid to my brief. If Savonarola is not stayed from preaching, I will lay Florence under an
interdict. I do not condemn him for his good teaching, but
because he preaches though excommunicated, and does not seek
absolution.' He looked at the letter of the magistrates and
declared that he recognised it as composed by Savonarola.

The Pope knew that the Florentine magistrates were beginning to give way. On March 9 he issued another brief which
was written with great moderation. He could not suffer an
excommunicated man to continue preaching, and he ordered the
magistrates to prevent him. 'As regards Fra Girolamo,' he
continued, ' we only demand that he should repent and come to
us: we will receive him readily, and after restoring him to the
Church by our absolution, will send him back to save souls in
your city by preaching the word of God.'[1] Savonarola's answer
to the brief was that he could not free himself from embarrass-
ment by trampling on his conscience; he was certain that his
teaching came from God.

The Florentine magistrates, on March 14, summoned a

---

[1] Gherardi, *Nuori Documenti*, 114–120, publishes this brief from the
Florentine Archives, and is of opinion that it is the original, as it bears the
same date as the Florentine envoy's letter from Rome. The brief, as given by
Villari and Perrens, is more violent, and seems to have been a first draft,
which was subsequently modified.

CHAP.
VIII.

Savonarola
forbidden
to preach
by the
magis-
trates.
March,
1498.

council to deliberate. There were various opinions; but the majority was in favour of suspending Savonarola from preaching. Still the magistrates held their hands, and on March 17 again summoned some of the chief citizens to give their advice. The general conclusion was to persuade Savonarola to abstain from preaching, but to answer that the other demands of the Pope were unworthy of the city.[1] On March 18 Savonarola preached his last sermon and took farewell of his congregation. For his own part, he said, he was glad to be relieved of the labour of preaching; he was glad to betake himself to study; he would carry on by his prayers the work which he had begun by his sermons; God would send another to take his place.

The letters of the Florentine magistrates telling of this resolution did not reach Rome till March 22. Alexander VI. was angry at this long delay, and had uttered many threats to the Florentine envoy who was relieved to have some answer to carry to the Pope. The answer fell far short of what Alexander VI. desired; Savonarola was not commanded, but only persuaded, to abstain from preaching; he was not sent to Rome to ask for absolution. Moreover the Pope had addressed a brief to the Florentine magistrates; he received no direct answer from them, but only a communication through their envoy. However, Alexander VI. received the answer in good part. He said, 'If Fra Girolamo will obey for a time and then ask for absolution, I will willingly give it him and give him liberty to preach. I do not condemn his doctrine, but only his preaching without absolution, his evil speaking of us, and his despite of our censures. If we endured such things there would be an end of the apostolic authority.'[2]

But though Alexander VI. spoke fairly, he was resolved to act resolutely. He was angered at hearing that though Savonarola's voice was silenced, his followers, chief of whom was Fra Domenico da Pescia, continued fervently to deliver their master's messages to the Florentine people. On March 31 he told the Florentine envoy that he purposed sending a prelate to Florence to demand that Savonarola should come to Rome and make his submission. The envoy saw in this a change from the

---

[1] For the exact relations of these deliberations see Cosci in *Archivio Storico Italiano*, vol. iv. (1879) p. 452.

[2] Gherardi, *Nuovi Documenti*, p. 130.

Pope's previous attitude of indifference ; and Alexander VI. had motives concerned with weightier matters than the political combinations of Italy, to urge him to deprive Savonarola of the power of attack.

Alexander VI. had many enemies who were ready to use against him any weapon that could be found. Cardinal Rovere had urged Charles VIII. to summon a Council and inquire into the simoniacal election of the Pope. Charles VIII. had shrunk from a task of such magnitude, from which he had little to gain, and for which his own character rendered him unfit. But in the end of 1497 a change came over Charles VIII. The death of his infant son had given him a shock, and he began to think more seriously of his duties. He laid before the Sorbonne a series of questions. Were the decrees of Constance for the summoning of future Councils binding on the Pope ? If the Pope did not summon a Council, could the scattered members of the Church gather together of themselves ? If other princes refused, could the King of France call together a Council for the good of the Church ? The Sorbonne replied in the affirmative to all these questions.

It was natural for Alexander VI. to dread this possible revival of the conciliar spirit. He knew how Charles VIII. had been impressed by Savonarola. He knew that Savonarola's prophetic claims, his moral earnestness, and his wonderful influence at Florence, made him an important personage. Savonarola had spoken boldly of the need of reform in the head of the Church and of the corruptions of the Roman Curia ; in a General Council he would prove a dangerous adversary. Alexander VI. had been willing to try and win him over ; when once he had broken with him it was necessary to reduce him to silence. There is no reason to think that he wished for more than Savonarola's submission ; but that he must have. Savonarola had called him a ' broken iron,' had rejected his excommunication as unjust, and when driven to extremities had approached the subject of a Council. On March 9 he said in his sermon, ' Tell me, Florence, what is a Council ? Men have forgotten ; but how comes it that your sons know nothing of it, and there is no Council now ? You answer, " Father, it cannot be gathered together." That is perhaps true. A Council is the Church, all good prelates, abbots, and scholars. But there is no Church

without the grace of the Holy Spirit ; and where is that to be
found ? Perhaps only in some obscure good man. And for this
reason you may say that there can be no Council. A Council
would have to make its own reformers. It would have to
punish all the evil clergy, and perhaps there would be left none
who were not deposed. This is why it is hard to summon a
Council. Pray the Lord that it may one day be possible.'

On the arrival of the Pope's last brief, Savonarola wrote a
dignified letter with his own hand to Alexander VI. He said
that he had laboured for the salvation of souls and the restoration of Christian discipline ; he had been assailed by many foes,
and had hoped for help and comfort from the Pope, but the
Pope had joined his enemies ; he could only submit himself
patiently to God, who sometimes 'chose the weak things of
this world to confound the mighty.' 'May your Holiness,' he
ended, ' make haste to provide for your own salvation.' After
this, there could only be avowed hostility between the Pope and
the ardent apostle of righteousness.

Savonarola knew that many of the Cardinals were in favour
of summoning a Council. He employed several of his friends
in Florence, who had relatives amongst the Florentine envoys
at foreign courts, to submit to them a memorandum on the
motives for summoning a General Council. This was sent to
the Emperor and the Kings of France, Spain, England and
Hungary. Meanwhile Savonarola in his cell was preparing
letters which would carry the matter farther.[1]

Savonarola had been driven into a position where he was
likely to create a movement in the ecclesiastical politics of
Europe. His weakness was that he was too closely identified
with the particular politics of Florence. He had begun as a moral
reformer in the great centre of the life of Italy. He had aimed
at regenerating Florence so that it should be a city set on a hill,
whose light would spread far and wide. He had interpreted
its political events as warnings from on high, and had led it

Isolation of Savonarola.

---

[1] I agree with Bayonne, *Nourelle Etude sur Savonarole*, 183–84, in thinking
that the letters of Savonarola to the Christian princes were never sent. They
are published by Perrens, by Meyer, and by Baluze, *Miscellanea*, vol. iv. They
accuse Alexander VI. of simony, and say that he is not a Christian but an
unbeliever. If these letters were the work of Savonarola at all, they were
merely rough drafts, which were never sent, and we cannot say how much
they were falsified by his enemies.

to adopt a political attitude which seemed to him to have
the sanction of God. This political attitude of Florence had
many political opponents. When they could not move Savonarola as a politician, they attacked him as a prophet. With some
difficulty they brought against him the authority of the head of
the Church, and forced him into collision with the ecclesiastical
system. Savonarola set to work to enlist on his side the long-
ings of the nations of Europe for ecclesiastical reform. Till
this could be done he rested on the approval of his own conscience, on his individual sense of a divine guidance. His
followers believed in him on the ground of his own assertions.
His enemies hastened to take advantage of his isolation, and
challenged him to bring to some clear and palpable test his
claims to a divine mission.

Savonarola in his later sermons had expressed his inmost
feelings of profound trust in God. Like the Hebrew Psalmist
he saw God on the side of the just; he perceived the nothingness
of the wicked; he believed that when troubles pressed most near
the hour of God's deliverance was close at hand. Now that he
was put to silence his enemies gathered round him and cried,
'There, there, so would we have it.' The deadly struggle of
the world against the righteous man raged round Savonarola,
and made him a hero of the eternal tragedy of the human
soul.

Attacks of
the Fran-
ciscan
preachers.

The dealings of the Florentine magistrates with the Pope,
the consultations of the citizens, the political intrigues, the
flying rumours, had awakened a feverish excitement in the city.
When Savonarola's voice was silenced the voices of smaller
men began to be heard. The enemies of Savonarola had
always been well represented in the pulpit. The Franciscans of
S. Croce had seen with jealousy the growing importance of the
Dominicans of S. Marco. The Franciscan preachers had always
been ready to point out the errors of Savonarola's teaching;
but hitherto their eloquence had met with little attention.
There was no case to be made against Savonarola; nothing that
could be offered as an equivalent to the interest attaching to
his bold and fervent treatment of religious and social questions.
But the papal excommunication and Savonarola's refusal to
heed it opened out a fertile field for polemics. Savonarola's
conduct might be justifiable, but it was certainly revolutionary.

Many men were undecided and wished to hear both sides before making up their minds. The Fransciscans had little to say that men cared to hear, so long as they attacked in Savonarola the moral reformer, the political regenerator of Florence ; but now a controversy concerning the meaning and limits of the power of excommunication was one in which every Florentine was willing to take a part. Hence came the importance of silencing Savonarola. So long as the stream of his impassioned eloquence continued, he could confirm the waverers, and his adversaries were little heeded. When Savonarola's voice was no longer heard his opponents redoubled their attacks, and the pulpit of S. Croce rang with denunciations of the false prophet, the heretic, the excommunicated monk.

Savonarola's friends waxed equally warm in his defence. Fra Domenico da Pescia was his chief champion, and on March 27. in an impassioned sermon, declared his readiness to enter into the fire to prove his belief in the truth of Savonarola's teaching. Next day he repeated his offer, and declared that many others of the brethren of S. Marco were ready to do likewise. Turning to his congregation he added, ' yes, and many of you would do so too.' Many women rose in their excitement and cried, ' I too am ready.' The Franciscan preacher, Francesco da Puglia, at once took up the challenge. ' I believe,' he said, ' that I shall be burned ; but I am ready to die to free this people. If Savonarola does not burn, you may believe him to be a true prophet.' He set aside the offer of Fra Domenico, and matched himself only with Savonarola.[1]

In the prevailing excitement the rhetoric of two contending preachers was seized upon by Savonarola's foes. The Compagnacci at a supper in the Pitti Palace resolved to use the opportunity. Their leader, Dolfo Spini, assured the Franciscans that they had nothing to fear : the trial would be pre-

---

[1] There is great doubt from which side the challenge first proceeded. I have followed Luca Landucci's account in his *Diario*, 166, 167, though the biographers of Savonarola and Nardi make the challenge proceed from the Franciscans. I think that Landucci's Diary is likely to give the most accurate account of the immediate facts. The challenge had probably been made before to Savonarola, and had been set aside by him. It had probably not been seriously meant ; but when Fra Domenico unwisely revived the recollection of it as a rhetorical artifice, it was at once seized upon by Savonarola's enemies.

vented and Savonarola would be ruined. He found it easy to stir up the populace to wild excitement about the proposal. He enlisted the magistrates on his side by showing them that it afforded a safe way out of their difficulties.

The trial by fire was a remnant of the old judicial system of the ordeal—a system which had been discountenanced by the Church, and had fallen out of use. But its memory still lingered in men's minds, and it seemed to them to apply to the exceptional case before them. Formal documents were drawn up and signed by the champions on either side. Savonarola refused to submit himself to the test. He had not challenged it; but if his champion failed, the consequences would fall upon him. He told his friends that he was sure that God was on his side and would work wonders for him; but He would do so in His own good time; he would not tempt God; the signs which he had already wrought by the results of his preaching were enough to convince those who were open to conviction.

When the news of the proposal reached Rome, Alexander VI. expressed his disapproval. The revival of the ordeal was against the laws of the Church. Moreover, the intention to submit directly to the judgment of God a case which had been called before the Pope's tribunal was in itself a denial of the Pope's spiritual authority. Alexander VI. protested against the ordeal to the Florentine envoy; but he did not send to Florence a formal prohibition. The envoy assured him that there was no means of stopping the trial by fire save by removing the excommunication of Savonarola. This Alexander VI. refused to do, and left things to take their course.[1]

On the morning of Saturday, April 7, the people of Florence thronged with eagerness to the Piazza de' Signori, where a platform, sixty yards long and ten yards broad, was erected and piled at either side with logs smeared with oil and pitch. At S. Marco Savonarola addressed his friends. Miracles, he said, were useless where reason could suffice; he went to the trial with a clear conscience, because he had been provoked and

---

[1] Gherardi, *Nuovi Documenti*, 135–140. Villari's assumption that Alexander VI. favoured this plot against Savonarola is entirely against the evidence. It would have been very awkward for him if by any chance Savonarola had been successful.

could not shrink back without betraying his cause. He committed himself to the hands of God, and besought his friends to stay and pray for him. The brethren of the convent, walking in procession two by two, advanced to the Piazza. Fra Domenico was vested in a chasuble, and by his side went Savonarola, in a white cope, bearing in his hand the consecrated host. As they went they sang the processional psalm, 'Let God arise and let his enemies be scattered,' and the vast throng that followed joined in the strains. They entered the Piazza and took up their position in the Loggia de' Lanzi, of which half was assigned to them and half to the Franciscans.

Fra Domenico was ready, but the Franciscan champion was in the Palazzo. Presently a message was brought demanding that Fra Domenico should lay aside his chasuble, on the ground that it had been enchanted by Savonarola, to whom his enemies wished to ascribe magical arts. Fra Domenico at once assented. Then came a second demand, that he should change his other clothes for a similar reason. Again he agreed, saying that he was ready to wear the dress of any of his brethren. He retired into the Palazzo to change his garments, and when he returned was carefully kept from the neighbourhood of Savonarola lest he should be enchanted afresh. The crowd meanwhile were weary of waiting. They had stood since the early morning and were fasting. A tumult arose, and a band of Compagnacci, who had been waiting their opportunity, made a rush for the Loggia. They were repulsed by the readiness of one of Savonarola's friends, who drew a line upon the ground and dared them to cross it. When order was restored, a heavy thunderstorm burst over the city and the torrents of rain gave a new pretext for delay.

At last the storm was over and preparations were again begun. The Franciscans asked Fra Domenico to lay aside the crucifix which he held in his hand. He did so and took in its stead the consecrated host. To this the Franciscans raised great objections; would he dare to expose the host to fire? This time Savonarola stood firm. His adversaries had done their utmost to show that if he succeeded in the trial it was due to magic; he claimed to be allowed to have God's presence in the Sacrament as a sign that God, and God only, was his defence.

He answered the objection to the possible desecration of the host, by saying that, in any case, only the accidents and not the substance of the Sacrament would be destroyed. The theological discussion occupied much time; at last the magistrates sent a message that the trial would not take place that day. The two bodies of monks retired to their convents.

The crowd angrily dispersed from the Piazza, and the Compagnacci used their opportunity of turning against Savonarola the popular disappointment. The bystanders had not understood what passed. Some of them had come to see a sight and had been disappointed. Many had come expecting to see the prophet give a clear sign of his divine mission. He had spoken of signs and wonders; he had foretold the purposes of God; his followers had gone readily to the trial. The Franciscans, on the other hand, had claimed no divine mission. They had from the first declared that they expected to be burned, and were content to be burned for the sake of unmasking an impostor. It was not for them to show a sign: it was for Savonarola. In the eyes of the people he had failed, and they lost all faith in their prophet; disappointment led to bitterness and a keen sense of deception.

Arrest of
Savona-
rola,
April 8,
1498.

The Compagnacci were well organised and resolved to take advantage of this change of the popular feeling. Next day, Palm Sunday, a body of Compagnacci raised a crowd which rushed to S. Marco, killed such of Savonarola's followers as they met, and stormed the convent with fire and sword. For a time the brethren offered a stubborn resistance, till the magistrates sent a body of men to arrest Savonarola, Fra Domenico, and Fra Silvestro; who were led to the Palazzo amid the shouts of the angry crowd, who heaped upon them every indignity and insult.

Delight of
Alexander
VI.

When the news of these events reached Rome, Alexander VI. was delighted. He had been longsuffering toward Savonarola at first; but when once he declared against him he was resolved upon his humiliation. He had protested against the trial by fire—he could scarcely do otherwise—but when it ended in Savonarola's fall he was quite satisfied. He wrote to the Franciscans and praised their holy zeal, which he would ever hold in grateful memory. He wrote to Fra Francesco da Puglia and incited him to 'persevere in this good and pious

CHAP.
VIII.

work till the evil were entirely destroyed.'[1] He wrote to the Florentine magistrates and praised their action. He absolved the city from all censures which had been incurred through any irregularities committed in the late tumults. The Florentine magistrates used the opportunity of the Pope's graciousness to ask for a grant of a tenth of ecclesiastical revenues, as their exchequer sorely needed replenishing. Alexander VI. replied by a request that Savonarola should be handed over to him for trial. Though the magistrates did not agree to this request, they were anxious in their conduct of the trial to gratify the Pope to the utmost.

The miserable story of Savonarola's trial may be briefly told. A commission of seventeen members was appointed to examine him. They put to the torture the nervous sensitive monk already worn out by asceticism and toil. They questioned him and reduced his incoherent answers to such shape as they pleased. When this did not seem enough to ruin his character they falsified the deposition, and when he heard it read in silence, extorted his signature and announced that he had confessed to being a deceiver of the people. Everything was carefully arranged to ruin him in popular estimation. It was the weakness of Savonarola's career that his efforts sprang too exclusively from a belief in his own individual mission. When his followers saw their prophet in the hands of his enemies they had not the courage to stand alone. The so-called confession of Savonarola sufficed for the time to dispel their faith. 'He confessed,' says one of them, 'that he was not a prophet and had not from God the things that he preached. He confessed that many things which happened during the course of his preaching were contrary to what he had represented. When I heard this confession read I stood in stupor and amazement. My soul was grieved to see so grand an edifice fall to the ground because it was built on the sorry foundation of a lie. I was waiting to see Florence a new Jerusalem, whence would go forth the laws and example of a good life; I was waiting for the renewal of the Church, the conversion of unbelievers, the consolation of the just. I felt that it was all the contrary, and could only heal my woe by the cry, "Lord, in Thy hands are all things."'[2]

Trial of Savonarola. April, 1498.

---

[1] Dated April 11, in Quetif, 462. [2] Luca Landucci, *Diario*, 173.

This sense of profound discouragement amongst Savonarola's followers was the result of the skilful way in which Savonarola's enemies had placed the issue before them. 'Savonarola,' they said, 'is a prophet with a special mission from God. We do not profess to be prophets. We know that the fire will burn us, but we are willing to be burned if he burns too. We are willing to do anything that may convince you that your prophet is no true prophet, and has no special mission.' Savonarola's entire position was made to depend exclusively on his prophetic claims. Amongst these claims was put, by the suggestion of his enemies and the excited feelings of his friends, the claim of working wonders which Savonarola himself had always repudiated. His entire faith in God's providence led him to face the trial so skilfully proposed. When he was found to be merely a man, like other men, his followers for the moment felt that they had been deceived. They did not stop to ask whether the deception was due to their own enthusiasm or to their master's assertions. Perplexed and disheartened, Savonarola's party melted away.

Even the brethren of S. Marco deserted their great leader, and wrote to the Pope begging his forgiveness. They pleaded that, in their simplicity, they had been beguiled by the commanding intellect and pretended sanctity of Savonarola. 'Let it suffice your Holiness to punish the head and front of this offence; we like sheep who have gone astray return to the true shepherd.' [1] No abasement could be more complete.

Papal
Commis-
sioners
sent to
Florence.
May, 1498.

The fate of Savonarola was the subject of much negotiation between the Pope and the Florentine magistrates. The Pope wished that he should be delivered to him for punishment; the Florentines urged that such a course was injurious to the dignity of their city. At last Alexander VI. agreed to send two commissaries to Florence who were to judge the spiritual offences of Savonarola, while he left the Florentines to judge his offences against the city. At the same time he granted them his permission to impose a tax of three-tenths upon ecclesiastical revenues. 'Three times ten make thirty,' said some of those who still remained true to Savonarola; 'our master is sold for thirty pieces like the Saviour.' [2]

On May 19 the papal commissioners arrived in Florence.

---

[1] Perrens, Appendix No. XVII.   [2] Luca Landucci, *Diario*, 175.

They were Gioacchino Torriano, General of the Dominicans, and Francesco Remolino, Bishop of Ilerda. Concerning Remolino we have the testimony of Cesare Borgia that ' he had no mind for ecclesiastical affairs; '[1] but the qualifications of the commissaries was not an important matter, as they made no secret that they came to condemn Savonarola, not to judge him. Again Savonarola was put to the torture to see if any further information could be obtained about his plan of summoning a General Council. The commissaries were anxious to find out if he had any confederates amongst the Cardinals; but they discovered nothing. On May 22 they declared him and his two companions guilty of heresy and gave sentence against them. Then they were condemned to death by the magistrates, and Savonarola as a last favour was allowed to see his two friends and gave them his benediction. On the morning of May 23 they met to receive the viaticum, and Savonarola was permitted to communicate with his own hands. He knelt and professed his faith, asked pardon for his sins, and committed himself to God.

The scaffold had been erected in the Piazza de' Signori. The gibbet on its projecting arm bore three nooses and three chains, while underneath was a pile of wood to burn the bodies. When first the gibbet was erected it looked like a cross, and the Piagnoni murmured, ' They are going to crucify him, like his Master.' One arm was sawn away to destroy the comparison.

The condemned descended the steps of the Palazzo, and were led to a tribunal where sat the Bishop who had been commissioned by the Pope to degrade them from their ecclesiastical rank. They were stripped of their vestments; their tonsures and their hands were scraped. The Bishop took Savonarola by the hand and in the confusion of the moment made an error in the words of degradation. ' I separate you,' he said, ' from the Church militant and triumphant.' ' Militant, not triumphant,' Savonarola corrected him; ' that is not in your power.' ' Amen,' said the Bishop; ' may God lead you there.' Then they passed to the next tribunal where the papal commissioners read the sentence which condemned them as ' heretics, schismatics, and

Execution of Savonarola, May 23, 1498.

---

[1] Cesare Borgia wrote in 1492 to Piero de' Medici, commending Remolino for a chair in canon law at the University of Pisa, as ' homo docto et virtuoso, maxime non havendo animo a le cose ecclesiastice.' Alvisi, *Cesare Borgia*, Appendix No. III.

despisers of the Holy See.' Remolino said, 'His Holiness is
pleased to deliver you from the pains of purgatory by granting you a plenary indulgence. Do you accept it?' They bowed
their heads in token of assent. Next they were handed over
to the civil power and were led to the last tribunal, where sat
the magistrates, who condemned them to be hanged and their
bodies burned. They moved onwards to the scaffold in silent
prayer. Savonarola had enjoined on his companions that they
should say nothing; he did not wish to justify himself in the
eyes of men, or say anything which might cause a tumult.
When a friend murmured words of comfort, Savonarola gently
answered, 'God only can console men at their last hour.'

Fra Silvestro was the first to suffer, exclaiming, 'Lord, into
Thy hands I commend my spirit.' Then Fra Domenico, with a
face of joy, seemed not so much to go to death as to a festival.
Last of all Savonarola cast his eyes for a moment over the
assembled crowd, who still held their breath in suspense, hoping
for some miracle. His lips moved, but nothing was audible.
Then a suppressed murmur ran through the crowd as they saw
his body hanging in the air. The corpses were hung in chains,
and the pile below was fired. The ashes were gathered and were
thrown into the Arno. Yet faithful souls scraped together some
precious relics of the charred fragments; and three days afterwards women so far forgot their fear as to kneel in passionate
devotion on the spot where their great teacher had been burned.
In spite of persecution there were many who loved Savonarola
because they knew what he had done for their souls. His books
were eagerly read, biographies of him were written, his defence
was passionately undertaken, the place of his execution was
crowned with flowers on the anniversary of his death.

Importance
of Savona-
rola.
The last days of Savonarola's life in prison were spent in
writing a meditation on the Fifty-first Psalm. This together
with his other devotional writings enjoyed a wide popularity
and went through many editions. It fell into the hands of
Luther, who republished it in 1523, with a preface in which he
claimed Savonarola as one of his predecessors in setting forth
the doctrine of justification by faith only. He writes in his
usual trenchant style: 'Though the feet of this holy man are
still soiled by theological mud, he nevertheless upheld justification by faith only without works, and therefore he was burned

by the Pope. But he lives in blessedness and Christ canonises him by our means, even though Pope and Papists burst with rage.' It is not worth while to examine the grounds of Luther's statement. Savonarola's words are full of ardent faith in Christ, but Luther's position was far from his mind. He taught nothing which was opposed to the accepted doctrines of the Church; he never denied the papal headship, and he received submissively the plenary indulgence which Alexander VI. granted him before his death. Savonarola was a great moral reformer, who was driven at the last to take up the position of an ecclesiastical reformer also; but he followed the lines of Gerson and Ailli, and wished to take up the work which the Council of Constance had failed to accomplish. His conception of moral reform led him into politics, and his political position brought him into collision with the Papacy. Rather than abandon his work he was prepared to face a conflict with the Papacy, but his enemies were too numerous and too watchful, and he fell before their combined force.

Savonarola's fate is a type of the dangers which beset a noble soul drawn by its Christian zeal into conflict with the world. More and more he was driven to fight the Lord's battle with carnal weapons, till the prophet and the statesman became inextricably entangled and the message of the new life was interwoven with the political attitude of the Florentine republic. Little by little he was driven into the open sea till his frail bark was swallowed by the tempest. He encouraged Florence to adhere to an untenable position till all who wished to bring Florence into union with Italian aspirations were driven to conspire for his downfall.[1]

This great tragic interest of the lofty soul overborne in its struggle against the world has made Savonarola a favourite character for biography, romance, and devotional literature. But the historical importance of Savonarola goes deeper than the greatness of his personal character or his political importance. Savonarola made a last attempt to bring the New Learning into harmony with the Christian life. He strove to inspire the Florence of Lorenzo, Ficino, and Pico with the conscious-

---

[1] For Machiavelli's opinion of Savonarola, see Tommasini, *Niccolò Machiavelli*, i. 161 &c.; for that of Ficino, see Passerini, *Documenti* in *Giornale Storico degli Archivi Toscani*, iii. 115.

ness of a great spiritual mission to the world. He aimed at setting up a commonwealth of which Christ was the only king; animated by the zeal of a reformed Church, the State was to guide men's aspirations towards a regenerate life. The individual force and passion of Savonarola was the offspring of the Renaissance, but it had to force its way to expression through the fetters of Scholasticism. Savonarola's sermons present a strange contrast of the forcible utterance of personal feeling with the trivialities of an artificial method of exposition. He palpitates with the desire to reconcile conflicting tendencies and enter into a larger world. He falls back upon the mysterious utterances of prophecy to point men's eyes to a larger future than he was able to define. His words are now vague to our ears, his political plans are seen to be dreams, his prophetic claims a delusion. But his character lives and is powerful as of one who strove to restore the harmony of man's distracted life.

It is unjust to Alexander VI. to represent him as the chief author of Savonarola's ruin; but he gave his sanction at the last to the schemes of Savonarola's foes. It is needless to discuss the technical points at issue between Savonarola and the Pope; it is enough that the papal policy in Italy demanded the destruction of a noble effort to make Christianity the animating principle of life. Even a Pope so purely secular as Alexander VI. is said in later years to have regretted Savonarola's death; Julius II. ordered Raffaelle to place him amongst the Doctors of the Church in his great fresco of the *Disputa*; and his claims to canonisation were more than once discussed.[1] The Church silently grieved over his loss when he was gone, when political difficulties had passed away, and the memory of the fervent preacher of righteousness alone remained.

[1] For the opinion of later Popes about Savonarola, see Bayonne, *Etude sur Jérôme Savonarole*, 236 &c.

CHAPTER IX.

ALEXANDER VI. AND THE PAPAL STATES.

1495–1499.

IN following the fate of Savonarola we have seen the resoluteness with which Alexander VI. pursued one great object of his policy, the union of Italy to resist French intervention. A second object which employed his care was the reduction of the Roman barons so as to secure the peace of the Papal States. Alexander VI. had felt his helplessness before the advance of Charles VIII., and had learned how many enemies he had to face at his own doors. The feeble rule of Innocent VIII. had reversed the resolute measures of Sixtus IV. ; Ostia was held against the Pope; the Orsini castles threatened him on every side ; Rome itself was a scene of constant feuds, and brawls and assassinations were common in its streets.

The first measure of Alexander VI. was to strengthen the fortifications of the Castle of S. Angelo and connect it more readily with the Vatican. He first gave it the appearance of a mediæval castle, with walls, towers, and ditches of defence. He caused the houses which had clustered round it to be pulled down, and laid out the street now called the Borgo Nuovo which leads from it to the Vatican. These works, which took some years to complete, were begun in 1495, and were a heavy drain on the papal treasury.

He next proceeded to strengthen himself in the College of Cardinals, where he had many enemies and where he encountered much opposition to his plans. On February 19, 1496, he announced the creation of four new Cardinals, all Spaniards, and one his nephew, Giovanni Borgia. As this raised the number of Spanish Cardinals to nine, much discontent was expressed, and many efforts were made to induce the Pope to create some Italian Cardinals. The Marquis of Mantua offered

16,000 ducats to have the dignity conferred upon his brother; [1]
but Alexander VI. steadily refused. He had seen the dangers
to which the Papacy was exposed from the introduction of the
political jealousies of Italy into its councils. It was enough
that the Sforza and the Medici were already powerful in Rome,
and that Cardinal Rovere led a political party of his own.
Alexander VI. was ready to meet his enemies with their own
weapons. He was resolved to form a strong party which
had no connexion with Italian politics, and he was willing
to face the unpopularity of pursuing an independent line of
action.

The downfall of the French power in Naples afforded
Alexander VI. an opportunity of striking a blow at the Roman
barons who had sided with the French king. Ferrante II. was
aided in expelling the French by the troops of Spain under the
leadership of the great general, Gonsalvo de Cordova. Gonsalvo's military skill and the awakened patriotism of the Neapolitans rapidly prevailed against the French, who received no
reinforcements from home. In August 1496 their last stronghold, Atella, capitulated; its garrison undertook to depart from
the kingdom, and a general amnesty was declared. Amongst
those included in this capitulation was Virginio, the head of
the Orsini house, who would fain have embarked with the
French, but Ferrante, at the Pope's request, kept him as
prisoner. Alexander VI. had prepared measures against the
Orsini. On June 1 he declared them rebels against the Church
and confiscated their goods; he summoned to his aid Guid-
ubaldo, Duke of Urbino, proclaimed the young Duke of Gandia
Gonfaloniere of the Church, and appointed the Cardinal of
Lunate as his legate for the war. On October 26 the Pope
blessed the standard which he handed to his son, and next day
the papal army set out from Rome.

At first the papal arms were successful, and ten castles of the
Orsini were captured within a month; but a determined resistance was offered by Bracciano, which was strong in its position
on the lake. Bartolommea Orsini, Virginio's sister, showed
masculine daring in baffling the besiegers, who suffered from
exposure to the winter weather. Moreover, she amused herself
at their expense. One day a donkey was driven out of the

---

[1] Marin Sanuto, *Diario*, i. 53.

castle bearing a placard 'Let me pass, for I go as ambassador
to the Duke of Gandia;' underneath its tail was fastened a
letter full of bitter mockery.[1] The siege of Bracciano was
raised in January, as the troops of the Orsini threatened Rome.
At last, on January 23, 1497, a battle was fought by Soriano
in which the Orsini were completely victorious. The Duke of
Urbino was taken prisoner; the Duke of Gandia was wounded
in the face; he and Cardinal Lunate with difficulty escaped
to Rome.

The position of Alexander VI. was now precarious. The
troops of the Orsini laid waste the Campagna and cut off
supplies from the city. Ostia, which commanded the approach
by sea, was garrisoned by French troops. Alexander VI.
turned for help to Gonsalvo de Cordova, who was sitting idly
in Naples; but the Venetian envoys urged upon him the
need of peace with the Orsini, and on February 5 an agreement was made. Anguillara and Cervetri were given up to
the Pope, and the Orsini were to retain the rest of their possessions on paying 50,000 ducats. Those who were in prison
at Naples were to be released; but this stipulation did not
affect Virginio, who had died in prison a few weeks before.
The Pope paid no heed to his captive ally, the Duke of Urbino,
who was left to negotiate his own ransom. The Pope was
shameless enough to leave the Orsini a victim from whom they
might extort the money which they were to pay to him. The
Duke of Urbino was childless, and Alexander VI. already
coveted his domains for one of his own sons.[2]

Alexander VI.'s first attempt at recovering the Papal States
had not been successful. He hoped for better things from his
next enterprise. On February 19 Gonsalvo de Cordova came
to Rome and undertook the reduction of Ostia, which was
bravely defended by a Biscayan corsair, Menaldo de Guerra.
Gonsalvo took with him 600 Spanish horse and 1,000 foot, so
badly armed and equipped that the Italians laughed at their
poor appearance. Gonsalvo answered, 'They are so naked that
the enemy has nothing to gain from them.' Ostia capitulated,

---

[1] Marin Sanuto, i. p. 410.

[2] *Ibid.*, i. 527: 'El pontifice feva acciò intervenisse qualcossa di lui,
perchè dicto ducha non ha figlioli, et hessendo il suo stato feudo di la
Chiesia, potesse darlo a' soi figlioli, a li qual haveva gran voglia di darli qualche
stato in Italia.'

and on March 15 Gonsalvo was welcomed with a revival of the old Roman triumph. Before him rode Menaldo in chains; he himself was escorted by the Duke of Gandia and the Pope's son-in-law, Giovanni of Pesaro. The procession swept along to the Vatican, where Alexander VI. received them seated on his throne. Menaldo threw himself before the Pope and asked for pardon; Alexander VI. made him no answer, but presently turning to Gonsalvo, left the fate of the captive in his hands.[1] Gonsalvo was generous and gave him his liberty.

Alexander VI. went the next day to Ostia to settle the affairs of his new possession. He bestowed on Gonsalvo every mark of his gratitude; but the haughty Spaniard refused on Palm Sunday to receive a palm from the Pope's hand because it was offered to him after the Duke of Gandia.[2] The Romans, so soon as the fear of their foes at Ostia was removed, looked with displeasure on the Spanish Pope with his Spanish army, and the solemnities of Holy Week were marred by riots between the Spanish soldiers and the people, who even threatened to stone the Pope as he went in procession through the streets.[3] Gonsalvo did not care to stay long in the ungrateful city, and went back to Naples at the end of March.

The Neapolitan restoration and the capture of Ostia restored Alexander VI. to power, and he was resolved to assert it. The Cardinals of the French party, Colonna and Savelli, returned to Rome; Orsini no longer dared to oppose the Pope; Rovere preferred exile to submission. The Cardinal of Gurk was ordered to return to Rome or confine himself to his diocese of Foligno; he stayed at Foligno, protesting to the Florentine

---

[1] Burchard, *Diarium*, ii. 354.

[2] This most probably is the foundation for the story that Gonsalvo rebuked the Pope for his evil life. Raynaldus, *Annales Ecclesiastici*, 1497, § 2, says so, and has been followed by subsequent writers; but he gives no reference, and I find no authority for the tale. Guicciardini says that Gonsalvo was presented with the golden rose; but this is not mentioned by Burchard, who was papal Master of Ceremonies, nor by Paulus Jovius, the biographer of Gonsalvo. In their silence I have dismissed Guicciardini's story.

[3] Marino Sanuto, i. 569, under date March 24: 'In Roma era seguito certa novità de' Spagnuoli con Romani in Campo de Fiorr, zoe con quelli di don Gonsalvo, e che ne era tra lhoro morti molti.' To this we may add the testimony of a German pilgrim, Arnold von Harff, quoted by Gregorovius, vii. 395: 'Die Romanen hetten den pays mit bestain doit zo slayn, so verhast was he zo deser szyt mit sinen freenden den Hispanioler.'

ambassador that he was not bound to follow the Pope to do evil. 'When I think,' he said, 'on the life of the Pope and some of the Cardinals, I have a horror of the court of Rome, and have no wish to return till God reforms His Church.'[1]

A bystander might indeed be pardoned for feeling some doubts about the Pope's intentions. The incidents of the life of his family gave rise to much scandal, and it was quite clear that the Pope was not careful of his own reputation or of the reputation of his office. In Holy Week men's tongues were set wagging by the sudden flight from Rome of Giovanni Sforza, lord of Pesaro, Lucrezia Borgia's husband. He went, on the pretext of performing his religious duties, to the Church of S. Onofrio, outside the Porta Romana. There a swift horse was ready for him; he mounted and rode in haste to Pesaro, leaving his wife at Rome.[2] The reason for this strange departure was not at first known; presently it appeared that there was a question of Giovanni's divorce from Lucrezia on the ground of impotence. Giovanni resisted the Pope's proposals that he should consent to a divorce, and judged it wise to leave Rome before the pressure became irresistible. He was a weak man, and had not been of much use to the Pope's policy; Alexander VI. was desirous of a more influential son-in-law. Giovanni Sforza gave out that he was in fear of his life, and trembled before the threats of Cardinal Cesare.[3] What was Lucrezia's attitude towards her husband we do not know; in the beginning of June she retired from Rome to the Convent of S. Sisto, preferring to remain in quiet till the matter was settled.

Meanwhile Alexander VI. pursued his policy of aggrandising his sons. Ferrante II. of Naples died childless and was succeeded by his uncle, Federigo, Prince of Altamura. The Pope used the opportunity afforded by the demand for his

Marginal notes: CHAP. IX. — Flight of Giovanni Sforza.

[1] Letter of Bracchio, from Perugia, April 8, 1497, printed in the Appendix to Thuasne's Burchard, ii. 668.

[2] Marino Sanuto, i. 569.

[3] Two chroniclers of Pesaro, quoted by Gregorovius, *Lucrezia Borgia*, 96, tell the story that Lucrezia concealed Giovanni's chamberlain in her room, while Cesare paid her visit, and unfolded a plot for Giovanni's death. Hereon Giovanni mounted an Arab horse and rode to Pesaro in twenty-four hours, and his horse fell dead as he dismounted. The ride from Rome to Pesaro in twenty-four hours and the death of the horse savours of romance. Gregorovius adds that these chronicles are incorrect in their dates and are full of errors.

BOOK
V.

coronation to revive some old claims of the Papacy; he erected Benevento into a duchy, comprising also Terracina and Pontecorvo, and conferred the duchy on the Duke of Gandia. None of the Cardinals dared to oppose him, save Cardinal Piccolomini, whose remonstrances were seconded by the Spanish ambassador. Even the opposition of all the Cardinals did not prevent the Pope from nominating his son Cesare as legate for the coronation. He resolutely sought the advancement of his children, and held everything else as secondary to that object.[1]

Murder of
the Duke
of Gandia,
June 14,
1497.

The Pope's schemes were doomed to a terrible disappointment, and Rome was suddenly startled by the news of the death of the Duke of Gandia by a mysterious murder. On the evening of June 14 he had gone to sup with his mother Vanozza in her house by the church of S. Pietro in Vincula. There was a large party, amongst whom were the Cardinals Cesare and Giovanni Borgia. It was night when the Duke of Gandia and Cesare mounted their horses, accompanied by a small retinue. When they arrived at the Palazzo Cesarini, where Cardinal Ascanio Sforza lived, the Duke of Gandia took leave of his brother, saying that he had some private business to transact. He dismissed all his attendants save one, and followed a masked figure, who had for the last month frequently visited him at the Vatican, and who had come to speak with him that night during supper. He turned back to the Piazza Giudea, and there ordered his one attendant to wait for him; if he did not soon return he was to make his way back to the Vatican. Then he took the masked figure on his mule and rode away. The servant, as he waited for his master, was attacked by armed men, from whom he with difficulty escaped with his life and was left speechless. In the morning the Pope was uneasy at his son's absence, but supposed that he had gone on some amorous intrigue and did not wish to leave the lady's house in daylight. But when the night did not bring him back Alexander VI. grew seriously alarmed, and sent the police to make inquiries. They found a Slavonian woodseller who gave them some information. He plied his trade on the Ripetta, near the Ospedale degli Sciavoni. He had unladen his cargo,

---

[1] Marino Sanuto, i. 650: 'E cussi Benevento el papa have per dicto suo fiol, per il quale se inzegnava di far ogni cossa per darli stado in Italia.'

and to protect his wares from theft was sleeping in the boat which was moored by the bank. He saw two men, about one o'clock in the morning, peer cautiously from the street on the left of the Ospedale. When they saw no one they returned, and were followed by two others who used equal caution. Seeing no one they made a sign. A horseman then came forward, riding on a white horse. Behind him was a corpse with the head hanging down on one side and the legs on the other; it was held in its place by the two men who had first appeared. They went to a spot where rubbish was shot into the Tiber, and there the horse was backed towards the river. The two men on foot seized the corpse and flung it into the water. The horseman asked if it had sunk, and was answered ' Yes, sir.' He looked round and saw the mantle floating on the surface, and one of the men pelted it with stones till it sank; then they all went away.

When this story was told to the Pope, he asked why the woodseller had not informed the police. The answer was that he had seen in his days a hundred corpses thrown into the river in that spot, and no questions had been asked about them. It was a terrible testimony to the condition of Rome under the papal government.

The fishermen and sailors of the Tiber were set to work to search the river. They discovered the body of the Duke of Gandia, with the throat cut, and eight wounds upon the head, legs, and body. He was fully dressed, and in his pocket was his purse containing thirty ducats. The corpse was placed on a barge and was conveyed to the Castle of S. Angelo, and thence was carried to the Church of S. Maria del Popolo, where it lay in state.[1]

When Alexander VI. heard that his son was dead, and thrown like dirt into the river, he gave way to passionate grief. He shut himself up in his chamber, and would admit no one. His terrified attendants stood by the door and listened to his sobs; for three days he refused all food. Inquiries were made throughout Rome; but nothing was discovered which could throw any light upon the murderers. Rumours were rife and

---

[1] I have followed Burchard, ii. 387 &c. The other accounts agree with his. There are several letters from Rome in Sanuto's *Diario*, i. 651.

many were suspected. Some accused the Orsini, especially Bartolommeo de Alviano,[1] others Giovanni Sforza of Pesaro, whose flight from Rome was explained on the most abominable grounds.[2] Others again considered that Cardinal Ascanio Sforza was the author of this act of vengeance, being irritated against the Duke of Gandia for having caused the assassination of his chamberlain, whose free speaking had given offence.[3] Ascanio was so much alarmed at the rumour about himself that he did not venture into the Pope's presence.

On June 19 the Pope appeared in a Consistory, and received the condolences of all the Cardinals, except Ascanio Sforza. The Pope spoke with difficulty : ' The Duke of Gandia is dead. Our grief is inexpressible because we loved him dearly. We no longer value the Papacy or anything else. If we had seven papacies we would give them all to restore him to life. Perhaps God has punished us for some sin ; it is not because he deserved so cruel a death. It is said that the lord of Pesaro has killed him ; we are sure that it is not so. Of the Prince of Squillace it is incredible. We are sure also of the Duke of Urbino. God pardon whoever it be. For ourselves we can attend to nothing, neither the Papacy nor our life. We think only of the Church and its government. For this purpose we institute a commission of six Cardinals, with two auditors of the rota, to set to work for its reformation, to see that benefices are given solely by merit, and that you Cardinals have your share in the councils of the Church.'[4]

Then the Spanish ambassador rose and explained the absence of Cardinal Ascanio ; he was afraid of the rumours

---

[1] Letter of the Ferrarese ambassador at Florence, quoting despatch from Rome dated August 8, in Capelli, *Atti e Memorie per le Provincie Parmesi*, iv. 385.

[2] Letter from Rome, June 17, in Malipiero, *Annali Veneti*, 490 : 'Si dice che 'l Signor Giovanni Sforza, Signor di Pesaro, ha fatto questo effetto, perchè il Duca usava con la sorela, sua consorte, la quale è filiola del Papa, ma d' un' altra donna.'

[3] Sanuto, under date June 19, gives the accusation ; also, i. 843, gives the cause. The Duke at dinner with Ascanio called the chamberlain a coward : he retorted by calling the Duke a bastard. See, too, letter of Bracchi in Thuasne's Burchard, ii. 672.

[4] Letter of Venetian envoy in Rome, June 20 ; Sanuto, i. 653. The ambassadors of the League were also present at this Consistory, so that there is no doubt of the substantial accuracy of this speech.

that he, as the head of the Orsini faction, had planned the Duke
of Gandia's murder. 'God forbid,' said the Pope, 'that I
should suspect him, for I hold him as a brother.' Then the
envoys in turn presented their condolences to the Pope, and
all went away amazed at his good intentions.

Alexander VI. wrote letters to all the princes of Europe,
telling them of his loss and of his sorrow. He received letters
of condolence from all sides, even from Savonarola and Cardinal
Rovere, who expressed their sorrow and counselled Christian
resignation to the Pope.[1] For a time Alexander VI. was sincere
in his desire to act more worthily of his office. Men heard
with astonishment of the proposals which the six commissioners for reform put forward. The sale of benefices was prohibited; they were to be conferred on worthy persons. The
revenues of a Cardinal were not to exceed 6,000 florins, nor
their households to contain more than eighty persons. No
Cardinal was to hold more than one bishopric; offenders against
this rule were at once to choose which they would resign;
pluralities were similarly forbidden to the inferior clergy. It
was even proposed that the decrees of the Council of Constance
should be made binding. There was also a noticeable provision
that the Pope should maintain five hundred foot and three
thousand horse to chastise the subjects of the Church.[2] These
were admirable proposals, and would have been welcomed by
Christendom with delight. But Alexander VI.'s interest in
ecclesiastical matters diminished with his sorrow. He was a
man of quick and strong feelings. The blow at first crushed
him, and he turned in his remorse to bethink himself of forgotten duties. But his natural disposition soon reasserted
itself; he regained his self-control, and returned to his original
plans. Reform of the Church meant loss of money, and money
was above all things necessary for his political projects. The
report of the reform commission was no sooner ready than

[1] Savonarola's letter is given in Perrens, Vie de Jérôme Savonarola, Appendix
ix, Rovere's in Gregorovius, Lucrezia Borgia, Appendix No. 14. They are
neither of them letters which would have been written by opponents to a man
whom they thought utterly abominable.

[2] These interesting details are given in a letter from Rome of July 8 in
Sanuto, i. 655.

BOOK
V.

Doubt
about the
murder of
the Duke
of Gandia.

it was set aside as derogatory to the privileges of the Papacy.[1]

Every effort was made to discover the murderer of the Duke of Gandia, but without avail. The suspicions of the police were especially directed against Count Antonio della Mirandola, whose house was not far distant from the place where the body was found. He had a daughter who was famous for her beauty, and it was conjectured that she was the bait by which the mysterious visitor allured the duke to put himself unattended in his hands. But nothing definite was discovered, and it was agreed that the assassination was a masterpiece in its way.[2] In the absence of any certainty, everyone was at liberty to form his own opinion about the murderer. Probably the most natural conjecture is the truest—that the Duke of Gandia fell a victim to the jealousy of some lover or husband whose honour he had attacked. The rumours current in Rome mentioned everyone who might possibly have an interest in the Duke of Gandia's death, amongst these his brother Gioffrè, Prince of Squillace, because he would presumably be his heir. When it appeared that Cardinal Cesare was to succeed to his place in the Pope's affections, rumour transferred the guilt to him. As Cesare became an object of dread in Italy men repeated this charge more constantly, and Guicciardini and Machiavelli have raised it to the dignity of an historical fact. But it was not preferred against Cesare till nearly nine months after the event, and it rests upon no better foundation than do the suspicions against the Orsini, Ascanio Sforza, Giovanni Sforza, Antonio della Mirandola, or Gioffrè Borgia. When so many rumours were afloat it is clear that they all rested on mere conjecture, and that it is impossible to pronounce any certain opinion.[3]

[1] Already on June 28 a letter from Rome announced: 'De li cardinali 6 eletti non fu facta altra mentione, adeo el pontefice era come mai a voler governar la sedia.' Sanuto, i. 671.

[2] 'In ogni modo si crede sia stato gran maestro.' Letter of Bracchi to Florence, June 17, in Thuasne's Burchard, ii. 669.

[3] The reader who wishes to follow this question further will find in Gregorovius, *Geschichte der Stadt Rom*, vii. 405-6, the authorities in favour of Cesare's guilt: in Alvisi, *Cesare Borgia*, 44-5, the opposite side. I have contented myself with separating the facts from the rumours, and the rumours which were contemporary from those of a later date.

In spite of the Pope's assurance that he entirely acquitted Ascanio Sforza of any share in the murder, Ascanio judged it prudent to retire from Rome to Grottaferrata, and when on July 22 Cardinal Cesare Borgia set out for Naples to crown Federigo, all Rome was convinced of Ascanio's guilt.[1] Cesare performed with splendour his duties of legate, and crowned the last Aragonese king of Naples at Capua on August 10. His stay in the kingdom was a source of expense to the impoverished treasury, and Federigo was glad to see his costly guest depart. On September 6 Cesare was received by all the Cardinals and was escorted to the Vatican. Alexander VI. was still so little master of himself that he could not trust himself to speak to his son, but greeted him in silence.[2]

Cesare
Borgia
crowns
Federigo of
Naples,
July 22,
1497.

Perhaps it was due to Cesare's influence that Alexander VI. rapidly recovered his spirits, and returned to his old plans, foremost amongst them the overthrow of the Orsini. He gathered troops, allied himself with the Colonna, and assumed such a threatening attitude that the Orsini sought the good offices of Venice. Venice warned the Pope that it took the Orsini under its protection, and Alexander VI. sullenly gave way to its remonstrances. The Romans changed their opinion about the murderer of the Duke of Gandia, and now were sure that his death was the work of the Orsini.[3]

Alexander VI. at the same time steadily pursued his family policy. He enriched Cardinal Cesare with the benefices of Cardinals who died, while he matured a plan for releasing him from ecclesiastical obligations and opening to him the career which the Duke of Gandia's death had left vacant. Similarly he prosecuted the divorce of Lucrezia from Giovanni of Pesaro,

---

[1] Marin Sanuto, i. 695, June 17 : 'El Cardinal Ascanio era pur fuor di Roma, e in imicizia col papa, zoè che per tutto si teneva certo esso cardinal fusse stato quello havesse facto amazar el ducha di Gandia.' If we are to listen to rumours it is only fair to note their fluctuations. Again, on August 8, Sanuto writes of Ascanio : 'Questo fu quello che judicio omnium fece amazar il fiol del papa.' Similarly on August 24.

[2] Burchard, ii. 404: 'Non dixit verbum Valentinus Pape nec Papa sibi, sed eo deosculato descendit de solio.' Those who hold that Cesare was the murderer of his brother see in this a proof of the Pope's knowledge of his guilt.

[3] Sanuto, i. 827, December: 'Questo faceva perchè tramava questo papa poi di ruinar li Orsini, e questo perchè li Orsini certo havia facto amazar suo fiol ducha di Gandia.'

which had been referred to a commission presided over by
two Cardinals. The alleged cause was Giovanni Sforza's impotence. Giovanni protested against it with all his might, as
besides the ridicule which it threw upon him, it involved the
restoration of Lucrezia's dowry, 31,000 ducats. He went to
Milan and implored Ludovico Il Moro to use his influence to
prevent it. But Ludovico and his brother Ascanio had no wish
to quarrel with the Pope;[1] they rather urged Giovanni to give
way and resign himself to what was inevitable. He was at last
driven to sign a paper in which he owned that Lucrezia was
still a virgin.[2] But he revenged himself for his discomfiture
by imputing to Alexander VI. the most abominable motives for
his conduct. The divorce was in itself a sufficiently scandalous
proceeding, and everything concerning it was rapidly spread
throughout Italy. Men made merry over the matter after
the manner of the time. Alexander VI.'s family affairs
had already become a subject of considerable amusement to
the wits of the day. A refined, scurrilous, and profligate
society could not have had a subject for conversation which
suited them better. The accusations of Giovanni Sforza had
an immediate success; they passed from mouth to mouth and
lost nothing in the telling. Alexander VI. was neither liked
nor respected, but he was dreaded. He was exactly the man
against whom scandalous stories were the only weapon available
for his victims. From this time forward stories of incest and
unnatural crime were rife about the Pope and his family.
Alexander VI. had done enough to make anything seem
credible about him. He had outraged public opinion in every
way, and the tongue of slander took its revenge. The death
of the Duke of Gandia, the divorce of Lucrezia, the proposed
dispensation of Cesare from the cardinalate—all these follow-

---

[1] It is true that Ludovico made a characteristic suggestion that Giovanni
should give the Pope's legate a visible proof of the falsity of the charge, but
Giovanni declined. 'Et mancho se è curato de fare prova de se qua con Done
per poterne chiare el Rᵐᵒ Legato che era qua, sebbene S. Exᵗⁱᵃ tastandolo
sopra ciò gli ne habbia facto offerta.' Letter of Ferrarese ambassador in
Milan, June 23, 1497, in Gregorovius, *Lucrezia Borgia*, 101.

[2] Letter of Collenuccio from Rome, December 25, 1497, *ibid*: 'El S. de
Pesaro ha scripto qua de sua mano; non haverla mai cognosciuta . . . et essere
impotente, alias la sententia non se potea dare. El prefato S. dice però aver
scripto cosi per obedire el Duca de Milano et Aschanio.'

ing one another in a few months filled men with bewilderment and made them ready to catch at any explanation however monstrous it might be.[1] In September these rumours had reached Rome and set men's tongues wagging freely. We may agree with the sagacious judgment of the Venetian envoy in Rome. 'Whatever may be the truth, one thing is certain; this Pope behaves in an outrageous and intolerable way.' It is bad enough that Alexander VI. gave a colourable pretext to such slanders. The slanders themselves rest on no evidence that justifies an impartial mind in believing them.

The corruption of the papal court was notorious, and was deplored on all sides. Not only Savonarola, but a churchman like Petrus Delfinus, General of the Order of the Camaldolensians, longed for reform and hailed Alexander VI.'s temporary repentance with joyful expectancy. On every side were murmurs. Charles VIII. of France expressed his regret that he had not used his opportunity and summoned a Council. The Spanish princes sent envoys to remonstrate with the Pope on his disorderly life.[2] The disorganisation of the Curia was shown by the sudden arrest on September 14 of the Pope's secretary, Bartolommeo Florido, Archbishop of Cosenza, on the charge of forging papal briefs. He had trafficked in dispensations and exemptions, and was said to have issued as many as 3,000 briefs on his own authority. One of them was issued in favour of a nun of the royal race of Portugal, and allowed her to leave the convent and marry a natural son of the late king. This act of audacity seems to have led to detection of the fraud,[3] and Florido was induced to confess his crimes. He was degraded from his ecclesiastical offices and was condemned to perpetual imprison-

Disorganisation in the Curia.

---

[1] The letter of the Ferrarese ambassador, quoted above, goes on to say that Giovanni Sforza told Ludovico about Lucrezia: 'Anzi averla conosciuta infinite volte, mal chel Papa non gelha tolta per altro se non per usare con lei; extendendose molto a carico di S. Beat⁰.' It will be observed that Giovanni did not accuse Alexander VI. in the past, but imputed a motive for his conduct in the future. This motive was shown to be false by the fact that the Pope instantly set to work to provide a new husband for Lucrezia. This was written on June 23. We can trace the progress of the scandal in Rome, where, on September 21, Sanuto reports: 'Ut intellexi, zà molti mesi questo Cardinal Valenza usava con la cognata. Sed quomodocunque res se habeat, di questo per Roma se ne parlava. . . . Unum est, che questo papa fa cosse excessive et intollerabili.'

[2] Raynaldus, 1498, No. 20, from Osorius and Mariana.

[3] Burchard, ii. 406, 411.

ment in a subterranean dungeon in the Castle of S. Angelo, where he was fed on bread and water, was supplied with oil for a lamp, and was allowed to have his breviary and a bible. He died after a few months' confinement.

Another mysterious death in Alexander VI.'s household again set men's tongues wagging. On February 14, 1498, the Pope's favourite chamberlain, Piero Caldes, known as Perotto, was found drowned in the Tiber.[1] Together with him, it was said, was the corpse of a maid in the service of Lucrezia. Again men darkly hinted that the drowned girl was a mistress of the Pope. In later times the death of Perotto was put down to Cesare Borgia, who is said to have killed with his own hand the wretched man, who clung to the Pope's mantle, while his blood spurted into the Pope's face.[2] Again we can trace the growth of an incredible story.

These frequent murders and the insecurity of life in Rome to some degree justify Alexander VI.'s desire for a strong position, where he might put down disorder and feel secure. Rome was in utter anarchy and the Pope was helpless in his own city. The feud between the Orsini and the Colonna raged violently, and the Pope was powerless to keep the peace. Federigo of Naples had confiscated the Orsini fiefs in his kingdom and conferred them on the Colonna. The Orsini could not brook to see their rivals increase in power ; both sides gathered armed men, and the Pope was driven at times to take refuge before their tumults in the Castle of S. Angelo. A desultory warfare was carried on in the Campagna, till on April 12, 1498, the Orsini met with a crushing defeat at Palombara. Both parties saw that a continuance of the struggle would only weaken themselves and benefit the Pope. They refused his offers of mediation and made peace in July, on the understanding that they would both unite against the Pope, would ally with the King of Naples, and submit their disputes to his decision. The union of these rival houses was felt to be a severe blow against Alexander VI. Mocking verses were found attached to a column of the Vatican, bidding the Pope prepare to find another victim

---

[1] Burchard, ii. 433: 'Cecidit in Tyberim non libenter; in eodem flumine repertus est.' Sanuto, i. 883: 'Sta trovato anegato nel fiume del Tevere.'
[2] Paolo Capelli, in Alberi, *Relazioni degli Ambasciatori Veneti*, Serie II. iii. 10. Capello came to Rome in May 1499.

offered to the Tiber, as the rest of the Borgia family were to
share the fate of the Duke of Gandia. The wits of Rome were
certainly cruel.[1]

Alexander VI. frankly accepted the situation, and resolutely
set himself to meet his enemies with their own weapons. In
the precarious condition of Italian politics allies were not to be
trusted unless their fidelity was secured by interested motives;
so Alexander VI. used the marriage connexions of his family as
a means to secure for himself a strong political party. He had
no one whom he could trust save his own children, whom he regarded as instruments for his own plans. If Italian politics
changed rapidly he was ready to change as rapidly as they. The
spiritual office of the Papacy afforded him a safe mooring; he
would use every opportunity that offered for increasing its temporal power. He was the first Pope who deliberately and con-
sciously recognised the advantages to be reaped in politics from
the papal office, and set himself to make the most of them.
For this reason he inspired dread in the minds of Italian statesmen like Machiavelli. He was an incalculable force in politics;
he was engaged in the same game as the rest of the players,
but none of them knew the exact nature of his resources.

The nepotism of Alexander VI. was not merely a passionate
and unreasoning desire for the advancement of his family, but
was founded on calculation and pursued with resoluteness. Marriage projects for Lucrezia were eagerly sought, and there were
many rumours about their progress. The death of the Duke of
Gandia made the Pope anxious to have another general whom he
could trust; but Cesare's resignation of the cardinalate involved
a considerable sacrifice. His ecclesiastical revenues amounted
to 35,000 ducats yearly, and it was not easy to find an equally
valuable position for a layman. Alexander V.'s first thoughts
turned to Naples. A firm alliance with Federigo would make
him secure in Rome, and would enable him to deal with the
overweening power of the Roman barons. He proposed Neapolitan marriages both for Lucrezia and Cesare; but Federigo

Marriage
of Lucrezia
Borgia
with
Alfonso,
Duke of
Biseglia.
August,
1498.

---

[1] The verses are given in Sanuto, i. 1016. They play upon the Borgia crest,
which was a bull. They end:

> 'Ausonios fines vastantem cædite taurum,
> Cornua monstrifero vellite torva bovi.
> Merge, Tyber, vitulos animosas ultor in undas;
> Bos cadat inferno victima magna Jovi.'

had no love for the Pope and dreaded his interference in the affairs of his kingdom. However, after much pressure from the Duke of Milan he consented to the marriage of Lucrezia with Don Alfonso, Duke of Biseglia, a natural son of Alfonso II.; and the marriage was quietly celebrated in the Vatican in August 1498. But he steadfastly resisted the further proposal of the Pope that he should give his daughter Carlotta to Cesare Borgia. He said at last: ' It does not seem to me that a Pope's son, who is a Cardinal, is in a position to marry my daughter, though he is the son of a Pope. Let him marry as a Cardinal and keep his hat; then I will give him my daughter.' [1]

While these negotiations were pending a change came over European politics owing to the death of Charles VIII. of France. He died suddenly in April from striking his head against a low doorway in his new castle of Amboise, which he was erecting as a reminiscence of the splendour he had seen in Italy. He was succeeded by his distant cousin Louis, Duke of Orleans, who had so persistently urged his own claims to the duchy of Milan, as representing the old Visconti house. Louis XII. was of mature years, and was likely to act more energetically than the feeble Charles VIII. He showed a pacific temper in France, and said, ' the king does not remember the wrongs done to the duke.' He was careful and thrifty, and showed from the beginning a resoluteness to assert his rights which filled Ludovico Sforza with alarm.

The downfall of Savonarola seemed to have secured the success of the Italian League against France. But the League held loosely together, and it needed very little to dissolve it. The Venetians and Ludovico Il Moro were mutually jealous, and each suspected the other of designs on Pisa; the Pope had little confidence in his Italian allies; Federigo of Naples was helpless; Maximilian had his grievances both against Milan and Venice. It was a question which of the allies should be first to use a new combination for his advantage.

Negotia-
tions of
Alexander
VI. with
Louis XII.
1498.

Fortune favoured Alexander VI. Louis XII. had been married to Jeanne, youngest daughter of Louis XI., when she was a child of nine years old. She bore her husband no children, and there was nothing in common between them. On the other hand, Charles VIII. left a young widow of twenty-one,

[1] Sanuto, i. 988; June 1498.

Anne of Brittany, whose hand carried with it the last great
fief which was not yet consolidated with the French crown.
Louis XII. wished to put away his wife and marry Anne in her
stead; and if ever the dissolution of a marriage could be justified on grounds of political expediency, the justification might
be urged in this case. Alexander VI. used the opportunity
offered by the application for a divorce. He proposed a close
alliance with France, and offered to send his son Cesare to
negotiate further. He left Cesare's marriage projects in the
hands of Louis XII., and employed Cardinal Rovere, who was at
Avignon, to prepare the way for his proposals.[1] It is a sign of
the astuteness of Alexander VI.'s policy that his determined
enemy found it useless any longer to oppose him. Cardinal
Rovere had urged Charles VIII. to invade Italy, to summon a
Council and depose the Pope; he had garrisoned Ostia to be
a thorn in Alexander's VI.'s side, and had retired haughtily to
France. Alexander VI. had escaped all Cardinal Rovere's
designs against him; he had taken Ostia, and thereby diminished the Cardinal's income, though he made some restitution
and offered to restore Ostia if the Cardinal would return to
Rome.[2] Rovere found himself neglected in France; he was
weary of his hopeless isolation, and judged it well to seek reconciliation with the Pope while he might still have something
to offer. Alexander VI. was not vindictive. He agreed to
restore Ostia and receive the Cardinal into his favour, provided
that he acted as his agent at the French court.

The Pope entertained great hopes of the fruits of a French
alliance, and gathered money to equip Cesare in splendour for
his embassy. When he showed some care for ecclesiastical
discipline, men said that he was moved by a desire to extort
money from the culprits. The Marrani who were expelled from
Spain flocked to Rome, and spread their heresies even in the
papal court. In April 1498 the aged Bishop of Calagorra,
steward of the Pope's household, was accused of heresy and
was committed to prison. The charge against him was that he
had relapsed into Judaism and denied the Christian revelation.[3]

[1] Letter of Cardinal Rovere, dated September 11, 1498: 'Curabo et enitar ut
omne debitum quod eidem v^{re} S^{ti} debeo cedat, et pro mea tenuitate persolvatur
in personam d^{ni} valentinensis.' Brosch, *Papst Julius II.* Appendix No. 3.

[2] Sanuto, i. 642.

[3] Burchard, iii. 15, gives the result of his examination in February 1500.

In July three hundred Marrani did public penance. Men laughed in Rome and said that all this was done to provide for Cesare's outfit.[1]

Cesare
Borgia
renounces
the cardi-
nalate,
August 17,
1498.

At last Cesare's preparations were made. In a secret Consistory on August 17 he rose and said that from his earliest years he had been inclined to secular pursuits; at the Pope's earnest wish he had become a churchman, had received deacon's orders, and had been laden with benefices; as he still found that the bent of his mind was secular, he besought the Pope to dispense him from his ecclesiastical obligations, and asked the Cardinals to agree to his request.[2] They readily consented to leave the matter in the Pope's hands. The dispensation followed in due form, and Alexander VI. declared that he granted it for the salvation of Cesare's soul.[3] It might be retorted that he should have considered that object before raising him to a position for which he was unfitted. On October 1, Cesare, magnificent in cloth of gold, set out from Rome on his journey to France. He took with him 200,000 ducats in money and in splendid attire.

Cesare's progress was marked with royal state. On December 18 he entered Chinon, where was the French king, with grandeur which long lived in the memory of the French. His robe was stiff with jewels; his steed's trappings were of finely wrought gold.[4] Louis XII. laughed at this vainglory and foolish boasting, and turned at once to business. The Pope's commissioners granted a dispensation from his marriage with Jeanne of France; and Cesare Borgia brought with him a cardinal's hat for the king's favourite, George of Amboise, Archbishop of Rouen, who received it on December 21 from the hands of Cardinal Rovere as the Pope's legate. Cesare had already received from the French king part of the reward of the Pope's compliance with his wishes. He had been invested with the counties of Valentinois and Diois, to which the Papacy had a long-standing claim on the ground of their bequest to the

---

[1] Sanuto, i. 1014-1029.   [2] Burchard, ii. 492.

[3] Letter to Archbishop Ximenes of Toledo, September 3: 'Causis et rationibus pro salute animæ suæ cum promoventibus,' quoted by Gregorovius, *Geschichte der Stadt Rom*, viii. 422.

[4] The account of this entry is given by Brantôme, *Vies des hommes illustres*, xlviii. The king called it 'la vaine gloire et bombance sotte de ce duc de Valentinois.' Sanuto's account, ii. 320, agrees with Brantôme's.

Church by the last Dauphin. There remained, however, the question of Cesare's marriage. He was still anxious to have for his wife Carlotta, daughter of Federigo of Naples, that thereby he might have a claim upon the Neapolitan throne. Federigo had refused; but Carlotta, who was the daughter of a French princess, was in France, and Cesare hoped to win her through the influence of the French king. Carlotta, however, remained firm in her refusal, sorely to the dismay of the Pope, who complained to Cardinal Rovere that he was made a laughing stock by this failure of his plans. In his disappointment he threatened to abandon the French alliance and join with Milan, Naples, and Spain.[1] To pacify him, Louis XII. offered Cesare a further choice of two French princesses, nieces of his own, the daughter of the Count of Foix or the sister of the King of Navarre. Cesare chose the beautiful Charlotte d'Albret, a girl of sixteen years. It was some time before the preliminaries of the marriage could be arranged, and Cesare had to undertake that a cardinal's hat should be bestowed on Aimon d'Albret, Charlotte's brother. At last, on May 22, 1499, Alexander VI. announced to the Cardinals that the marriage had been celebrated, and Rome blazed with bonfires at the news, 'to the great scandal,' says Burchard, 'of the Church and the Apostolic seat.'

The good understanding between Alexander VI. and France was viewed with alarm by other powers, and led to remonstrance with the Pope. Ascanio Sforza saw his brother menaced in Milan, and feared for his own influence in Rome. Alexander VI. never discouraged plain speaking, and was ready to answer with equal plainness. In a Consistory in December 1498, Ascanio told the Pope that his French alliance would be the ruin of Italy. Alexander VI. answered, 'It was your brother who first summoned the French.' Warm words passed between them, and Ascanio went away threatening to call on Maximilian and Spain to join in convoking a General Council.[2] The threat of a Council was now a common device in Italian politics, and Alexander VI. knew its futility. His ecclesiastical position was entirely

---

[1] Sanuto, ii. 531, March 1499: 'Soa santità va scorando . . . et si non havesse il fiol in Franza si acorderia con Milan.'

[2] *Ibid.* ii. 217: 'Si detono di denti molto forti,' he says of the Pope and Ascanio.

secondary to his political importance, and so long as he had a place in the combinations of Italian affairs he was safe enough. He did not even show any resentment against Ascanio. He was not the man to strike one whose doom was being prepared by others.

The remonstrances of Spain were more serious than those of Cardinal Ascanio. The Spanish sovereigns were not strong enough to oppose the schemes of Louis XII. in Italy, and judged it prudent to make a treaty of neutrality with France. But they hoped that the Italian powers would unite in resisting him, and were alarmed at his alliance with the Pope. The Spanish envoy, Garcilasso de la Vega, presented a letter from his sovereigns on December 18, in which they complained of the corruption of the papal court, and hinted at the summons of a Council. The Pope angrily answered that they were misled by false information sent by their ambassador from Rome. Garcilasso went on to refer to the promises held out by the Pope after the death of the Duke of Gandia, and their failure before his scheme for promoting Cesare. Alexander VI. with increasing bitterness said, 'Your royal house has been afflicted by God, who has deprived it of posterity; this is because they have laid impious hands on the possessions of the Church.' In January 1499 there was a still more stormy scene. Alexander VI. tried to tear the paper from Garcilasso's hands, and threatened to have him thrown into the Tiber; he accused Queen Isabella of unchastity. The envoys wished to make a formal protest in the Pope's presence, but were not allowed.[1]

Venice joins the French alliance. February, 1499.

Alexander VI. knew himself to be strong enough to defy remonstrances. His league with France was joined by Venice, who wished to have a share of the dominions of Milan and to rid itself of a troublesome neighbour. Their alliance with France was secretly sworn on February 9, and was published on April 15. Cesare Borgia was present at the ceremony, and Cardinal Rovere held the missal on which the oath was taken. It was an eventful moment for Italy. The gates were opened by her own hand for foreign intervention, and the knell of Italian independence was sounded. The self-seeking of Venice and the desire of the

[1] This is told by Sanuto, ii. 280, 385 ; Zurita, *Historia del Rey Hernando*, i. bk. 3, ch. xxxiii. 35, and Burchard, ii. 506, agree: 'Habita sunt inter eos verba valde clamosa tam per Papam quam per oratores et injuriosa.'

Pope for a strong ally overpowered all larger considerations. There was no national feeling, no sense of patriotism or of consistency. Savonarola had been sacrificed that the French might be shut out of Italy; now the very men who worked for his overthrow adopted his politics which they had condemned. The Italian League had faded away. Old foes were reconciled by new motives of self-interest. Cardinal Rovere had sought French help to drive Alexander VI. from his seat; when that failed, he aided Alexander VI. to seek the help of France to establish himself more securely.

CHAP. IX.

Alexander VI., however, did not openly declare his alliance with France, but watched the progress of Cesare's marriage projects with uneasiness. Even after he was satisfied on that score, his attitude was so ambiguous that it was not till July 14 that Ascanio Sforza became certain of his hostility. He fled from Rome in the early morning, pretending to be going out hunting, and made his way to Milan, where his brother Ludovico was making preparations to resist his foes. Ludovico was cunning and vainglorious; but he mistook craft and self-assertion for statesmanship. After the retreat of Charles VIII. he had exulted in the success of his schemes. He boasted that he had the Pope for his chaplain, the Venetians for his treasurers, Maximilian for his condottieri general, and the King of France for his messenger to come and go at his pleasure. Now in the hour of his peril Ludovico found himself without allies. Federigo of Naples was trembling for himself; Maximilian was engaged in war against the Swiss; Florence was still busied with Pisa. The only device that Ludovico could find was the dastardly plan of instigating the Turks to make a diversion in his favour. This helped him little. When the French troops advanced on the west, and the Venetians on the east, Ludovico could offer no resistance. The cities in his territory opened their gates to the invaders. Only the citadel of Milan professed to hold out, and that was betrayed by its commander. Ludovico fled into the Tyrol, and on October 6 Louis XII. entered Milan amidst the joyous shouts of the crowd. With him rode the Duke of Valentinois and Cardinal Rovere, both prepared to reap what advantage they could from the success of France.

Louis XII. captures Milan. October. 1499.

Alexander VI. meanwhile was engaged in adjusting his plans

to match the change of his political attitude. The Neapolitan
marriage of Lucrezia was now of no use to him, and his son-in-
law the Prince of Biseglia felt himself out of place in the
Vatican. Early in August he secretly left Rome and went
to Naples, whence he sent word to the Pope that he could not
stay in the Vatican which was filled with partizans of France
who spoke ill of the Neapolitans.[1] Federigo summoned also
the Prince of Squillace and his Neapolitan wife to return to their
possessions. The Pope sent away Dona Sancia and refused to
give her any money for the journey ; the Prince of Squillace
stayed at Rome. The Neapolitan marriages were now a trouble to
the Pope. Lucrezia needed her husband's care and wept over
his absence ;[2] to distract her mind and make Alfonso's return
more easy, Alexander VI. on August 8 appointed his daughter
regent of Spoleto. Spoleto was one of the few cities in the
Papal States which had not fallen under a tyranny, but was
governed by a papal legate, generally a Cardinal. Alexander VI.
was so heedless of precedent or decorum that he did not scruple
to send as its governor a girl of nineteen, his own daughter.
He was absolutely unfettered by the traditions of his office ; and
others did not feel bound to be more careful of his reputation
than he was himself.

Soon the Pope gave another sign of his affection for his
daughter. Ascanio Sforza was driven to resign his office as
regent of Nepi, and Nepi also was conferred on Lucrezia.
Her husband rejoined her at Spoleto, and on September 25
Alexander VI. left Rome to meet Alfonso and Lucrezia at
Nepi, whither she went to take possession. In the middle
of October Lucrezia returned to Rome, where she gave
birth to a son on November 1. This event seems to have reconciled the Pope and his son-in-law ; and the brilliant life of
the papal household was happily resumed.[3]

----

[1] So the Pope told the Venetian envoy : ' Et soa Santità rispose poco curarsi
di lui.' Sanuto, ii. 1135.
[2] ' A lassa la moglie gravida di 6 mese, la qual di continuo pianse.' Sanuto,
ii. 1049.
[3] Burchard, iii. 4, describes a public appearance of the Pope with Lucrezia
and her husband on January 1, 1500.

APPENDIX.

APPENDIX.

1. *Paul II.*

(1) CHIEF amongst the authorities for the pontificate of Paul II. is Cardinal AMMANNATI, who has been spoken of in vol. ii. 496 of this work. On the death of Pius II. Ammannati undertook to continue the *Commentarii* of his patron, and carried on the work to the end of 1469. This continuation is printed at the end of the Frankfort edition (1614) of Pius II.'s *Commentarii*. It is obvious at once to the reader that Ammannati's task was not congenial to him, and his attempt to imitate the style of Pius II. is not successful. In fact, Ammannati was merely a man of letters; he had little of the instincts of a statesman or of an historian. Hence he becomes lost in fine writing, which neither tells the result of his own observations nor rises to the method of a continuous history. His account of Bohemian affairs is the best part of his work. In Italy nothing of importance occurred, yet Ammannati narrates at length trivial events without any sense of perspective. Except a few remarks on Paul II.'s election, he says little which throws light on his character or policy.

More interesting than his *Commentarii* are his letters, which are also printed in the Frankfort edition of *Pii II. Commentarii*, under the title of *Cardinalis Papiensis Epistolae*. We see from these letters the character of Ammannati; he was easy, good-natured, flexible, and vain, honourable and well-intentioned, but swayed by personal motives. He bore a grudge against Paul II. for his treatment of the Cardinals, and had besides a special grievance of his own. Under Pius II. he had enjoyed the sweets of papal favour, and found it hard to assume a humbler position under Paul II. Added to this, he was aggrieved because Paul II. refused to take his part in a quarrel which he had with the Duke of Milan concerning his ecclesiastical revenues. Many of his letters, especially those to Bessarion, bear signs of personal spleen and disappointment. His

         T

pen was ready, and reproduced his passing moods. Thus letter 188 is an utterance of sudden spite ; letter 374 is a good instance of a man who gets rid of his ill-humour by putting it on paper. Several of his letters addressed to the Pope seem to me to be merely literary compositions which were never sent, especially No. 281, in which he reproves Paul II. for his too great desire for fame. It is clear that Ammannati did not like nor understand Paul II. ; but he gives us much interesting information about him, and draws a picture of the ordinary life of the Curia, which is much more pleasant than anything that we meet with again for half a century at least.

(2) GASPAR VERONENSIS *De Gestis Pauli secundi.* This work is divided into four books, of which the last three are published in MURATORI, *Rerum Italicarum Scriptores*, iii. pt. ii. 1024 &c. The first book was printed in 1784 by MARINI, *Archiatri Pontificii*, ii. 178. Gaspar, as we gather from his own pages, was a teacher in Rome, and numbered amongst his pupils Rodrigo Borgia, who, however, showed him little gratitude. He was also the teacher of Aldus Manutius, who speaks of him honourably in his dedication to Theocritus. Gaspar was made a papal secretary by Calixtus III., but did not continue in that office under Pius II., and we know nothing more than he tells us of himself. His commentary does not rise to the rank of a history. It has no arrangement, and wanders into digressions about his personal friends. The first book deals with the election of Paul II., his general character, and his treatment of the Curia. Gaspar writes as a panegyrist, and had a private cause for gratitude towards Paul II., who, while a Cardinal, sent his household to extinguish a fire which had broken out in Gaspar's house, and carefully guarded Gaspar's effects from pillage. The second book gives a valuable account of the Cardinals at Rome on the accession of Paul II. The third book similarly wanders into praises of the Pope's secretaries, and the fourth book is concerned with the Pope's relatives. Gaspar has given so much time to his preface that he never reached the history. His general account of the condition of the Curia harmonises with that of Ammannati. Unfortunately he tells us nothing of the breach between Paul II. and the men of letters, though what he does tell is more than enough to defend Paul II. from the sneers of Platina, who does his best to represent him as an illiterate barbarian.

(3) The Life of Paul II., by PLATINA, is a very finished piece of writing, and may serve as a conspicuous example of the revenge taken by a man of letters on one whom he had cause for disliking. Platina, without saying anything that is obviously untrue, has contrived to suggest a conception of Paul II. which is entirely contrary

to known facts, yet which is so vivid, so definite, so intelligible, that it bears the stamp of reality. Platina so far succeeded, that his representation of Paul II. was for a long time currently accepted. On the whole, considering the malignity of Platina, it is a great testimony to the virtues of Paul II. that there was nothing worse to be said about him. Platina and Pomponius Lætus were men who enjoyed so high a literary reputation that no one ventured to contradict them by name. Michael Canensius makes no mention of Platina in his life of Paul II., and though he alludes to Pomponius, he says, ' Hujus sectæ principem pro honestate hic nominare minime intendimus.' How thoroughly the Roman men of letters succeeded in defaming Paul II. we learn from a letter of Filelfo to Sixtus IV., *Epistolæ* (ed. Venice, 1502), bk. xxiii., where Filelfo defends Paul II. from the charges of gluttony, avarice, and ambition.

(4) The best authority for the pontificate of Paul is MICHAEL CANENSIUS, *Vita Pauli secundi*, published in part by Muratori, *Rer. Ital. Scrip.* iii. pt. ii. 993 &c. and fully by Quirini, *Pauli II. Veneti Pont. Max. Vita.* (Rome, 1740). Canensio was a native of Viterbo, learned in canon law, and a canon of SS. Lorenzo and Damaso in Rome. He was made Bishop of Castro in 1474 and died in that office in 1482. His *Vita Pauli secundi* was written, as he says in his preface, ' dum a frequenti curiæ sollicitudine ac nostra superata ambitione ad ecclesiam meam Castrensem, tamquam ad quemdam tranquillum amœnumque portum declinassem.' It is dedicated, not to any of the nephews of Paul II., but to Cardinal Estouteville ; at the end of the work is a promise of writing also the Life of Sixtus IV., a promise which was apparently not fulfilled. Canensio writes with discernment and deserves to rank as the chief authority for the pontificate of Paul II. Quirini has prefaced his edition with *Vindiciæ* in which he discusses at length the various charges brought against the Pope and argues temperately in his behalf.

(5) For the affairs of Bohemia we have the documents in Palacky, *Urkundliche Beiträge zur Geschichte Böhmens im Zeitalter Georg's von Podiebrad* ; Höfler, *Böhmische Studien* in *Archiv für Oesterreichische Geschichtskunde*, xii. 328 &c; Klose, *Documentirte Geschichte von Breslau*, iii. These are illustrated from other sources by Palacky, *Geschichte von Böhmen*, iv., and Jordan, *Das Königthum Georg's von Podiebrad*.

(6) I have gleaned much information about Paul II. and his successors from PAOLO CORTESE, *De Cardinalatu*. Cortese was born in Rome in 1465 ; he was a learned theologian and enjoyed the friendship of the chief scholars of Italy, of whom his work *De Hominibus Doctis* gives much interesting information. The *De*

Cardinalatu was published immediately after his death in 1510 by Raffaelle Volterrano, who dedicated it to Julius II. The book has not been reprinted and is now very rare, which probably accounts for the small attention that has been paid to it.

Equally valuable is the *Commentarii Urbani* of RAFFAELLE VOLATERRANO. His family name was Maffei; he was born at Volterra in 1451 and died in Rome in 1522. His *Commentarii* is mostly devoted to geography; but book xxii. is entitled *Anthropologia*, and amongst other things contains a series of characters of the Popes. His account of Paul II. shows how his own observation was at variance with the presentation given by Platina : ' Præter necessarias auditiones dies totos aut voluptati aut nummis pensitandis aut veterum numismatis sive gemmis sive imaginibus spectandis tradebat. Inter hæc tamen vitia hanc animi integritatem custodiit ut nullam rem ecclesiasticam liceretur, justitiam quoque publice sectaretur, severus nec tamen crudelis in delinquentes.'

---

2. *Letters of Pomponius Lætus to Rodrigo de Arevalo, Castellan of S. Angelo, during his imprisonment.* (*Corpus Christi College, Cambridge, MS. No.* 161.)

1. POMPONIUS TO RODRIGO.

Salvus sis, sanctissime et religiosissime pater Roderice. Si pro innumeris in nos beneficiis essem bonitati vestre gratias habiturus, que cumulatissima sunt, neque possem neque valerem. Undique enim se aperit ad benefaciendum prestantia vestra ; que quanta sit, et quanti existimata, et quam fidelis, Paulus summus pontifex judicavit, cum Romane arcis, que tocius ditionis ecclesiastice retinacula habenasque possidet, te custodem elegit et prefecit. Nec mirum ; nam pius et sanctus princeps secum habere nisi bonos nisi probatos non potuit. De cujus pietate, misericordia, clementia, sanctitate si sermo mihi habendus esset, deficerent vires, deficeret loquendi vena, hebesceret ingenium ad tanti pontificis contemplationem. Habemus ante oculos quod in tanta rerum suspicione et discrimine, ubi de lesa majestate inquirendum erat, immobilis mansit et imperturbatus. Cedat huic T. Cæsar, qui conjuratis pepercit ; cedat in clementia et misericordia Trajanus, inque pietate Antoninus, in gravitate Tacitus; quos profecto omnes longe majore constantia, animo, dignitate antecellit unus Paulus Pontifex maximus ; cujus virtus admiranda quantum sit in officio divinitus delegato facile cognosci potest. Vicem summi Dei in terris merito gerit unde et Christi Vicarius appellatur cum ligandi et cogendi potestate, quod insigne precipuum

Christus Dominus noster Petro et ejus successoribus concessit. Placuit hec dixisse ut aperirem bonitati vestre mentem meam, quid sentiam de tanto pontifice, celitus dato, divinitus electo, quem sine divino numine nichil efficere putandum est. Dicet quis presens facinus ascribendum innocentie nostre, ego vero clementie pontificis reor ; nam in similibus discriminibus non solet queri ratio : pro quo atque aliis innumeris sanctissime gestis audeo omnibus pontificibus qui fuerunt aut futuri sunt facile sanctissimo judicio anteponere. Annon tibi Christum videtur imitatus qui cum ictum manus vultu cepisset tulit quam humanissime ? Sic in presentia Paulus a quodam scelerato apertissime lesus pontificali innata atque ingenita secum gravitate et constantia usus est. Jam finem facio ; pro tantis enim laudibus longam exposui orationem si modo materies longitudine non defutura mihi sit. Valeat eternum bonitas vestra, cui captivitatem nostram commendarem nisi scirem nihil habere in animo commendatius. iiii. Kl. Aprilis.

2. Rodrigo to Pomponius.

Delate ad me sunt litere tue, Pomponi carissime, et plurimum gavisus sum tui incolumitate et illarum suavitate. Tanta enim in illis est dicendi vis, tanta verborum elegantia, sententiarum pulchra ac solida auctoritas, ut illos priscos divinosque viros quos imitari cupis facile superes. Agis itaque, eloquentissime vir, mihi ultra condignum grates quod humanitatis et charitatis officia impenderim, qua re agis tu morem prudentis egroti qui ignoto medico gratias agit, non pro eo quod ante prestiterit sed pro illo quod futuro merebitur. Fateor, doctissime Pomponi, optaverim ego te visere, tecum in laudatis studiis quibus refertissimus es conversari, summaque aviditate ardebam ut ex tuo meum ingenium illustraretur, non quidem ut ex meo tuum corpus servaretur. Sed ita ordinata est Providentia, que suos probat, que calamitatibus exercet, nec aliquem exceptum relinquit nisi a se exceptum. Venit enim ad quosdam diu felices sua porcio : et ut michi semper visum est, quisquis in hominum conspectu dimissus videtur dilatus est. Quid enim in te unum sevire fortune rabies poterat, quem non locupletem nisi literis, non in principum aulis, non mollibus vestibus, non in excelsis honoribus tumescentem, non delicias, non enervatam felicitatem sectantem (invenit) ? Sed verum est quia belua illa furibunda, quam fortunam vocant, majoribus bonis invidet : doluit de tua humanitate, doluit de tua virtute, de varia literarum supellectili. Sed confortare, disertissime Pomponi : mentita est iniquitas sibi. Fecit ut patereris quantum humana natura posset pati ; sed efficere id valet, videlicet ut quo acerbiore dolore concutitur, eo notior sit virtus tua, constantia animi tui. In eo quippe certamine fortior simul et notior evades : opus enim erat ut hominibus experimentum tui faceres. Non comparatur virtus sine certamine : quicquid possumus non sine congrediendo cognoscimus. Fuere quidem multi, quos tu legisti, qui se ultra grassantibus malis obtulerunt et virtuti latenti et, ut ita dixerim, in obscurum tendenti occasionem per quam innotesceret quesiverunt. Tu igitur, eam volens, non traheris, quippe qui pro luce doctrine et virtutis tue, si cessisses, a te cessisses. A volente queret fortuna quicquid a te petierit ; maluisses offerre quam tradere. Ceterum plurima digna laude de nostri Pont. Max. laudibus attulisti, de pietate, de misericordia, clementia, sanctitate—in qua re ad dicendum magnus campus est. Major enim est omni laude nec laus sufficit laudanti ; quia scriptum est *Scrutator majestatis opprimitur a gloria.* Jacta igitur in eum unum curam tuam ; ora altissimum Deum cujus vices in terra gerit, ut placabilem tibi reddat quem in te iratum arbitraris. Vale, Pomponi.

3. POMPONIUS TO RODRIGO.

Scripseram, religiosissime episcope, non ut vicem redderes literarum tuarum, quibus me dignum non puto, sed ut tantum haberes, teneres, cognosceres animum meum. Qui cum a delatoribus nimis petulans asseratur, placuit judicio dignitatis vestre comprobari qualis sit. Sed humanitas vestra tanta est ut vel minimo cuique respondere dignetur ; ita mihi homunculo non modo literas sed sempiternam consolationem invenisti : cujus rei ergo quanti humanitatem vestram judicem explicari non potest, ingenio modo presertim adhuc obtuso. Fecisti me participem oris tui, quod ad laudem pontificum et principum semper accommodatum fuit ; donasti mihi his unis literis immortalitatem, et de quo silentium futurum erat jam celebritas expectanda est. Ideo satis mei memor fui cum scripsi : inveni enim medicum, ut exemplo vestro utar, cujus ope captivitas mea liberanda foret. Alii medici nisi lotionibus, nisi mercibus Arabum quicquid assequi possunt : dignitas vero vestra verbis, litteris, consilio, verius ac securius egrotantibus prodest. Egrotos dico, quod duplici de causa egrotant, aut animo aut corpore ; et illis potissimum opem affert vestra humanitas quos litterarum studiosos et amatores novit. Inde cum ex rivulo ingenii mei flumen tuum purgari cupiebas, scribis pro ingenita humanitate et sanctimonia. Nam scriptum est *Qui se humiliat exaltabitur,* ut vester calamus, auctoritatum locupletissimus, alibi non abs re notavit. Hec etiam Chrisostomi sententia fuit, cujus suavitas et dicendi lepos aureum os appellari meruit. Postea scribit dignitas vestra quod virtus nisi collata discriminibus que et quanta sit videri non potest. O aurea verba ; o proverbium satis annotandum. Sic et sentire videtur Silius Italicus cum ait, *Aurea virtutem profert via*, hec est, frugalitatis meritum. Ideo accommodatissime subjungis quid in me sevire fortune rabies poterat. Egenus sum rerum omnium, vestium et divitiarum contemptor, nullius felicitatis appetens nisi illius que post fata venire solet. Alii aulas principum pro lege habent, singulis diebus salutare, circuire fora, ambitiones inquirere, noctem pro foribus magnatum vigilare. Ipsa vero dignitas rectum judicium afferre potest. Nulla re moveor nisi litterarum appetitu, qui profundus, immensus, insatiabilis ita est ut non tantum me incitet sed obruat ; addo, quod et calamitosius est, votum meum explere non licet. Experiar tamen hac vestra consolatoria epistola, qua mirum in modum oblector, an hec studiorum dilatio constantiam meam expugnatura sit. Sed, ut arbitror, me turbatum et omni spe destitutum statim littere vestre reducent et in meliorem statum reformabunt. Erit aliquando hic congressus, qui nunc tantum calamitatis afferre videtur, velut in certaminibus, sic jucundus, delectabilis et cum prospera alea futurus, que in omni re optima desideratur ; et tunc id me passum fuisse noluisse affirmavero. Non tradam oblivioni omnem vestram sententiam, ad quam observandam non opus est, ut in me, exhortatione. Huc accessi libens ; nam, si voluissem, in alio terrarum orbe nunc degerem. Sed, quod nichil preter quod majestati pontificis conferret egerim, non dubitavi, non timui, non erubui huc venire ; neque penitet venisse neque peniteret si adhuc venturus essem. Videbit misericordia pontificis innocentiam meam ; miserebit inopie et calamitatis ; cognoscet fraudes delatorum. Pro cujus pietatis observantia mihi ad dicendum, ut dignitatis vestre verbis utar, magnus offertur campus ; in quo utinam latitudine agri non deficiam. Nam quis posset de tanta majestate loquens non obmutire, nisi vestra vis eloquentie hoc ipsum aggrediatur, que satis idonea est ad id exequendum ? Ego vero nec possum nec, si possem, tentarem, cum ita abjectissimus sim ut ad laudes tanti Principis os offerre non audeam, qui relictum adeo mitissimo nutu imperium feliciter gubernat. Valeat dominatio vestra eternum, cui captivi nos omnes deditissime commendamus. Postremo humanitatem vestram etiam atque etiam exoro ut Lactantium et Saturnalia Macrobi commodo dare dignetur. Audeo hec petere cum humanitatem vestram semper fuisse et futuram esse erga omnes studiosos proclivem noverim. Pridie Kl. April.

4. POMPONIUS TO RODRIGO.

Calamitate non pauca oppressus, perturbato litterarum studio, libellum summa diligentia in officina vestra architectatum non

solum legi, sed pro inexplicabili erga me utilitate exscripsi ; in quo
malignum illum, seu potius dicam malignitatem ipsam, approbantem
iniquas seditiones Basiliensis Concilii comprimis et extinguis, et que
ad summi pontificatus electionem pertinere videntur (demonstras).
Tum lepore, tum mira exemplorum congerie cumulas struisque ;
uteris et ea modestia qua antea Quintilianus, nationis vestre, usus
est, scilicet nomen illius quem reprehendis silentio mandas ; qua in
re quantum bonitatis et simplicitatis habeas ex hoc uno inspici licet.
Illum non mordes sed castigas ; non laceras sed mordes ; non evisceras
sed ut taceat cogis. Sic erga filium pater esse solet ; et si merebatur
a doctrina vestra imprehensibiliter dilaniari, quod utile erat fidei
Christiane, quia in Romanum Pontificem jure et sanctimonia
electum illatraverat, et bonitatem vestram clam, more vulpecule,
fedato pollutoque ore insectabatur, tamen sua peculiari iniquitate
tantam sobrietatem expugnare non potuit. Quid dicam de copia,
de ordine et de illa inexpugnabili conclusione ubi electionem
Amadei, servato oratoris officio et honesto dicendi more, confutas, in
qua majores nostros superare videris? Illi namque quotienscum-
que in alios invehebant caninis dentibus infremebant, ut Cicero
in Antonium et Verrem, Calvus in Vatinium fecere. Sed aliud
opinonem vestram decebat ; Christianus es, religiosus es, et presagus
rerum futurarum, omnia in te Sancto Spiritu revelante. Nam cum
electionem Smi Eugenii quarti probas, hoc portendere ingenio vestro
divinitus dabatur, scilicet ex electis Cardinalibus ab Eugenio
futurum Paulum secundum ejus nepotem, qui in presentia pontificatum clementissime gubernat, quo nihil unquam in terris sanctius fuit
futurumque est. Et ut fidelitas vestra arci Romane presideret
scriptum est, quod et Spiritus Sanctus per linguas hominum loquitur.
Optassem et voluissem te vidisse tante molis orationem pronuncian-
tem ; tunc afflatus numine videbare, ut arbitror, humano major.
Cognosco tamen effingendo imaginem vestram tunc concionantem,
ab omni sismate abhorrentem, ex acumine sententiarum, verborum
nervis et totius solute orationis vehementi cursu. Ita fieri solet ut
hominem ex scriptis, non solum qualis sit, sed etiam quantus et quis
judicemus. Undique gravis, concitatus, ardens, vehemens es ; et
erga Romanam ecclesiam mirum amorem ostendis, pro qua et illa
felicissima legatione ad varios principes, apud quos sigillatim contion-
atus es, multos labores volens subisti et adhuc in probatissima
senectute subires, ferresque vigilias, labores, sudores, cruciatus pro
ecclesie ratione observanda. De quo tam amplo facinore ipse
Christianorum minimus summopere desidero ut Christus, summus
parens, salutem vestram ad auxilium Christiani nominis tuto con-
servet. Valeat ergo eternum integritas vestra. Kl. April.

5. Pomponius to Rodrigo.

Plinius Secundus in epistolis mirum in modum solitudinem laudat quam vult esse peculium poetarum, sed eam que in silvis usurpatur, ubi concentus avium amenitatem, ubi frondose arbores jucundissimam opacitatem, ubi virentes herbe natalem et delectabilem stratum prebent prestantque. Mira res: multa hic inveniunt; multa dictant suggeruntque, et verum secretum musarum appellatur. Nunc silve carminibus sonant; nunc antra remugiunt; denique loca omnia Calliopen referre videntur. Utinam michi in presentia id contingeret. Sed parietibus circumdor, summota libertate, ubi celum videre nisi per exigua foramina non conceditur et solus per testudineam cellam vagor. Oro pietatem vestram, que immensa est, unum det comitem hilarem, scilicet cujus confabulatione tristitia mea, que plurima est, leniatur. Scriptum est enim, *Alius alius onera portate, et sic implebitis legem Christi.* Si secus fiet profecto invalescente hac mestitia cadam. Quare summopere obsecro ut a conversatione alicujus me non addicas; nam si studium poetarum sector solitudo in hoc mihi non placet. Verum pietas vestra cum qua et littere jocari solent, faciat ut libet. Kl. April.

6. Rodrigo to Pomponius.

Legi epistolam tuam plenam certe facetie et risus perpulchri. Nam in eos invehis qui solitudinem laudant, quia etsi quibusdam feris, ut ais, hominibus ea pergrata aliquando esse potest, putas talem esse que in silvis usurpatur, ubi concentus avium frondoseque arbores amenitatem non parvam afferunt. Non utique quam tu pateris solitudinem laudandam arbitrare, quippe, ut ais, inter muros vivis, et, ut ita dixerim, sepultus videare. Nisi itaque, disertissime Pomponi, jocose ea a te dicta arbitrarer, non parvum animo dolerem. Judicarem quidem tibi docto viro ea divina atque superne contemplationi et speculationi accommodatissima monimenta permodesta fore, que a cunctis sapientibus concupita quam maxime fuere. Taceo, ut bona pace tua dixerim, quia tibi ipsi non parum contrarius videris; quum paulo ante confessus es nullius temporalis felicitatis te appetentem, cunctarum rerum nisi litterarum contemptorem, hominum denique consorcia fugientem. Vide igitur, Pomponi disertissime, quid velis cum hujuscemodi solitudinis querelis. Quid enim oro tibi aut solaminis aut remedii esse potest cum hominibus maxime vulgaribus conversari, quorum turba nata est impedire bonorum virorum consolationem? Hinc noster Anneus Seneca, *Quo major est populus cui commisceris, eo periculi plus est.* Nec te latet quod hominum societas quam maxime aut impedire aut certe interrumpere solet mentis nostre ad altiora progressum.　Quo enim pacto solus esse potest vir bonus, ut tu, et doctus qui, continuis et bonis cogitationibus sociatus, preclaris studiis stipatus existit, qui divinas sanctasque meditaciones comites habet, qui, ut aiunt, nunquam solus sibi minus videtur quam cum solus?　Hinc alter ex Grecis sapientibus contendebat sapientem solum esse non posse; habet enim secum eos omnes qui sunt vel fuerunt boni, et quod corpore non potest cogitatione amplectitur; et si hominum illi copia deerit loquitur cum Deo, quodque si murorum angustia corpus coartat eo magis mente superna considerat, ad que tanto anhelat ferventius quanto in terra premitur sevius.　Non ergo te cruciet parva angustaque mansio.　Illud tui familiarissimi Valerii Maximi in mentem veniat *Humile tugurium virtutes, angustus locus magnarum virtutum turbam capit.*　Mihi crede, Pomponi charissime, longe sanctius est sociari turba virtutum quam hominum; quod et ipse Valerius joco virtuoso patientissimi Diogenis ostendit, cum ait Diogenem ipsum, cum torqueretur in dolio, domum volubilem habere letari, et secum temporibus comitantem non abhorrere.　Rursus quid tibi afferre potest hominum confabulatio, qui plerumque garruli sunt, ne dixerim fastidiosi, nec quempiam consolantur?　Quin potius mestum reddunt, quod patientissimus Job expertus ad amicos dicebat *Consolatores onerosi estis vos.* Illud utique vellem consideres, Pomponi charissime, quia quanto quisque ab humanis colloquiis est separatus, tanto Deo est propinquior; idque rex et propheta David fassus est, *Elongavi,* inquit, *fugiens et mansi in solitudine;* et sequitur, *Audiam quid loquatur in me Deus, audiam, inquam, videlicet remotus ab hominibus.* Adde quia, ut Scriptura sacra edocemur, illi viri Israelite cum fuerunt in solitudine, gloria Domini eis in nube apparuit.　Denique ne crucieris quod solus sis, qui potiora vite tue solatia recte in libris litterisque reponis.　Nam et in libro Machabeorum legimus illos sanctissimos viros dixisse, *Nos nullo indigemus humano solatio, habentes libros et copiosos annales;* que res agit ut homines ad confabulandum necesse non existimem, quia et libri et littere ipse hominum supplent vices, que verius uberiusque consolantur.　Vale, mihi frater amantissime.

7. POMPONIUS TO RODRIGO.

Accepi litteras vestras quibus rides opinioni mee, que solitudinem, id est, heredium poetarum, paulo antea accusavit.　Id me non nisi joco fecisse scribis; amorem meum erga litteras damnare videris; quare mirum in modum doleo magisque angerer si cognoscerem pietatem vestram sic animo sentire.　Sed facis pro ingenita bonitate ut

quibusdam salibus et jocis captivitatem hanc aliquantulum leves ;
et in hac parietina solitudine me solari non desinis, tum suaviloquio,
tum doctissimorum hominum exemplis, ut moris est erga omnes
vestri. Que laudabili memoria retines et his, veluti fulchris, omnia
roboras, unde cum tam memorioso et copioso scriptore de rerum
varietate contendere pertimesco. Esset enim ingenium meum frustrari
potius quam acuere certando, cum tam promptum tamque velox non
sit ut se conferre vestro audeat. Scribo et ipse tamen ut non
a solito, id est, rudi et simplici dicendi stylo recedam, qui mihi
semper supra omne dicendi genus placuit. Sed ad me redeo ne mei
oblitus videar. Seneca diligentie vestre testis est, ut arbitror, de
sedicione quam ex turba oriri intelligit ; sed de solitudine, eam in
mente habuit que in libertate usurpatur, et quam liberi homines pro
voluntate excolunt. Sed captivi quo pacto solitudinem nisi inviti
ferre possint judicet doctrina vestra. Quid captivus preter libertatem cogitare potest, ut piscator de piscibus, navita de ventis, arator
de bobus, et sic singuli quique ad res sibi necessarias animum diri-
gunt ? Egroti nulla alia suavi cogitatione detinentur nisi ut aut in
fontibus sint aut in vinariis cellis ubi appetitum expleant ; nec
invenies valetudinarium hominem qui sitim laudat, et contra qui
bene valet intemperantiam in potu. Et si quis libertate privatus
solitudinem laudat, non ex corde sentit, et si profiteretur, non est
illi adhibenda fides. Captivus similis illi videtur qui, cum sponte
religionem ingreditur, post aliquot dies, cum videt se naturali voto
exutum dolet et interdum ingente solitudine in desperationem
adductus suspendio vitam finit. Quis quod benignitas nature tribuit
negligit nisi mentis inops ? Filios uxores cruciant ; laniant que non
habent ; paupertatem divites multis millibus versuum amplectendam
nepotibus suaserunt ; mendicus nunquam repertus qui egestatem
non vituperet. Si Cynico Diogeni termini constituti fuissent, quos
preterire et superare non licuisset, profecto tanti philosophi animus
singulis momentis singula remedia ad libertatem excogitavisset,
studio sapientie neglecto ; itaque liber seriolum domicilium suum
modo huc, modo illuc devolvebat. Mortales omnes hujus sunt
nature ut appetentius ea ipsa cupiant que negentur, et que habeant
despernant ; ut Ovidius bonus vite trutinator testimonium offert,
Nitimur in vetitum semper cupimusque negata. Igitur prudentia
vestra, cognita singulorum necessitate, in locum unum miseros con-
gregavit ut alius alium consolaretur animumque ad patientiam
incitaret. Captivitas nulla esse videtur que amicorum confabula-
tionibus transigitur, ut fit in itinere, in jejunio ; non est molesta
longitudo viarum, non fames, non sitis, si mutui sermones blandi et
delectabiles et a facetiis non protinus abhorrentes intersunt. Sed nos

in presentia scelere unius perturbatos, de historiis humanis, de divinis narratio excitat, labemque omnem imminentem rejicit et repellit ; qua ex re unanimes omnes bonitati et pietati vestre gratias habemus meritas, et immensas habituri semper erimus, si modo tanti simus qui cumulatissimis beneficiis vestris gratias habendo reddere queamus. Vale, pater. Non. April.

3. *Sixtus IV.*

(1) It is difficult to say if the *Vita Sixti IV.* in Muratori, iii. pt. ii. 1053, and in Panvinius' continuation of Platina's *Vitæ Pontificum*, is the work of PLATINA. It ends about the time of Platina's death in 1481 ; on the other hand there are differences between its style and the other lives written by Platina. This, however, may be accounted for by regarding it as a rough draft which Platina meant to revise if he outlived Sixtus IV. It reads as if it were meant to form part of a series. Thus, speaking of the fall of the Ponte di S. Angelo, the writer says: ' quemadmodum Nicolai V. tempore, *ut diximus,* in Adriani ponte contigit.' The personal reference to ' preceptor meus Johannes Argyropylus ' does not help us much, as many could claim to have attended the lectures of Argyropylus at some time or another. On the whole I incline to regard it as a rough draft of Platina. It is chiefly valuable for the information which it gives of the early career of Sixtus IV.

(2) From 1481 to 1492 we have the *Diario di Roma* of a Roman citizen known as the NOTAJO DI NANTIPORTO, in Muratori, iii. pt. ii. 1071 &c. Who this notary was, or where the district known as Nantiporto was situated, cannot be said. But the diary is the account written from time to time by a plain man who recounts facts as he saw them and indulges in no comments of his own. His account is of great interest for the condition of Rome under Sixtus IV. and Innocent VIII., and gives a picture of continuous disturbance.

(3) More important is the *Diario della Citta di Roma* of STEFANO INFESSURA, scribe of the senate and people of Rome, as he styles himself. This diary begins in the year 1394, and the early part of it is compiled from family records. But with the accession of Sixtus IV. we feel ourselves in contact with a vigorous man of decided opinions. Infessura was an ardent republican, and looked upon the papal government of Rome with unfriendly eyes. He felt the hopelessness of mending matters, and is comparable to Tacitus surveying the iniquities of the Roman Empire. Infessura is an authority of the highest value, but allowance must be made for his strong bias in

admitting his personal judgments. So violent is he against Sixtus IV. that Muratori long doubted whether he should publish his diary, and says 'pauca mihi placuit expungere quæ fœdiora mihi visa sunt atque indigna quæ honestis auribus atque oculis offerantur.' *Rerum Italicarum Scriptores*, iii. pt. ii. 1110. Infessura, however, had been previously published by Eccard, *Corpus Historicum Medii Ævi*, ii. 1865 &c. in an unexpurgated form. I cannot attach any weight to Infessura's attack upon the private life of Sixtus IV., but his pages give a vivid picture of the nature and extent of the antagonism which the Pope's policy awakened. When Infessura says of the death of Sixtus IV., 'Nec visus fuit homo, qui de eo bene dixerit nisi quidam frater Sancti Francisci,' we feel that he is overshooting the mark.

(4) Far different from Infessura is the *Diarium Romanum* of JACOPO VOLATERRANO, printed by Muratori, xxiii. 88 &c. Jacopo Gherardi, as his family name was, came to Rome as secretary of Cardinal Ammannati, in whose service he tells us that he learned the habit of writing. After Ammannati's death he was made a papal secretary by Sixtus IV., and remained at the papal court till his death in 1516, aged 82, shortly before which time he was made Bishop of Segni by Leo X. Jacopo Volaterrano begins abruptly in 1472, but breaks off in 1473, and begins again in a more detailed form in 1479, when he entered the papal service; he ends with the death of Sixtus IV. Jacopo may be regarded as the ancestor of Burchard and Paris de Grassis. He recounts events as they occurred with the method of an official. He does not rise to the position of an historian, but takes only an outside view of affairs and tells about ceremonies and other details of the life of the Curia as they struck himself, and as he was concerned with them. For this reason he is especially valuable, and his absence of literary pretentiousness is most refreshing.

(5) SIGISMONDO DE' CONTI, was a man of good family in Foligno, where he held the office of Chancellor under Paul II. He was famous as a Humanist, and came in 1476 to improve his fortunes in Rome, where he was made one of the secretaries of the Curia. He attended Cardinal Giuliano della Rovere in an embassy to Germany in 1480, and in 1482 was made one of the secretaries of the Pope. This office he held till 1502, when he retired; but Julius II. appointed him his private secretary, and he died in Rome in 1512. He is famous in the history of art as the donor whose portrait was painted by Raffaelle in the great picture of the 'Madonna di Foligno,' which was painted by his order. Sigismondo's *Historia suorum Temporum* was much used by other writers, and has been

often quoted in parts, but was published for the first time at Rome in 1883. It covers the period from 1475 to 1509, and has the advantage of being written by one who was well conversant with affairs. Sigismondo, however, was a Humanist above all things, and cares for style and arrangement rather than for the substance of his narration. He begins with a preface in the style of Tacitus, and finds the war of Sixtus IV. against Florence a good starting point. His history has many literary merits; the narrative is clear and well arranged, and events naturally follow one another. Yet the book is disappointing on the whole from its want of historical insight. Sigismondo wrote to obtain the praise of a literary circle, and cared more about style than matter. Moreover he was an official as well as a man of letters, and if he wished for immediate fame was bound not to pass the limits of official discretion. He can scarcely be said ever to give judgments or opinions of his own, but merely represented gracefully the views which were current. His history was obviously written and circulated from time to time amongst his friends in the Curia. His summaries of character are therefore little more than official panegyrics, and we can trace the way in which Sigismondo turned from the setting to the rising sun. Thus he goes beyond every other apologist in acquitting Girolamo Riario from any complicity even in the Conspiracy of the Pazzi, and says: 'Præterea neque in vultu neque in moribus Hieronymi quicquam sævum aut atrox fuit; contra omnia plena tranquillitatis, plena clementiæ, plena innocentiæ, plena beneficentiæ,' &c. (i. 27). This was clearly written and circulated while Sixtus IV. was alive and Girolamo was powerful. Book iii. was written probably after the death of Sixtus IV; there we read (i. 114): 'Sixtus cupiditati Hieronymi obsecutus, Hieronymum ipsum populo Foroliviensi imposuit . . . usque adeo difficile est pietatem justitiamque servare, cum in regni cupiditatem incideris.' Finally, when Girolamo is put to death (i. 315) Sigismondo has not a good word to say for him, but sneers at his avarice and thinks that he was rightly served for standing in the way of Innocent VIII.

A work written under these conditions cannot be of great weight as an authority on doubtful points. Sigismondo has none of the qualities of a statesman or of a political critic. He was satisfied with things as they were, and made the best of them in his pages. But his position in Rome gave him access to good sources of information, and he incorporates documents and mentions facts which are not given elsewhere. He has enabled me to record more fully than has been done before several important facts, especially the feud of the Santa Croce and Della Valle families and the general condition of Rome under Sixtus IV.

Of modern books dealing with the Period of Sixtus IV., the most important are Roscoe, *Life of Lorenzo de' Medici* ; Fabroni, *Vita Laurentii* ; Reumont, *Lorenzo il Magnifico* ; Buser, *Die Beziehungen der Medicaer mit Frankreich* ; and Frantz, *Sixtus IV. und die Republik Florenz* (1880), which contains ample references to the chief subsidiary sources of information ; for artistic records Müntz, *Les Arts à la Cour des Papes* is excellent.

4. *The Synod of Florence*, 1478.

The *Synodus Florentina* is given in Fabroni, ii. 136 ; Roscoe's *Life of Lorenzo*, Appendix xxvii. ; and Pignotti, *Storia di Toscana*, iv., Appendix ii. The document is in the form of an ecclesiastical protest, and ends : 'Datum in ecclesia nostra Cathedrali S. Reparatæ 23 Julii 1478.' Only two copies of the document are known, one in the hand of Gentile, Bishop of Arezzo, in the Florentine archives, another at Venice in type which might be of contemporary date (described in Pignotti). It is a question if we are to regard this document as really the production of a synod or as a pamphlet, to which possibly a synod might have given occasion. It is hard to believe that any body of clergy would have given their assent to such an indecorous document. Capponi, *Storia di Firenze*, ii. 126, agrees with Fabroni in thinking that it was not the production of a synod, but was perhaps the work of Gentile of Arezzo. Reumont, *Lorenzo il Magnifico*, i. 440, suggests that the address from the Cathedral of S. Reparata would more naturally attribute it to the Archbishop of Florence, Rinaldo Orsini. Frantz, *Sixtus IV. und die Republik von Florenz*, believes it to have come from a synod ; but his reason is a wish to prove that the manifest corruption of the Florentine clergy under the Medici justified the action of Sixtus IV. The disappearance of any records of this synod gives good ground for suspecting the authenticity of the document : though it is urged on the other side that the Florentine clergy were ashamed of themselves and suppressed all the copies they could in later times. The strongest positive argument against it is supplied by the letter of Sixtus IV. to the Duke of Este, in Sigismondo de' Conti, *Historia*, i. 40. This was written after war had begun, probably about the end of August. If the Pope had believed in this synod he would not have written of Lorenzo, 'fœdissima scripta in sugillationem honoris nostri disseminavit,' without some further explanation. The indecorum of the Florentine clergy would have supplied an additional argument to his appeal : 'Vultis populi Florentini dignitati et libertati prospicere? Detrahite ei hominis iniquissimi jugum.'

5. *The Attempt at a Council in* 1482.

The proceedings of Andrew Archbishop of Krain are amply illustrated by Sigismondo de' Conti and the letter of Sixtus IV., i. 410; also by the Archbishop's secretary, Peter Numagen, in Hottinger, *Historia Ecclesiastica,* iv. 347 &c., and more recently by Burchard, *Der Erzbischof Andreas von Krain* (1852), which is founded on a search amongst the Basel archives. The following letter of an official of the Curia seemed to me to be of interest as showing the views entertained by canonists on the validity of Constance decrees. The opinions which it expresses are important for the history of the fall of the Conciliar principle. The document is copied from a rare Roman print of 1482, in the Cambridge University Library.

*Leonellus Chieregatus Epus Arbensis, S. D. N. Pape Referend-
arius, Georgio Jurisconsulto ecclesie Sancti Petri Basiliensis Proposito
Salutem plurimam:*—

Ex literis tuis nuper accepi quantis in augustiis, ut tuis verbis utar, sis constitutus; et prout meus in te amor ac jus inter nos hospitii apud majores nostros sanctissimum exstitit, non mediocriter tibi condolui; statuique, cum urbis vestre tum domus domini zelo ductus, quid de hac nova apud vos ecclesie turbatione orta sentiam, quidve pro vestra communique tranquillitate a vobis agendum censeam tibi significare, veritus ne hec parva scintilla magnum quicquam quod et vos comprehendat emittat incendium. Verum ne te diutius detineam dicam libere quid optarim. Nollem insignem illam vestram Basiliensium civitatem—cui omnia prospera cupio, cum multa nos, quando ad eam divertimus, prosequuta fuerit benignitate—veterem sibi inustam maculam, que omni conatu delenda erat innovare. Nollem ipsam nunc velut canem ad vomitum regredi. Nollem in antiquam erga sanctam sedem apostolicam rebellionem prolabi. Nollem denique tantam apud cunctos catholicos populos infamiam incurrere, ut de ea dici possit, quod de Boemis ubique non sine nota divulgatur, ut quicumque seditiosus, quicumque fugitivus, quicumque sceleratus in Dei ecclesia turbas, schismata, hereses excitare voluerit, tutum apud Basilienses perfugium inveniat. Fugiendum est hoc probrum; detergenda est ista macula; hec infamia est abolenda. Quanto gloriosior est urbs ipsi vicina Constantia. Illa enim inveteratum in ecclesia Dei schisma sedavit; illa pacem populo Christi et unionem peperit ejus ecclesiis; hec idolum adorandum in loco sancto erigere, hec tunicam Domini inconsutilem, quam ipsius etiam crucifixores scindere noluerunt, in partes dividere non expavit. Potuit tunc forte sacrorum Constantiensis et Senensis conciliorum ac Martini quinti et Eugenii quarti summorum pontificum auctoritatem erratis suis excusatorium obtendere. At nunc Dei ecclesia in pace quiescente, sedente in ea Sixto quarto unico indubitato Romano pontifice, qui et sacra doctrina et orthodoxa religione, et candida anteactæ vitæ puritate, concordi amplissimi ordinis consensu ad tanti apostolatus apicem ascendit, qui cunctis reipublicæ imminentibus necessitatibus, una cum sacro senatu salubriter prospicere non cessat, quam causam—quam auctoritatem jure probatam ejus tranquillitatem turbandi pretendere velit ignoro. Neque enim Constantiensis concilii, quod apud vos, ut audio, profertur in medium, me hac in re decret movet auctoritas, qua freti ecclesiasticæ pacis turbatores isti, sub specie congregandi concilii ut ejusmodi decreto obtemperetur, turbato reipublicæ statu, et criminum suorum meritas pœnas evadere et ambitioni suæ inservire, ac se novarum molitione rerum alere nituntur. Nam postquam in ecclesiis, sicut in Romano imperio, aucta est avaritia, et crevit ambitio, fuere semper in eis homines hipocritæ, quibus nullæ opes nulla virtus adest. Qui veterum suarumque rerum odio et studio novarum mutari omnia cupientes, ut sibi placeant, prepositum sibi episcopum superbo tumore contemnunt, maledictis lacerant, et cunctis machinationibus impugnare non desinunt. Hinc heresium initia scaturiunt, hinc schismaticorum conatus erumpunt; sic (ut inquit Ciprianus) de ecclesia receditur, sic altare prophanum foris collocatur, sic contra pacem Christi et ordinationem atque unitatem Dei rebellatur. Non mirum si beatus Hieronimus, vir in omni doctrinarum genere consummatissimus, veteres (ut ipse testatur) scrutans historias, neminem scidisse ecclesiam et de domo Domini populos seduxisse potuit invenire præter eos, qui a Deo positi fuerant sacerdotes, qui cum in laqueum tortuosum fuerint conversi omnibus in locis scandala ponunt.

Dixi (ut eo redeam unde diverti) me hoc sacræ Constantiensis synodi decreto hac in re non moveri ; quod audacter dictum forte putabis. Sed id non temere dixisse facile comprobabo. Quamvis enim tempora generalibus conciliis a sancta Constantiensi synodo fuerunt prefixa, quibus advenientibus qui concilio interesse tenentur debent in eo absque alia vocatione comparere, cum terminus juris pro homine quemlibet interpellet—nemo tamen meo exili judicio posset nunc absque superioris interpellatione legitimum universalis ecclesiæ concilium Basileæ aut indicere aut se pro eo celebrando exhibere. Cum enim canon ille ita generalia concilia jubeat celebrari ut primum a fine ipsius Constantiensis concilii in quinquennium immediate sequens ; cui termino habita Senis universalis synodus satisfecit. Secundum vero a fine illius immediate sequentis concilii in septennium ; quod Basileæ, Ferrariæ, Florentiæ, ac demum Laterani implevit Eugenius. Et deinceps de decennio in decennium perpetuo celebratur in locis que summus pontifex approbante et consentiente concilio, vel eo deficiente ipsum concilium assignaverit. Nec ab initio Basiliensis concilii—sive (ut modo dicebam) ab Eugenio Romano Pontifice non sine ipsius synodi consensu Ferrariam primo, deinde Florentiam, inde Romam, sive ab Amedeo, in sua obedientia Felice tunc appellato, Lausanam translati—pluribus jam (ut ipsimet turbatores aiunt) decursis decenniis ullo in loco quispiam celebrandi generalis concilii causa usque ad hanc temporum temeritatem comparuerit. Clarum est illius auctores decreti eundem terminum contrario facto revocasse, aut saltem pericula et scandala unioni et quieti fidelium, experientia comprobante, ex ejusmodi conciliis verisimiliter proventura formidantes declarasse nolle hac vice generale concilium celebrare. Nihil est enim, secundum sanctissimum jus quo utimur, tam naturale quam unumquodque vinculum eo modo solvi quo fuerat ligatum ; majoremque vim habent procul dubio facta quam verba, nec tacitum regulariter differt ab expresso. Prelati ecclesiarum (ut hoc lucidius dicam) in Constantiensi synodo congregati terminum illum conciliis generalibus celebrandis statuerunt : iidem ecclesiarum prelati, ex quibus concilia constituuntur, in termino lapsi primi decennii nec tot annorum curriculis post unquam ad synodum venientes videntur ipsum terminum abrogasse.

Nec moveat quempiam quod finis decennii a die dissolutionis concilii Basiliensis numerandi sit initium novi concilii celebrandi, itaque quod sancti presules post decennium possint quandocunque generalis concilii celebrationis causa simul convenire. Nam licet hec consideratio videatur his ecclesiastice pacis turbatoribus applaudere, non tamen potest conatus eorum confirmare. Ex ea enim si admitteretur, absurdum hoc ingens sequeretur, quod quandoque, etiam longo tempore post decennium, vel paucissimi patres congregati possent, accusata reliquorum contumacia, ad concilii celebrationem procedere, et universo orbe legem imponere : quo quid absurdius excogitari possit ignoro. Nam cum in termino decennii nemo comparuerit, nec tam longo tempore post quisquam se obtulerit, non potest aliquis negligens estimari ita ut nonnulli postea venientes absentium contumaciam valeant accusare, quod, cum in termino totque annis post ipsum nemo comparuerit, non coguntur aliorum tam diuturno tempore post comparentium adventum divinare. Nec, ut dixi, venire tenentur ; neque negligentiæ aut contumaciæ possunt accusari, cum terminus ipse universali consensu per non comparationem memoratam videatur esse sublatus : sed nova opus est superioris ad quem jure pertinet vocatione. Sic enim prodidere jureconsulti, quod si per me non stetit quominus creditori in termino satisfacerem non possum absque nova interpellatione in mora constitui : quam interpellationem ad hos pacis ecclesiæ turbatores faciendam haudquaquam spectare nemo est qui nesciat.

Nec mihi quisquam opponat undecimæ Basiliensis synodi sessionis decretum quo caveri videtur, ut quamvis in principio termini non comparuerint prelati, facultas tamen celebrandi concilii per ipsos non expiret, sed quanto citius fieri potest celebretur. Nam decretum illud etiamsi foret observandum, quantum ex ejus verbis colligi potest, congregandorum patrum commoditatem consideravit ; ipsisque commodum post diem termini spatium veniendi concessit : non autem facultatem ejusmodi quæ civiliter est intelligenda usque in consummationem seculorum ipsis prorogasse videtur. Non obviat igitur quin tanto tempore post terminum prelati non comparentes, quo pluries commoditas conveniendi potuit ipsis adesse, censeantur hac vice (ut ante dixi) congregandi se concilii causa terminum revocasse. Decretum illud preterea [de] eo casu loqui manifestum est, quo in precedenti concilio locus pro futuro fuerit assignatus. Clarum est enim loci definitionem fore necessariam ut sciant cuncti quo debeant proficisci, et ubi pro celebrando concilio debeant commorari. Quod ita esse (ut antiquiora relinquam) tam Constantiensis quam ipsius Basiliensis synodi decreta demonstrant. Quæ loci constitutio, si in precedenti concilio facta non fuerit, non dubium est sanctos presules ad conveniendum ejusmodi decretis non artari, eamque ad summi Pontificis arbitrium pertinere. Cum igitur non constet ante dissolutum Basiliense, sive, ut rectius loquar, Lateranense concilium aliquem pro futura universali synodo locum fuisse deputatum, nec propterea tam Constantiensis quam Basiliensis synodi decretis ecclesiarum prelati nunc ad generale concilium aliquo commeare cogantur ; quod omnia superius dicta confirmat. Mirandum est certe pariterque dolendum nonnullos id quod Romani pontificis [est] temere sibi usurpare non erubescere.

Quod si concilium Basiliense nunquam nec alio translatum nec ullo pacto dissolutum fuisse non verentur affirmare ; et quamvis jam diu post cunctorum patrum discessum istic non viguerit, cum tamen negotia in eo cœpta non fuerint finita, ipsis redeuntibus ex primeva institutione eodem in loco absque nova Romani pontificis convocatione celebrari posse impudenter asseverant, intelligant concilium generale esse de his quæ ad existentiam sui requirunt non solum habitum sed etiam actus exercitium, quo deficiente non sufficit habitus. Verum cum a tot annorum curriculis non conciliaris actus exercitium modo defecerit, sed etiam habitus ipse, discedentibus cunctis prioribus et nullo presidente perseverante, in quibus et actus et habitus consistebat, evanuerit, nemo sanæ mentis dicere auderet Basileæ nunc sine nova Romani Pontificis loci assignatione et ad eum locum prelatorum vocatione generale concilium celebrari posse. Cavendum est enim (ut est in sacris literis) ne holocausta nostra in omni loco quem viderimus, sed in eo quem elegerit Dominus, offeramus.

Desinat igitur insignis ista civitas vestra his facinorosis hominibus qui altare contra altare [statuere] non expavescunt favere ; declinat hos vineæ Domini eversores tutari, extollere, nutrire. Odiat malignantium conciliabula et impiorum conventicula abominetur ; plurisque faciat Deum et ejus ecclesiæ sanctam pacem et unitatem quam sperati alicujus temporalis commodi usum. Recordetur non solum Choræ, Datan et Abiron, qui sibi contra Moysem et Aaron sacerdotem sacrificandi [jus] ausi sunt usurpare, hiatu terræ absortos meritas illius tam sacrilegi [facti] penas luisse, verum etiam ceteros ducentos quinquaginta, qui se ab ipsis separare noluerint ignem a Domino prorumpentem consumpsisse. Quo exemplo, ut Cyprianus inquit, edocemur omnes obnoxios culpæ et penæ futuros, qui se schismaticis contra prepositos et sacerdotes suos irreligiosa temeritate miscuerint. Nam non solum duces et autores, verum etiam tanquam hujus furoris participes supplicio destinant, qui se a communione malorum non segregaverint, precipiente per Moysem Domino et dicente, *Separamini a tabernaculis hominum istorum durissimorum, et nolite tangere de omnibus quæ sunt eorum, ne simul pereatis in peccatis eorum.* Clamat etiam per Osee prophetam Spiritus Sanctus et dicit, *Sacrificia eorum tanquam panis luctus, et omnes qui manducant ea contaminabuntur,* indicans omnes omnino cum auctoribus suis supplicio conjungi, et qui fuerint eorum peccatis contaminati. Auferte igitur, ut ad vos Moyses vociferatur, malum de medio vestri, et expellite ejusmodi homines, ne ipsorum peccatis contaminati una cum ipsis pereatis.

Quod si tantæ non estis potentiæ vos qui bene sentitis, quid agere debeatis eloquia sacra vos instruunt : *Recedite et exite inde, et immundum ne tetigeritis.* An vobis non ingens crimen esse videtur his hominibus adherere, hos nutrire, cum his conversari, his tutelam prestare, qui preposito suo, qui summo Pontifici, qui Christo Domino palam maledicere, qui ecclesiam Dei scindere, qui innumeros errores in agro dominico serere non reformidant ? Quid vobis commune cum istis qui Salomonem non audiunt in Spiritu Sancto dicentem, *Ex tota anima tua time Deum, et sacerdotes ejus sanctifica* ; et iterum commonentem, *Honora Deum ex tota anima tua et honorifica sacerdotes ejus ?* Quid sustinetis hos falsos fratres divini Apostoli Pauli haudquaquam memores, qui cum sibi dictum esset, *Sic in sacerdotem Dei maledicendo irruis*, ipseque respondisset, *Nesciebam, fratres, quia pontifex est, scriptum est enim, Principem populi tui non maledices*, sic de pontifice cujus jam sacerdotium cessaverat loquens, nos profecto voluit erudire non esse veris pontificibus detrahendum? Quid tolleratis, quid alitis ejusmodi personatos hypocritas, qui, non a Deo vocati tanquam Aaron, honorem sibi sua temeritate assumere presumunt; qui calumnias, qui turbas, qui conventicula conflare moliuntur adversus Dominum et adversus Christum ejus; cum debuissent, juxta veterem probatamque beati Gregorii sententiam, si quid habebant contra ipsum, si eum redarguere volebant, vel extra auctoritatem facere contendebant, ad apostolicam sedem venire, ut ibi ante confessionem beati Petri cum eo juste decertarent. Sic Damasus, sic Sixtus, Symmachus et Leo, summi Pontifices, non in conciliabulis calumniantium sed in synodis a se legitime apud apostolicam sedem indictis malignantium calumnias diluerunt.

Sed quid isti contra unicum indubitatum sanctumque Pontificem pretendere velint non video, nec, ut arbitror, licet latrare non cessent, ipsi noverunt; cujus si bene facta vellem nunc recensere, et epistolæ modum excederem, et quæ universo orbi notissima sunt commemorans nil tibi novi significarem. At cum magnis in rebus administrandis difficile sit unicuique posse placere; cum in reddenda justicia ut plurimum alteri partium displiceat, unde illud vulgatum *Summum jus, summa injuria*; ideo qui presunt jurisdictioni, quibus ex officio incumbit arguere, increpare, suspendere et ligare, aliisque cohortionibus uti, Innocentio III. Romano Pontifice teste, frequenter incurrunt odium plurimorum, et insidias sepenumero patiuntur. Cumque sint tanquam signum ad sagittam positi, nunquam desunt subditi qui de ipsis conquirantur, qui ipsis maledicant, et adversum eos crimina confingant. Non debent tamen, ut Cornelius Romanæ urbis episcopus est auctor, conviciis perditorum moveri quominus a via recta et a certa regula non recedant, quam et Apostolus instituit dicens, *Si hominibus placerem, Christi servus non essem.* Fugiendi sunt nihilominus hi pestiferi detractores; his nequaquam est communicandum; non refugium concedendum, si hujus seculi honore tangimur, si Dei timore et amore movemur.

Hæc, mi Georgi, liberius diffusiusque quam ab initio statueram dictavi, impetum calami, ne dicam spiritus, retinere non volens; qui absque ulla librorum revolutione, quicquid in buccam venit, ut aiunt, exaravit. Quod in bonam partem accipias queso, cum a benevolentissimo animo erga te patriamque tuam proficiscatur, quos nollem tantis involucris quæ, nisi vobis caveritis, videre videor implicari: quibus nescio quando poteris si in ea incideris extricari. Nollem

etiam sanctam ecclesiam catholicam in partes a nephandis turbatoribus istis discerpi : et apud vos presertim hujus impietatis offici-
nam preparari. Quibus malis omni suasione, industria, diligentia,
conatu et auctoritate, quantum poteris (poteris autem multum) ut
occurras et hortor et rogo motus solius Dei et ejus ecclesiæ zelo ac
tuæ patriæque tuæ causa, non ut alicui potentiori complaceam.

Vale. Rome XV. Kal. Novembris MCCCCLXXXII.

Hecque impressa est epistola per honorabilem et discretum nec-
non ingeniosum virum Magistrum Bartholomeum Gudinbeck de
Sultz. Laus Deo.

------

6. *Innocent VIII.*

With the accession of Innocent VIII. we enter upon the
possession of a new source of information, the *Diary* of JOHN
BURCHARD, which was partly published by Leibnitz in 1696, and
more fully by Eccard in *Corpus Historicum Medii Ævi*, ii. In 1854
a complete edition was undertaken by Generelli at Florence, but was
not finished : recently the entire work has been excellently edited
by M. Thuasne (Paris, 1883–5). Burchard was largely used by
Raynaldus in his *Annales Ecclesiastici*; but it was long maintained
that the German MSS. used by Leibnitz and Eccard had been
interpolated with scandalous stories about Alexander VI. No
evidence has been produced in support of this supposition, and the
character of Alexander VI. rests upon other testimony than that
merely supplied by Burchard, who records in a dull manner, without
comment, such events in the Curia as struck him.

Burchard was a native of Haslach, near Strasburg, and in 1481
left his canonry of Strasburg for Rome, where he bought an office in
the Curia, and in 1483 succeeded Agostino Patrizzi as Master of
Ceremonies. In this capacity he began to keep a diary to serve as a
collection of precedents for the due performance of the duties of his
office. During the pontificate of Innocent VIII. the diary is concerned with little else than ceremonial ; but in the more stirring
times of Alexander VI. it becomes fuller. The selection, however,
of piquant extracts, made by Leibnitz and Eccard, gave a false impression of the work, and tended to discredit Burchard as a malignant
gossip. This impression disappears when Burchard's diary is read
as a whole. He merely relates facts as they came before him,
and neither imputes motives nor makes any attempt to depict
characters. The value of Burchard's information on several points

is open to discussion, but there is no reason to suspect his good faith.
He was an official who served his master with zeal and diligence, and
never thought of criticising his doings. He certainly gives a striking
picture of Alexander VI.'s diligence in attending to the formal duties
of his office.

Burchard was made Bishop of Orte by Pius III. in 1503, but
continued in his office of Master of Ceremonies till his death in 1506.
He set the example of an official diary kept by the Master of the
Ceremonies. His colleague, Paris de Grassis, continued Burchard's
work, and a comparison of the two writers is convincing for Burchard's
good faith. Paris is often quoted as a witness against Burchard's
veracity ; but I think without any reason. Paris de Grassis became
Burchard's colleague in May 1504, contrary to Burchard's wishes.
There was no love lost between the two officials, and Paris loses no
opportunity of denouncing Burchard's malignity. These expressions
have been taken to refer to the facts stated in Burchard's diary, but
this is an entire mistake, and would be dispelled at once by reading
Paris de Grassis as a whole. He objected to Burchard's ill-will
towards himself, which led him to treat his inexperienced colleague
with disdain and refuse to help him in learning the complicated
duties of his office. 'Non invideant scripta mea,' he says in his preface, ' maligni detractores, presertim ille meus collega Joannes
Brucardus multo magis socius in offitio quam amicus in charitate, que
nulla est in eo.' On Burchard's death, Paris de Grassis abuses him in
no measured terms and says : ' Libros quos ex talibus inscripserat
nemo intelligere potest nisi diabolus assertor ejus aut saltem Sibilla '
(Thuasne, Burchard, iii. 426), but this refers only to ' nostre ceremonie
que conculcate et implicite et obscurate fuerunt.' That this is so
is clear from his introductory remarks to a 'Tractatus de Creatione
Cardinalium,' which is inserted in his diary. Paris says that Burchard
gave him a formula for the creations of Cardinals, which on due reflection he found unintelligible. ' Tractatus Cardinalium quem senior
magister idemque collega meus unicus, Brocardus, mihi ad id muneris
quam recentissime ascito, velut alterum legalium Pandectarum elo-
quium, sive divinum potius evangelium, crebro indesistensque studen-
dum et imitandum proposuit; admonens quam maxime et super omnia
illius traditionem e manibus nunquam illabi paterer, sed, sicut Afri-
canus Scipio Pediam Cyri et Ciprianus Tertullianum et Hieronimus
Ciceronem, nullam diem sine lectione pretereuntes, ita ego scienter
addicerem, complecterer anxie atque illibate custodirem. Et propteres
effectum est ut ego, qui earum rerum imperitus et ceremonialium
legum omnino discipulus iis credidi simplicillus ne dicam stolidus—
preter sensum et doctrinam etiam ipsissima verba prout erant linea-

APP.

tim et dictionatim cum ipso libro articulata, composita in memoria sculpserim solidissime, atque iterum insculpserim ; et quibus jam modis, non oblivionis mee interpres sed mee memorie nescius fiam, aut qua arte nescire possim quod scio nescio. Ac, bone Deus, quot in eo libro ineptias, quot nenias, ut appellat Hieronymus, habeas. Prorsus nugas Hispanicas legi et deprehendi; nempe ut ego ipse magister ideoque discipulus eidem mihi discipulo duo preterea obedienda indiderim; primum ut non eius autori, scilicet magistro meo collegae Brucardo, tanquam mendaci et nugatori ambagioso ulla in re credam, tanquam a virtute absoluto et a communi observatione dissonante. Corrigere rei veritate voluero cuncta profecto . . . sed meo iuditio numquam, medius fidius, tractatus ille enodatius castigatiusque corrigetur absque lucubrationibus et calumniis, quam si denique flammis totum opus illud corrigatur, presertim ille ipse tractatus de creatione cardinalium.'

The criticisms of Paris are concerned with Burchard's ceremonial, not with his testimony to facts. His own diary is more open to criticism for its gossip than is that of Burchard. Whatever might be his intentions, the German was not a match in curiosity for the Italian.

Burchard's diary, with the documents collected by Generelli and Thuasne, is the chief source of information about Innocent VIII. We still have Infessura and Sigismondo de' Conti, together with the documents given by Fabroni, *Vita Laurentii*, and Roscoe, *Life of Lorenzo de' Medic*. About Neapolitan affairs we have Volpicella, *Regis Ferdinandi primi Institutionum Liber*, and Porzio's *Congiura de' baroni del Regno di Napoli*, which was not, however, published till 1565. Most important as showing the relations between Lorenzo de' Medici and the Pope and Lorenzo's steady desire to keep the peace of Italy are the letters of Jacopo Volaterrano, published by Tabarini in *Archivio Storico Italiano*, terza serie, vols. vii. and x. They concern the years 1487–8 when Innocent VIII. was seeking allies for war against Naples : Lorenzo first used his influence to make peace between Milan and Naples, and then to prevent the revolution at Forlì from setting Milan at variance with the Pope.

7. *The Deathbed of Lorenzo de' Medici.*

There are two accounts of the last interview of Savonarola and Lorenzo. They are irreconcilable with one another, and the question is, which is to be adopted. The one which I have followed is given by Poliziano in a letter to his friend Jacopo Antiquario, dated from

Fiesole, May 18, 1492. The other account is given by the biographers of Savonarola, Pico and Burlamacchi. According to them, Lorenzo, in a condition of profound remorse, sent for Savonarola, saying, ' I know no true friar save him.' When Savonarola came, Lorenzo confessed himself to him ; he deplored three great sins, the sack of Volterra, the dowry money taken from the Monti di Pietà, and the bloodshed after the conspiracy of the Pazzi. Savonarola consoled him during his confession by repeating ' God is gracious : God is gracious.' When Lorenzo had ended he said, ' Three things are required of you. First, to have a lively faith in God's mercy.' ' I have,' said Lorenzo. ' Secondly, to restore what you have unjustly taken ; to bind your sons to make restitution.' Lorenzo paused for a moment, then bowed his head. Then Savonarola drew himself to his full height and said, ' Lastly, to restore liberty to Florence.' Lorenzo shrugged his shoulders and did not speak ; Savonarola departed without giving him absolution.

Which of these accounts we adopt depends on our opinion of the trustworthiness of the respective sources. Poliziano was at Lorenzo's bedside, and his account was written six weeks after Lorenzo's death. The biographers of Savonarola were not eyewitnesses, and wrote after Savonarola's death. There is no evidence that Pico, the earliest of them, had written his book before 1520 ; whether Burlamacchi wrote independently or merely re-edited Pico is a question open to discussion (see Villari in *Rivista Storica Italiana*, i. 7. &c.) ; but I think that the biographers anyhow represent the story current amongst Savonarola's followers, and however numerous they may be can only count as one authority. It may be urged that their account of this matter must have come from Savonarola himself. But we may be pardoned for sparing Savonarola's fame the supposition that he made political capital for his own glorification out of the secrets of the confessional ; still less probable is it that the tale was revealed by Lorenzo in an agony of remorse—after Savonarola's departure and just before his death.

The two accounts agree in some points and differ in others. It is not difficult to suppose that in the stirring times that followed on the expulsion of the Medici the facts recorded by Poliziano were exaggerated into those recorded by Burlamacchi. It is more difficult to suppose that Poliziano, directly after Lorenzo's death, hearing rumours of Savonarola's story, explained it away and gave his own version to the world in the form of a letter to a friend. Poliziano's account is not contradicted on any point except the interview with Savonarola. Its details are circumstantial and quite probable. They certainly do not show a man racked with remorse to the degree that

was necessary to induce him to send for Savonarola. Just before
Savonarola's entrance, he had made the remark to Pico that he was
sorry to die without finishing his library.

Moreover the two accounts differ in one important point. Poliziano makes Savonarola come to visit Lorenzo ; Savonarola's biographers make him come to hear his confession. There are great
difficulties in the way of supposing that Lorenzo wished to make
another confession after having received the sacrament. If it was a
confession, we cannot suppose that Poliziano and the attendants were
in the room ; yet Poliziano agrees with Burlamacchi and the rest in
saying that Savonarola exhorted Lorenzo to three things. The
accounts may easily be harmonised about the first two. The third,
Poliziano says, was an exhortation to endure death with constancy ;
Savonarola's biographers say that it was a demand for the restoration of liberty to Florence. Reumont, *Lorenzo Il Magnifico*, ii. 590,
remarks that Poliziano's account makes this third exhortation of
Savonarola rather an unworthy commonplace. But some version of
the prayer, ' Suffer us not at our last hour for any pains of death to
fall from Thee,' is surely not commonplace in a priest's mouth. On
the other hand, Burlamacchi's request, if we consider it, is unworthy
of the political capacity of Lorenzo and Savonarola alike. How
could Savonarola suppose that any words of a dying man could
restore liberty to Florence ? How could he hope that such a request
would impose upon a keen politician like Lorenzo ? What immediate and practical steps could have been taken for the purpose ?
If we accept this story we must suppose that Savonarola talked
clap-trap and that Lorenzo was deceived by it. Villari, *Storia di
Savonarola*, book i. note to chapter ix., gives his reasons for following
Savonarola's biographers. It is one thing to regard them as the
supreme authority for the general influence of Savonarola's life and
character ; it is another thing to assume that their testimony to
actual facts overrides all other sources of information. The biographers read into the early life of Savonarola all the greatness of
his subsequent career, and their account of the early part of his life
at Florence seems to me to exaggerate his importance. They represent him as forming at once a party which avowed political
hostility to the Medici. Lorenzo certainly did not think so, or he
would have taken steps to remove Savonarola ; he did not much
object to Savonarola for standing aloof, and treated him with respect.
If Savonarola had been regarded as a decided enemy of the Medici,
it is inconceivable that Piero de' Medici should have helped
him to procure the papal Bull which made the Florentine Dominicans independent of the Lombard Congregation.

8. *Alexander VI.*

The period which begins with the French invasion of Italy is marked by a vast increase in the materials for history. Not only does the number of literary histories increase, but diplomacy was developed and its records were more continuously preserved. I cannot do more than mention some of the chief authorities for this eventful period. The best informed historians are undoubtedly Guicciardini, *Storia d'Italia*, and Zurita, *Historia del Rey Don Hernando el Catolico*, who had access to documents which they used with much discernment. The publication of Guicciardini's *Opere Inedite* has brought to light much that supplements his History. Of the other Florentine writers, Nardi, *Istoria della Città di Firenze*; Pitti, *Storia di Firenze* in *Archivio Storico Italiano*, first series, i.; Ceretani and Parenti, quoted by Villari, *Storia di Savonarola*, and Ranke, *Historisch-biographische Studien*, may be mentioned as the chief. On the Pisan side is Portoveneri, *Memoriale*, in *Archivio Storico Italiano*, first series, vol. vi. Besides, there is Senegara, *De Rebus Genuensibus*, in Muratori, xxiv.; Allegretti, *Diari Senesi*, in Muratori, xxiii.; Matarazzo, *Cronica di Perugia* in *Archivio Storico Italiano*, first series, xvi. More important still are the Venetian sources, *De Bello Gallico* in Muratori, xxiv., which is there ascribed to Marino Sanuto, but which Fulin has shown to be the work of Priuli; Malipiero, *Annali Veneti* in *Archivio Storico Italiano*, first series, vii.; Sanuto, *La Spedizione di Carlo VIII.*, edited by Fulin, who in his introduction gives the literary history of the work; Sanuto's *Diario*, which begins in 1496 and is continued to 1535. This diary has long been known as a mine of information; Sanuto apparently learned that he was more fitted to be a diarist than a chronicler; he contented himself with writing day by day an abstract of the news which reached Venice from its ambassadors or from private correspondents in various parts of Europe, together with a record of the proceedings of the Venetian senate. Further information about Sanuto is to be found in Rawdon Brown's *Ragguagli sulla Vita e sulle Opere di Marino Sanudo*. This diary of Sanuto has been supplemented by Villari's publication of the *Dispacci* of the Venetian envoy Giustinian, who was at Rome in 1503-4. Besides these sources of information we have also a collection of papers concerning Naples in Trincherà, *Codice Aragonese*, and the French accounts—Commines' *Mémoires*; Kervyn de Lettenhove, *Négotiations de Philippe de Commines*; Vigné, *Le Vergier d'honneur*; Pillorgerie, *Campagnes et Bulletins de la Grande Armée*. These sources of information have been commented upon by

Cherrier, *Histoire de Charles VIII.* For affairs in Rome itself we have Sigismondo de' Conti and Burchard's *Diarium*, with the valuable appendices of Thuasne. I have printed in the Appendix to vol. iv. extracts from the *Diary* of Sebastiano Branca di Talini, and from the *Historia* of Ægidius of Viterbo.

Several details of this period have been made the subject of exhaustive treatment in late years, and important documents are scattered about in numerous works. The whole question of the Borgia family and its relationships, as well as the character of Alexander VI., has been warmly discussed. Cerri, *Borgia ossia Alessandro VI., Papa*, 1858 ; Antonelli, *Lucrezia Borgia in Ferrara*, 1867 ; Olivier, *Le Pape Alexandre VI.* ; Citadella, *Saggio di Albero Genealogico della Famiglia Borgia*, 1872, made many suggestions and raised many questions. Gregorovius, *Lucrezia Borgia*, 1874, overthrew the apologists for Alexander VI. and Cesare, but defended Lucrezia ; his account of the Borgia in *Geschichte der Stadt Rom*, vii., deserves careful attention. Nemec, *Papst Alexander VI., eine Rechtfertigung*, 1879, returned to the defence, and was followed by Leonetti, *Papa Alessandro VI.*, 1880. Leonetti's work is distinguished above that of the other apologists by its erudition ; but it is deficient in a critical estimate of authorities as a whole, and is an ingenious piece of special pleading constructed by exaggerating every word that can be wrested into his service, concealing everything that makes against him, and attacking ruthlessly all witnesses who cannot be silenced or pressed into his favour. Leonetti's book drew forth an article by Comte Henri d'Epinois in the *Revue des Questions Historiques*, April 1881, which is characterised by an admirable sobriety of judgment, and to which I would refer those who are interested in this controversy. Since then two French writers have attacked the conclusions of M. d'Epinois ; Vebron, *Les Borgia*, 1882, and Maricourt, *Le Procès des Borgia*, 1883. I have given the arguments of these writers the consideration which I thought they deserved, but it would be impossible in a volume of this scale to enter into my reasons for differing from them, or to defend in detail every conclusion which I have put forward. It is sufficient for me to say that I have given my best attention to all the arguments which have been adduced.

---

9. *Correspondence of Alexander VI. with Bajazet II.*

The genuineness of the letters of Bajazet has been often called in question. Ranke *Zur Kritik neuerer Geschichtsschreiber*, 108, points out (1) that the letters of Bajazet speak of a Turkish envoy being sent back with the Pope's envoy, while nothing is said of his capture, nor was he produced as evidence. (2) The letters call this envoy *Cassimen*, whereas Turkish authorities call him *Mustapha Beg*. (3) The letters are dated 'anno a Jesu prophete nativitate,' which was improbable for a Turk. (4) Bajazet is represented as writing, 'juravi super evangelia nostra,' an expression which a Turk would not use for the Koran. These arguments so far weigh with Gregorovius, *Geschichte der Stadt Rom*, vii. 353, note 1, that he says ' The letters do not seem genuine in composition, but were they genuine in contents?' Brosch, *Papst Julius II.*, 61–2, thinks that the matter still rests where Ranke left it, and that the reasons for regarding the letters as forgeries preponderate. On the other hand, Heidenheimer, in an elaborate article, *Korrespondenz Bajazet II's mit Alexander VI.*, in *Zeitschrift für Kirchengeschichte*, v. 511 &c. (1882) strongly maintains the authenticity of the letters.

Heidenheimer's article is so full that little need be added to it. I had arrived at the same conclusion before I saw Heidenheimer's exhaustive article. The sources of information which have been opened since Heidenheimer wrote, strengthen his arguments, which I propose briefly to condense and supplement.

The answers to Ranke's objections are tolerably simple :—(1) The Turkish envoy who was travelling with Buzardo escaped from Sinigaglia to Ancona ; so Cardinal Rovere told the Ferrarese envoy, Manfredi, at the time (Letter of November 24 in *Atti e Monumenti per le provincie Parmesi e Modenesi*, iv. 334). We further know that he made his way from Ancona to Ferrara, and thence to Venice, where he complained to the Doge of the treatment which he had received (Sanuto, *Spedizione di Carlo VIII.* 125–180).

(2) It is true that the Turkish authorities, followed by Leunclavius, *Historie Musulmanæ Turkarum*, 653, say that Bajazet II. sent into Italy *Mustapha Beg*, not *Cassimen*, as Buchard's document calls him, to carry the Pope's pension, and murder Djem, which he succeeded in doing. This story is not accurate about the fact ; is it accurate about the name ? Sigismondo de' Conti, ii. 22, mentions a Turkish envoy in 1490 called *Mustafa* ; but he tells us, ii. 27, that the envoy who brought the Holy Lance in 1492 was called *Zaus Cassiminus*, and quotes Bajazet's letter giving him that name. We are justified in inferring that the two envoys who went between Constantinople and Rome were *Mustafa* and *Cassimen*. If the letters were forged, the forgers would not have made a mistake about a name ; if there is a discrepancy, it is quite likely that the mistake may have been made by the Turkish writers.

(3) The extent to which international courtesy had affected

APP.

Turkish diplomacy was unknown to Ranke. Sigismondo de' Conti, ii. 23, gives a letter of Bajazet to Innocent VIII. in 1490, addressed 'domino Innocentio divina providentia Romanæ ecclesiæ summo Pontifici,' and dated 'scriptum Constantinopoli Maii septimo decimo a generatione Jesu anno 1490.' An extract from a letter book of the time of Julius II. is in the British Museum, Harleian MSS. 3462. it is headed 'Tituli quibus utitur pro se Soldanus et quibus scribit ad Sm D. N. Papam, ad serm regem Catholicum et ad serm Ducem Venetiarum.' The address to the Pope runs thus : 'S. P. D. sanctissimo Pno nostro Pape Julio Sanctitati Papæ,—eximii, sanctmi, spiritualis Deum timentis et bonum operantis Papæ—Romani, maxi-mi in secta Christianorum antiqua—inter fideles Jesus Regis regum Nazarenorum—Christianorum—conservantis ac dominantis maria et sinus maritimos—patris patriarcharum et episcoporum, perlegentis evangelia, scientis in secta sua quæ sint licita et quæ non licita, benevoli regibus et principibus, et regnum Romanum possidentis, cujus gloriam Deus augmentet.' It is clear that the courtesy of the Turkish chancery knew no limits.

(4) As the Turkish secretaries had no objection to phrases, there is nothing unlikely in their carrying their complaisance so far as to render 'our holy law' by the words 'evangelia nostra.'

These arguments show that there is no internal evidence which is conclusive against the letters. At the same time it must be admitted that Alexander VI.'s enemies were numerous, and that forgery is by no means improbable. There is no doubt, however, about the fact of the embassy to Constantinople, or the capture of Buzardo, or the seizure by Giovanni della Rovere of the money which Buzardo was carrying. The only question is whether or no the letters themselves are genuine.

The letters are given by Burchard, *Diarium*, ed. Thuasne, ii. 202, under date December 16. They are also given by Sanuto, *Spedizione di Carlo VIII*, 42. Their contents were known to Malipiero, *Annali Veneti*, 146. Burchard tells us that he had them from Raymond Perraud, Cardinal of Gurk, who was one of the Pope's great enemies. Burchard was also told, on January 22, 1495, by the Cardinal of Gurk, that he had reproved the Pope : 'Pontifici sua crimina objecit ; . . . informationem magno Turco missam et mutuam intelligentiam' (Thuasne, ii. 233). Gurk repeated these statements to the Florentine Bracci at Perugia in April 1497, and Bracci wrote an account of them to the Florentine Government (Burchard, Thuasne, ii. 668). Cardinal Perraud on this last occasion was certainly inaccurate, for Bracci writes : 'Et havera visto Brevi di Sa Sta scripti al Turcho et risposte del Turcho ad Sa Beatitudine ; et ultimamente copia di certi capitoli et conventione hine inde. Poteva sapeva chel Turcho li haveva offerto CC mila Ducati se faceva morire il Fratello.' The sum offered for the murder of Djem was 300,000 ducats.

However much Cardinal Ferrand may have spread the knowledge of these documents, he did not forge them himself. They were sent by Giovanni della Rovere to his brother the Cardinal at Florence. A letter of the Ferrarese envoy, Manfredi, dated November 24, tells how he had an interview with Cardinal Rovere, who showed him a letter from Giovanni dated November 20, informing him of the seizure of the 40,000 ducats: ' Similiter li remetteva le instructioni che havea dato el Papa ad un mess. Georgio suo commissario mandato al Turcho, le quali instructioni altramente non ne fece vedere sua Sig.ria; la lettera del Sig. Prefecto conteneva che ermo de qualità che era stupenda cosa et pericolosa alla christianitade. Dimostra che el tenesse pratiche da vendere el fratello del Turcho, che è a Roma, al gran Turcho, et recevrie lo agiuto et favore suo contro questo Christianiss. Re.' (Capelli, *Atti e Memorie per le provincie Parmesi e Modenesi*, iv. 331.) From this we learn that the letters were sent from Sinigaglia on November 20, and probably reached Florence on November 22. The copies and translations afterwards circulated bear date November 25, and are confirmed by the instrument of the translators and copyist. It is noticeable that Manfredi says that Cardinal Rovere showed him his brother's letter: ' fece vedere una lettera che in quel punto lo havea hauto del Signor Prefecto suo fratello del xx del presente;' but he did not show him the documents enclosed, probably because they were already in the hands of translators. This makes it clear that the forgery, if forgery there was, did not take place in Florence. In fact, forgery was not a weapon which Cardinal Rovere was likely to use. His brother sent him the letters, with an account of their contents: he had them translated and copied at once.

If the letters were forged the forgery was the work of Giovanni della Rovere at Sinigaglia. The letters of Bajazet are dated Constantinople, September 15 and September 18. If we are to follow Sanuto's date, forgery would be difficult. He writes (*Spedizione di Carlo VIII.*, 124): ' Zorzi Buzardo orator dil Pontifice ... smontato in Ancona per andar per terra a Roma, a presso Sinigaja a dì 20 Novembris dal prefetto di Roma ... fo assaltato e tolti li diri ducati 40 milia et alcune lettere trovo in le man dil predetto Buzardo el qual etiam lui fo preso et conclusive fece un bon butino.' It may be that Sanuto's date, November 20, was that on which the news reached Venice. Cardinal Rovere told Manfredi, at the same time as he showed him the Prefect's letter, that the Pope had sent his confessor, Gratiano, to Florence with a letter to himself, asking him to procure from his brother the restitution of the 40,000 ducats and offering him his friendship. Anyhow, the capture of Buzardo was known in Rome, in Venice, and in Florence on November 20 or 21, and the documents themselves were in Cardinal Rovere's hands immediately. There is little time for the execution of an elaborate and circumstantial forgery.

If a forgery were committed, we have to assume that it was committed at Sinigaglia immediately on the chance capture of the Pope's messenger. In that case Buzardo must have acted as the accomplice of Giovanni della Rovere, and between them they either fabricated or altered the documents which were sent to Florence.

The documents themselves are not such as an ordinary forger could have invented. They are : (1) The Pope's instructions, in Latin, to Buzardo, which Buzardo confirms by testifying that they were given him in July. (2) Four letters in Turkish from Bajazet to the Pope, dated September 18. They acknowledge the mission of Buzardo, give him leave to depart, and signify the sending of Cassi-men as an envoy to the Pope. The fourth is more remarkable, for it recommends Niccolo Cibò, Archbishop of Arles, for the dignity of Cardinal. These letters were translated into Latin at Florence by a Greek, Lascarus, Ludovico Pico, Bishop of Famagosta, and Marcellus of Constantinople, secretary to the Prince of Salerno. (3) A private letter to the Pope suggesting the murder of Djem, dated September 15. It is described as written ' in charta oblonga more Turcarum que habebat in capite signum magni Turce aureum, in calce nigrum.'

The two Latin documents (1) and (3) are those which tell against Alexander VI.; this is an additional proof that the documents were not tampered with at Florence. We might have regarded with suspicion Florentine translations of Turkish letters ; but the evidence against Alexander VI. lies in his own instructions to Buzardo, and Bajazet's Latin answer, which must have been drawn up with Buzardo's privity. The copy of the instructions, as given in Buzardo, is attested by Buzardo : ' Ego, Georgius Busardus, per presens scriptum et suscriptum manu mea propria fidem facio et confiteor supra dicta habuisse in commissione ab ore prefate sanctitatis Rome de mense julii MCCCCLXXXXIIII, et executum fuisse ad magnum Turcam in quantum fuit mihi ordinatum' (Burchard, ii. 205). On the supposition of a forgery, Buzardo, either through fear, or in complicity with Giovanni della Rovere, put his hand to a fabrication. Now Alexander VI. was not the man to forgive an act of shameless perfidy directed against himself. If there had been forgery he

App.

would have done his utmost to punish the culprits in later days. True he excommunicated Giovanni della Rovere for seizing his money. True he complained of his conduct in his instructions to his ambassadors to Louis XII. of France on his accession. He complains that he robbed him of 40,000 ducats, that he warred against the Papal States, 'and what we bore most ill, he has endeavoured to defile our good name by false devices,—*falsis machinationibus contra nos fingens quod cum Turcis sentiemus.*' This reads as if it was thrown in as an after-thought; and further, we must not suppose that statesmen of previous times did not weigh their words in making disavowals as carefully as do the statesmen of the present day. Alexander VI. was within the truth when he denied the charge, 'quod cum Turcis sentiremus:' but this does not show that he had not asked the Turks to come to his help. He did not love the Turks in themselves, but at a particular time he asked them to help him against France. This he does not deny.

Moreover, however much his good name may have suffered, he was not specially angry with Giovanni della Rovere. He was reconciled to him in 1499, absolved him from his excommunication, and further left him in possession of the 40,000 ducats which he had seized. Giovanni claimed that he had taken them in payment of a debt due to him from the Pope, and his claim was allowed. This was certainly charitable conduct towards a traitorous forger, if such Giovanni had been.

Similarly, Buzardo seems to have gone back to Rome and to have resumed his occupation in the papal service with all the signs of conscious innocence. The Venetian diarist, Malipiero, records on February 28, 1496, that Buzardo again went to Constantinople as the envoy of Alexander VI. This treatment of the only two men who could have been guilty of the forgery seems strong evidence against the forgery having taken place.

Finally, there is corroborative testimony to the fact that Alexander VI. appealed to the Sultan to use his influence with Venice. The records of the Venetian Senate contain an answer given to an envoy of the Sultan on December 2, 1494. 'As regards the request of his Highness the Grand Signor, respecting the help and favour which he desires us to give to the Pope and King Alfonso, we cannot but commend his laudable object; nevertheless, being at peace with his Majesty the King of France we are unable,' &c. (Brosch, *Papst Julius II.*, 315). Thus it appears that Bajazet II. did actually do one of the things which the Pope's envoy was instructed to ask him to do. He applied to Venice that it should help the Pope. So long as the letters in Burchard stood alone, and were read only as referring to poisoning Djem, they might be regarded with suspicion, as being an attempt to explain Djem's death afterwards. But the documents published by Lamansky, *Secrets d'État de Venise*, show us that proposals about poisoning Djem constantly recurred in the Turkish diplomacy of this period. The documents found on Buzardo harmonise with all similar documents, and the history of their capture and circulation is perfectly clear. I see no sufficient grounds for questioning their genuineness.

10. *Savonarola.*

The story of Savonarola has attracted much attention in recent times, but it has been my task to approach it only from the side of estimating the relations of Savonarola to the Papacy. The early biographies of Savonarola by Giovan Francesco Pico and Burlamacchii formed the basis of subsequent works, such as Barsanti, *Della Storia del Padre Girolamo Savonarola*, 1782. Pico's *Vita Savonarolae* was edited by Quetif in 1674 with illustrative documents, and our knowledge of Savonarola has grown since then by the search for new documents bearing on his career. Chief amongst the works which have each made some new contribution to our knowledge, are Meier, *Girolamo Savonarola*, 1836; Perrens, *Jérome Savonarole*, 1852; Marchese, *Documenti intorno a Savonarola in Archivio Storico Italiano*, Appendix, vols. vii, viii.; and *Storia del Convento di San Marco*. Villari's *Storia di Girolamo Savonarola*, 1859, drew together the results of previous labours and brought to light a great deal of fresh material. Still the field of research was by no means exhausted, and additional documents were published by Capello in *Atti e Memorie per le Provincie Modenesi et Parmesi*, iii.; by Del Lungo in *Archivio Storico Italiano*, 1863; by Lupi in *Archivio Storico Italiano*, 1866; and by Portioli in *Archivio Storico Lombardo*, 1874. In 1877 Ranke, in his *Historisch-biographische Studien*, devoted a paper to Savonarola in which he raised a doubt whether the two early biographies by Pico and Burlamacchii were independent, or Burlamacchi was founded on Pico. This was answered by Villari in No. 1 of the *Rivista Storica Italiana*, 1884; but not, I think, convincingly. At all events the early biographies which Villari takes as the basis of his history represent the Savonarola of his own adherents, not the personage who interested the politicians of Europe, amongst whom was Alexander VI. In cases where the biography, even of Pico, contradicts the statements of strictly contemporary documents, I have preferred to adhere to the documents. Finally, a number of documents which were especially useful for my purpose were published by Gherardi, *Nuovi Documenti intorno a Savonarola*, 1878. These were commented on by Cosci in *Archivio Storico Italiano*, 1879, and form the basis of Bayonne, *Etude sur Jérome Savonarole*, 1879. The publication of the *Diario* of Luca Landucci (1883), a Florentine apothecary who was a follower of Savonarola, gives us a vivid and truthful picture of the influence exercised by him on the minds of the Florentines.

END OF THE THIRD VOLUME.